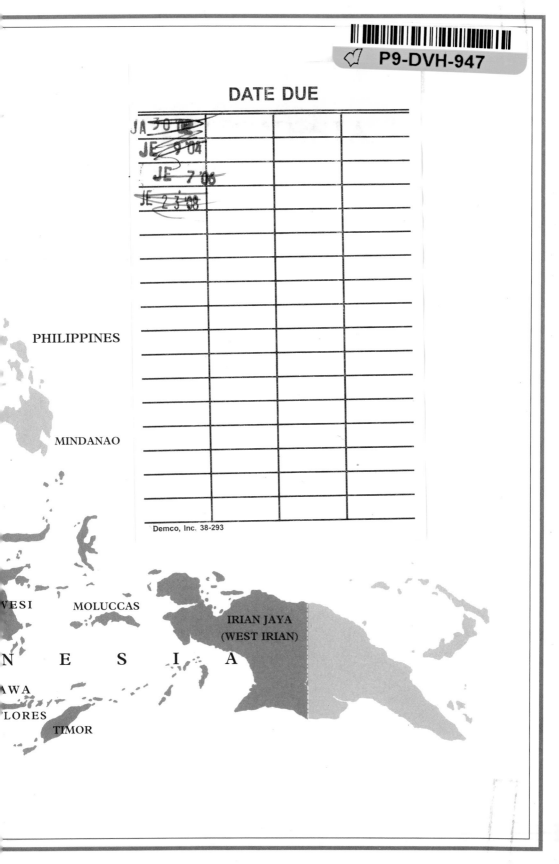

DATE DUE

JA 30 02			
JE 9 04			
JE 7 06			
JE 23 08			

PHILIPPINES

MINDANAO

VESI

MOLUCCAS

IRIAN JAYA
(WEST IRIAN)

N   E   S   I   A

AWA

LORES

TIMOR

INDONESIA'S STRUGGLE FOR ECONOMIC
DEVELOPMENT

INDONESIA'S STRUGGLE FOR ECONOMIC DEVELOPMENT

Pragmatism in Action

RADIUS PRAWIRO

KUALA LUMPUR
OXFORD UNIVERSITY PRESS
OXFORD SINGAPORE NEW YORK
1998

ORD

TY PRESS
en U1, 40150 Shah Alam,
hsan, Malaysia

nent of the University of Oxford.
It furthers the University's objective of excellence in research, scholarship,
and education by publishing worldwide in

Oxford New York

Athens Auckland Bangkok Bogotá Buenos Aires Calcutta
Cape Town Chennai Dar es Salaam Delhi Florence Hong Kong Istanbul
Karachi Kuala Lumpur Madrid Melbourne Mexico City Mumbai
Nairobi Paris São Paulo Singapore Taipei Tokyo Toronto Warsaw
with associated companies in Berlin Ibadan

Oxford is a registered trade mark of Oxford University Press
in the UK and in certain other countries

Published in the United States
by Oxford University Press, New York

© Oxford University Press 1998
First published 1998
Second impression 2001

British Library Cataloguing in Publication Data
Data Available

Library of Congress Cataloging-in-Publication Data
Prawiro, Radius.
Indonesia's Struggle for economic development: pragmatism in
action/Radius Prawiro.
p.   cm.
Includes bibliographical references and index.
ISBN 983 56 0053 8
1. Indonesia—Economic conditions—1945– 2. Indonesia—Economic
policy. I. Title.
HC447.P738 1998
388.9598—dc21
98–10656
CIP

Typeset by Indah Photosetting Centre Sdn. Bhd., Malaysia
Printed by KHL Printing Co. (S) Pte, Ltd., Singapore
Published by Penerbit Fajar Bakti Sdn. Bhd. (008974-T)
under licence from Oxford University Press

For Leonie, for a lifetime of love, friendship, and support, even during those years when I had so little time for our family life.
And for my children. While it is a father's job to care for his children, it is you who have given me strength and inspiration.

Foreword

INDONESIA'S Struggle for Economic Development is one of the most significant books to be published on Asian economic development in recent decades, and the most important book on the Indonesian economy since 1966.

Were the author completely unknown, this volume would still be judged highly as a scholarly, balanced, and comprehensive account of Indonesian economic development over this period. But what renders the book really remarkable is, obviously, its authorship. Radius Prawiro has occupied positions at the highest level of policymaking in his country for almost three decades, culminating in a stint as Co-ordinating Economics Minister (1989–93). Although not always included among the so-called 'Berkeley Mafia'—he studied accounting in the Netherlands—he is regarded as one of the key architects of the dramatic transformation of the Indonesian economy over this period. Moreover, unique among New Order Cabinet members of any duration, he also held Cabinet rank in the late years of President Sukarno's rule, thus enhancing still further the authority of the observations contained in this book.

After a long and distinguished career of public service, Radius Prawiro was entitled more than most to 'hang up his boots' and enjoy a peaceful retirement. But clearly—and fortunately for scholars of Indonesia—he believed he had a story to tell, and he thus embarked on the ambitious project which culminated in this book. As a colleague remarked, it is difficult to think of another example of a leading policymaker writing about his country's economic development and policy with such professional competence. Anyone with an interest in Asian economic development—and these days that just about includes everyone—will be in Radius' debt for not just concentrating on his golf handicap since 1994. This most readable book will influence the way we all look at Indonesia. To the next generation of Indonesian students, it will set the standard of works to follow, especially as there are still all-too-few scholarly analyses of the country by its own nationals. The volume will undoubtedly be adopted in university courses on South-East Asian studies and economic development the world over, and it will be read by diplomats, journalists, and investors seeking a primer on the country. Policymakers in other developing countries will also find this an invaluable guide in reflecting on the lessons from Indonesia's economic development.

While the book is scholarly in tone, it is also enriched by many insights which draw on the author's extraordinary breadth of experience. Readers will want to sample these according to their taste. Among those I found of particular interest are the account of President Sukarno, the transition era of 1965–7, and the shift towards an export-oriented, deregulated economy in the 1980s. But there are many more.

There are also a few (in fact tantalizingly few) personal vignettes and comments on the author's life and career, some interlaced with a wry sense of humour. For example, there is some recollection of his childhood, and the endemic poverty of much of rural Java at that time. We also learn that Radius occupied a central position in some high-level policy discussions in the mid-1960s, not only because he was Central Bank Governor but also because he had one of the very few air-conditioned offices in the country then!

But in general, the author is admirably modest in his account of developments. Rarely does his own rule intrude beyond some understated remarks here and there. What may be regarded as a 'Javanese' approach to authorship in this instance is a refreshing change from the many examples of books by recently retired top officials which verge on self-promotion (or at least justification). Of course, Radius is justifiably proud of his country's record of economic management during his tenure, and he writes as a humane and committed nationalist. But he is obviously reluctant to take personal credit, preferring instead to ascribe the record to a talented team of ministers and senior officials advising President Soeharto.

Indeed, Indonesia's technocrats were an outstandingly successful group of policymakers for so long not just because they were technically competent and politically astute, but also because they have been interested in broader socio-economic issues and impacts beyond the immediate confines of their portfolios. These broader interests are amply illustrated in this volume, with the discussion of issues related to poverty alleviation, demography, health, and education being deeper than would normally be expected of a former Finance Minister and Central Bank Governor. Such an approach, exemplified by this volume, is in fact very much in the tradition of Indonesian technocrats and their commitment to intellectual endeavours: one thinks for example of Widjojo Nitisastro's classic *Population Trends in Indonesia*, Sumitro Djojohadikusumo's *Perkembangan Pemikiran Ekonomi* and other writings, Mohammad Sadli's extensive writings, and Suhadi Mangkusuwondo's editorship of *Ekonomi and Keuangan Indonesia* for many years.

Notwithstanding his essentially positive tone, Radius Prawiro also touches on some of the country's problems and challenges, including ethnic and religious tensions, quality of education, the legal system, and the environment. Some readers may have wanted more discussion of these issues. Indeed, history has been rather unkind to the author. Between completion of the manuscript and its publication, Indonesia has experienced its most serious economic crisis since 1966 (which has also witnessed the return of Radius to the public limelight in early 1998). But the author may reasonably contend that this book relates up to the completion of his period of active government service in 1993, well before the onset of the crisis. Moreover, any notion that the current difficulties are the result of the technocrats' governance is preposterous—the problems arose not from their policy prescriptions but rather from the fact that, in the 1990s, they have not been listened to enough. There will clearly be a need to have another generation of Radius Prawiros and his contemporaries to overcome the current crisis and to regain the momentum of rapid socio-economic development in Indonesia and elsewhere in East Asia.

I am sure that you the reader will enjoy, and learn from, this book as much as I have. *Selamat membaca*!

Canberra   HAL HILL
February 1998   Department of Economics
Research School of Pacific and Asian Studies
Australian National University

Preface

SINCE 1945, when I was part of an embryonic army fighting for national independence from colonial rule, until this day, I have had the privilege to serve the nation and people of Indonesia. Starting in the early 1960s, I began working in the government, and for almost three decades I held ministerial portfolios and worked with a remarkable team that guided Indonesia's economic policy. When one is in the midst of creating economic policy for a rapidly developing country, events transpire with such speed and urgency that there is seldom time to stop and formulate a cohesive and systematic review of what has occurred and why. Over the years, however, many friends, colleagues, and scholars encouraged me to share my perspective on Indonesia's economic policymaking during these important years. This book tries to respond to those urgings. This book is above all a testimony to the stamina and resourcefulness of the people of Indonesia. My intention was to write a book that would be of value to Indonesians as well as to students of economic development and to policymakers around the world. To this end, I spent many months reviewing materials in my personal archives, holding discussions with my former colleagues and old friends, and studying many insightful articles written by Indonesian and foreign scholars of the Indonesian economy. Many of these articles helped give me the 'outsider's' perspective, which was useful in determining how to frame my analysis. I thought it noteworthy that Indonesian writers often appeared more critical of the government's policies in writings intended for local consumption than in their writings intended for external audiences. Since I intended to write for both domestic and international audiences, I tried to balance the sympathetic understanding of an insider with the detached objectivity of outside observers.

This book, like economic development itself, was a collaborative process. Most of the ideas that appear in this work reflect discussions and experiences shared with my colleagues who formed the team of economic policymakers during my time in public office. Today, as throughout this period, I remain particularly indebted to my esteemed colleague, Dr Widjojo Nitisastro. For well over thirty years, Pak Widjojo has not only been a dear friend but also a wise mentor and brilliant policymaker. More than anyone, he has helped me to understand the subtlety and beauty of economic development, and he has been most gracious in continuing to share his knowledge and understanding with me after I retired from office in 1993. I would also like to thank my other distinguished colleagues who were part of the original economic team that came together in the 1960s, including Dr Ali Wardhana, Dr Mohammad Sadli, Dr Emil Salim, Dr Subroto, Drs Rachmat Saleh, Dr Saleh Afiff, and Dr J. B. Sumarlin. I would also like to gratefully acknowledge the other economists and policymakers who later joined the economic team, most notably Dr Suhadi Mangkusu-wondo, Dr Arifin Siregar, Dr A. Mooy, Dr Soedradjat Djiwandono, and Dr B. S. Muljana. It was the lessons I learned in the company of such able policymakers and dedicated nationalists that are reflected in every page of this book.

Several people provided me with commendable assistance in this project. In particular, I would like to thank Faisal Harahap and Yudhistira Yewangoe who spent countless days and months researching archives, visiting libraries, and even plying the Internet to collect data. This information served to both stimulate my memory and corroborated my personal recollections while also giving me a better understanding of the academic perspectives on Indonesia's economic development process. Bakti Prawiro, my eldest son, studied a draft of this work with an eye to add clarification where needed.

I am very grateful to Dr Hal Hill, the editor of the *Bulletin of Indonesian Economic Studies* and head of the Indonesia Project at Australia National University in Canberra, for graciously agreeing to write a foreword to this book. I would also like to express my appreciation to Robert McNulty who provided me with valuable editorial and research assistance, and to Dr Catherine Sokil, who carefully reviewed an earlier draft of this work and gave many useful recommendations.

Finally, and most importantly, I would like to thank my wife, Leonie, for her patience in dealing with the disruption caused by the project. Without her support, this book might never have been completed.

This work includes a broad range of topics over an extensive period. Covering so much material has been a challenging, albeit satisfying task. To confine this book to a reasonable length, every chapter involved a difficult choice concerning what to include and what to omit. I have striven to be as fair and objective as I could be in the selection and interpretation of events and ideas. While I appreciate the assistance many people provided me on this project, as the author, all the discussions and conclusions of this work are my responsibility. If readers identify facts or ideas that they believe would enhance this work, I would be happy to receive their suggestions.

Jakarta   RADIUS PRAWIRO
January 1998

Contents

Tables

Figures

Abbreviations and Acronyms

ABRI	Angkatan Bersenjata Republik Indonesia or Indonesian Armed Forces
ADB	Asian Development Bank
AFTA	ASEAN Free Trade Area
APEC	Asia Pacific Economic Co-operation
ASEAN	Association of South-East Asian Nations
ASEM	Asia–Europe Meeting
Bappenas	Badan Perencanaan Pembangun Nasional or National Development Planning Agency
BE	Bonus Ekspor or Export Bonus
BEJ	PT Bursa Efek Jakarta
Bimas	Bimbingan masal or Mass Guidance Programme
BKK	Badan Kredit Kecamatan or Subdistrict Credit Agency
BKKBN	Badan Koordinasi Keluarga Berencana Nasional or Family Planning Co-ordinating Board
BKPM	Badan Koordinasi Penanaman Modal or Investment Co-ordinating Board
BLLD	Biro Lalu Lintas Devisa or Foreign Exchange Bureau
BNI	Bank Negara Indonesia
bpd	barrels per day
BPK	Badan Pemeriksa Keuangan or Supreme Audit Council
BPS	Biro Pusat Statistik or Central Bureau of Statistics
BRI	Bank Rakyat Indonesia
BTN	Bank Tabungan Negara
Bulog	Badan Urusan Logistik or National Logistics Board
BUUD	Badan Usaha Unit Desa
CGI	Consultative Group on Indonesia
CIA	Central Intelligence Agency
COLT	Commercial Offshore Loan Team
Conefo	Conference of Newly Emerging Forces
DG	director-general

DICS	Debt for Investment Conversion Scheme
DNI	Daftar Negatif Investasi or Investment Negative List
DP	Devisa Pelengkap or Complementary Foreign Exchange
DPR	Dewan Perwakilan Rakyat or Parliament
DSP	Daftar Skala Prioritas or Investment Priority List
EU	European Union
FAO	Food and Agriculture Organization
FCDT	Foreign Commercial Debt Team
FY	fiscal year
GATT	General Agreement on Tariffs and Trade
GBHN	Garis-garis Besar Haluan or The Broad Outline of the Nation's Direction
GDP	gross domestic product
GNP	gross national product
HDI	human development index
ICOR	incremental capital/output ratio
IGGI	Inter-Governmental Group on Indonesia
IMF	International Monetary Fund
Inpres	Instruksi Presiden or Presidential Instruction
IPM	Integrated Pest Management
IRRI	International Rice Research Institute
JSX	Jakarta Stock Exchange
KIK	Kredit Investasi Kecil or Small Scale Investment Credit
KMKP	Kredit Modal Kerja Permanen or Working Capital Credit Scheme
Kostrad	Komando Strategis Angkatan Darat or Army Strategic Command
KUD	Koperasi Unit Desa or village co-operatives
Kupedes	Kredit Umum Pedesaan or General Rural Credit
LDC	less developed country
LNG	liquefied natural gas
MAPA	Manila Action Plan for APEC
MCK	*Mandi, Cuci, Kakus* or bathing, cleaning, toilet
MFA	Multi-Fiber Agreement
MITI	Ministry of International Trade and Industry, Japan
MPR	Majelis Permusyawaratan Rakyat or People's Consultative Assembly
MPRS	Majelis Permusyawaratan Rakyat Sementara or Provisional People's Consultative Assembly

NAFED	National Agency for Export Development
NAFTA	North American Free Trade Agreement
NAM	Non-Aligned Movement
Nasakom	Nasionalisme, Agama, Komunisme or Nationalism, Religion, Communism
NEFO	Newly Emerging Forces
NIC	newly industrializing country
NNP	net national product
NTB	non-tariff barriers
OECD	Organization for Economic Cooperation and Development
OLDEFO	Old Established Forces
OPEC	Organization of Petroleum Exporting Countries
P4BM	Pusat Pengolahan Pembebasan dan Pengembalian Bea Masuk or Centre for the Management of Import Duty Exemption and Restitution
Pakdes	Paket Desember or 'the December Reform Package'
Pakto	Paket Oktober or 'the October Reform Package'
PKI	Partai Komunis Indonesia or Indonesian Communist Party
PKK	Pendidikan Kesejahtraan Keluarga or Family Welfare Movement
PKMD	Pelayanan Kesehatan Masuk Desa or Village Community Health Development
PN	Perusahan Negara or state-owned company
PNI	Partai Nasionalis Indonesia or Indonesian Nationalist Party
Posyandu	Pos Pelayanan Terpadu or Integrated Health Service Posts
PRC	People's Republic of China
PT	Perseroan Terbatas or limited liability company
Puskesmas	Pusat Kesehatan Masyarakat or Community Health Centres
Puskesmas Pembantu	Auxiliary Puskesmas or Health Subcentres
Repelita	Rencana Pembangunan Lima Tahun or Five-Year Development Plan
SBI	Sertifikat Bank Indonesia
SBPU	Surat Berharga Pasar Uang or government promissory notes
Simpedes	Simpanan Pedesaan or General Rural Savings Accounts

SSIFT	South-South Initiative in Free Trade
Supersemar	Surat Perintah Sebelas Maret or The Authorization Letter of 11 March
Tabanas	Tabungan Pembangunan Nasional or Savings Programme for National Development
Taman Gizi	'Nutrition Gardens' or 'Weighing Posts'
Taska	Tabungan Asuransi Berjanka or Twelve Month Savings Programme for Life Insurance
UNCTAD	United Nations Conference on Trade and Development
UNDP	United Nations Development Programme
UNICEF	United Nations Children's Fund
UPGK	Usaha Penbaikan Gizi Keluarga or Family Nutrition Improvement Programme
UPPKA	Usaha Peningkatan Pendapatan Keluarga Akseptor or Efforts to Increase the Income of Acceptor Families
VAT	value added tax
WHO	World Health Organization
WTO	World Trade Organization

A Note on the Use of Statistics

Throughout this book, unless otherwise stated, figures are drawn from official Indonesian government sources, specifically the Central Bureau of Statistics, Bank Indonesia, or the appendices to the President's annual budget addresses. When numbers appear in the text that have been drawn from these sources no specific citation is given. When tables or charts are provided, the data source is identified. In those instances when data are drawn from World Bank publications or other non-governmental publications, the source is identified in brackets or in a footnote.

The abbreviation 'Rp' represents Indonesia's national currency, the rupiah. Unless otherwise specified, the word 'dollar' and the '$' symbol refer to US dollars. Throughout this work, the word 'billion' follows American conventions, meaning a thousand million, rather than the British convention according to which a billion is a million million.

Introduction

As recently as the mid-1960s, Indonesia was ranked by the World Bank as the poorest country in Asia, and among the very poorest in the world. By the year 2020, however, the Bank predicts that Indonesia will be the fifth largest economy in the world after China, the United States, Japan, and India. Today, in the late 1990s, Indonesia is still a poor country, but during the thirty years from the mid-1960s to the mid-1990s, the country travelled rapidly along the long and difficult road to join the ranks of the world's newly industrializing economies. This book tries to shed some light on how this economic transformation was possible from the perspective of someone who was present and participating in the economic policymaking process during this period.

This is a book about economic development in the context of three extraordinary decades—a period that corresponds to my own 28-year career as a Cabinet member and economic policymaker in the successive governments of President Sukarno and President Soeharto. In 1965, as vice-chairman of the Supreme Audit Board, I was one of the youngest ministers in the final Cabinet of the Sukarno era. Beginning in 1966, with the change in government that followed the abortive *coup* in October 1965, I held a series of Cabinet posts beginning as Governor of Bank Indonesia, then as Minister of Trade, Minister of Finance, and finally, ended my ministerial career in 1993 as co-ordinating minister for the economy, finance, industry and development supervision, Indonesia's equivalent to what would be a deputy prime minister for economic affairs in some other governments.

This was a period of astonishing change for Indonesia, and as fate would have it, I had the privilege to observe the Indonesian drama unfold from centre stage. My observations and assessments of the key economic issues of this time form the foundation of this book. What I have written here, however, is neither a biography, nor an economics textbook, nor a history: it is a bit of all of these and more. This is a book based on the premise that economics is a discipline that is best studied in context. Equipped with empirical studies, complex mathematical models, and a host of supporting analytic tools, economics is the most scientific of all the social sciences. Yet for all its sophistication, I believe the most meaningful lessons from economics can be obtained by observing economic phenomena in the real market-place of human history. Because every country, every period, and every economic situation is unique, there is never a perfect match between theory and reality. Reality will always be more complex than our economic models. It is also true, however, that human progress depends upon the development and transmission of knowledge from one generation to another. Despite its limitations, the field of economics has progressed quickly and contributed greatly to the increasingly effective management of economies. This book tries to bridge economic theory and practice during a period when Indonesia's economic development progressed at a remarkable pace and encountered a host of challenges.

As a member of the team responsible for Indonesia's economic policies during this period, I had to continually ask the question, 'What are the lessons we can learn from our past challenges that can help us guide future development?' That same question lies at the heart of this book. It is my attempt to respond to the adage that 'those who do not learn the lessons of the past, will be condemned to repeat them'. I believe firmly that progress in economic development requires that we heed well the lessons of the past, not out of nostalgic attachment to the 'old days', but to ensure that we are able to live better in the future. In this book, I have tried to distill some of the important lessons of Indonesia's economic development over a critical period in its history.

The story of economic development in post-independence Indonesia is one of great drama, full of both triumph and tragedy. In the mid-1960s, the body of knowledge on economic development was relatively small, and the systematic study of Indonesia's economy was virtually non-existent. Around 1966, however, a group of young Indonesian economists had recently finished their advanced degrees and came together to assist the new government to formulate its economic policies. External observers soon began to call this group the 'technocrats', and among themselves, the group was simply called 'the economic team'. The team had a simple goal: to help Indonesia rid itself of poverty by introducing economic policies supportive of rapid economic development. Over the next twenty-five years, Indonesia's economic team was able to remain in place as a stable and constant force, as the core members gained in seniority and new members joined the team. The guiding principle of the economic team was 'pragmatism'. In practical terms, this displayed itself in a genuinely open, experimental attitude rather than one dominated by political ideologies or economic dogma.

In this book, I attempt to investigate the theoretical and practical considerations that led to Indonesia's choice of economic policies as well as the outcomes of those policies.

I consider economic development to be a special branch of economics. Rather than simply describing economic phenomena, economic development should respond to the question, 'How can we make life better?' In response to this question, the developmental economist must consider a broad array of issues that touch human life. For practical reasons, I have confined the focus of this book to the most prominent issues in Indonesia's developmental experience. These issues unfold in broad, progressive stages: first, the pursuit of economic stability in the late 1960s; next, the effort to build the foundation of the economy in the 1970s; and then, the effort to reinvigorate the economy through deregulation from the mid-1980s to the early-1990s. In the Epilogue, I discuss the significance of the economic turbulence that affected Indonesia and several of its Asian neighbours beginning in mid-1997. In the last two chapters I reflect on the role of globalization and other issues that will influence Indonesia's economic development in the years ahead. In every chapter, I attempt to consider the issues of development from a historical and theoretical perspective. For Indonesia's economic team, textbook theories, while helpful, were never sufficient to formulate economic policy. For this reason, I have tried in every chapter to assess the issues with historical impartiality, while remembering these were real events involving living human beings. Throughout the book, I have included notes that either add supplemental details or illustrate the text with my own experiences as a member of Indonesia's economic policymaking team.

In the pages that follow, I have endeavoured to distill many of the essential lessons from this period in the hope that this will be of value to a broad audience from Indonesia-watchers, to historians and futurologists, scholars and practitioners, specialists and laymen. Indonesia's march from poverty is a powerful example of humanity's ability to overcome adversity through hard work, intelligent policies, and collective goodwill. The story is far from over. None the less, already there are great treasures to be mined from this early period of Indonesia's development. This book tells the part of the story to which I was a witness.

Prologue:
Development in the Crucible
of Revolution

NINETEEN sixty-five was a bleak year for Indonesia. For centuries, the people who made up what is present-day Indonesia had seen the rise and fall of kingdoms, the ebb and flow of human migrations, and periods of relative wealth and poverty. However, the extent to which the systems of social and commercial exchange had now broken down was without precedent. The independence revolution that just two decades earlier was born out of hope and pride was now crumbling into pieces, incapable of resisting the forces of chaos it had unleashed. Suddenly the kindness, civility, and culture that were at the heart of the Indonesian character seemed to evaporate as the country slid into a conflagration of economic ruin, bloodshed, and despair.

Twenty years earlier, in 1945, Indonesia had forcibly and painfully extracted itself from three and a half centuries of Dutch colonial rule. With its voracious economic appetite and cultural arrogance, colonialism had taken its toll on a proud and ancient culture. Everywhere, Indonesians now appeared as second-class citizens in their own homeland.

In reaction to this bitter legacy, there was a natural tendency after independence to want to discard all remnants of the colonial past. There was a deep and widespread suspicion among many Indonesians that the roots of colonialism could be traced to the economic and social philosophies embodied in liberal capitalism. Part of Indonesia's response to this concern was embodied in Article 33 of the 1945 Constitution which states that the economy of independent Indonesia should reflect the values embodied in the family.[1] The constitution was not designed to regulate the specifics of the nation's commercial life. However, the intent of Article 33 was clear: the familial and community ties that link Indonesians so tightly one to another should serve as the basis for an alternative model to *laissez-faire* or 'free-fight' capitalism. There was nothing in the 'family-model of economics' (*economi kekeluargaan*), however, that discouraged entrepreneurship, trade, or other forms of commerce. The intention of the framers of the Indonesian constitution was to model the economy on the family as a way of softening the hard edge of market forces—such as the drive for profits and productivity—with more humanistic values such as caring and mutual help (*gotong royong*). The Indonesian alternative implies that the pursuit of economic advancement should be tempered by an abiding concern for the well-being of all Indonesians.

The changes in Indonesian society have been so rapid and pervasive over the last fifty years that these economic ideals have been severely tested. From the founding of the Republic, Indonesia's political life was turbulent and the economy unstable. Between 1949 and 1957, eight different coalition governments led the country. Factional fighting among the political parties was intense and divisive. A group known as the 'Konstituante' was elected in 1955 with the stated mission of writing a new constitution for the country. After several years of unending debate and discussions, Indonesia's founding president, Sukarno,[2] dissolved the Konstituante and declared that the nation should return to the 1945 Constitution. This decision, on 5 July 1959, marked the beginning of Indonesia's period known as 'Guided Democracy'. Guided Democracy ended the contentious wrangling that had brought near paralysis to the Indonesian political system. In the process, however, Indonesia's experiment in liberal democracy ended and virtually all government power was ceded to the President.

THE RADICALIZATION AND DECLINE OF THE INDONESIAN ECONOMY

In a country built upon diversity, Sukarno was the quintessential synchronist. He collected ideas from East and West, North and South, and developed a blend that was uniquely Indonesian and of enormous appeal to the country's masses and intellectuals alike.[3] Outside Indonesia, Sukarno's philosophy and charisma inspired unparalleled co-operation and solidarity among people from the Third World. The Non-Aligned Movement (NAM) owes its existence to Sukarno, together with five other great leaders of that time: Jawaharlal Nehru from India, U Nu from Burma (now called Myanmar), Josip Broz Tito from Yugoslavia, Gamal Abdel Nasser from Egypt, and Kwame Nkrumah from Ghana.

Among the many ideas and ideologies that circulated among Indonesia's pre-independence intellectuals, the philosophy of Karl Marx held a place of prominence. The political party Sukarno founded in July 1927, the Partai Nasionalis Indonesia[4] (PNI or Indonesian Nationalist Party) was left of centre, but far from communist. But, as Indonesia's fragile economy began to deteriorate in the early to mid-1960s, socialists and communists gained greater control over the government and exerted increasing influence over Sukarno. The leftist leaders in power were disinterested in formal economic theories or any policy recommendations that reflected a capitalist outlook.[5] What followed was a series of economic policy actions, all of which contributed to an unavoidable and disastrous decline in the economy.

The Monetary Origins of Indonesia's Economic Decline

During those years, the government subordinated economic policies for political objectives in many arenas, but perhaps the most serious was in the field of banking and monetary policy. Indonesia's central bank had grown out of the former colonial bank known as De Javasche Bank (the Bank of Java). In 1953 the bank was renamed Bank Indonesia. Bank Indonesia had the exclusive right to print bank notes and was responsible for supervising the banking and credit systems and for maintaining the stability of the nation's currency. Originally, Bank Indonesia had maintained a level of independence from political decision-making not unlike that of central banks in most other market-oriented economies. By law, money in circulation was not to exceed five times the total central bank holdings of gold and foreign exchange reserves. In 1957, however, in the name of 'Guided Economy', Bank Indonesia's independence ended. Bank Indonesia became a *de facto* instrument of central government administration, printing more and more money in contravention of restrictions on deficit spending. As surely as night follows day, government spending increased dramatically, but without corresponding increases in revenues.

By removing Bank Indonesia's independence, the government disregarded the sound counsel of an earlier Governor of the Bank, Sjafruddin Prawiranegara. In 1952 he said: 'If the Government were given the key to the Central Bank, there would be a great danger that the government would be tempted to operate outside the budget, since it would always be in a position to create new funds' (Javasche Bank, 1953: 17). Sjafruddin resigned as governor in February 1958 and, regrettably, his predictions were entirely correct. In 1960, Bank Indonesia stopped publishing its weekly, quarterly, and annual financial reports, and the monetary affairs of the country became a matter of state secrecy rather than public record. In 1961, the PNI parliamentarian Jusuf Muda Dalam became Minister for Central Bank Affairs and Governor of Bank Indonesia.

Governor Jusuf Muda Dalam further contributed to the destabilization of Indonesia's banking system by merging all the state banks directly into the central bank, thereby eliminating any competition among banks—the life-blood of an efficient banking sector.[6] By merging Bank Indonesia and the state banks, the central bank became the country's primary commercial bank, and the distinction between regulator and regulated was entirely eliminated. Bank Indonesia was renamed Bank Negara Indonesia (BNI) Unit I and the former state banks were called BNI Unit II, BNI Unit III, and so forth. Under this arrangement, the government guided, if not entirely controlled, virtually all banking activities in the country from consumer deposits and commercial loans to interest rate management. The central bank was no longer a lender of last resort, but essentially the only significant lender in the country. Furthermore, since the central bank no longer issued banking statistics, the country faced a near-total black-out on banking and financial information. Perhaps more than any other policies, the elimination of central bank independence from political decision-making, coupled with the elimination of competitive behaviour among banks, marked the initial step in a cycle of decline in the Indonesian economy. Indeed, this policy gave the government 'the key' (in Sjafruddin's words) to launch all sorts of programmes and policies that were entirely untenable from the perspective of macroeconomics or generally accepted principles of accounting.

The Loss of Fiscal Restraint and Focus

Despite the government's limited revenues, expenditures mushroomed. From 1958 onward, the 'Old Order' government[7] engaged in tremendous deficit spending.

1. *Military Spending*. Government spending for military actions in-creased when, in December 1961, the government launched the campaign to liberate West Irian[8] (later known as Irian Jaya). This was followed in 1963 by the 'Confrontation' (*Konfrontasi*) with Malaysia as well as do-mestic military actions to quell several regional uprisings. Indonesia had moved to a war economy, which bled the country of its limited resources.

2. *Rice Imports*. Despite the government's professed objective to achieve rice self-sufficiency, extreme supply shortages persisted throughout the 1957–65 period. Rice was so important to the Indonesian diet that, despite its poverty, Indonesia became one of the world's largest rice importers. This caused a massive drain on the country's foreign exchange reserves. To confront this problem, Sukarno, during his Independence Day speech on 17 August 1964, announced that he was forthwith banning the importation of rice. This led to panic buying, which greatly exacerbated the country's inflation. In the end, the government reversed itself, but the levels of rice imported fell well below the amount needed to meet the country's food requirements. This severely undermined public confidence in the economic management of the country.

3. *Subsidies*. As a hedge against inflation, the government provided enormous subsidies on many consumer goods, especially petroleum

products and rice. In 1965, over one-fifth of the government's revenues went to subsidize petroleum products.[9] The government tried to reduce subsidies on petroleum products, but when the public protested, the government again retreated and cancelled the proposed cuts.

4. *Prestige Projects*. Despite the size of its budget deficits in the early 1960s, the government was committed to a massive programme of constructing public monuments and 'prestige projects'. Work began on a large building to serve the 'Conference of Newly Emerging Forces' (Conefo). Several imposing statues in the socialist–realism mode were constructed, as were a huge sports stadium (Senayan) and Monas, the 'National Monument'.[10]

5. *Discretionary Funds*. Ministries and projects obtained funds to a large extent according to presidential discretion. Ministries were given supplementary budgets by presidential directive. A special fund, called the 'Revolution Fund', was created to finance miscellaneous projects and to reward friends of the regime. This fund was for use by the president and some of his close advisers, who would disburse large sums of foreign exchange to government agencies and individuals entirely on their personal authority. These discretionary funds were outside the budget yet drew on state funds.[11]

What is missing from the above list, of course, is spending for the economic development of the country—more specifically, investments in such things as schools, hospitals, roads, irrigation systems, and all those things that would contribute to the creation of a strong economy that responded to the needs of Indonesia's citizens. There existed a small degree of infrastructure upgrading, but the amount was minor and insufficient to address even Indonesia's most basic and urgent needs for development. The government had lost its focus. It spent beyond its means and seemed oblivious to the potential consequences of its actions. There was no earnest effort to bring revenues in balance with expenditures. For example, although the government drew a considerable portion of its revenues from taxes on imports and exports, it instituted several policies that had a negative impact on trade. In so doing the government, in effect, cut its own revenues. Yet, despite the Indonesian government's large budget deficits, in 1964 the government decided to show its generosity by exempting all civil servants from having to pay income taxes for the year. In these and other ways, the government demonstrated that it had lost control of the budgetary process. This was leading the country to a state of economic anarchy.

The Vicious Cycle of Decline

The country's budgetary mismanagement gravely imperiled the economy, while several related policies reinforced the cycle of economic decline.

1. *The Nationalization of Foreign Enterprises and Rejection of Foreign Investment.* The Indonesian policy that drew the greatest criticism from abroad was the nationalization of foreign enterprises. In 1957, the movement to nationalize foreign companies began with selected Dutch trading firms and then spread to others. Over time, a large collection of banks, plantations, factories, and mines moved from the hands of foreign investors to those of the Indonesian government. In May 1965, the law guaranteeing foreign investment was repealed and many of the remaining foreign business holdings were nationalized. Only oil companies were shielded from this policy.

To Indonesians, the government's move to nationalize foreign industries appeared justified in the wake of years of colonial economics. The conflict between Indonesia and the Netherlands over West Irian exacerbated hostilities between the two countries and reinforced the government's position that there could be no role for the Dutch in the Indonesian economy. To foreign governments and industries the actions confirmed their worst fears about the shift to the left in Indonesia. Increasingly, the view from abroad was that Indonesia was unsuitable as a site for investment; consequently, foreign capital needed for industrial development ceased to flow into the country. In this case, the domestic and international perspectives were irreconcilable.

The nationalization policy failed to achieve its intended economic results. Indonesia took control of firms without having the qualified personnel to manage them. The production of goods, both for the domestic market and for exports, declined, further reducing Indonesia's foreign exchange earnings. In the process, these firms were transformed from tax revenue-providers to subsidy-absorbers. In fact, the economy suffered because of nationalization.

2. *Decline of Trade and Pretensions of Autarky.* By the mid-1960s, the government had already experienced several years of extraordinary budget shortfalls. To finance its habit of deficit spending, the government depleted its foreign reserves. Purportedly to maintain monetary stability, the rupiah exchange rate was maintained, in turn, at an artificially high level. This policy served to drive up the price of Indonesian export goods, which reduced their competitiveness in international markets. The ill effects were compounded by a complementary policy of trying to build industry by taxing agricultural exports. Apart from oil—which at this point still occupied a relatively small portion of Indonesia's economy—Indonesia's

primary trade products were rubber, coffee, palm oil, and a few other agricultural products. When the government imposed taxes on agricultural exports, traders could not increase the price of exports and still compete in international markets. Nor were the traders willing to absorb the additional export costs themselves, because they often had narrow profit margins on their goods. In the end, this meant that Indonesian farmers had to bear the brunt of the export taxes and overvalued currency. Hence, the overall effect of these policies was to push farmers out of the export sector, and this further contributed to the shrinking of foreign exchange reserves.

In 1964, the government further added to the country's troubles by launching Berdikari, the 'Standing on Our Own Feet' campaign. This sought to arrest the depletion of the country's foreign exchange reserves by pressing for the development of import-substitution industries. The August 1964 ban on rice imports grew out of the Berdikari movement and set the stage for food shortages. Indonesia aspired to a more self-sufficient—or autarkic—economy, but these policies only aggravated the desperate conditions in the country.

3. *Hyperinflation.*[12] There are many causes of inflation, but in the simplest terms, inflation generally originates from two sources—a *shortage in the supply of goods* or *a surplus in market demand* created most often by excessive money supply growth. By the mid-1960s, Indonesia had both types and in the extreme. The country's annual inflation rate in 1965 was over 650 per cent. Hyperinflation performed a trick on all consumers: in the time it took to put a rupiah in one's pocket and take it out a significant portion of the value had disappeared. Once this fact became widely recognized by Indonesian consumers, it created an expectation that exacerbated inflation. This spread deep insecurity throughout the economy.

4. *Declining National Income.* The net result of these factors was that the country grew steadily poorer. When measured in the local currency, in real terms, the country's per capita income[13] showed an actual decline by 3.7 per cent between 1961 and 1965. If one were to measure Indonesia's per capita income against a foreign currency, such as the dollar, the drop in income was far more drastic, since the value of the rupiah to the dollar declined from Rp 186 to the dollar in 1961 to Rp 14,000 to the dollar in 1965. For a wealthy, industrialized country, an economic downturn of this magnitude would spark a governmental crisis and would necessitate that the population exercise greater frugality. In the mid-1960s, most Indonesians were already living at a subsistence level. Frugality was meaningless in the face of abject poverty. For many, personal survival was at stake.

Although Indonesia had recently been freed from the bondage of colonialism, through its own policies the country was slipping back to pre-colonial economic conditions of several centuries earlier. Many Indonesians responded to the growing economic crisis by abandoning the cities altogether and returning to the countryside. This urban exodus was prompted by a belief that the chances for personal survival were stronger by staying closer to the land and relying upon the community spirit of rural Indonesians. By 1965, however, the country had a population of 107 million, and Indonesians were still using traditional farming techniques. The simple demographic reality was that the land could no longer support a nation of subsistence farmers.

Alone and Indebted to the Wrong Friends

The nationalization of foreign companies not only destroyed the country's standing as a destination for foreign investment, it antagonized foreign governments and unnerved foreign corporations. Especially in the West, Indonesia was increasingly being looked upon as a pariah state. The country's international isolation reached a nadir when Indonesia withdrew from the United Nations in January 1965.[14] By withdrawing from the United Nations, Indonesia automatically rescinded its membership in the International Monetary Fund (IMF) and the World Bank, two institutions that could have been particularly helpful to Indonesia in trying to heal the damaged economy.

Indonesia's rejection of ties with the West was counterbalanced by a growing *rapprochement* with the socialist regimes. On 11 April 1965, Sukarno pronounced to the Majelis Permusyawaratan Rakyat Sementara (MPRS) or Provisional People's Consultative Assembly that 'the national–democratic' phase of the Indonesian revolution was almost finished: 'We are now entering the next stage ... the stage of Indonesian Socialism.'[15]

The drift toward socialism was accompanied by *rapprochement* with the Soviet Union and the People's Republic of China (PRC). When Indonesia's foreign minister, Dr Subandrio, was on a state visit to China, the 23 January 1965 edition of the *People's Daily* gave him a warm welcome with the following words: 'The Chinese and Indonesian people have cemented a militant friendship in their protracted anti-imperialist struggle; they have always supported and inspired each other and advanced shoulder to shoulder.' The closeness between Indonesia and its socialist comrades was not only rhetorical. Indonesia was amassing considerable debt from Eastern Bloc countries primarily for the purchase of arms—used mainly in its military operations against the Dutch in West Irian and in the confrontation campaign against Malaysia.

No country can sustain a continuous expansion of debt and ever-increasing deficits. This, however, is what Indonesia tried to do. Whether realizing it or not, the then governor of the central bank ensured that the country's economic collapse would be deep and protracted by authorizing ever-increasing levels of debt while simultaneously presiding over a rapid and unreplenishable depletion of the country's foreign reserves.[16]

Although hyperinflation was the most visible and devastating testimony that the government had lost control of the economy, even more dangerous and insidious was the growing strength of the communist party and its influence on the government. In 1965, the Partai Komunis Indonesia (PKI or Indonesian Communist Party) was the third largest communist party in the world, after China and the Soviet Union. Although the majority of Indonesians did not support communism, its influence, however, was widespread. Even within the Cabinet, there was a deep division between the communists and the anti-communists and this division was exacerbated by the breakdown in the economy. The recommended policies for restoring health to the economy was polarized along ideological lines. The conditions were ripe for a major eruption.

THE FAILED *COUP* THAT TOPPLED
A GOVERNMENT

On 17 August 1964, Indonesia's Independence Day, President Sukarno gave his famous 'Year of Living Dangerously' (*Tahun Vivere Pericoloso*) speech. In fiery prose he invoked the 'three absolute conditions' of Indonesia's revolutionary spirit: 'Romanticism, dynamism and dialecticalism', which he said were the 'raving inspiration of Indonesian history'. Eight months later President Sukarno gave another landmark speech called 'Turning the Wheel' (*Banting Stir*) in which he proclaimed: 'My economic philosophy is thunderous revolutionary spirit combined with down-to-earth handling of problems as they arise.' In these speeches Sukarno may have reached a pinnacle in his use of rhetoric. His economic policies, however, were by no means 'down-to-earth'. The country had all but slipped into chaos.

Late in the night of 30 September 1965, a subversive group went to the homes of six of the nation's top military leaders—all of whom were known to be avid anti-communists. The *coup* plotters, who later identified themselves as the '30 September Movement', forced the generals from their beds, and brought them—some alive and some already killed—to an airbase on the outskirts of Jakarta. Soon thereafter all the generals were executed and their bodies dumped in a well. A seventh general, Minister of Defence General Abdul Haris Nasution, saved himself only by escaping over the garden wall of his home and hiding at the neighbouring residence of the Iraqi ambassador. A statement by the *coup* leaders, dated 1 October 1966, appeared the next day in the left-wing newspaper, *Harian Rakjat*

('People's Daily'). In the statement, the *coup* leader, Lieutenant-Colonel Untung, and other signatories claimed that the purge of what they called 'the Council of Generals' was necessary to pre-empt an anticipated *coup* against the government of Indonesia sponsored by the Central Intelligence Agency (CIA) of the United States. They proclaimed the establishment of the 'Indonesian Revolutionary Council', into which, they asserted, all state power had been transferred. Furthermore, they declared that the actions carried out in Jakarta would be repeated against 'lackeys and sympathizers' of the Council of Generals throughout Indonesia. The same paper, *Harian Rakjat*, published an editorial on 2 October denouncing the murdered generals for their 'condemnable and counter-revolutionary act' of plotting a *coup*. The support of the people, the paper asserted, was with the patriotic 30 September Movement.

The strategy was classic 'decapitation'. The *coup* leaders apparently believed that if they could eliminate the principal anti-communists among the military's top leadership, their subordinates would either join the 30 September Movement or be so disorganized and disunited that seizing control of the military would be achievable. What they had not anticipated was that Maj. Gen. Soeharto, then a commander of the Komando Strategis Angkatan Darat (Kostrad or Army Strategic Command) would quickly assemble the forces to counter the attempted *coup* and quickly restore relative order to the capital, Jakarta. As it turned out, the conflict was more protracted outside Jakarta, especially in Central Java, where there was a larger base of PKI support.[17]

The attempted *coup* was a turning point in Indonesia's economic history. At least three major changes occurred in the country's political climate in the aftermath of the attempted *coup*: first, Indonesia's infatuation with communism turned sour; second, through large-scale protests, people demanded that the government take action to rebuild the economy; and third, Soeharto was thrust into prominence as the *de facto* leader of the military although General Nasution retained the title of Minister of Defence.

A GOVERNMENT UNREFORMED

The attempted *coup* and the public outcry that followed should have been the government's final wake-up call. This message, however, continued to fall upon deaf ears. On 22 November 1965, Indonesia's budget and associated policies were enunciated in Presidential Instruction (Inpres) No. 26. On the positive side, the instruction contained measures intended to restore stability to the country's economy. Overall, however, the plan continued to be misguided and there was no indication that the government was any more serious about implementing this budget than any previous ones.

The most problematic aspect of the 1965 Presidential Instruction was the decision that imports could no longer be financed with short-term credit. The Instruction put Indonesia's international trade on a cash-and-carry basis. Since the country had exhausted its foreign exchange reserves, the policy was understandable. However, because it effectively stopped imports of many needed consumer as well as producer goods, it created great hardship for Indonesian citizens as well as unmanageable bottlenecks in industrial production.

In the ensuing months, until March 1966, the government's policies under Sukarno's leadership were roughly in the same mould as before:

- In November 1965 Indonesia went ahead with the paid nationalization of Shell Oil's holdings in Indonesia;
- Non-productive projects for 'national character building' continued;
- In January 1966, at Lebaran, the Muslim celebration that concludes the fasting month, the government issued an enormous bonus to all government employees, which had the effect of escalating the hyperinflation that was decimating the value of Indonesia's currency;[18]
- The government defaulted on its trade credit obligations;
- The confrontation with Malaysia continued;
- The government continued to promote Nasakom (Nasionalisme, Agama, Komunisme or Nationalism, Religion, Communism)—the proposed united front among the nationalist, religious, and communist forces.

There was nothing in any of the economic policies of this period that suggested that the government intended to reform itself and rehabilitate the economy. Indonesians, however, had grown weary and disillusioned with revolutionary ideology. They wanted food, clothing and they wanted a renewed form of money that represented a serious medium of exchange. This dissatisfaction was made evident through numerous public demonstrations. One such protest in Jakarta in November—explicitly directed against the PKI—had thousands of protesters. The scale of public disaffection with socialism, and whatever was behind the current breakdown in the economy, was enormous.

On 11 March 1966, with angry protesters filling the streets outside the presidential palace, Sukarno abruptly terminated a Cabinet meeting then in progress and left by helicopter for his residence in Bogor.[19] Later that day he met with three army generals, Amir Machmud, Basuki Rachmat, and Andi Muhammad Jusuf. The content of their discussions is not known, but it is widely believed that they pressed Sukarno to recognize that the current state of the country was untenable, and that without significant change, the current level of chaos could reel further out of control with dire consequences. Later that day, the generals returned to Jakarta with a letter from Sukarno, which was referred to in Indonesian as Supersemar (Surat Perintah Sebelas Maret or The Authorization Letter of 11 March). The letter empowered Maj.-Gen. Soeharto to 'take all steps deemed necessary to guarantee the security, tranquillity and stability for the smooth function of the government and the course of revolution, and to safeguard the personal safety and the authority of the leadership of the President'. This letter opened the door for the most significant reorientation of Indonesia's politics and economic policies since independence.

SUKARNO'S DEVELOPMENTAL LEGACY

History is like a great river of humanity and cultures moving forward under the momentum of time and tradition. Occasionally there are those prophets, revolutionaries, and geniuses with gifts of discernment and charisma, who recognize they are called to do what seems impossible and change the course of history. Sukarno was such a man—a true revolutionary. Indonesia's sovereignty was not granted. It was won, and Sukarno led the battle. He was the proclaimer of Indonesia's independence and throughout his life, when he spoke, the intensity of his passion and conviction virtually set his audience on fire. He unified a huge nation of over a hundred million people, spread over 17,000 islands. He woke the people from their colonial slumber and created the opportunity for the birth of an independent nation.

Revolutionaries, however, often do not make ideal statesmen. Their ability to inspire does not qualify them to govern. The economic policies of Sukarno's government, especially since the early 1960s, were so misguided that they nearly pushed the country into a catastrophic abyss. Sukarno, until the end of his life—through the confrontation with Malaysia, the withdrawal from the United Nations, in his dangerous flirtation with communism, among others—was fighting the ghosts of neocolonialism. What he failed to see was that the world had changed, and there were new battles to fight and new enemies to defeat.

Sukarno believed everything could be accomplished through a passionate political will. He did not recognize that markets and economic behaviour could not be commanded by revolutionary fiat. He never realized he could undo his life's extraordinary achievements with something as pedestrian as inflation. Yet, by allowing the country to slip into near bankruptcy, he undermined his political platform and damaged his credibility with the people. For these reasons, although he was able to open the door for a new nation, he was unable to cross the threshold.

Revolutions are like crucibles in which societies are heated up, traditions and class structures are melted down, novel ideas are alloyed with time-worn customs, and new ways of living take shape. Revolutions provide the concentrated sparks of energy that engender millennial changes in societies that have become rule-bound, brittle, and stagnant. Revolutions, however, are fundamentally inhospitable environments, and unconducive to the long-term painstaking process of development. Economic development takes the protracted patience of evolution.

The challenge Indonesia faced in 1966 would continue for many years to come. Indonesia's new challenge was the battle against poverty, against stymied expectations, against life cut short through malnutrition and disease, and human spirits left in darkness through want of education. Indonesia's new struggle was that of economic development—a challenge that remains to this day. For the upcoming thirty years, economic development would serve as the focal point of almost all government efforts and its fundamental *raison d'être*. As in all long-term endeavours, the road was not straight and smooth, but rough and winding. The government made many mistakes, some small, some enormous. It also had notable victories. Along the way, experience was a most generous teacher. The lessons of these years should prove useful to future generations of Indonesians and to people in other countries concerned with the challenge of economic development. The following pages review many of these lessons in their historical and economic context. The lessons will need further reflection, analysis, and refinement. The journey is far from complete. This book is being written from the road.

1. The wording of Article 33 of the 1945 Constitutions is, 'The economy shall be organized as a co-operative effort founded upon the basis of family spirit' (see Simorangkir and Say, 1980: 94).

2. In Indonesia, many people, like Sukarno, have only one name. Furthermore, in many parts of Indonesia, there is no such thing as a 'family name'. Although a person may be given two names, he might just as well be addressed by his first name or second name. The only way to tell which name should be used is through usage. Use of the first name, therefore, denotes neither familiarity nor formality.

3. Regarding Indonesian synchronism and its early influences on Sukarno, see Dahm (1969: 9). Therein, Dahm cites a passage from the Spring 1921 edition of the journal *Utusan Hindia*, to which Sukarno was a contributor: 'Socialism, communism, incarnations of Vishnu Murti, awaken everywhere! Abolish capitalism, propped up by the imperialism that is its slave. God grant Islam the strength that it may succeed.' Dahm rightly points out

that 'this Hinduized Communist Manifesto and Islamic oath could certainly not have appeared in any place on earth but Java'. It may well be in this eclecticism that we find the intellectual origins of 'Nasakom', Sukarno's bold but ill-fated effort to form an ideological synthesis based on nationalism, religion, and communism.

4. To be more precise, in July 1927 Sukarno founded the Perserikatan Nasional Indonesia (Indonesian National Association). In May 1928, the name was changed to Partai Nasional Indonesia (Indonesian National Party) to make the political intention more explicit.

5. At the time, in early 1965, I was the vice-chairman of the Badan Pemeriksa Keuangan (BPK or Supreme Audit Board) reporting to Sultan Hamengkubuwono IX. Although I had completed postgraduate studies in economics in Rotterdam, the Netherlands, it was my earlier training in accountancy that permitted me to obtain a position as one of the youngest members in Sukarno's Cabinet. My credentials as an economist were ignored until there was a change in governments.

6. In Indonesia, as in many countries, banking is carried out by private commercial banks and banks owned by the government. In Indonesia, the state banks were organized along functional lines to ensure that different sectors of the economy had access to credit. During this period of Indonesia's history, almost all banking was with state banks. State banks will be discussed in more detail later.

7. The 'Old Order' (Orde Lama) government is a term used to refer to the governments during the Sukarno era (1945–65). This contrasts with the 'New Order' (Orde Baru), which began when government control was passed to Soeharto in March 1965.

8. West Irian was the name then given to the easternmost province of Indonesia. Although this territory had been a part of the Dutch colonial holdings along with the rest of Indonesia, after the Dutch recognized Indonesian independence in 1949 they tried to maintain their control of West Irian. Later, however, when the territory was integrated into Indonesia in 1969, the name was changed to Irian Jaya.

9. According to estimates in the *Bulletin of Indonesian Economic Studies*, Indonesian subsidies on petroleum products amounted to Rp 150 billion in 1965 while the entire government revenue for that year was about Rp 671 billion (Penny, 1966b).

10. Monas, now the centre-point of modern Jakarta, is in the form of an enormous obelisk with a huge sculpted flame covered in gold at its top. Sukarno's original intention was to have the monument topped with a gigantic real flame, perpetually fuelled with Indonesia's natural gas. Only after some persuasion did he agree to a golden representation instead.

11. The use of these discretionary funds along with a disregard for budgeting made the auditing process impossible. This problem was particularly evident to me, given my responsibilities as the government's auditor. It was not until I was appointed Governor of Bank Indonesia that a serious audit was possible and the scale of these discretionary funds was revealed.

12. Indonesia's hyperinflation and its causes are discussed in detail in Chapter 1.

13. Measured as Net National Product (NNP). NNP is obtained by subtracting capital goods depreciation from Gross National Product (GNP) figures, that is, NNP = GNP − Depreciation.

14. The 21 January 1965 edition of the newspaper *Harian Rakjat* reports that Indonesia's Supreme Advisory Council explained its decision to withdraw from the United Nations as representing, 'the will and desire of the Indonesian people, as a position inevitably bound up with the struggle of the Indonesian people to crush the neo-colonialist

Malaysia project, and to effect a world-wide struggle of the NEFO [Newly Emerging Forces] against the OLDEFO [Old Established Forces] forces'.

15. While the term in use was socialism, the intent was communism in the Marxist sense of the word, and as espoused by the leading proponents, the Soviet Union and China. In an interview the following month, Chairul Saleh, Indonesia's third deputy prime minister and spokesman on economic affairs, was quoted as saying, 'In the economic sphere, our aim is to bring about a kind of synthesis of two contrasting philosophies, liberal humanism and Marxism, within the framework of what we have described as Indonesian Socialism' (Ali, 1964).

16. Following the abortive *coup*, Governor Jusuf Muda Dalam was sentenced to death for subversion. Although the sentence was never executed, Jusuf remained in jail until his death. His actions as governor of the central bank were so blatantly and extremely wrong that the inescapable conclusion by the courts at the time was that he was engaging in a deliberate effort to destabilize the economy. His purpose for so doing seems to have been to fuel social unrest and thereby create a climate more conducive for a leftist seizure of power. In the same vein, the PKI elements of the Sukarno Cabinet were among the staunchest supporters of the confrontation with Malaysia. They consistently encouraged Sukarno to fight neo-colonialism despite the obvious fact that such conflicts were damaging Indonesia's reputation, causing needless suffering, and ruining the economy. Certainly, many others outside the PKI endorsed these conflicts, but few could rival the PKI in terms of the militancy and fervour with which they supported these conflicts. Here again, the PKI's intention may have been to destabilize the country, thereby facilitating a take-over of the government.

17. It is most unfortunate that so many of the details of the attempted *coup* remain unclear to this day. There is an enormous discrepancy, for example, in the number of casualties associated with the havoc that followed the attempted *coup*. Some scholars suggest that the PKI was not even behind the troubles. As someone who personally witnessed this catastrophe, I have no doubt that the attempted *coup* was, indeed, led by communists. For an official summary of the events associated with the attempted *coup*, see Indonesia, State Ministry (1994), *Gerakan 30 September Pemberontakan Partai Komunis Indonesia: Latar Belakang, Aksi, dan Penumpasannya*.

18. See *Kompas*, 9 December 1965 for a discussion of this measure.

19. Along with other members of the Cabinet, I was summoned to this meeting at 6.00 a.m. in order to avoid the street demonstrations. The situation on the streets became so chaotic that General Sukendro arrived late because he had to abandon his car and continue to the palace on bicycle. Most of the communist members of the Cabinet did not show up for the meeting, perhaps because they anticipated that trouble was at hand. Although the atmosphere was tense, we proceeded with the meeting until one of the President's adjutants handed him a note that said the palace was encircled with unidentified troops. Sukarno abruptly decided to leave the palace, although the meeting had not been adjourned. Subandrio followed Sukarno in such a rush that he left with only one shoe on. Thereafter, the meeting quickly ended and we all managed to get home.

PART I

1966–1970
SEEKING STABILITY AT THE
TURNING POINT

Introduction

THE world that Indonesia's new government entered in 1966 was in a state of millennial transition. Three great trends marked the post-Second World War period: the collapse of colonialism, and the rise of two competing economic philosophies, totalitarian communism and capitalistic democracy. Across Asia and Africa, countries that for generations had been ruled from afar were gaining independence. The leaders of these newly emerging countries were forced to choose between not only communism and capitalism, they were also ineluctably drawn into a cold war that polarized virtually all international affairs and political and economic thinking in general. With declarations of non-alignment, Indonesia and other newly independent countries asserted their intention to dissociate themselves from this dichotomy. However, the net of superpower confrontation was cast wide, and no country was untouched.

The schism in world affairs went beyond the East–West showdown. The 1950s, and especially the 1960s, was a period of manic mood swings. In the 1950s, the Marshall Plan stimulated rapid growth on a global scale. However, the irrepressible optimism of this period gave way to a chaotic turmoil of the 1960s. It was as if the changes associated with the end of the millennium had arrived some forty years ahead of schedule. In South-East Asia, the full impact of the communist–capitalist collision had exploded into the war in Vietnam.

As this conflict spilled over into the neighbouring countries of Laos and Cambodia, there were signs that civilization itself was unraveling. Youths in the United States held massive anti-war demonstrations and expressed virulent antagonism toward the 'establishment' that most of the world had regarded as a model for modern society. In China, Mao Zedong launched his Great Cultural Revolution—a movement that brought destructive fanaticism and brutality to a new height by promising to do to Chinese culture what communism had done to free enterprise. In France, a showdown between the political left and right brought the country to its knees in the massive paralyzing strike of 1968. Among developing countries everywhere, the traditions and cultural norms that for centuries had provided social cohesion and security seemed anachronistic in the post-colonial period. A relatively new invention, the television, was being mass produced at very low cost and started to appear just in time for rural folks to catch a glimpse of the upheaval outside their villages. The world they saw was brutal but seductive. The cultural dislocations of modernity knew no national or economic boundaries. Centuries-old religious traditions were under attack or merely scorned as irrelevant. The masses were offered the utopian promises of Marx, or the hyperconsumerism of capitalism repackaged by advertising agencies. For the intellectuals, in the place of two millennia of religion and philosophy, Western philosophers offered the emptiness of existentialism or the anti-metaphysical logical positivism.

During this period, nothing seemed solid. Yet, the upheavals that were transforming societies around the globe were less visible in the field of economics. The monumental pre-war economic thinking of John Maynard Keynes still dominated. The Bretton Woods system that he championed was in its twilight years, but still served as the foundation of the non-communist international economy. A new monetarist vision was starting to vie for the hearts of the community of economists, but Keynes was still the guiding star against which all market-oriented theories were compared.

The field of development economics was itself underdeveloped. It was rooted in the assumption that problems developing countries faced were roughly the same as those of the industrialized countries a hundred years earlier. Besides a few scholars, such as W. W. Rostow and Paul N. Rosenstein-Rodan, development economics remained a competition between Marxism in the Soviet planning mode and Keynesian macroeconomics. Neither, however, was adequate in addressing the difficulties faced by many impoverished and underindustrialized countries. This was a problem for the leaderships of newly independent former colonies, such as Indonesia.

Outside the university, theories paled as politicians and revolutionaries struggled for the hearts and minds of people. With a world divided rather neatly into two camps, the allure of Marx was dangerously strong. Marx offered hope for classless equality to the millions of impoverished and indigent people who counted rice by the grain, relied on their feet for transportation, and rankled at the disparities in wealth that seemed to come hand-in-hand with liberal capitalism. In Indonesia, however, the failed communist *coup* of 1965 effectively closed the door on the communist alternative—at least for the moment. Yet, the Keynesian capitalist alternative was not entirely adequate to meet the country's conditions or disposition. The government's goal, therefore, was to devise a model of economic development suitable to Indonesia at its current stage of development and to tame the extreme hyperinflation that was devastating the economy. In its place, Indonesia urgently needed to achieve some portion of the stability that had eluded it for decades.

1
Stabilization: The Prerequisite
of Development

WHEN the new government began its work in 1966, one of the great puzzles of everyday life in Indonesia was how the average citizen managed to survive. For the overwhelming majority, incomes were barely sufficient to sustain subsistence levels of consumption. With inflation running over 650 per cent per year, money ceased to hold meaningful value. Ideas of social progress and personal betterment had faded. The focus of daily life was how to persevere in conditions of economic collapse.

No one trusted the economy. No one felt confident that basic necessities would be available from one day to the next. One of the few economic certainties was that a rupiah tomorrow would buy far less than it did today. The dysfunction in the economy was so extreme that people were literally dying as a result. Hunger was spreading, and unpredictable shortages of food had become a fact of life. Inflation was not just a hardship, it was dangerous.

Many interwoven factors and circumstances contributed to the breakdown of the Indonesian economy; inflation, however, had moved to centre stage. While poverty had slowed commerce to a crawl, inflation reeled forward at an ever-increasing pace. For most Indonesians, economic life had become a bewildering paradox: the economy was simultaneously overheating and lurching to a halt. Although the term had not yet been coined, this was Indonesia's period of great stagflation.

To begin the fight against inflation, the government needed to understand its nature, its habits, from where it derived its power and how it sustained itself over time. Inflation will vary according to the environment; in general, five factors contribute to inflation:[1]

1. *Growth in Money Supply*. If growth in the money supply exceeds the current demand for money, given the level of goods and services being created by an economy,[2] then prices rise as the currency is cheapened.

2. *Scarcity of Goods*. If final goods are in short supply, prices rise.

3. *Inflationary Expectations*. If buyers and sellers come to expect that inflation is an inherent aspect of an economy, then that mentality

feeds inflationary behaviour and creates resistance to anti-inflationary measures.

4. *Imported Inflation.* This occurs when the price of imports increases because of inflation in the country of origin, or due to a reduction in the value of the home currency. The importing country, as it were, imports inflation.

5. *Cost Push.* This occurs when costs of intermediate goods or labour increase, due largely to market imperfections or interventions, such as when governments impose a minimum wage or agree to hikes in utility rates.

Although all of these factors played a role in Indonesia's hyperinflation to some extent, the overwhelmingly dominant factor was an excessive supply of money created to finance the government's deficit. Indonesia had run budget deficits continually from the founding of the Republic until after the new government took office in 1966.[3] In 1964 and 1965, the size of the budget deficits had grown beyond the size of government revenues. In other words, deficits ran above 100 per cent (Table 1.1).

The seriousness of the deficit was even greater than the numbers suggest. Despite the erosion of the rupiah's value and the government's dwindling revenues, the military confrontation with Malaysia and the construction of 'prestige projects' continued. The government attempted to create 'wealth' by printing money, which accelerated inflation. Confusion grew along with the money supply. Uncertainty was so rife that it was virtually impossible to tell if one were getting richer or poorer as inflation ate away at the value of people's holdings day-by-day, hour-by-hour. People were initially in a state of shock. It did not take too long, however, before inflationary expectations were also running at hyperspeed. There was dire need for a resynchronization between the growth of the money supply and the country's production of goods and services.

At the close of the Sukarno years, Indonesia had completely exhausted its foreign exchange, which meant that access to the imports needed to assist in agricultural and industrial rehabilitation was tightly constrained.

TABLE 1.1
Indonesia's Governmental Revenues and Expenditures, 1964–1965 (Rp. millions)

	Revenues		Expenditures		Deficit	
Year	Budget	Actual	Budget	Actual	Actual	As Percentage of Revenues
1964	200	283	688	681	398	141
1965	671	923	965	2,526	1,603	174

Source: Bank Indonesia annual reports.

Yet without imports, farms were without fertilizer, pesticides, new seed varieties, and most farm machinery, and industries lacked machinery and essential inputs and components such as yarn for textile spinning. Industry and agriculture stagnated.

Life's essentials were in extremely short supply. People on fixed incomes (*penghasilan tetap*)[4] were especially hurt. As in most economically difficult periods, they were particularly vulnerable. This scarcity in essential goods was the most urgent problem the government faced. When hunger and shortages of essentials such as clothing become endemic to an economy, social unrest is not far away and the survival of the government is at stake.

THE MESSAGE OF THE PEOPLE'S SUFFERING

In keeping with the Indonesian tradition of giving a defining name to every Cabinet, in early 1966, Sukarno's last government was called 'Dwikora' which means 'The People's Twofold Command'. The name came from a slogan in the campaign against Malaysia and was reflective of the government's preoccupation with the fight against neo-colonialism. During the first quarter of 1966, as conditions in the country steadily deteriorated, the Dwikora government vainly tried to carry on business as usual. The government made feeble efforts to reform itself. It devised a half-hearted stabilization programme and then proceeded to ignore its own recommendations. Politics continued to dominate. In February 1966 the confrontation with Malaysia was escalated with the 'Crush Malaysia Campaign' (Kogam). Socialists and communists still dominated the Sukarno Cabinet.

When Sukarno authorized Soeharto to take effective control of the government, he was responding to a wave of public discontent that had gained an overwhelming momentum. It was clear that the ground on which the nation was founded was shifting—everyone was affected. What was not clear was where the upheaval would lead. The sequence of events was *change first, plan later*.

In such a moment, strong leaders are needed. Soeharto was the man of the moment. His sense of timing and political instincts were acute. This was a defining moment in Indonesia's history. The country needed a change in course. The people's message was a call for food and for a functioning economy. Soeharto immediately set a course that helped to channel the discontent of people toward productive ends.

On 12 March 1966, the day after he was authorized to lead the government, Soeharto's first official act was to ban the communist party from the government.[5] On 25 July 1966, with the sanction of the MPRS, Soeharto formed a new Cabinet.[6] This government was founded in response to a nation in distress, and the name it gave itself was the 'Ampera Cabinet', that is, the Cabinet of 'The Message of the People's Suffering'.

Sukarno remained President until February 1967. Despite this, the government was actually led by a 'presidium' of three, informally referred to as the 'Triumvirate'. Soeharto was the chairman, Adam Malik was in charge of foreign affairs, and the Sultan of Yogjakarta, Hamengkubuwono IX, was responsible for economic affairs. The Cabinet, like the three senior leaders, was comprised primarily of political and economic centrists. On 12 March 1967, Soeharto was installed as acting president and one year later, on 27 March 1968, Soeharto was appointed president of Indonesia by the MPRS.

From it origins on 11 March 1966, the new government staked its existence on its ability to respond to the nation's distress. At the time, the prospects for success were remote. In an attempt to manage popular expectations, Sultan Hamengkubuwono said in April 1966, 'We do not want to make promises which may create unrealistic hopes among the people. This could lead to disappointments if the improvements fail to meet expectations. The only promise we give is that we will work hard to meet the challenge' (Hamengkubuwono, 1966).

SUBDUING THE MAD ELEPHANT OF INFLATION

During the first fifteen years of the Republic, people did not automatically take inflation into account and hence their behaviour was little affected by it. However, when the country slipped into prolonged hyperinflation economic behaviour changed significantly. By the early 1960s, Indonesia had become a nation of hoarders. Consumers hoarded to avoid the inevitable price increases that constantly outpaced wage increases. Shopkeepers hoarded with the idea that they could maximize their profits by holding goods as long as possible. Given the extreme circumstances, this seemed like rational economic behaviour, but, needless to say, it only further exacerbated the economic crisis and exacted an even greater penalty on those who could not afford anything, the great number of 'have nots'.

The only group benefiting from these conditions were the speculators. With goods in limited supply, both consumers and manufacturers could be held hostage by speculators who successfully retained stocks of needed goods in short supply. The nation's principal harbour, Tanjung Priok, in Jakarta, had become a depot for speculators.[7]

If the new government was going to be able to defeat inflation it needed to gain control of the financial system that hitherto had eluded it. Perhaps even more difficult, Indonesia's leadership had to change the minds, behaviour, and emotions of every Indonesian. The government had to prove to the citizenry that this war on inflation was serious and now the government had the capacity and determination to reform the economy. The economic team knew that the window of opportunity was small. It had two to three years at most to bring inflation under control. If it succeeded, it would have accomplished a major step in resuscitating an economy that was showing every sign of utter disintegration. It would also have laid the groundwork for moving to the next stage of the developmental process: economic growth. If the team was unable to defeat hyperinflation, the continued existence of Indonesia as a functioning nation was in doubt.

As the new Cabinet was about to begin this task, I remembered the fragment of a story that some visiting African officials had told me several months earlier. As the story went, a gigantic elephant went insane. He went on a rampage throughout the jungle killing and destroying everything in his path. Even the lions were terrified of the elephant. One day a courageous rabbit decided that he had to save the jungle community so he determined to subdue the elephant by outsmarting him. As he began his quest to challenge the mad elephant, a bird in a tree sang out, 'Rabbit, rabbit, where are you going? Where are you going?' 'I'm going to subdue the elephant', said the rabbit. 'Can you do it? Can you do it?' sang the bird. 'I will try. I will try', replied the rabbit. With that, he went on his way.

I did not know how the story ended. Nor did I know if we could subdue the raging elephant of inflation that was destroying our country. All that was certain was that a small group of men had come together with the objective of restoring stability to the economy that was out of control. Our commitment and the sense of urgency were strong and intense. To succeed we would need the full support of the government and the people as well as a plan that could 'outsmart' inflation.

Planning the Attack

Soon after its formation, the economic team began work on what would eventually become the stabilization plan. The plan should be looked at from two perspectives: first, there were the strategic or contextual elements that were not formally part of the plan itself, but without which the plan would never have succeeded. Second, there was the formal plan itself. The next few paragraphs review some of the contextual aspects that supported the plan.

1. *Restructuring of the Government Apparatus.* Before the government could embark on an effort to restructure the economy, it had to take steps to put its own house in order. The new government undertook a major effort

to restructure itself. Some ministries were merged with others, and other ministries were streamlined. A key element was the central bank which had been incapacitated by the former governor. Restoration of the central bank was particularly important as it would have a focal role—in close co-operation with the Ministry of Finance—in a complex, multifaceted plan to return order to the economy.

2. *A Single-minded Attack on Inflation*. The government gave undivided priority to the stabilization effort. Everything else was secondary. This was more difficult than it sounds. Under ordinary circumstances, the job of government is to respond to the many demands from the full range of the electorate. By definition, it is a government's responsibility to listen to those constituencies and respond in the best and most appropriate way possible. However, for a period, the government deliberately had to limit its focus to what was most essential for recovery. All plans for government programmes were evaluated in terms of their contribution to the stabilization effort. The order of priority that the government set was consummately clear and simple: the first need was to stabilize the economy. Only thereafter could it broaden its efforts to attend to issues of longer-term growth and development.

3. *The Soft Shock*. How long could the government maintain a single-minded attack on inflation? No one knew, but certainly, it could not be too long, perhaps two or three years. The government needed quick results both because delays were dangerous—since the country's decline could continue or accelerate—and because, undoubtedly, the stabilization process would inflict new pains on the people. People will endure the pain of going to the dentist knowing that an hour of discomfort will result in long-term benefit. Similarly, people would bear a painful stabilization programme if they believed it was only a temporary transition. If, however, the pain were drawn out, it could engender disillusionment and unrest before the 'medicine' had its effect. The programme could be easily derailed. Therefore, instead of a gradual approach to stabilization, the government opted for a 'soft shock', that is, a firm and intensive change in the course of the economy, tempered by policies intended to stimulate economic growth to the fullest extent possible.

4. *Trusting in the Wisdom of the Market*. The previous government had moved steadily toward the socialization of the economy. This course had deprived the private sector of its strength. The new government moved decisively to restore conditions conducive to the growth of the private sector.

5. *Growing Through the Crisis*. Stabilization is generally a painful process in which governments try to arrest inflation through policies that limit demand. In other words, stabilization programmes impose strict austerity

on economies that are usually already poor. Stabilization programmes, therefore, are most often accompanied by economic contraction. The stabilization plan developed by the new economic team was unorthodox and radical; it created a tight link between stabilization and stimulation policies. In effect, the government's policy attempted to influence both the supply and demand sides of the economy in an aggressive manner. The first priority was to reduce inflation, plain and simple. However, the government's plan also aimed at stimulating production. Policies to achieve these objectives would run in parallel and be directed at different aspects of the economy. Indonesia's planners hoped that the country could grow through the stabilization process. To some, this idea was preposterous. To the economic planners, however, stabilization without growth was tantamount to finishing fourth in the Olympics—no medals, no parades, just a glorious achievement perceived as a failure.

The 3 October Plan

Less than seven months in office and following weeks of intensive preparation, on 3 October 1966, the government officially launched its stabilization programme. Remarkably, the programme was created without the benefit of a similar model to draw from. Several developing countries had successfully travelled the road from economic underdevelopment to achieve the stature of middle income countries. Moreover, there were countries, like Germany between the wars, that had experiences of hyperinflation. However, there was no model Indonesia could emulate of a country that had emerged simultaneously from such a low level of economic development and extreme hyperinflation. Indonesia had to break new ground.

Commenting on this period, Malcolm Gillis (1984: 244), a scholar on Indonesian economics, wrote:

What was unusual [in the stabilization measures adopted in Indonesia] was, first, the tenacity with which the policies were implemented, and second, the virtually complete absence of any empirical basis for predicting their success or failure. The reforms that were adopted were chosen not after examining the results of simulations or alternative policies in an econometric model, but because the training and experience of members of the economic team led them to expect that economic agents would ultimately respond to liberalized policies in ways beneficial to the economy.

The stabilization programme constituted the new government's first major set of economic policies. The public was hopeful, but skeptical. It did not know whether the government was seriously committed or if it even had the capability to execute its own policies. No one—not even the economic team—knew whether the measures would work. The policies were created with equal measures of science and faith. The essential elements of the programme were as follows:

1. *Fiscal Policy*. On the fiscal side, Indonesia set out to eliminate deficit financing and restrict itself to a balanced budget by discontinuing non-productive projects. It would concentrate on supporting revenue-generating activities and reorganizing its antiquated and inefficient taxation system.

2. *Monetary Policy*. The government tried to implement monetary policy that would slow the expansion of the money supply without putting an excessive squeeze on the economy. In essence, Indonesia would attempt a somewhat paradoxical policy of having a tight money policy—including generally tight credit—while simultaneously directing ample credit toward selected types of investment, such as the rehabilitation of existing production facilities or projects with the greatest potential to expand the country's productive capacity.

3. *Balance of Payments Policy*. The government would attempt to improve the country's balance of payments position by gradually building foreign reserves and moving toward a unified exchange rate. In the longer run, this would enable Indonesia to pursue international trade more aggressively.

4. *Debt Management*. The enormous foreign debt accumulated during the previous two decades represented both a drain on the country's resources and an obstacle to expansion. As part of the stabilization effort, the new government had to give top priority to debt management. Furthermore, the government needed to rebuild the nation's productive capacity. To do so required a new infusion of foreign resources, which was accomplished through the assistance of a consortium of creditors known as the Inter-Governmental Group on Indonesia (IGGI).[8]

The implementation of the programme was complex and risky. In the broadest terms, the various policies can be described as either 'stabilizing' ('demand regulating') or 'stimulating' ('supply-enhancing'). This distinction, though useful, must be qualified because most policies influence both supply and demand to some extent. In broad terms, however, this analysis holds. The details are described in the following sections.

RESTRAINING DEMAND

To eliminate hyperinflation, Indonesia focused on restraining domestic demand. On the macroeconomic level, disciplined fiscal policy required that the government first control its own overall spending. Now, after twenty years as an independent nation, Indonesia had to put aside its undisciplined spending habits and focus on the more sober and difficult task of living within its means. On a more micro-economic level, the government instituted policies that were intended to bring back to the formal economy those people who had become economically disenfranchised. In so doing, the economic life of the country would be able to rely on standard channels of commerce rather than the black market and the barter economy.

Living on a Budget

Nowhere were the economic policies of the new government in more stark contrast with those of the former regime than in the case of fiscal policies. The socialist orientation of the Sukarno government had led the government to control or tightly regulate almost every aspect of the economy, from public services to manufacturing and trade. The government apparatus and the economy itself had become almost indistinguishable. The government had overreached its capacity.

In December 1966, the Dewan Perwakilan Rakyat (DPR or Indonesia's Parliament) ratified the first budget of the new government. The budget document declares, 'The 1967 Budget is said to be the Balanced Budget, meaning the Government's expenditures are limited by the State's revenues, so that the deficit is eliminated as much as possible' (Indonesia, Departemen Keuangan, 1967: 17). With this simple statement, the New Order asserted a fundamental break with the past.

A schematic summary of the new format of the Indonesian government adopted for its budgets appears in Table 1.2. According to this formula, foreign aid is added to the list of standard government revenues along with oil, taxes, and miscellaneous proceeds such as remittances from state-owned enterprises. Furthermore, debt service is categorized as a routine expense along with personnel costs and other costs of running the government. When foreign aid is received to finance development projects, it is listed under 'development revenues'. What this means is that Indonesia's concept of balanced budget is not entirely standard since the government considers foreign aid as a *revenue*, even though foreign aid generally constitutes new *debt*. Although the classification of revenues and expenditures deviated from existing norms, it has served a very important function: it meant that the government never budgeted beyond what it expected to collect from taxes, foreign aid, and revenues from oil and state-owned enterprises.

TABLE 1.2
A Schematic Summary of the Indonesian Government's Budget

Revenues	*Expenditures*
Domestic Revenues	Routine Expenditures
Proceeds from oil and state	Personnel, material, subsidies, and others
enterprises	Debt service payment
Taxes	Development Expenditures
Development Revenues	Ministries and institutes including security
Programme aid	and defense
Project aid	Regional development including Inpres
	Development budget reserves
	Project aid

The 'balanced budget' demanded uncustomary fiscal discipline. Previous budgets had been more of a chronicle of funds spent rather than a tool for economic management. By contrast, the 1967 budget began with an analysis of the country's economic conditions. Based thereon, the government created a budget in which the projected revenues of Rp 81.3 billion were matched by an equivalent amount in expenditures. Expenditures were divided between 'routine' and 'development'. All special or supplementary budgets were eliminated. By a presidential decree signed on 31 December 1966, on a quarterly basis the government was required to produce a report on the realization of the budget, credit, debt conditions, and so on. This report evolved into the accountability reports that are still produced on a semi-annual basis. This report is audited by the Supreme Audit Board.

One assumption included in the 1967 budget was that the inflation rate could be brought down to 30 per cent over the course of the year. Although that inflation target was not reached, the budget did succeed in staying essentially in balance. When the year was over, the total receipts were Rp 84.9 billion and total expenditures were Rp 87.5 billion, a discrepancy of a mere 3 per cent.

The commitment to a balanced budget has been one of the cornerstones of the government's economic policy since the transition of power to the New Order. To this day, the government's only exception to this rule has been special funds for calamities—chiefly earthquakes or floods.

The government knew its credibility would depend largely on whether it could mobilize the resources needed to operate within the self-imposed strictures of the balanced budget. Yet, the nation's foreign exchange was exhausted, trade was crippled, and the taxation system was incapable of performing its function. The commitment to a balanced budget created an immediate dilemma—a balanced budget requires a base of revenues, but Indonesia was impoverished and its capacity to raise revenues was weak.

Taxes are the economic lifeblood of government. However, when a country has a per capita income of $60, tax collection is like a blood drive among the anaemic and those awaiting operations. Fair taxation in a period of hyperinflation is almost impossible. For example, if a shopkeeper purchases a product for Rp 100 and sells it a month later for Rp 200, he appears to have made Rp 100 in profit and should be taxed accordingly. But if the inflation rate is running at 100 per cent per month, then in fact the shopkeeper has simply broken even. Moreover, if the inflation rate is running at 75 per cent, the shopkeeper may have earned a minimal profit, but in a matter of days that profit will be rendered inconsequential. How much, therefore, should the shopkeeper be taxed? What should be a simple question, is rendered a paradox.

Despite the hyperinflation, Indonesia had no alternative; it had to tax. Indonesia's challenge was how to tax effectively in conditions inhospitable to taxation. Taxes can be divided into two categories: indirect taxes, such as duties on traded items, and direct taxes, such as corporate and personal income taxes. Indirect taxes constituted 49.6 per cent of Indonesia's total tax revenues in 1967. Foreign trade, although small, played an important role in the government's budgetary process. During this period, oil played a relatively insignificant role as a contributor to governmental revenues, contributing only 8.7 per cent in 1967. The relatively heavy reliance on indirect taxes is typical of developing countries at a stage of development similar to that of Indonesia.

On a practical level, the entire system of taxation, from assessment to collection, was deficient. The country desperately needed to thoroughly revamp the entire system of taxation. However, in the early days of the New Order, the government decided to pick its battles selectively. For this reason, serious tax reform was not implemented until nearly twenty years later, in the 1980s. In the late 1960s, the most important measure taken to improve tax collection was to increase the salaries of tax officials and to place more effort in independent audits, as imprecise as they were under the circumstances.

During this early period, the best that can be said is that the government managed to make a dysfunctional system work more efficiently. Over the years, there were many instances when makeshift solutions had to suffice. Sometimes the art of politics relies on leveraging maximum benefit from deficient conditions. In this case, despite the limitations of Indonesia's taxation system, the government managed to coax from it the revenues needed to keep the budget in balance. Tax revenues progressively rose, moving in nominal terms from Rp 12.5 billion in 1966 to Rp 240.5 billion in 1970.[9]

Managing government expenditures, the economic team discovered, was fraught with difficulties comparable to those encountered in managing revenue collection. In a patriarchal society such as Indonesia, the government had become the ultimate patron. There was almost no element of the economy that was not directly touched by the government. For a non-communist country, Indonesia under the Old Order had come about as close as one gets to a command economy. The omnipresence of the government in the economy brought with it many of the problems frequently associated with socialist governments: the government was far too big, both in terms of the number of employees and in its pervasive presence in commerce and industry. The economy was dominated by highly inefficient state enterprises. Government spending was based largely on political motives, with little attention to economics. Moreover, every point of economic interaction within the government was a new opportunity for patronage or corruption.

In 1966, the new government urgently needed to establish priorities so that it could operate within its budget. Cutting expenditures proved to be very difficult. It is impossible to cut expenditures without adversely affecting some group, and each group fought and lobbied to retain its benefits. Even at this stage of development, budget cutting launched a vigorous and complicated political struggle among various factions. The process was arduous and time consuming, but unavoidable.

To balance the budget, the government had to be firm, bordering on ruthless, in cutting expenditures. The 1967 budget itemized the essence of the budget reductions. Cuts fell into six categories:[10]

1. Reduction in personnel costs both in the civil and the military services;

2. Halt in the purchase of land, building, and other related items for the civil and the military services;

3. Halt in subsidies from the central government to the regions;

4. Halt in subsidies to state-owned enterprises;

5. Halt or postponement of projects still in early stages that would not bear quick financial benefit to the state;

6. Prohibition of new projects that place a burden on Indonesia's domestic currency, the rupiah, or foreign exchange reserves.

These six can be further summarized as restrictions on the size of the government, rescheduling or cancellation of capital projects, and reductions in subsidies.

1. *Managing the Size of the Government.* Since independence,

Indonesia's central and local governments had become the principle providers of employment outside of the agricultural sector. Even the most casual observation of government operations revealed a major surplus of labour and extreme inefficiency. Inefficient or not, for both cultural and political reasons, massive lay-offs were not considered an option for balancing the budget. Therefore, aside from the removal of declared communists from the bureaucracy, the government's primary method for payroll reduction was through attrition. Although there was evidence that this did lead to a reduction in the number of employees, the costs of maintaining Indonesia's government, given the level of its gross national product (GNP) was among the highest in the world. Generally, about 36 per cent of the state budget was allocated to cover the cost of state employees. As Indonesia's crisis eased in the early 1970s, the number of government employees eventually grew again, although new employees were generally added in services that were previously underdeveloped, such as health care and education. The State Ministry for Administrative Reform was later established to prevent an uncontrolled expansion in government agencies and employees.

In the 1967 budget, the government mandated that each ministry create an itemized list of its annual funding requirements. After the budget was passed by the Parliament, ministries had to operate within their approved budgets. In contrast to previous practices, there was very little room for adjustment, and budgets were no longer 'negotiated' during the course of a fiscal year.

2. *Rescheduling or Cancelling Projects.* The new government decided to halt funding immediately to all non-essential projects. The statement made by Soeharto on behalf of the Indonesian government at the Multilateral Conference in Tokyo on 17 September 1966 provided a clear guideline for approving or cancelling projects. There he said, 'my government is determined as part of the stabilization programme to curtail expenditures on investments temporarily, although it is vitally important in providing for wider employment opportunities. Projects which are not expected to yield economic results in a short time have to be postponed or will be abandoned altogether. If in appropriate cases, private business has shown interest in completing these projects on their own account, my government will welcome such interest' (Soeharto, 1966: 8–9).

The government gave funding priority for rehabilitation of infrastructure and productive facilities that had fallen into disrepair. The strategy was to restrict appropriations only to those projects that promised a very quick return on investment. All 'prestige projects' that were not very close to completion were halted. The basic methodology used to determine if a project would be funded or terminated was as follows: the government began with a basic assumption that all projects would be cut. A project was 'guilty until proven innocent'. Then each project was evaluated on a case-by-case basis. Unless compelling economic arguments could be made for the continuation of a project, the policy to suspend or terminate remained.

Cutting a project, however, is expensive. If a project were suspended, but not terminated, costs were incurred simply by keeping the work on hold. If a project were cancelled, the government often had to pay cancellation fees. To avoid cancellation or rescheduling costs, the government wanted to sell projects rather than close them. Unfortunately, the private sector was generally disinterested in buying projects rejected by the government. Therefore, the full financial brunt of cancelling or rescheduling a project fell upon the government. The only consolation was the costs of cancellation or rescheduling were less than the cost of completing the projects. These savings came at a price, but without sacrifice, the budget would not have balanced.

3. *Reduction in Subsidies*. The new government also decided to attack the politically sensitive issue of subsidies. This was done with some trepidation, since violent public opposition to cuts in subsidies contributed to the fall of the Old Order. None the less, the new government took a bold step of cutting significantly the subsidies to state-owned enterprises and the armed forces. Furthermore, the government decided to reduce subsidies for petrol. According to a government inquiry, in early 1966 an Indonesian taxi driver probably *paid more for a cup of tea than for a litre of petrol*. The government's intention was to maintain some subsidies on essential products, such as rice and kerosene, but to cut back as much as possible. In April 1968, the subsidy on petrol was removed, causing a 400 per cent price increase, from Rp 4 to Rp 16 per litre. The price increase was felt throughout the economy, yet the overall inflationary impact was not very significant as there were no new costs. Instead, the cost of petrol was passed from the government to the consumers. Widespread angry protests did follow; they were the strongest manifestations of dissatisfaction against the new government so far encountered. Still, the government held firm in its position and this policy ultimately proved anti-inflationary and for the benefit of the country. By cutting the petrol subsidy, a major drain on government resources was eliminated. The reduction in subsidies was an inevitable manifestation of the balanced budget policy.

Restoring the Central Bank

Although the prominent cause of Indonesia's hyperinflation was 'hyper-deficit spending', there were various manifestations of monetary policy that also had a role. Establishing appropriate monetary policies was one of the most difficult and important aspects of Indonesia's stabilization effort. To restore value to Indonesia's money, Indonesia had to take charge of the money supply and rebuild the country's financial institutions—above all the central bank.

In the final years of the Old Order, the independence and institutional integrity of the central bank was profoundly compromised. The central bank relinquished its three principal duties: preserving the value of the Indonesian currency, maintaining stability of the banking system, and serving as the lender of last resort. For Indonesia to regain control of the economy, the banking system had to be reconstructed at great speed. This effort was integrated into the October 1966 stabilization programme.

The first and most important step in reforming the banking system focused above all on the central bank, then called Bank Negara Indonesia. Since the state-owned commercial banks had been merged into the central bank, Indonesia's central bank reform necessarily included reform of the entire commercial banking sector. The six-year period during which Indonesia's financial data had not been made public served as a screen of ignorance that hid a multitude of sins. The new government had to get behind that screen and establish with much more rigour the true financial position of the country. Soon after the Ampera Cabinet had been installed, an internal audit of the central bank and the commercial banks was launched. The first objective of the audit was to gain an understanding of the current financial state of the central bank and, secondly, to reconstruct retroactively the accounting records that had been neglected or falsified during the previous years. Besides revealing pervasive patterns of graft, corruption, and sabotage, the audit brought to light the full extent to which the country's foreign exchange reserves had been depleted and the magnitude of the country's debt. Besides helping to create an accurate picture of the country's finances, the audit was also instrumental in identifying those personnel who had engaged in fraud or other corrupt or illegal activities associated with the central bank.[11]

Following the audit, a system of acceptable banking practices had to be created—first, for implementation at the level of the central bank and secondly for commercial banks. The most important reform policy was the restoration of limited central bank autonomy. It should be noted that although the reformed banking laws were not passed until 31 December 1968, as early as 1966, the central bank began operating informally under the rules that would later become law. The essence of the banking reform law of 1968 included the following:

- The state banking conglomerate, Bank Negara Indonesia, was to be reorganized by returning the state commercial banks to their former status. The commercial banks regained their previous names and were expected to lend based on expected profit. The commercial banks resumed their specializations in agriculture, trade, industry, and so on. The central bank would exert control over the commercial banks via instruments such as fractional reserve requirements and the discount rate;
- The central bank, renamed Bank Negara Indonesia Unit I in 1965, regained its original name, Bank Indonesia;
- Bank Indonesia became the monitor of the country's entire banking system, with oversight responsibility for all commercial banking activities in Indonesia;
- Bank Indonesia was again charged with responsibility for safeguarding the integrity of the nation's currency;
- Monetary policy would be determined through a 'Monetary Council' comprising the governor of Bank Indonesia, the Minister of Finance, and the Minister of Trade;
- Bank Indonesia was restricted in the amount it could lend to the government based on the budget approved by the Parliament. The Bank would lend money to the government at a rate of 3 per cent per annum or at a rate to be determined by the Monetary Council;
- Bank Indonesia would begin publishing annual reports and monthly financial updates. These reports were intended to supply information essential in assessing the condition of the economy.

The bank reforms implemented during this period constituted an important step in returning Indonesian banking to a state of relative normalcy. Commercial interest again became the guiding principle for the country's commercial banks. The environment was again suitable for foreign banks to operate in a commercially viable manner. While the reforms did represent an important step forward, by modern banking standards, they were still deficient. Compared to many industrialized economies, Indonesia's central bank still lacked sufficient autonomy. Furthermore, foreign and domestic banks were so tightly regulated that their ability to respond effectively to the country's banking needs was severely constrained. None the less, the reforms enhanced stability, diversity, and limited competition among commercial banks. These reforms were essential in creating a banking system that could meet the basic needs of Indonesia's evolving economy.

By restoring order to Indonesia's banking system, the government was better able to reassert control over the money supply. Monetary management is one of the most important components in any programme to control inflation. Indonesia was no exception to this principle. What was unusual in Indonesia's case were the creative and aggressive measures the government took to bring discipline to a monetary system that under the influence of hyperinflation had grown perversely resistant to stability.

To understand this process we will first review the background and strategy for managing the money supply in Indonesia's attack on inflation. We will then look at supporting policies, such as credit, savings, and balance of payments policies.

Restoring Value to Money Through Money Supply Regulation

The growth in Indonesia's money supply during the early 1960s was a kind of vicious cycle, where excessive growth in the money supply triggered inflation, which then required a larger volume of money. In 1965, the government increased the money supply three-fold. Then in the first quarter of 1966, the money supply doubled again.

Soon after the Ampera Cabinet was installed in July 1966, it began its attack on inflation by focusing on money supply management and development of the nation's productive sectors. The goal of the country's monetary policy was to regulate the money supply in a manner that neither strangled economic growth nor fed inflation. As was stated earlier, the government did not want to take a 'gradualist' approach to inflation reduction. Since the government had decided on a 'soft-shock' approach, the policies were intended to bear results fairly quickly. This meant that the government would have one chance to implement policies that were correct and effective. There would be few opportunities for mid-course corrections. The economy was wounded and its health precarious. If the anti-inflationary measures were too loose, inflation might be weakened but not defeated. If the measures were too strict, the country could slip into a deep and devastating depression.

Monetarists such as Milton Friedman in the United States saw monetary policy as one of the essential elements in influencing economic stability and growth. Indonesia's economic team tended to agree. In his article on inflation and money supply, Friedman (1968: 3) states:

[In the period prior to the great depression] the US monetary authorities followed highly deflationary policies. The quantity of money in the United States fell by one-third in the course of the contraction. And it fell not because there were no willing borrowers—not because the horse would not drink. It fell because the Federal Reserve System forced or permitted a sharp reduction in the monetary base, because it failed to exercise the responsibilities assigned to it in the Federal

Reserve Act to provide liquidity to the banking system. The Great Contraction is tragic testimony to the power of monetary policy—not as Keynes and so many of his contemporaries believed, evidence of its impotence.

The Great Depression resulted from many factors most of which had no parallel in Indonesia's economy in the 1960s. Friedman's words, however, aptly identified the potentially devastating effect of a mismanaged monetary policy which was at the heart of Indonesia's hyperinflation.

Indonesia's central bank was acutely aware that it had to walk a fine line between a money supply that was too tight or too loose. Every central bank faces this problem, but for Indonesia in the mid- to late-1960s the problems were of a different order. Monetary management in hyperinflation is like operating in a typhoon—although there is no progress, monetary affairs are spinning very quickly. Good judgements require reasonably accurate data. The country's capacity for gathering statistics was primitive and inadequate. No one in Indonesia was able to gauge accurately the size and the rate of growth of the money supply. Since the needed information simply was not available, the central bank had to bring the money supply back on track based on 'educated guesses' extrapolated from provisional and unreliable data.

A second related problem in managing the money supply pertained to timing. After implementing measures to expand or contract the money supply, the government needed to estimate the impact on inflation and the country's overall economic activity. Based on that, the central bank would implement subsequent measures with the objective of systematically reducing inflation. However, statistics supplied to the central bank were *four to six months old*. To combat Indonesia's hyperinflation, the central bank needed information that accurately described *current changes* in money supply on a day-to-day basis, not historic information. Under these circumstances, it was very difficult to establish causal links between policies and movements in the economy. Yet, there was constant pressure to implement corrective measures quickly even though, under hyperinflation, a quick and wrong action today could be greatly magnified over a short period and result in a cumulative effect that grossly overshot or undershot the money supply targets set by the central bank.

Consumer prices in various markets, mainly Jakarta, were monitored by spot checks on the fluctuating prices of a basket of sixty-two goods and services. However, the analysis of this information and other complex calculations were done by hand. To address this problem, Bank Indonesia obtained an IBM mainframe computer and sent several employees abroad to learn how to operate it. A year later, when the machine was up and running, the Bank was only able to draw on about half of its capacity. It was not until 1971 that the machine was fully functional.[12] Yet, surprisingly, the Bank's policies were generally correct. What the Bank lacked in terms of precise data, it made up for with its consistency and persistence in policy implementation.

A third problem in regulating the money supply resulted from the fact that so much of Indonesia's population operated outside the formal economy. Both the black market and the barter market were so big that they added to the distortions of an already highly distorted economy. To deal directly with this problem, the government implemented savings policies that served as an incentive for people to enter the formal economy. This will be discussed further below.

During the 1967–70 period, the government endured vociferous criticism from all sides for monetary policies that were described simultaneously as too tight and too loose. Those who argued for looser monetary policies were primarily domestic merchants and, to some extent, consumers who wanted easier access to credit and expanded salaries. Academic and institutional analysts tended to regard Indonesia's money supply policy as too expansionary. There was no simple solution. Indonesia's money supply had grown in nominal terms, but in real terms, the money supply had contracted. According to an excellent analysis by Heinz Arndt, the real money supply peaked in 1960 and by 1966 had fallen to less than one quarter of that value. As he explains,

The outstanding feature of the money situation in Indonesia in the last three years [i.e. 1964–1966] has been the paradoxical characteristics of all hyperinflations: shortages of money. The basic reason for the paradox is simple enough. As prices run ahead of expansion of money supply with increasing loss of confidence in the currency, the 'real' value or purchasing power of the money supply shrinks (1966: 58).

The essence of the government's method for restoring value to the nation's currency was to decrease the rate of growth of the money supply while simultaneously endeavouring to limit and direct credit to productive sectors. In absolute terms, Indonesia's monetary policy appeared expansionary. However, because the rate of growth had slowed, the monetary policy was perceived as being very tight.[13]

In certain respects the money supply was tightened and loosened simultaneously. The government tried to allow the money supply to grow sufficiently to maintain growth in designated sectors. In other areas, however, money seemed very tight indeed. Initially, much available credit went to supply the needs of the government and state-owned enterprises as well as the agricultural sector. What was most important is that money was not being 'created' to finance ever-increasing deficits by the government. In fact, the entity that was hit hardest by the tight monetary policy was the government itself. Prestige projects, such as the Borobudur Hotel and the Senayan sports complex were postponed, and others were cancelled altogether. This is as it should have been, because the government had been the primary generator of inflation.

By controlling the money supply, the government took an important step in neutralizing inflation and restoring value to money. Indonesia's money supply policy was effective, however, because this policy was integrated into a broader set of highly unorthodox measures intended to give some power to the government's anti-inflationary 'shock treatment'. These measure included steps to expand bank deposits and manage credit flows in a selective manner.

From Hoarders to Savers: Bringing People Back to the Bank

In the attack on inflation, an unusual campaign took place at the point where macroeconomic policy meets micro-economics. For a brief period, Indonesia's banks took on a radical role as the front line in Indonesia's war on inflation. The strategy, in essence, was to arrest inflation by getting people to stop spending money and save it instead. This removed money from circulation, slowed monetary velocity, and provided the banks with the liquidity that could be later channelled to productive investments.

In the mid-1960s, Indonesia had fourteen private savings banks and one state savings bank, Bank Tabungan Negara (BTN). Indonesia's banks—private and state alike—were focused on commercial banking rather than personal savings. The typical Indonesian citizen had no access to any banking services whatsoever. Nor did banks have much incentive to service individual depositors. Their accounts were too small and there were too few of them. Furthermore, the economy was so unstable that it discouraged people from using banks. Hyperinflation is a powerful disincentive to using money. By holding money, one sacrifices one's wealth to hyperinflation. To avoid this, people tried to keep their wealth either as tradable goods, such as rice or livestock, or even land. A bag of rice retained its value, rupiah did not. There were many drawbacks, though, to holding one's wealth in-kind: it provided no interest or security, it strengthened the barter system, and it slowed the development of a sophisticated economy.

To get Indonesians through the doors to conduct business, banks needed strong enticements. This was done by raising interest rates on one-year time deposits to 6 per cent *per month* and by keeping all deposits and interest tax-free. Depositors were not required to declare the origins of deposit. At the time, inflation was still running higher than the interest rates, so the consumers still lost money in real terms. None the less, the security of holding one's money in a bank at an annual interest rate of 72 per cent proved irresistible.

Table 1.3 summarizes the monthly interest rates offered on savings accounts.

These policies had a major impact on every member of the economy, from the very poor to the very rich. In record numbers, the urban labourers and small farmers opened bank accounts for the first time in their lives. Wealthy Indonesians who had gone to great lengths to keep their capital in foreign currency, tradable assets, or in offshore accounts, held more and more money in rupiah and in Indonesian banks. In 1969, state banks and many private banks participated in a savings campaign called Tabungan Berhadiah (Savings with Prizes). People who opened savings accounts were automatically entered into a lottery. Two other programmes were launched in 1971, the Tabungan Pembangunan Nasional (Tabanas or Savings Programme for National Development) and the Tabungan Asuransi Berjanka (Taska or Twelve Month Savings Programme for Life Insurance). Programmes such as these helped to create a *culture of savings*. This was a crucial step in creating a whole new 'economic culture' that could lead to sustainable economic development.[14]

Initially, the interest rates on time deposits were higher than commercial lending rates. This was possible because Bank Indonesia would lend to banks at subsidized rates as a means of continuing the flow of credit at the same time that deposits were pouring in. The Bank's monetary policies were so successful in building deposits that it considered the subsidy to be a very worthwhile investment.

Deposits sky-rocketed. Between October and December 1968, time deposits rose from Rp 3 billion to Rp 4.5 billion. In the process, Indonesia had moved from a nation of hoarders to a nation of savers. As Malcolm

TABLE 1.3
Indonesia's Monthly Interest Rates on Deposits,
October 1968–January 1970

As of	1-month deposit	3-month deposits	6-month deposits	12-month deposits
1 October 1968	1.5	4.0	5.00	6.0
17 March 1969	1.5	4.0	4.00	5.0
1 May 1969	1.0	2.0	3.00	4.0
10 July 1969	1.0	1.5	2.50	3.0
15 September 1969	1.0	1.5	2.00	2.5
1 January 1970	1.0	1.5	1.75	2.0

Source: *Bank Indonesia Report 1969/70*, p. 38.

Gillis points out, 'The effects [of the savings scheme] were immediate and sizable: within a year the public was holding about 25 per cent of its liquid assets in such deposits. One result was that the ratio of liquid assets to GDP rose from below 6 per cent in 1968 to almost 16 per cent by 1975' (1984: 255). This is certainly one of the largest increases in savings ever recorded.

The policy was not welcomed by all, however. Because government credit favoured certain sectors over others, those who did not receive preferential treatment regarded the policy as economic discrimination and misguided interventionism. By the late 1960s, traders and industrialists were continually demanding a looser monetary policy. Their request would be fulfilled eventually as savings were translated into loans for productive investments. Change, however, came too gradually for many, but the process was needed to maintain stability as the economy was being nursed back to health.

The increased savings absorbed liquidity from the market which created tremendous deflationary pressure. Earlier, people would be inclined to spend money on non-essential products simply as a way of keeping their exposure to currency at a minimum. With deposit rates so high, people again had an incentive to save. Flush with cash, banks were in a better position to lend, although, by government policy, they were required to regulate their lending according to special government guidelines, known as the selective credit scheme. This is discussed below.

STIMULATING SUPPLY

By themselves, the stabilization policies might have arrested inflation. However, if the policies ended there, economic growth and productivity might have been crushed along with inflation. Indonesia's economic development was very 'thin'. In the late 1960s, industry was negligible and foreign investment was almost non-existent. The stabilization policies alone were insufficient. They needed the counterbalance of policies that would stimulate production. Conceptually, the transition from stabilization to growth is simple. Practically speaking, however, the transition was exceedingly complex and risky. Miscalculated efforts to stimulate production could easily re-energize inflation. The situation could be likened to trying to drive a manual shift motor car up a very steep mountain road under monsoon rains. Under rampant hyperinflation, the motor car was sliding backwards down the slippery road. Stabilization was like applying the brake which halted the regression. The trick, then, was to shift the motor car into gear to resume the ascent. Of course, this can be done, but as soon as one lifts one's foot off the brake, the motor car can easily stall or start to backslide forcing one to apply the brake again. One has to try to move forward, but under such conditions, the attempt is dangerous and nerve-racking.

Improving Food Production and Distribution

Rice shortages produced more than inflation: they caused hunger, fear, social upheavals, and sometimes even death. It would be wrong to reduce Indonesia's agricultural sector to rice alone. Plantation crops, such as rubber and coffee, were the nation's principal exports and, therefore, of enormous importance for the country's economic restoration. Rice, however, served as an unofficial barometer of national well-being. Especially because Indonesia's foreign exchange reserves were so low, importing rice became particularly problematic. The correlation between rice shortages and inflation was unnervingly direct. When rice supplies fell, rice prices rose and—as if by some inexplicable law of physics—prices throughout the economy moved in concert. Then the all too familiar cycle of a troubled economy began: shortages led to hoarding, hoarding led to speculation, and speculation to public discontent. In 1967, the government set rice self-sufficiency as one of its economic goals. In fact, it took Indonesia an additional seventeen years to achieve this goal. This effort will be discussed in Chapter 5. What was critical for the government during the stabilization period was to keep rice supplies adequate for consumption needs and to maintain relative price stability.

Poverty and lack of industrial and transportation infrastructure exacerbated Indonesia's rice shortages. The immediate need in the mid- to late-1960s was to obtain and distribute fertilizer. The country had one fertilizer factory with a production capacity of 100,000 tonnes per year—plainly insufficient to meet the nation's needs. With foreign exchange reserves depleted, the country lacked the means to import the fertilizer that could have greatly improved production. Even when fertilizers were obtainable, distribution was severely constrained due to inadequate infrastructure. Fortunately, during some critical periods, Indonesia was able to obtain rice supplies primarily through the PL 480 food aid from the United States and food aid programmes from Japan and other IGGI countries. The shortage of foreign exchange, however, proved to be a serious impediment to the short-term provision of adequate rice supplies.

The government approached the logistical problem of managing rice supplies primarily through two vehicles, *money supply management* and the *operation of a national food agency* (or logistics board), called by the Indonesian abbreviation, 'Bulog'.[15]

Money supply management was linked to rice production by recognizing the cyclical nature of the Indonesian economy. Every year, the country's main rice harvest came in the November–January period. There was a corresponding increase in economic activity in this period as traders purchased rice stock and farmers purchased many of their supplies for the upcoming year. Although the central bank tried to constrain the growth in the money supply, it still needed to be expanded on an annual basis to ensure there was sufficient liquidity to support a burst of economic activity during this critical time of year. The problem then arose regarding how to manage the money supply after the harvest period was over. This is where Indonesia's deposit scheme helped to absorb the excess liquidity and keep downward pressure on inflation.

It was specifically in response to this economic cycle that Indonesia moved in 1970 to change the beginning of its fiscal year to 1 April.[16] Although the December–January period represented the peak period in economic activity, the increase flow of tax revenues that resulted would not find their way to government coffers until February and March. The government decided that it was best, therefore, to begin the budget year with revenues relatively replete, which was the case in April. By recognizing this agrarian cycle and shifting the fiscal year to begin in April, the government was better able to balance the supply of money with the demand for money.

The other stabilizing tool in the government's arsenal was the creation of the Badan Urusan Logistik (Bulog or the National Logistics Board) responsible for managing strategic food supplies such as rice. Bulog traces its origin to the food agency used by the Old Order to oversee food distribution.[17] In the early days of the New Order, Bulog's official responsibilities were as follows: first, to co-ordinate the activities of the entities engaged in the supply and distribution of essential commodities, or things closely related to those commodities, such as fertilizer for rice; second, to supply and distribute rice in accordance with the regulations established by the government, particularly to civil servants, personnel of state enterprises, and the armed forces; and third, to execute the instructions from the Chairman of the Presidium with matters pertaining to logistics. The mandate of this agency was to build and maintain a buffer stock of rice, manage rice distribution throughout the country, and engage in market intervention in order to preserve price stability for rice. The agency could and did extend its responsibility to other products, but rice has always been the commodity that dominated Bulog's activities. The essential elements of this policy were adopted in 1968 and have been in effect ever since.

The impact of Bulog on the economy was generally positive although, as will be discussed later, it encountered problems along the way. Despite the difficulties, however, the creation of Bulog helped to boost confidence

among consumers and producers alike. Eventually, the deep-seated fear of
ever-looming food shortages diminished. This reduced food speculation
and led to greater stability throughout the economy.

Pervasive Need and Selective Credit

The biggest problem faced by the new government was pervasive poverty.
Indonesia's poverty was unbearable; it stretched from the farmers in the
fields to the depleted treasury of the central government. Stabilized poverty would constitute a miserable victory. One of the most fundamental
questions the government faced was how to create purchasing power from
almost nothing. The government's answer was 'selective credit'.

Indonesia's selective credit policy may have been the most important
step taken to move the economy from stability back to growth. The strategy behind the selective credit policy was 'leveraged economics'. Since the
country had so little money, the government had to 'cultivate' wealth by
shrewdly investing the country's limited funds and foreign aid in those
programmes that would yield the maximum return. That would then have
to be reinvested, and eventually, it was hoped Indonesia's potential wealth
could start to materialize. In the very beginning, however, the government
had to take exceptional measures. To qualify for credit, a project should
meet at least one of the following criteria: there should be a quick return
on investment; the investment should be in food production or an export
industry; and the investment should be for the rehabilitation of an existing
facility, rather than a new project.

Since capital was very constrained, banks prioritized their loans based
on the above criteria. The lending rate was also determined according to
the type of investment. High priority projects were given loans at lower
rates than projects in low priority areas. Furthermore, the 3 October stabilization programme instructed banks to no longer discriminate between
private sector businesses and state-owned enterprises.[18]

The selective credit policy allowed the government to channel the
country's limited funds to those sectors of the economy that could help to
reduce scarcity in essential goods and rehabilitate infrastructure and
industrial capacity. In so doing the government was able to allow much of
the nation's wealth to remain in the hands of the private sector while concentrating and directing the flow of resources to support national reconstruction. Because the interest rates on credit were below the inflation rate,
banks were lending at a loss. Ultimately this loss was carried by the central
bank, which deliberately lent money at below market rates as a way of
stimulating investment in priority sectors. This notwithstanding, some
critics insisted that official interest rates were still too high. Bruce

Glassburner (1978: 36), one of the leading scholars on Indonesia, provided an appropriate response to the critics:

[T]he assertion that interest rates were high in the years of the stabilization policy is based on a quite simple failure to distinguish between nominal and real rates.... In 1965–66, in informal markets, even among personal friends, rates were 16–20 per cent *per month*, a rate which roughly matched the rate of inflation, hence approximately sustained the real value of the money lent. The state banks were charging 25 to 50 per cent *per annum*, depending on the class of loan, which implied a subsidy of virtually the entire amount of the loan.

He then goes on to state: 'It is true, of course, that private entrepreneurs complained bitterly about the "liquidity crisis" and the high cost of money. Liquidity was scarce, having been largely destroyed by inflation. But in fact, the real value of money in circulation, which had fallen by 70 per cent between 1960 and 1965, began to rise immediately in 1966, and had risen by 180 per cent by 1970' (1978: 37).

Rethinking Foreign Investment

As late as December 1965, the move to nationalize foreign holdings was continuing, although by that time, most remaining foreign assets in Indonesia had been expropriated already by the state. On paper, the government's wealth had increased slightly. However, Indonesia had so decisively turned away from the acceptable norms of international investment that it had imposed on itself a kind of economic quarantine. Indonesia was not a country in which foreigners wanted to invest. This isolation had the unintended effect of consolidating and extending the reach of poverty. As an essential part of the programme to reintegrate Indonesia into the world economy, Indonesia recommitted itself to welcoming foreign investment. The most important measure for achieving this was the foreign investment law of 27 January 1967. The law took a bold step to reverse Indonesia's earlier anti-investment posture and to create a hospitable environment in which foreign investment could grow. Despite the positive signals from the new government, foreign investors were continuing to leave the country faster than they came. In 1966, net foreign investment declined by $16 million. In 1967, despite new foreign investment, net foreign investment declined by $12 million and in 1968, the loss was $3 million. With the new investment law, however, investor confidence in Indonesia gradually began to return. By fiscal year, 1969/70 there was a net increase in foreign investment of $39 million. The trend continued, and by 1973/4 net foreign investment increased by $318 million.[19]

To assist in the efforts to stabilize and rehabilitate the economy, Indonesia's investment law specified that the government would give priority to foreign investments that helped advance specific economic goals. These included investments that achieved the following: to increase foreign exchange earnings, decrease imports or bring quick economic returns (less than two years), provide meaningful employment, assist in the transfer of skills and technologies, and enhance efficiency. The law provided tax incentives for investments meeting certain requirements, such as foreign exchange generation. To further encourage the quick flow of investment into the country, the law even awarded 'pioneer status', with certain privileges, to companies that invested in Indonesia between 1967–8.

Soon after the implementation of the law, steps were taken to return some businesses to their previous owners. Within months, investment agreements were reached. One of the oldest and most durable was the investment of the Freeport McMoran Company for copper mining in Irian Jaya. The investment continues today and has expanded to include extensive operations in gold mining.

Similar principles were applied to foreign banks. By early 1968, a number of banks were ready to set up operations in Indonesia. The first wave of foreign banks in Indonesia were the following: from the United States, Chase Manhattan Bank, Bank of America, American Express, and First National City Bank of New York (Citibank); from Europe, The Chartered Bank of London, Pierson and Heldring, Algemeene Bank Nederland; from Asia there was the Hongkong and Shanghai Banking Corporation, the Bank of Tokyo, and the Bangkok Bank.

The return of international direct investment in the areas of commerce and finance was very valuable in reestablishing the credibility of the country in its international financial relations. Although the initial financial impact on the economy was small, in this early stage of development, these contributions were important in rehabilitating the economy and injecting economic life into sectors that had been starved for funding, technology, and skills.

The Near Death and Resurrection of Foreign Trade

From 1960 to 1965, Indonesia's total gold and foreign reserves had fallen from $408.9 million to *negative* $4.5 million. Default was inevitable. In December 1965, the central bank was unable to honour a $2 million letter of credit to Japanese exporters. Thereupon, the Japanese Ministry of International Trade and Industry (MITI) refused to insure shipments to Indonesia. Suddenly, Indonesia found its access to trade significantly curtailed. The move by Japan was accompanied by a general downgrading of Indonesia's credit rating. The country was forced by its trading partners to conduct foreign trade on a cash basis. Emergency measures were adopted to pull the country through the crisis. The government implemented policies to 'buy time' while it gradually tried to rebuild its foreign exchange position. To do so would require a revamping of the country's foreign exchange system.

In the years leading up to 1966, the government had devised a complex multiple exchange rate system that was intended to strengthen the country's balance of payments position. The results, however, were precisely the opposite. Indonesia's exchange rate system led to overvaluation of the rupiah, which damaged the nation's exports. Indonesia, then, steadily depleted its foreign exchange reserves. The country, in effect, lived off its savings. In early 1966, when the central bank was unable to pay its letters of credit, economic reality caught up with the country. Indonesia was broke.

In April 1966, when Sultan Hamengkubuwono IX, who was in charge of economic affairs, made his important statement on the state of the economy, he confirmed a desire to return greater authority and autonomy to the central bank and to restore the country's balance of payment position. Besides this general commitment, however, no system had yet been devised to restore the health of the nation's exchange rate system.

The stabilization programme introduced in October 1966 took steps to simplify the multiple exchange rate system, though it did not eliminate it entirely. Indonesia initially continued to maintain foreign exchange controls because it had no choice. The government was overburdened with long-term debt. To this was added the weight of short-term debt to pay for current letters of credit. With Indonesia's foreign exchange reserves negative, the country was in no position to have an open foreign exchange regime.

Foreign exchange is vital for trade and national reconstruction. Indonesia, therefore, had to devise a means that ultimately amounted to a foreign exchange rationing system. The rationing was done through a simplified multiple exchange rate system and by specifically allocating foreign exchange on a tender basis to parties who intended to use the foreign exchange for purposes designated as economically useful. Foreign exchange was reserved for imports in priority areas. These measures were the first step in a systematic movement toward a unified exchange rate. The exchange rate system that was developed under the 1966 stabilization policy pegged the rupiah exchange to the dollar at two basic rates: one called BE (Bonus Ekspor or Export Bonus) and the other DP (Devisa Pelengkap or Complementary Foreign Exchange). The multiple exchange rate system, also called the 'BE system' for short, was the methodology used by Indonesia to replenish the country's foreign exchange reserves and move toward a unified exchange rate system.

In essence, the system worked as follows: If a trader exported products, the proceeds of his sale would be in two forms, export bonus, BE, and complementary foreign exchange, DP. The extent to which BE and DP were apportioned varied over time. The split, for example, could be 70 per cent in the form of BE and 30 per cent in DP. The BE was restricted for use in the importation or purchase of designated priority goods. DP, on the other hand, could be used for anything, including foreign travel or the purchase of non-essential goods. The exchange rate for the BE was considerably lower than the free market exchange rate, whereas the DP rate was closer to the free market rate. The dollars a trader received were the same for BE and DP, but one got more rupiah at the DP exchange rate and one had complete freedom to spend DP dollars on anything. The whole system was designed to be an incentive to export, but in fact, it was a kind of tax. However, because foreign exchange was in such short supply and foreign goods were in such demand, any vehicle that provided a systematic method of getting foreign exchange was valued.

Additional controls were added by categorizing exports into three groups. Group I consisted of major export commodities and included tin, tobacco, rubber, copra, pepper, and tea; Group II consisted of coffee and less well established primary products including kapok and essential oils; and Group III included handicrafts and miscellaneous other products such as rattan and vanilla. The amount of DP an exporter received depended on the category of goods exported. It happened that the government wanted to encourage the exportation of Group III, and hence the largest percentage of DP was given for sales of goods in that category.

Despite its restrictiveness, the BE multiple exchange rate system helped to add some stability and predictability to the country's exchange rate regime. Furthermore, besides regulating foreign exchange levels, the BE system gave the government another tool, in addition to selective credit, to direct private sector funds toward productive investments instead of luxury goods or consumption. Over the next three and a half years, the BE system underwent a steady and systematic series of modifications that brought the BE and DP rates closer to a unified rate. Concurrently, the nation's foreign exchange reserves rose from *negative* $98.8 million in 1966 to $22.6 million in 1971. These developments cultivated a confidence in the currency that had long been absent. Finally, on 17 April 1970 Indonesia's multiple exchange rate system was eliminated.[20] The BE and DP were unified at the rate of Rp 378 = $1. This reform was a milestone. The complicated exchange rate system that had served to regulate and limit trade had been eliminated, and foreign exchange reserves returned to levels that permitted the normal conduct of international commerce.

AFTER THE HONEYMOON: THE LAST YEAR
OF THE PEOPLE'S PATIENCE

Of all the causes of inflation, none may have been more obstinate than human expectations. Money supply, credit policies, even exchange rates, could be controlled or guided through government policy. Popular confidence, by contrast, needed to be coaxed, persuaded, and even seduced. It could not be decreed. The depth of the people's inflationary expectation was inversely proportional to their previous level of trust in the currency. Once people's trust in the currency was betrayed by hyper-inflation and violated by speculation, regaining public confidence in the currency would take more than patience. It would require bulldog tenacity in the face of an economy that had grown endemically resistant to price stability.

The inflation rate dropped from over 650 per cent in the first quarter of 1966 to 120 per cent by the end of 1967. With almost two years since Sukarno entrusted Soeharto with the leadership of the government, inflation was still unacceptably high and economic growth too low. Intellectually, the people may have been prepared for the pain needed to stabilize the economy, but after two years, the practical implications began to set in. The pain was becoming too much and the outcome woefully insufficient. To make matters worse, in late 1967 and early 1968 Indonesia faced a severe rice shortage and deteriorating terms of trade. Even the scholars that had approved of the government's measures seemed to have lost confidence. In February 1968, the *Bulletin of Indonesian Economic Studies* stated that the changes implemented since Soeharto had come to power 'are all in the right direction. But they have as yet been insufficient to permit the achievement of even the modest goals the new government has set for itself in the quest for economic stabilization, the prerequisite for economic development' (Panglaykim and Penny, 1968: 1–2).

This was a politically intense period. Sukarno was still the President and many believed he would try to reinstate himself as 'supreme leader'. There were about a dozen political parties actively seeking to gain control of the country's political and economic agenda. The political left still maintained a moral high ground for a sizeable segment of the population, and they were vociferous and relentless in their condemnation of the new govern-ment and its stabilization policies. Factions within the government and military continued to rally for sustained 'Confrontation' with Malaysia. Soeharto's political currency was at one of its lowest points. Yet, many eco-nomic indicators led the economic team to believe that the worst was over. The team could see the 'light at the end of the tunnel'. We zealously believed that stabilization was, indeed, the prerequisite for economic development and that stability was within our reach. Only a few more months were needed. The honeymoon, however, was over and everywhere there were calls for a divorce.

A weaker government would have capitulated to the widespread demands to abandon the stabilization policies. Soeharto publicly acknowledged the people's discontent in a speech in which he stated that 1968 was 'the last year of the people's patience'. Nevertheless, based on the advice of the economic team, the government remained steadfast in its commitment to the stabilization programme.

A few months later, on 7 November the Indonesian wire service Antara ran a report that, in understated terms, acknowledged what amounted to a landmark in the country's economic history. 'In the last 10-month period,' the report stated, 'the rate of inflation averaged 6.2 per cent per month. Excluding the month of January 1968, the rate of inflation was 2.2 per cent per month in the 10 months of 1968. If only the last 7 months are considered, the inflation rate averaged 1.4 per cent per month. In spite of this, the Trade Department is fully prepared for whatever may happen in November and December of 1968 and January of 1969.' The final statistics placed the inflation rate for 1968 at 85 percent. Too high, to be sure, but the trend was unmistakable. By 1969, inflation for the year had dropped to 9.89 per cent. The rabbit, it seemed, had ultimately succeeded in subduing the mad elephant.

The firmness with which the government cleaved to its policies may have been exasperating to many, but this firmness may well have been the most important factor in defeating inflation. The government communicated its position time and time again in speeches, press conferences, and at every public forum possible. When there was positive statistical data, we would bring it to the attention of the public. The government said publicly what it was going to do and it did it, even when its policies evoked emotional criticism. This firmness was a direct assault on the psychological foundations of inflation. Even a token retreat from the stabilization policies could have had devastating effects on the credibility and effectiveness of the programme. In the end, the validity of the policies, together with the consistently supportive actions, was sufficient to change deeply held public attitudes and defeat inflation.

THE END OF STABILIZATION

The decline in inflation continued (Figure 1.1). The inflation rate for 1970 was 8.88 per cent and for 1971 the annual rate was 2.47 per cent, a rate that has never since been matched. Indonesia reduced its inflation rate

FIGURE 1.1
Rate of Inflation, 1965–1971

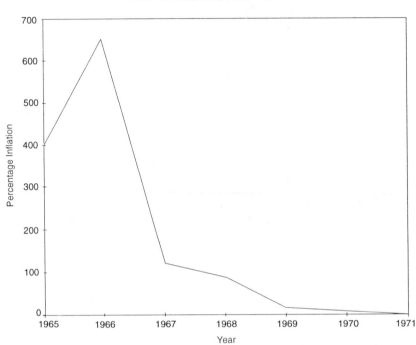

Source: Indonesia, Central Bureau of Statistics.

by about 650 per cent in four years. But what is even more noteworthy is that during the 1966 to 1970 period, not only did inflation decline, but trade grew, and Indonesia's GDP grew at a real rate of 5.8 per cent. Indonesia is one of the few, if not sole, examples of a country that managed to accelerate growth while it was destroying hyperinflation. This extraordinary accomplishment was possible because of the tight link and co-ordination of monetary and fiscal policies and the remarkable collaboration between all members of the stabilization team and the government. These various measures, when taken together, formed a policy phalanx that subdued inflation, revitalized a moribund economy, and instilled a sense of confidence among the people that their economy would function in a rational manner.

The economy was still very weak and fragile. However, in April 1970 the rupiah was devalued in order to strength the country's trading position, the multiple exchange rate system was dismantled for a unitary rate, Indonesia's creditors agreed to provide Indonesia with $600 million in loans, and a breakthrough was accomplished in how to manage Indonesia's outstanding debt. The year 1970 marked the end of Indonesia's stabilization period. Most important, the stage had been set for the government to turn its attention from short-term stabilization efforts to the long-term endeavour of building an economy and developing the country.

FINAL REFLECTIONS ON THE STRUGGLE FOR INDONESIA'S ECONOMIC STABILIZATION

The stabilization effort was a colossal lesson. Indonesia's economic leaders undertook the most comprehensive and concentrated effort to effect structural change the economy ever experienced. The 650-point drop in inflation to an annual level under 3 per cent was an irrefutable testimony of the power of sound macro and micro-economic policies. However, the methodologies employed by the economic team were by no means conventional, 'textbook' strategies. Policies such as the selective credit programme and the subsidized deposit/credit schemes broke every rule on good monetary management. They worked because unconventional problems sometimes require unconventional solutions.

The term 'stagflation' is derived from the two terms 'stagnation' and 'inflation'. The term was coined in the mid-1970s when the United States was experiencing a recession with high inflation. Most economists attribute America's stagflation to the combination of high deficits and high energy costs. For Indonesia, the causes—huge deficits with a crippled productive sector—were quite different. Indonesia's combination of 'tight and loose' monetary policy was in some ways the economic equivalent of 'unscrambling an egg'. The government tried, rather successfully, to use macroeconomic policy with the sectoral precision usually reserved for micro-economics. The entire economy suffered from inflation. To this, the government applied a generally tight money policy. The productive sector was stagnating. To this, the government applied a selectively loose money policy.

The selective credit system placed the government in a position of determining how and where to allocate resources, a principle that has been as thoroughly discredited as Soviet-style economics. In general, this type of policy was anathema to the market orientation of the new economic team. None the less, in a time of crisis, pragmatism dictated that the government exercise policy options that would have been flatly rejected in periods when the economy was operating healthily. Under conditions of economic health, or even normal degrees of economic 'sickness', such measures, without doubt, would do more harm than good. These measures were deliberate distortions to the market process that should be avoided at all costs. Only in such cases as when the market has been deeply and unnaturally thrown out of kilter should such policies be considered and then, only as temporary measures.

While Indonesia's unconventional stabilization policies achieved a stunning success, it is important to recognize that this success was a special case that confirmed the power of sound and prudent macroeconomic policies, especially the commitment to a balanced budget and the re-establishment of a sound banking system. Although these policies were insufficient in themselves to tame Indonesia's hyperinflation, they made several fundamental contributions to the stabilization effort. Specifically they:

- Created a banking system that supported balanced growth throughout the economy;
- Brought to an end the self-defeating practice of using the printing press to compensate for budgetary shortfalls;
- Created a climate of certainty and predictability that was essential to economic stability;
- Forced the government to prioritize its spending and allocate funds based on available resources;
- Eliminated the most important cause of hyperinflation: deficit-spending.

In the final analysis, the success of Indonesia's stabilization policies may have been due primarily to the firmness and consistency with which the government adhered to a set of clear and sound economic principles, above all the balanced budget rule. Over the years, the government has held to the balanced budget rule with such stringency that it has gained the moral force of law. This is as it should be.

Indonesia's 'tight and loose' monetary policy can serve as an important lesson for economic policymakers facing situations of hyperinflation or stagflation. The more important lesson, however, may be to recognize the strength of economic policies developed through the creative and intelligent teamwork of government leaders empowered by the support of the people. Indonesia's stabilization was a collective accomplishment achieved by a nation with a renewed sense of hope and purpose.

1. This discussion draws on ideas that were presented in a paper delivered by me in August 1966 at the Second Army Seminar held in Bandung, described in Chapter 3 (see Radius Prawiro, 1966).

2. Assuming no change in velocity.

3. The only thing close to a balanced budget occurred in 1951 when—due to a boom in exports resulting from the Korean War—Indonesia's economy was relatively healthy and the country ran a very small budget deficit.

4. The term *penghasilan tetap* is translated as fixed income. In Indonesia, it refers to salaried employees. This is because although salaries can be adjusted, in most cases, espe-

cially during the period under consideration, there were no automatic adjustments for inflation. When salaries were adjusted, they always lagged considerably behind inflation. Entrepreneurs, traders, and speculators were less affected by inflation, as were those who relied heavily on barter.

5. The Presidential decision to ban the Communist Party was further reinforced by the MPRS decree of 5 July 1966 (see State Ministry Republic of Indonesia, 1994, Appendix 21 and 24).

6. Until this point, I was serving as the deputy chairman of the Supreme Audit Board. In that capacity, I had urged Sukarno, the Sultan, Adam Malik, and Sumarno, the then Minister of Finance, to grant the central bank greater independence. I also met Soeharto at that time accompanied by Col. Barekah at Kostrad, and advised him to be especially careful regarding the central bank because if it were poorly managed it had the capacity to ruin the economy. The central bank was still led by Jusuf Muda Dalam, who was strongly affiliated with the PKI. I knew that Soeharto would implement a comprehensive 'house cleaning' in the Cabinet, and I was mentally preparing myself for a new life in the private sector. In early July, I returned home after work and turned on the television to watch the news. The lead story was that the new members of the Cabinet had been designated. I was listed as Governor of Bank Indonesia! I had not been informed and to this day, the appointment remains the greatest surprise of my life. I continued to serve the next twenty-seven years in various Cabinet positions with economic portfolios.

7. See, for example, *Sinar Harapan*, 12 December 1965. In 1963, I had to contend personally with the speculators. At that time, I was a junior official in the Ministry of Finance and had three small children. My wife and I were unable to find milk for our babies anywhere in the city. Finally, I was told to meet someone near the public cemetery, Menteng Pulo. There, in secrecy and at grossly inflated prices, I obtained the milk. I was informed that the origin of this contraband was the emergency food aid from the United States. Although it was intended for free distribution, it was being sold to the highest bidders by the unscrupulous speculators who had no qualms even about using foreign aid as a means to profit from the misery of others.

8. Managing Indonesia's foreign debt and the development of the IGGI was such a complex and important issue that this subject will be covered in detail in the next chapter.

9. Based on various Bank Indonesia reports.

10. This is drawn from Ministry of Finance documents (see Indonesia, Departemen Keuangan, 1967: 17–18).

11. This was my first responsibility as Governor of Bank Indonesia. The Bank was deeply divided between those who had achieved their position through the patronage of the former governor, Jusuf Muda Dalam, and all other employees. Quite a few bank employees had much to lose by an audit and they, therefore, obstructed the audit and resisted all change. None the less, the audit and reforms were carried out without degenerating into a 'witch-hunt'. In the end, very few people were forced to leave the Bank. Such upheavals are incompatible with the community and consensus orientation of the Indonesian culture. This made the process particularly tense and unsettling. The audit and changes in personnel were an unavoidable but painful experience for the Bank.

12. The decision to computerize Bank Indonesia's operations was one that I pushed for personally, despite the advice of many knowledgeable consultants who felt that at Indonesia's level of development such an investment was ill-advised. The computer represented a huge investment for Indonesia given its financial difficulties, but I insisted, believing that Indonesia could not afford to waste a moment's time in gaining the tools to collect, compile, and analyze data more efficiently. The study of economic development is

rife with examples of governments plowing money into technologies that cannot be absorbed locally. It was in opposition to such technological waste that the 'appropriate technology' movement was founded in the 1970s. 'Appropriate technology' is a wise and valuable concept for developing countries. In this case, however, I believe that the investment in the computer was essential to enable Bank Indonesia become a more effective central bank.

13. The tight monetary policy was accompanied by stricter controls over Indonesia's commercial banks by Bank Indonesia. Many banks were found to be 'unsound', and after the central bank gave these banks warnings, twenty-one banks were unable to meet the government's requirements and were suspended. This decision was not without political ramifications. Each political party had its own bank, and they were equally subject to these regulations. At that time, Soeharto was the chairman of one of the foundations that owned one of the suspended banks, Bank Gemari. I informed Soeharto personally of the problems with the bank and without hesitation, he agreed that the measure was appropriate. This bank, along with several others, never recovered from the suspension. They were forced into liquidation or mergers.

14. The drive to promote savings led Bank Indonesia to think and act in ways never before dreamed. For the first time, Bank Indonesia approached problems as 'marketing' challenges. For example, traditionally, less affluent Indonesians would try to hold their savings in gold since it was considered inflation-resistant. Even though it made more sense to hold gold than rupiah, even gold tends to lose value, and holding gold at home is not as safe as in a bank. To liken savings accounts with gold, the government encouraged banks to give deposit books for savings a yellow cover that was supposed to symbolize gold. The savings record was called the 'Golden Book'. The golden books were guaranteed against loss or theft. So depositors trusted the system and felt increasingly secure holding their money in banks. In addition, the government created a poster to promote savings that featured Indonesia's most famous and beautiful film star, Widyowati. The posters were given freely to savings account holders. The posters were wildly popular and appeared everywhere across the country, in shops, private homes, or anywhere that a bare wall could be adorned by an actress promoting savings.

15. Of course, besides the logistics of rice supply management, there were important issues in rice production, such as seed use, fertilizer applications, and others. They will be described in Chapter 5.

16. It is for this reason that throughout this book and in government documents when referring to items measured in fiscal years, from 1 April to 31 March, we use the '/' convention, that is, 1970/1, which should be read as 'fiscal year 1970–1971'.

17. Bulog resulted from the merger of the Badan Pelaksana Urusan Pangan (Food Agency) and the Kolognas (National Logistics Command) in 1967. For more information see Bank Indonesia Report 1966/7, pp. 146–7.

18. This policy of impartiality between private and state-run sectors did not last, and eventually, the state owned enterprises again found themselves with more protection than other sectors of the economy.

19. These figures represent realized foreign investment, rather than the investment approvals that are usually reported. The negative figures from 1966 to 1968 indicate that disinvestment exceeded investment (see Bank Indonesia *Annual Reports* from various years).

20. As governor of the central bank, I was *ex officio* chairman of the board of the Biro Lalu Lintas Devisa (BLLD or Foreign Exchange Bureau), the body required by law to monitor and control the distribution of foreign exchange. However, because we had an

enormous insufficiency of foreign exchange reserves, there was little to distribute, and because of the scarcity of trained personnel, many BLLD staff could put their talents to greater service in the more pressing tasks at the central bank. By the time foreign exchange controls were officially eliminated, the country had already *de facto* operated without them for three years.

2
Indebted Beyond Poverty:
Seeking Collaborative Solutions to
Indonesia's Debt Crisis

UNDER A MOUNTAIN OF DEBT

THE piles of stark statistics emerging from Bank Indonesia and the Central Bureau of Statistics could not convey the depth of Indonesia's economic catastrophe. The country was not only poor and essentially bankrupt; it was carrying a debt burden that threatened to keep it impoverished for decades to come. In 1966, the initial instalment on twenty years of past borrowing was coming due. The country could not pay. This, in turn, disqualified Indonesia from new loans. New investment was cut off and the country was growing steadily poorer. Indonesia had fallen into the debt trap that has ensnared so many poor and disadvantaged countries.

Indonesia's export earnings in 1966 were $679 million. This was just barely enough to cover the repayment of debt then coming due; and yet, Indonesia's imports in the same year were $527 million: these, too, had to be paid for. The terrible burden of this debt was compounded by the extreme underdevelopment of the economy. The country had virtually no money to build roads, hospitals, or schools. There was no foreign exchange to import yarn for textiles, medicine for the sick, or food for the nation's hungry. All prospects for economic progress were being crushed under the country's mountain of debt. With a small and weak private sector, Indonesia had no alternative but to rely on the government to lead the effort to revive the economy. The government's options were severely constrained by the inheritance of poverty. The tragedy of Indonesia's indebtedness, however, was that it threatened to serve as a virtual guarantee that the country would remain impoverished for generations to come.[1]

THE FOREIGN AID DILEMMA

Almost two decades before the world would experience the 'third world debt crisis', Indonesia had already fallen victim to a problem that two decades later would threaten to destabilize the world economy. Indonesia had been the willingly recipient of loans for which it had no capacity to pay. During the 1950s and 1960s, many countries granted Indonesia loans with the largesse of great benefactors, with little regard for how the funds would affect the country's long term economic health. It was not until the loans reached maturity that the implications of non-repayment became evident.

Foreign aid poses a dilemma from the start. For government planners, aid offers itself as pure opportunity; a tool to offset some of the injustices of history and inequities of international economics. What leader of an impoverished country would refuse the offer of developmental assistance? Yet, if foreign aid is not used wisely it can be one of the easiest routes to financial perdition, the national equivalent to an intemperate day at the casino. From its founding in 1945, Indonesia was a willing participant in the complex political and economic game of foreign aid. Indonesia's first vice-president, Mohammad Hatta, articulated guidelines to ascertain when loans were appropriate in serving the nation's developmental efforts:

[A]ny foreign loan can only be regarded as development aid', he said, 'if it bears the interest rate of 3 to 3.5 per cent per annum and has a long repayment period. For industries of various types, the repayment period of such a loan should be 10 to 20 years. The repayment period of loans for infrastructure such as dam, irrigation and electric power [sic] should be longer than 20 years. Any loan with repayment period less than 10 years and with the interest rate higher than 5 per cent per annum, cannot be classified as development aid. Any foreign loan can only be classified as development aid if this loan really promotes a sustained national development.... It should be free from political strings of whatever forms and the granting of loan should not be followed by foreign intervention in domestic affairs of the aid receiving country.... As a matter of principle, national economic development of a developing country should be largely based on its own resources in line with the objective of self-help and self-reliance.... The amortization and interest of the loan should be covered by the results of economic growth.... It can be utilized efficiently if the implementation of the projects financed by the loan is in line with the general economic strategy of Indonesia (Arief and Sasono, 1987: x–xi).[2]

Vice-President Hatta described a very prudent and sensible approach to managing foreign aid. The government, however, did not follow his recommendations. Instead, it relied on foreign aid to mask weaknesses in the economy and deficiencies in fiscal management. By the late 1950s and early 1960s, Indonesia saw its eligibility for foreign loans diminish in proportion to the decline in its foreign reserves. The government responded by cutting imports, encouraging import substitution, and borrowing money from whatever external sources it could find. Import substitution failed to meet the country's needs and Indonesia found itself more susceptible to the political influences of aid givers. What initially looked like a route to 'easy money' proved to be a dangerous labyrinth with no clear exit.

SEEKING SAFE PASSAGE FROM THE LABYRINTH OF DEBT

Indonesia's new economic team needed to find new solutions to deal with what seemed to be an unresolvable problem. One of the government's first steps was to send abroad two delegations, one to the Western creditor countries and one to the Eastern bloc creditors. Their purpose was to 'test the waters', to see how various options would be received and to reconcile figures for outstanding debts. This division not only reflected the international political realities of the cold war, but also reflected the fact that the composition of indebtedness to the two groups was significantly different. The delegation to the Western countries was headed by an economist, Professor Widjojo Nitisastro, because the focus was on sovereign borrowing and commercial debt used for civilian purposes. Initially, the delegation to the Eastern bloc countries was led by General Suprayogi, who had been Minister of Production in the final Sukarno Cabinet, because those loans were mostly for military hardware and support. The solutions that eventually emerged from these and other efforts were the product of an evolutionary process. Coming to terms with the country's debt required Indonesia first to confront squarely what constitutes legitimate sovereign debt, after which it could determine the appropriate procedures for dealing with that debt.

To Pay or Not to Pay?: Assessing What Constitutes Legitimate Sovereign Debt

When the economic team confronted the enormity of Indonesia's debt problem, the first policy dilemma that had to be addressed was whether it should honour the debt at all. The economic team considered a variety of options. The decision was not straightforward. The team had to consider historical precedent, current political conditions, and 'gut feelings' about what was right and best for Indonesia.

There were four main alternatives to this problem:

1. *Complete Repudiation of Past Debt.* If Indonesia decided to unilaterally default on its loans or repudiate them outright it could point to many examples of defaults among sovereign debtors. In 1839, for example, the states of Mississippi and Louisiana defaulted on debts to Britain. In the 1870s, many Latin American countries, as well as Turkey and Egypt,

defaulted on debts. The 1930s witnessed a wave of defaults by seventeen Latin American countries as commodity prices tumbled in the wake of the Depression. The number of countries that never repaid their debts from the era after the First World War and the Second World War is high; Finland, which did pay its debts, even took to advertising itself as an honourable exception to the practice of avoiding repayment (Corbridge, 1993). As a further argument, the new government had come to power in the wake of a traumatic and violent national upheaval, and hence Indonesia could refuse to pay the debt of the Sukarno era since the new government had nothing to do with creating it. Indonesia took the view, however, that walking away from old debts would not have been consistent with the character of the new government, which regarded itself as the legitimate and constitutional successor to the old one. The new government could not insist on its legitimacy and at the same time repudiate the debts of its predecessor. Such a position could have been viewed as a gesture of bad faith toward the nations with which Indonesia hoped to establish renewed economic relations.

2. *Repudiate Debt to Communist Bloc.* Indonesia could repudiate a considerable part of the debt owed to the communist bloc countries while paying the debt owed to Japan and the Western industrialized countries. There were two justifications for such a policy. First, the communist bloc aid was predominantly military equipment that was never used and served no productive purpose, not even national defence. Second, following the attempted *coup*—which was linked to the PKI and may have been supported by communist states—the new government had outlawed the communist party and rejected everything associated with it. Rejecting the debts to the communist countries might have been accepted, even applauded, by some Western countries, but Indonesia felt such a move would retain the stigma of unilateral debt repudiation.

3. *Differential Debt Settlements.* Indonesia could strike deals individually with various creditors or with groups of creditors, such as communist, non-communists, and commercial creditors. Most of the debt was 'sovereign borrowing', that is, obligations of the government. Part of the outstanding debt, however, was commercial loans, for which the government had no legal obligation to pay. Commercial lenders knew this, and wanted to be repaid as quickly as possible, even with a discount, rather than wait for full repayment. The disadvantage of this policy is that it would create the impression that Indonesia was not treating its various creditors equally.

4. *Debt Discount.* A fourth consideration was to try to pool all outstanding debt and insist on paying it at a steep discount, a few cents on the dollar. This method might succeed in creating a kind of debt resolution, but at a considerable cost to Indonesia's creditors.

There were drawbacks to all of these approaches. The ideal solution would have been simply to pay off the debts according to their original terms. Since this was not possible, Indonesia's economic team hoped to find alternative solutions that would be acceptable to all parties concerned.

The 1966 Tokyo and Paris Meetings

Indonesia's international debt accumulated during the Sukarno period is summarized in Table 2.1:[3]

Indonesia's creditors understood well the country's plight.[4] This, however, did not diminish their desire for repayment. In some instances, Indonesia's creditors reacted to the crisis by becoming more insistent that debts be repaid. Although there were problems with a differential debt settlement, Indonesia was initially inclined to try to negotiate individually with each creditor. This would have required more time and effort, but it was possible that if Indonesia achieved a significant breakthrough with one country, it could leverage the precedent to its advantage in negotiations with other creditors. Conversely, if Indonesia had to deal collectively with its creditors, this could seriously weaken the country's

TABLE 2.1
Indonesia's External Debt from the Sukarno Period

Creditor (Countries)	Amount	Total
Western Countries[a] and Japan		1,557.7
Eastern Bloc Countries[b]		1,172.5
Other Countries[c]		157.1
Other Liabilities		245.7
Total		3,133.0
Payment Due		
1969–73	948.5	
1974–78	1,082.7	
1979–83	664.7	
1984–88	164.6	
1989 and later	272.5	
Total		3,133.0

Source: Data derived from H. Abs, 'The Problem of Indonesia's External Debt and Reflections on its Solution', Unpublished report for the Indonesian Government and Creditor Countries, 30 July 1969.
[a]United States, Federal Republic of Germany, Italy, France.
[b]Soviet Union, Poland, Czechoslovakia, East Germany, China.
[c]Denmark, India, Yugoslavia, Austria, Pakistan, Panama, Sweden, Switzerland, Tanzania, U.A.R.

negotiating position. The prospect of one poor and deeply indebted country facing a group of the world's richest and most powerful countries in a dispute over debt was decidedly uninviting. None the less, Japan and the Western creditors insisted that debt discussions be held collectively, and Indonesia complied.

Then, as now, there existed two fora for negotiating settlements of international debt problems: the London Club, which focuses on the resolution of disputes involving private commercial debt, and the Paris Club, which focuses on debt problems among national governments. Japan and the Western countries to which Indonesia was indebted were known as the 'Paris Club countries'. The Indonesian delegation first met with this group in Tokyo on 16 September 1966. Along with Indonesia, the countries in attendance were Japan, the United States, Britain, France, West Germany, Italy, and the Netherlands. The IMF and Australia sent delegations while Canada, New Zealand, and Switzerland sent observers. The communist countries were invited to join the meeting, but they chose not to, preferring to hold their own series of meetings without the Paris Club countries. Indonesia's delegation to Tokyo was led by Sultan Hamengkubuwono IX. The meeting was significant because it was the first opportunity for Indonesia's government to outline the economic policies that would guide the country in the post-Sukarno era. The preparations and research for the meeting were extensive. The delegation in Tokyo presented a plan that was stripped of anti-colonial rhetoric and grandiose spending projects driven by political objectives. In the plan, the government articulated a comprehensive and well-reasoned vision for the country's economic future.

The plan was foremost a frontal assault on hyperinflation. Underlying the plan was something of equal importance: the new government outlined an approach to economic management in which budgets were balanced and planning priority was given to investments that promised maximum economic development at minimum costs. The country's economic plans—though reflecting the government's political objectives— were developed with a rigorous adherence to principles of macro- and micro-economics. The meeting served as a rite of passage for the new government, a fresh start in Indonesia's international relations. It would take time, however, for Indonesia's creditors to be convinced that the changes in Indonesia would be lasting. The tone of the meeting, therefore, was cautiously sympathetic. Japan and the Western creditors were generally supportive, but wanted more information on the country's stabilization plan.[5] The IMF recommended that Indonesia's creditors agree to reschedule Indonesia's debt and supply fresh loans to help Indonesia through its current balance of payments crisis. The meeting ended, however, without firm commitments to provide Indonesia with the desperately needed aid. Participants at the meeting did agree, however, to hold another meeting in Paris before the end of the year. The meeting would try to come to terms with the issues of debt rescheduling and the need for additional aid.

The December 1966 meeting took place as planned. Indonesia had since introduced its stabilization programme, and initial signs of improvement were starting to emerge. At the meeting, Indonesia's creditors agreed to reschedule payments on Indonesia's loans coming due in 1966 and 1967. The new terms provided a three-year grace period, after which Indonesia had to repay its outstanding debts over an eight-year period. The group also agreed to its next meeting in Amsterdam in February 1967.

The Formation of the Inter-Governmental Group on Indonesia[6]

While some progress was made regarding Indonesia's debt situation during the February meeting, the more significant event was that this meeting gave birth to the IGGI. The IGGI was not the first example of an organization founded to resolve serious problems in sovereign debt. The World Bank chaired an aid consortium when India faced a financial crisis in 1958. Similar arrangements were later made for Pakistan and Columbia.[7] Very quickly, however, the IGGI distinguished itself as a remarkable forum for dealing with Indonesia's complex debt problems. One of the organization's greatest strengths was its relative informality. The IGGI had no official charter. It was not established through any binding legal agreements. It had no permanent secretariat or any of the institutional trappings to confer it the status of an 'official organization'. Nor was it designed to be an international 'collection agency' for outstanding foreign debt. It was an international body that imposed nothing on its members. The purpose of the IGGI was simply to serve as a forum to facilitate coordinated action among its members and the exchange of views.

Besides Indonesia, the participants in the first IGGI meeting were Australia, Belgium, France, West Germany, Italy, Japan, the Netherlands, the United Kingdom, and the United States. Observers included Austria, Canada, New Zealand, Norway, Switzerland, the World Bank, the IMF, and the United Nations Development Programme (UNDP), the Organization for Economic Cooperation and Development (OECD), and the Asian Development Bank (ADB). According to IGGI estimates of the time, Indonesia needed $200 million in foreign assistance to cover its projected foreign exchange gap for 1967. The United States pledged to provide one third of the amount if other members agreed to supply the remainder. On this Posthumus (1971: 18) states, 'This one-third formula was unilaterally announced by the US but Japan later accepted the challenge which this implied by offering the same amount of assistance. Thus, a rough "sharing of burden" formula for international aid to Indonesia developed, which has played a significant role ever since.' After a few years, aid allocations ceased to follow this original formula. However, through this agreement, Indonesia with its creditors achieved a breakthrough in managing Indonesia's debt problems.

All the IGGI members had a stake in Indonesia's debt crisis. At a minimum, the creditors wanted to recoup as much as possible on their loans. There was, of course, more to Indonesia's debt problems than money. Some countries—particularly the Netherlands, Japan, and the United States—had strong political interests in seeing stability return to Indonesia. The Netherlands wanted to restore smoothly functioning relations with its former colony. The Dutch previously had considerable economic interests in Indonesia, from plantations to oil production and even manufacturing. After Indonesia declared its independence, it found itself in a direct struggle with the Netherlands. Additional tensions between the two countries arose when the Old Order government nationalized many Dutch investments. The conflict was exacerbated when Indonesia fought the Netherlands in order to integrate Irian Jaya (then called 'West Irian') into the Republic. The IGGI offered an opportunity for a fresh start in Indonesian–Dutch relations. Both sides welcomed the possibilities.

Indonesia–Japan relations too were in need of renewal. During the Second World War Japan had invaded Indonesia, and its three-and-a-half-year control of the country had left many bitter memories. While most Indonesians were prepared to 'forgive and forget', still, the two countries had to take deliberate steps to create a new working relationship based on mutual respect between sovereign states. Besides wanting to see peace return to Asia, Japan also was interested in Indonesia for its natural resources that Japan needed to sustain its industrial output. Furthermore, Indonesia, with its huge population and proximity, was a logical market for Japanese goods. Japan now hoped to rely upon the vehicle of commerce to build relations that benefited both countries.

As for the United States, it was steadily being drawn more deeply into the war in Vietnam. In 1966, the United States still believed firmly in the 'domino theory', that is, that the 'fall' of one country to communism could lead to the fall of its neighbour. Indonesia's 1965 abortive *coup* cast a stark light on the country's political vulnerability. No matter how impoverished Indonesia may have been, the United States had no interest in seeing the sphere of Sino-Soviet communist influence further extended in South-East Asia.

Indonesia, of course, had its own political interests. Above all, it wanted to see stability and strength return to the country. To do so, it needed to remove the yoke of debt from its neck. Indonesians, however, still carried with them vivid memories of colonial domination. Despite Indonesia's trouble, the government was adamant that it would not compromise its political independence for financial assistance. The government was prepared to default on its debts before it would negotiate away its sovereignty and the dignities this implied. This principle was well understood and accepted by all IGGI members.

In forging the IGGI, Indonesia was neither a pawn in cold war *realpolitik* nor was the government in Jakarta engaging in its own Machiavellian game of playing the 'anti-Communist card' to its financial advantage. Both Indonesia and its creditors dealt with the debt crisis with cool-headed pragmatism. For Indonesia, the stakes were too grave for guile and intrigue. The new government was risking its existence on the idea that sound economic policies could restore the economy despite decades of neglect. However, to realize the objective of stabilization and rehabilitation, Indonesia's policymakers firmly believed that Indonesia had to find a resolution to its overwhelming debt burden. To this end, Indonesia's negotiators adopted a working style that built solidarity and trust. They were very candid and straightforward in discussing the country's debt problems, plans for remedying the situation, and prospects for improvement. Indonesia's creditors responded likewise and, consequently, all were spared the tedium of discussions prolonged through artful posturing and tactical deadlocks.

The IGGI was originally created for one purpose only: to find a solution to Indonesia's debt crisis. No one expected the organization to have a long life span. Indonesia, however, more than any other party, had much at stake in seeing the IGGI succeed. Indonesia realized that whatever country or organization served as the chair of the IGGI would have a decisive role in the outcome of the negotiations and the organization's ongoing development. By this time, the co-ordination of international aid usually fell to international institutions, often the World Bank. Indonesia would have preferred having the World Bank chair the IGGI because it is relatively neutral in its politics, technically adept, and 'by definition' committed to economic development. In the case of Indonesia, however, the World Bank was prohibited from assuming such a role because Indonesia did not fulfil certain World Bank requirements—in particular, the requirement that the prospective country must be eligible for World Bank loans. Indonesia did not satisfy this condition because it was currently in arrears on its World Bank loans. Another possible candidate, the ADB, had only recently been established and was not yet prepared to accept this responsibility. Although Indonesia's relations with the United States were increasingly positive, they were not so close that Indonesia considered the United States to be the most suitable chair. Furthermore, having the United States chair the IGGI might appear to violate Indonesia's professed commitment to political non-alignment. The two prime candidates were Japan and the Netherlands. The Japanese had initially been reluctant to support efforts to reschedule Indonesia's debt. Furthermore, Japan had already become the dominant economy in Asia. In 1966, it was unclear just how Japan would manage its role as economic superpower. The Netherlands, on the other hand, was a small country that had just lost its colonial holdings and was trying to stake out a new position for itself in world affairs. Indonesia believed that the Dutch would be an earnest and sympathetic leader. For these reasons, Indonesia supported having the Dutch chair the IGGI. Holland accepted this responsibility and, until the disbanding of the IGGI in 1992, it played a highly valued role in leading what was perhaps the world's most effective organization in bilateral and multilateral economic relations.

Pursuing a Lasting Solution to Indonesia's Debt Crisis

The establishment of the IGGI was laudable, but a cloud of uncertainty and crisis still hung over Indonesia. The country's debt problems still seemed almost insurmountable. Until 1970, Indonesia continued to meet with its creditors in what threatened to be a never-ending series of meetings at which grace periods were extended one year at a time. There seemed to be no closure, no meaningful resolution. The meetings were valuable, but Indonesia's negotiators began to see themselves as the financial equivalent of Sisyphus—every time Indonesia's debt problem appeared resolved, it reappeared and again required a great effort. Negotiations brought temporary relief, but it was weak aspirin for a persistent headache. Despite the initial signs of recovery in Indonesia's economy, in 1969 the country was no more capable of resolving its debt burden than it was in 1966. Indonesia needed a lasting resolution that was acceptable to all parties.

To reach a solution, Indonesia, with the support of its IGGI creditors, turned to the distinguished German banker, Hermann J. Abs, to act as a kind of arbiter and 'honest broker'. Abs had been the chairman of the Deutsche Bank, had an essential role in the settlement of Germany's war debt, and had handled a number of other difficult problems involving international debt.[8] He was one of the few people that was so widely respected that all the parties involved were confident that he could find an acceptable solution. In July 1969, Abs issued a report that became the basis for Indonesia's debt settlement. Drawing on information supplied by

Bank Indonesia, Abs began his report by estimating that at the end of 1968 Indonesia's external debt amounted to $3.1 billion. Commenting on this, he stated:

Even under very optimistic assumptions regarding both Indonesia's future balance of payments and budgetary development, and assuming a continuing high level of foreign aid, I cannot but agree with the general conclusion of the International Monetary Fund and International Bank for Reconstruction and Development to the effect that debt service payments of such an order of magnitude are, and will for years to come be, beyond Indonesia's financial capacity (1969: 4).

Abs' skill was evident in his ability to understand Indonesia's debt problem in its full complexity and yet simultaneously to grasp the essence in its utmost simplicity. He identified a fundamental objective to which he felt all parties should subscribe, namely:

The first and principal aim of a debt rescheduling exercise should be the restoration of Indonesia's creditworthiness. The year-to-year debt rescheduling negotiations in the period from 1966 until today as well as the rescheduling negotiations with the Eastern Bloc countries did not have the restoration of creditworthiness as their primary aim; rather first priority had to be given to granting relief to a debtor country at a time where restoration of its creditworthiness seemed as yet impossible.

Once the monetary stabilization period is successfully concluded, Indonesia in my view has a chance to reestablish its international creditworthiness, provided an adequate solution can be found for the settlement of its old debt, i.e. the external debt accumulated through June 30, 1966 (1969: 7).

The re-establishment of Indonesia's creditworthiness, Abs argued, would restore freedom and sovereignty to the government of Indonesia on matters of economic policy; make Indonesia eligible for loans by international lending agencies; enable Indonesia to make greater use of credit facilities to finance foreign trade; and re-establish Indonesia as an important partner in world trade, which would lead to the eventual decline in need for foreign aid.

To achieve these objectives Abs proposed three broad guidelines:[9]

1. A 'once-and-for-all' long-term debt settlement should replace the annual debt negotiations.

2. The settlement should restore Indonesia's creditworthiness.

3. The settlement should be based on the principle of non-discrimination, that is, the terms of settlement should apply equally to all of Indonesia's creditors.

After almost another year of negotiations, in April 1970, Indonesia and its creditors agreed to the following terms:

1. Debt principal was to be *repaid* over a 30-year period from 1970 to 1999.

2. Contractual interest was to be *repaid* over a 15-year period, beginning in 1985.

3. No additional interest would be *charged* on the amounts *deferred*.

4. Indonesia was given the option to *defer repayment* of part of its principal due during the first eight years to the last eight years, that is, 1992 to 1999. An interest charge of 4 per cent *would* be added to the deferred principal.

The settlement brought enormous relief to Indonesia. To complete the process, however, Indonesia also had to arrive at a resolution with the communist bloc countries, especially Indonesia's largest creditor, the Soviet Union. Indonesia's negotiations with the Soviet Union were difficult. The Soviets had wanted Indonesia to adhere to the terms of an earlier agreement that would have required Indonesia to settle its debts relatively quickly, with $25 million paid on 1 April 1969, and the remaining balance—some $500 million—paid over the next twelve years.[10] Adam Malik had assumed leadership of Indonesia's negotiations with the Eastern bloc countries. Indonesia had hoped to keep its debt negotiations from becoming an extension of cold war tensions. That notwithstanding, in 1966 the Soviet Union had already begun to criticize Indonesia's debt negotiations with Japan and its Western creditors. The Soviet Union contended that the West was trying to use debt concessions as a way of pressuring Indonesia to abandon its longstanding anti-colonial policy. Since the Eastern bloc did not participate in the IGGI meetings, Indonesia brought the terms of the IGGI settlement to its negotiations with the Eastern bloc and emphasized the principle of non-discrimination. The socialist creditors initially balked at Indonesia's proposals. However, in 1971 the Soviet Union, East Germany, Czechoslovakia, Poland, and Romania concluded an agreement with Indonesia with terms similar to those of the Abs settlement.

Commenting on this settlement, one economist, Henry J. Bitterman, concluded:

The Paris Club, which had previously pursued a relatively cautious and basically commercial approach, displayed a flexible and imaginative attitude in dealing with Indonesia.... Ironically, the very large debt owed to the socialist bloc facilitated the liberal treatment by Western creditors who were concerned that otherwise, their newly resumed aid programmes would in effect help to pay off Indonesia's heavy indebtedness to the socialist bloc which had discontinued lending after Sukarno's downfall. Thus, the Paris Club credits required Indonesia to supp̄ the agreed-upon terms of all creditors, including those outside of the Paris C⁻ This condition was a key requirement (1973: 219).

Bitterman also notes (1973: 220) that Indonesia was the only case in which the entire debt incurred before a given date was covered by such an agreement, rather than merely the payments accruing in a specified period of years. Post-Sukarno debt, however, was excluded from the agreement.

The terms of the Paris Agreement were later extended to Indonesia's remaining communist debt. With this, the settlement removed from Indonesia's shoulders the two burdens of debt and uncertainty. The country had a chance to reconstruct itself while still satisfying its debt obligations. The settlement transcended the zero-sum game. Instead of sacrificing development for debt repayment, the settlement integrated debt repayment into programme that satisfied Indonesia's creditors while permitting the country to focus its efforts on development.

In addition to sovereign debt, another issue that needed to be addressed was its smaller but hardly negligible commercial debt. In lieu of a series of London Club meetings to settle this matter, Indonesia introduced what became known as the Debt for Investment Conversion Scheme (DICS) programme. Although Indonesia did not have the foreign exchange to repay the debt to commercial investors, it did have a wealth of natural resources and other commercial opportunities that could be transformed into investment credits. Under the DICS programme, a creditor or someone acting on behalf of a creditor would be repaid for an outstanding debt in rupiah provided that the proceeds were immediately invested in Indonesia under the conditions stipulated by the 1967 foreign investment law. The list of creditors was made public in order to create a market for these outstanding credits. The DICS system transformed debt problems into a winning situation where creditors, who otherwise would have been forced to write off the debt or sell it at a very steep discount, were able to recoup some of their previous investment. The return on the investment was late and often smaller than originally expected, but the debts were settled. For its part, the government was able to settle obligations in rupiah rather than scarce foreign exchange. In the process, these investments brought new capital and skills into the country.

FROM DEBT RELIEF TO CONSTRUCTIVE AID

The Abs settlement gave Indonesia 'breathing space', a period of years during which the country could function without the nagging demands of debt repayment, threats of defaults, or countless rounds of debt negotiations. In itself, however, the Abs settlement was not a solution to Indonesia's larger problems. Indonesia needed to break the cycle of poverty and move the economy onto a path of long-term growth. The economy needed to be completely overhauled. To achieve this, Indonesia still needed a

method to intervene in the economy to 'jump-start' growth. This was where Indonesia's economic policymakers held foreign development assistance had the potential to make a decisive difference in the nation's development.

Redefining the IGGI

In 1968, Indonesia's government leaders believed that the stabilization policies were succeeding, but that the government had to move quickly and aggressively to stimulate greater production in the economy. A failure to move from stabilization to stimulation could squander the growing economic momentum and undo the fragile stability that was starting to take hold in the economy. Therefore, although Indonesia's debt crisis was still unresolved, the government turned to the IGGI as a forum not just for debt management but for the larger ongoing matter of developmental assistance. At this point, several delegations immediately balked, stating that the requests for aid were too high and that they wanted to bring aid discussions back to a purely bilateral level.[11]

This was a critical juncture in the history of the IGGI. At stake was the organization's fundamental mission. If the IGGI was to continue as an organization that existed solely to resolve Indonesia's debt crisis, then the time was approaching to begin a process of self-dissolution since the end of the debt crisis was almost within reach. However, Indonesia and several other Group members had come to believe that the IGGI offered an exceptionally efficient vehicle for the management of development assistance. Already, the IGGI had developed into a forum in which creditor countries and multilateral institutions, such as the IMF and World Bank, could work in a spirit of collaboration with Indonesia to seek effective means for putting aid resources to work. The IGGI was unusual in its transparency and efficiency. All members received the same information. They knew the amount and terms of development assistance that was going to Indonesia, and they knew how the aid was used. No other organization worked quite like it. In this way, although the IGGI was founded for one purpose—to respond to a debt crisis—it broke new ground to serve as a model for an expanded mission, that is, the effective disbursement of development aid. In this way, the IGGI evolved organically into a collaborative forum on the use of foreign aid to assist Indonesia in its economic development process.

Foreign Aid and Economic Development[12]

What is the purpose of foreign aid? Critics of a cynical bent have suggested that aid is often a form of economic entrapment. According to this perspective, creditor countries are sinister manipulators who only feign generosity. The unsuspecting developing country accepts the so-called aid and then is drawn into a dependency relationship with the aid giver that is reinforced when the poorer country cannot repay its debts. Some critics might try to portray Indonesia as an example of aid victimization. This would be wrong. There are, however, many examples of foreign aid that does fall far short of humanitarian or altruistic intentions. From the perspective of the recipient country, problems with foreign aid are generally of three types:

- Aid is given with too many political conditions. In such circumstances, the recipient country may be put in a position where aid amounts to an infringement of national sovereignty.
- Aid is given with little concern or guidance regarding the use to which the aid is put. If the recipient country spends the aid on non-productive ends, then it may be setting itself up for eventual default when the debt repayment comes due.
- Aid is given more as a means of benefiting private business interests in the creditor countries rather than responding to the economic needs of the overall population in the recipient countries.

Of these three varieties of misdirected aid, Indonesia previously suffered most from the second: the country accepted aid money with little concern for how to repay the loans. Now that it had come to terms with its creditors, Indonesia could ill afford to repeat the same mistake. If the country again allowed itself to slip into a new debt trap, its creditors might not be so forgiving a second time. This time, Indonesia had to adopt more secure and sophisticated methods for managing its debt.

Pressure to avoid debt mismanagement came not only from Indonesia's creditors. Some of the most severe critics of Indonesia's borrowing policies came from within the country. The role of foreign aid has always been somewhat controversial among Indonesians.[13] Even among the country's economic advisors, there was some debate regarding what was the appropriate level and role of foreign aid. Since Indonesia's early experience had been so negative, some officials and critics of the government suggested that Indonesia should avoid further indebtedness at all costs. This view has generally found support within a prominent stream of modern Indonesian politico-economic thinking which holds that Indonesia should seek greater economic self-reliance, bordering on autarky.

In the late 1960s, the new government was trying to resolve its outstanding problems with creditors, while at the same time it wanted to move the economy onto a higher growth trajectory. Indonesia's economic team believed that foreign aid offered the country an unrivaled opportunity to break down the wall of poverty. The theoretical justification used by Indonesia's economic policymakers for drawing on foreign aid has remained virtually the same since the late-1960s. Aid is essential to accelerate capital formation in a poor economy. Capital formation consists of productivity-increasing public or private sector investments. Particularly in the early stages of development, public sector capital formation is of critical importance for both human resource development and physical infrastructure development.[14] Without capital formation, an economy will stagnate at the subsistence level.

There are four major sources of capital formation: private savings, public savings, foreign investment, and foreign assistance. As with most developing countries, in the early years of the New Order, Indonesia's saving to GNP ratio was very low. Public savings were very low due to the low per capita income levels of Indonesians and the country's inadequate tax collection capabilities. In 1967, Indonesia promulgated the foreign investment law to stimulate the flow of direct foreign investment. (Foreign portfolio investment was not an option until December 1987.) Public and private savings and foreign investment were all, however, insufficient to meet the country's capital needs. The government sought foreign aid to compensate for this shortfall.

Bappenas: Creating the Institutional Capacity to Put Loans to Work

Indonesia learned the hard way that the incautious use of foreign aid can lead to economic ruin. Indonesia was determined not to permit a repetition of earlier mistakes. To ensure that its development funds were put to good use, Indonesia relied on a renewed and strengthened National Development Planning Agency, known by the abbreviation Bappenas (Badan Perencanaan Pembangunan Nasional).

Bappenas—the same organization that later would develop Indonesia's five year development plans, the cornerstone of the country's budget planning process—was responsible for proposing and overseeing government development projects. Bappenas was founded during the Sukarno period, but it was not until power was transferred to Soeharto that Bappenas was headed by trained economists responsible for committing development funds to projects that promised maximum benefits to the country. From the outset, Bappenas has had responsibility for the portion of the government budget dedicated to economic development. Over the years, a significant portion of this budget has been derived from foreign aid. This aid comes in a variety of forms, but is generally divided into two categories— programme aid and project aid. Programme aid is not directed at specific projects, but is usually provided by the creditor country as a means to offset shortages in foreign exchange. Project aid, on the other hand, is generally tied to specific projects. Furthermore, donors often provide aid with the stipulation that projects draw on goods and services from the creditor country ('tied aid').

Beginning with the New Order, Bappenas set about its work with renewed discipline and vigour. Bappenas began with macroeconomic analysis to determine the levels of foreign aid it would seek. After aid levels were set, Bappenas would then use micro-economic analysis to plan and regulate the project funded by the development assistance. Through the Bappenas methodology, the management of development funds was one of the few areas of economics where macroeconomic and micro-economic analysis were both needed and tightly integrated. In the macroeconomic stage of the analysis, the government would begin by estimating a realistic growth rate that would bring about a real increase in per capita income. This estimated rate of growth became the target used in government planning. To achieve the target, the government analysis would identify a certain rate of capital formation, or investment expenditures as a percentage of national income. The required investment would have to be matched by savings, both public and private; any shortfalls would come from foreign investment and/or foreign borrowing.

Public (or government) savings are defined as the positive difference between the government's revenues and expenditures. Estimates of government savings were obtained based on historical data and projected tax revenues. Private savings, meanwhile, were estimated based on historical savings propensities throughout the non-government sector. Combined, the shortfall in capital from domestic sources and foreign investment yielded an estimate of Indonesia's foreign aid needs.

After the macroeconomic analysis led the government to identify a targeted level of investment, micro-economics was used to guide project planning. Bappenas would set criteria for investment selection to identify necessary and desirable investment projects. A detailed accounting of how much domestic and foreign capital each project required would ensure that the planned investment did not surpass the overall ceiling set in the macroeconomic analysis. Thus computed, every year Bappenas prepared estimates on the amount of foreign assistance needed. These were presented to the members of the IGGI for discussion to determine the levels of aid creditor countries were willing to commit. Besides developing Indonesia's economic plans and formulating aid requests, Bappenas became a 'bottom-line' agency responsible for ensuring that aid funds are put to use according to plan. The agency recommends projects based on their potential to offer employment opportunities, increase income, and satisfy domestic demand for products or to generate foreign exchange through the production and sale of exports.

It should be noted that planning according to the Bappenas model was entirely different from the Soviet model. The Soviets also used sophistic-ated analytic tools to plan the economy. The important difference, how-ever, is that Bappenas never tried to plan the economy outright. Instead, it accepted that the economy would generally move according to its own forces. Bappenas tried to identify those areas of the economy where it could effectively make selective and strategic intervention that would remove impediments to development. For this reason, most of the Bappenas work focused on physical and social infrastructure, such as school development, irrigation systems for communities of farmers, and road development. Through such investments, Bappenas could stimulate economic development without trying to replace the free market with a state-controlled market in which it served as the economic arbiter.

Once its mission was clearly delineated under the new government, Bappenas assumed an overarching responsibility to monitor every step as projects progressed from proposals to completed operations. It is a job requiring detailed analysis and technical expertise across a wide spectrum of economic sectors. Based on this far-reaching responsibility, Bappenas has been headed by some of the country's best economists and supported by a team of specialists with diverse backgrounds. Over the years, Bappenas has been invaluable in guiding Indonesia's economic develop-ment in a way that proceeds in broad conformity to plans and that development projects benefit the country according to the original project proposals.

THE INDONESIAN MODEL OF DEBT RESOLUTION AND AID UTILIZATION

The resolution of Indonesia's debt crisis is an outstanding example of a collaborative solution to a complex international problem. The outcome was particularly noteworthy, given that many other indebted countries have defaulted in the past, even when there was no change in government. In their study, Peter H. Lindert and Peter J. Morton (1989) reported that historically lenders have not punished governments with a prior default history, nor have investors tended to pay close attention to past repayment records of borrowing governments. The fact is, Indonesia, may indeed not have lost its ability to borrow even if it had repudiated its previous debt.

In retrospect, however, the IGGI debt agreement was clearly the best option for Indonesia and the international financial community as a whole. Indonesia's creditors demonstrated their support through their willingness to confront the debt crisis with creativity, initiative, and gen-erosity. In this, the Abs settlement, described above, remains a break-through. It was a victory for international collaboration in crisis management. It offered a new model in debt settlement that avoided the extremes of frustrated unilateral repudiation or submissive compliance to overly burdensome terms. That said, it must be remembered that the settlement was controversial. One of the points to which the Paris Club countries insisted was that the Indonesian settlement should not set a broadly applied precedent in debt settlement. This concern was understandable because the settlement provided much better terms than those contained in the original loans. If debt rescheduling became commonplace on a global basis, the entire lending process could break down.

On this point, however, Indonesia's behaviour, both then and now, deserves special mention. Following the 1970 settlement, Indonesia has never had to reschedule its debt or renegotiate the terms of its multilateral or bilateral borrowing. More than thirty years later, Indonesia continues to comply with both the letter and spirit of the Abs settlement. The settlement achieved its goals. It provided Indonesia with the opportunity to rebuild its economy, and this permitted the country to honour its debts. The financial payments on Sukarno period loans were less than that specified in the original terms, but the loans *were* repaid. Furthermore, the ultimate objective of the Abs agreement—restoration of creditworthiness—was realized. This allowed Indonesia to resume normal bilateral and multilateral economic exchanges. The country obtained access to the funds needed for infrastructure and industrial development. Equally important, the settlement made it possible for Indonesia to assume a position as a full partner in the world of international economics. To this day, the settlement remains an example of international co-operation at its best.

To summarize, some of the principal reasons why the IGGI performed so admirably as a vehicle of bilateral and multilateral cooperation: a) the organization was efficient, unencumbered with bureaucracy, and flexible; b) all IGGI members were committed to the idea that it was in their collective best interests politically and economically for Indonesia to resolve its debt crisis and move onto a higher growth trajectory; c) aside from the period when the IGGI made the transition from a focus on the debt crisis to development assistance, the goals and methodologies of the organization were always well understood; d) the IGGI was able to make a graceful transition from an institution designed to resolve a debt crisis to one that focused on foreign aid and economic development; and e) the IGGI focused on the constructive role of aid without forcing political confrontation or submissiveness on matters pertaining to Indonesia's internal political affairs. This did not mean that Indonesia's internal policies were taboo, but discussions thereon were conducted in a spirit of mutual respect. The lasting legacy of the IGGI was the vital role it played in helping Indonesia remove itself from a prolonged trap of debt and economic decline.

There were many other important lessons garnered by Indonesia in its efforts to achieve a resolution to the debt crisis. The following reflections summarize some of the prominent reasons why Indonesia was able to weather its debt crisis and emerge even stronger at the other end:

- The 'once-and-for-all' agreement was a *sine qua non* for a lasting settlement. If Indonesia had to engage in seemingly endless rounds of extensions and renegotiations, the process would likely have collapsed from exhaustion.

- Indonesia was very careful to avoid creating a new debt trap for itself by ensuring that new loans were applied to projects that brought long-term economic benefit to the country.

- Although the Bappenas model of planning was highly centralized, it has been much more successful than superficially similar models in socialist economies. The reason for the success was that Bappenas benefited greatly from the rapid advances then being made in macro- and microeconomics, including Leontief's input-output models and ICOR (incremental capital/output ratio) estimates. Despite the country's relative poverty, from the beginning of the New Order, Indonesia distinguished itself by its use of state-of-the-art analytical techniques in its planning.

Overall, in global terms, efforts to accelerate the development process through international aid-based interventions have borne mixed results among recipient countries. Parties on all sides of the issue—aid givers, aid recipients, and scholars focusing on the role of aid in development—tend to be a disillusioned lot. Foreign aid has rarely provided the level of return donors or recipients hoped for or projected. None the less, the IGGI collaboration may be a noteworthy example of a forum for debt and aid negotiations that lived up to its mandate. Due to political tensions between Indonesia and the Netherlands, at Indonesia's initiative the IGGI was dissolved in 1992 and replaced by a similar organization known as the Consultative Group on Indonesia (CGI), chaired by the World Bank. Throughout its existence, however, the IGGI distinguished itself as an effective forum for debt and foreign aid management in the service of economic development. The CGI retained this spirit and has continued to act as a valued partner to Indonesia as its economy moves to a new stage of development.

1. Indonesia's debt coming due in the late 1960s, $3.1 billion, is not a large amount by today's standards. In 1967, however, Indonesia had no foreign exchange and the economy was not growing in such a way that it looked promising that the country would be able to cover its debt repayment. The mistake of the Sukarno regime was not so much the size of the debt but Indonesia's inability to generate sufficient foreign exchange to service the debt.

2. Quoted in the foreword of a book by Hatta's son-in-law, Sri-Edi Swasono (see Arief and Sasono, 1987).

3. Figures based on the report on Indonesian debt to the Western creditor countries by Herman Abs (1969: attachment #4). Note that the sums listed under the subtotals do not add up to the subtotals. The reason for this is not stated in the Abs Report, but presumably, this is because only a partial list of creditors are given, although the figures represent the actual totals. China, therefore, is listed among the Eastern Bloc countries but the amount owed to China is not specified.

4. Although debt and aid negotiations did not officially begin until September 1966, soon after my appointment as Governor of Bank Indonesia, in July 1966, I made a trip to Tokyo to lay the groundwork for the September creditors' meeting. The trip was initiated after we did a review of the nation's foreign exchange reserves and realized the extent of the financial crisis the country faced. With the support of the Presidium, I set out to meet with Japan's Minister of Finance Takeo Fukuda. Transition issues in Indonesia's government were still unsettled. Embassy staff appointed under Sukarno, for example, was still in place and how they would work with the new government was unclear. For this reason, I completely bypassed the Indonesian embassy and every other agency that, according to protocol, should have been involved in arranging the meeting. I met individually with Minister Fukuda and informed him of the conditions we faced and the dire consequences that could result if prompt and adequate actions were not taken. Thus apprised, Minister Fukuda gave Indonesia his personal support to ensure that Japan would help Indonesia in this time of duress. Without Minister Fukuda's initiative and determined effort, it is unlikely that Japan would have been able to support Indonesia in that moment of crisis. To my mind, Minister Fukuda—who went on to become Japan's Prime Minister in 1976 and passed away in July 1995—represents the model of a politician, statesman, and leader of the highest caliber.

5. The origins of the IGGI was studied by G. A. Posthumus (1971). For more detail, please see his study.

6. This section refers to my work (see Radius Prawiro, 1990), which provides a summary of the history and mechanics of the IGGI.

7. For more information see de Vries (1986: 74–5), as well as Posthumus (1971: 13).

8. For more information, see Pohl (1983).

9. The following paragraphs draw on the summary of the Abs settlement as described in the article by Widjojo (1994: 3–4).

10. This was discussed in an article by Roeder (1966).

11. For more, see Posthumus (1971: 36).

12. For more on this, please see the work by Machtarudin Siregar (1990) in which he discusses the role and significance of foreign aid to Indonesia.

13. Certainly, when President Sukarno in March 1964 told US Ambassador Howard Jones that the United States could 'go to hell' with its aid, he was giving voice to a deepseated resentment of what he perceived to be the unacceptably onerous conditions of foreign aid; see Penders (1974: 180) for a review of this event in the context of Sukarno era politics.

14. For more on this topic, see Musgrave (1983: 790–2).

3
Genesis of a New Economic Order

DURING the stabilization period, Indonesia created a new political and economic environment in which roller-coaster extremism was replaced with a steadier pragmatism. This is not to suggest that the government was lacking in a strong ideological perspective. Indeed, as mentioned, on 12 March 1966, the day after President Sukarno transferred *de facto* executive power to General Soeharto, Soeharto's first act was to ban the PKI. However, despite the new government's opposition to communism, it consciously tried to avoid the far left or right, hoping instead to remain open and flexible, especially in terms of its economic policies.

As mentioned in the Prologue, the government that succeeded Sukarno's became known as the 'New Order'. The difference implied by the name was not simply the change in leadership. The New Order represented a significant philosophical shift regarding what constituted the fundamental mission of the government and what the appropriate methods were for achieving that mission. For the New Order, the mission could be summarized with the words 'economic development'. In this pursuit, the discipline of economics—including the tools of macro- and micro-economic analysis—gained a prominence that was almost unimaginable in Indonesia's earlier years. Indeed, the rescue of the Indonesian economy would not have been possible without these strong and well-crafted economic policies. In themselves, however, these new policies were insufficient to bring about the changes so vitally necessary. In addition, a broad array of political, cultural, and social factors also played a key role in Indonesia's recovery. The next few pages reflect on some of the salient non-economic features that permitted Indonesia's New Order to create a new economic culture.

THE NEW LEADERSHIP

Throughout history, progress and development have never been possible without strong and effective leadership. Indonesia's successful programme of economic stabilization—without which further development could not have proceeded—confirms the truth of this principle. Many individuals and groups contributed to the effort to resurrect Indonesia's economy, but the three key principal forces that played the most compelling role in the events that ensued in the weeks and months that followed the establishment of the new government were the President, the economic team, and the armed forces.

An Executive Focus on Economics

The New Order staked its existence on its ability to build the Indonesian economy. If it failed in this effort, its credibility and the basic platform on which it was founded would have been destroyed. Though never formally articulated, the leadership of the country understood this idea from the beginning. During the first three years of the new government, there were successive changes in executive power. Initially, Indonesia was led by a presidium—comprising Soeharto as the chairman, Sultan Hamengkubuwono IX as the chief economic minister, and Adam Malik in charge of foreign affairs. The presidium led the country for one year, until March 1967. Two of the three members of the presidium, Sultan Hamengkubuwono IX and Adam Malik, had worked with President Sukarno in earlier cabinets. Sukarno supported the participation of these men in the presidium as a way of continuing his own influence. The Sultan was an extremely popular national figure in his own right. During the fight for independence from the Dutch in 1945, the Sultan provided assistance to Indonesia's central government when it was transferred from Jakarta to Yogjakarta and Sukarno and Mohammad Hatta had been taken into custody by the Dutch in 1948.

In later Sukarno cabinets, the Sultan was respected and admired as a voice of wisdom and moderation. As a member of the presidium, he served again as a crucial transitional figure during the precarious time between the Old Order and the New Order governments. He imbued the new government with moral authority and legitimacy, both at home and abroad. The high regard leaders in international circles had for the Sultan was very important as he endeavoured to help Indonesia re-establish positive working relationships with its overseas creditors. Similarly, Adam Malik, the new foreign minister, had served in many positions overseas. Leaders in Moscow and Washington knew and trusted him. Malik, too, was popular throughout the country. He was also sensitive to economic matters, although they were not his specific bailiwick.

The change in executive power, from Sukarno to the presidium and then to Soeharto, occurred with great finesse. During this transition, a concentrated focus on economics was maintained despite the political agitation of the time. In March 1967, the MPRS, Indonesia's representative body responsible for electing a president, chose Soeharto to be acting-president. A year later, the MPRS elected Soeharto full President, and in June 1968, he appointed a new Cabinet. Indonesia then reformed the political process and the MPRS was replaced with the Majelis Permusyawaratan Rakyat (MPR or People's Consultative Assembly) as a permanent element in Indonesia's political process.[1] The MPR consists of all the elected members of the DPR, together with representatives from various other sectors of the society. The MPR is assembled once every five years to elect the President. In 1973, after a five-year term, Soeharto was again elected President by the MPR, which was installed after the first general elections held in Indonesia since the New Order came to power.

From 1966 to 1970, the new government operated as if in a state of emergency. Although the primary enemy was hyperinflation, the government's broader objective was to create the conditions for sustainable economic growth. When Soeharto took the reigns of government, he and his team worked long and grueling hours in an effort to stabilize the economy. Although Soeharto was not an economist, he listened carefully to the recommendations of his economic advisers and studied the economic policy options they proposed. Only after thorough deliberations, frequently with substantive revisions, did he give his final endorsement. Thereafter, he would staunchly support the policy, even in the face of intense opposition. He would favour the economic policies that supported sustainable economic development rather than adopting politically expedient policies. Given the instability in Indonesia's society at the time, this commitment to sound economic management was remarkable.

The Economic Team

From the start, there was a close relationship between Indonesia's top leadership and the economists that served as policy advisers. In support of an economics-driven political agenda, Indonesia's new leadership adopted a management style that allowed the economic team to have an unusual degree of freedom and manoeuvrability. The presidium, and later President Soeharto, stood firmly in support of the government's economic team and their recommendations, even when the policies were politically unpopular.

The government did not create economic policy on a ministry-by-ministry basis. The Ministry of Trade, for example, did not act independently of the Ministry of Industry. Nor was economic policy made by arbitrary presidential command. Economic policy was a collective endeavour and the co-ordination and teamwork was exceptional. What was particularly unusual, however, is that before the installation of the 1968

Cabinet, two distinct groups worked in close co-operation to develop economic policy.

In addition to the Cabinet ministers who had the responsibility for developing government policy, Soeharto appointed two groups of special advisers (*staf ahli*): one for politics and one for economics. The political advisers were drawn from prominent intellectuals from various fields and especially from the military. The economic advisers were economists from the faculty at the University of Indonesia. The special advisory team on politics was dissolved in 1968. In one form or another, the economic team has continued to have a role in economic policy until this day.

In 1966, the Cabinet ministers with economic portfolios included the Minister of Finance, Frans Seda, and Mayjen Ashari Danudirodjo who served as the Minister of Trade and the Minister of Light Industries. M. Yusuf was Minister for Basic and Intermediate Industries, Sanusi was the Minister for Textile Industries, and I served as Governor of Bank Indonesia. Soeharto's special economic advisory group consisted of several academic economists who had received their training overseas. This group evolved into what became popularly known as the 'technocrats' and sometimes, more jocularly, the 'Berkeley Mafia', a name derived from the fact that several of its members had studied at the University of California at Berkeley. Separate from the Cabinet, the team of special advisers to the President included Widjojo Nitisastro, Ali Wardhana, Mohammad Sadli, Subroto, and Emil Salim, all of whom were faculty members in the department of economics at the University of Indonesia.[2] Together, these early minister, as well as the special advisors, were the original group of 'technocrats', but over time, others were added to the informal 'technocratic' team, including Rachmat Saleh, Arifin Siregar, J. B. Sumarlin, and myself. In 1968, Sumitro Djojohadikusumo joined the group when he was given the portfolio as Minister of Trade.

This arrangement, with two groups focusing on economic policy—ministers and advisers—could have led easily to factional battles and policymaking paralysis. These, however, were exceptional times, and national interest prevailed over fractiousness or differences of views. The two groups joined forces in the urgent task of creating policies that met sector-specific needs and macroeconomic objectives. In 1968, after the stabilization programme was well under way, the government was reorganized and in the second Cabinet, members of the special advisory team were given Cabinet portfolios or put in charge of government agencies. Widjojo was put in charge of planning as chairman of Bappenas, Wardhana was appointed Minister of Finance, Frans Seda was Minister of Communications, and I continued as Governor of Bank Indonesia. Mohammad Sadli, Subroto, and Emil Salim would be given ministerial portfolios in the next Cabinet. Most of the technocrats would remain in the highest ranks of government for many years to come. This continuity was invaluable because it meant that many of the lessons in the early years of the New Order were not lost when new problems were faced in subsequent years.

Throughout the stabilization period, Soeharto's advisory group and the economic ministers were mobilized by a sense of crisis. This infused both groups—the special advisers and ministers—with a shared sense of commitment to national recovery that exceeded personal self-interest or factional divisiveness. Since the technocrats were fresh from academia, they were relatively inexperienced in the art of politics. The period in which they were acting as advisers served as their political apprenticeship. It was, indeed, a 'trial by fire'. The *esprit de corps* among the economic team was exceptional.[3] This was possible because we were all economists with similar training and shared a common set of beliefs regarding the principles of sound economic management. We were also very young: all of us were in our thirties and full of confidence that we could find solutions to restore Indonesia to economic health. When the group held its strategy and planning meetings—which took place at least once a week—there was a relatively high degree of efficiency because the participants all spoke the same intellectual language. All of the team members shared very similar assumptions on the economy and used the same abbreviated economic jargon. There were almost no instances of irreconcilable differences. With all members in agreement on the fundamentals of good economics, the team was able to focus on the best strategies and tactics for achieving stabilization.

All the people in the economic team were intelligent and dynamic men with no shortage of self-esteem. It was Widjojo, however, who quickly became the unofficial yet acknowledged head of the group. Widjojo was an expert in both demographics and economics. He was a brilliant strategist and a person of vision with a long-term focus. He was an excellent listener and without resorting to domination or relying on the authority of conferred title, Widjojo was able to guide a team comprising many of Indonesia's most capable and influential economists. He brought out the best in each member. He kept meetings moving without imposing rigid procedures or formality. Widjojo was a natural leader. Throughout his career, he deliberately kept a low profile and yet if there is anyone who deserves the title of 'architect' of Indonesia's economic development, it is Widjojo.[4]

Commenting on the economic team at this time, the economist, Bruce Glassburner (1971), observed that Indonesia 'is now placing a frighteningly heavy bet on a handful of economists to bring order out of economic chaos', and he was somewhat alarmed that 'these economists have placed their heaviest bets on the revival of the market system'. In hindsight, the success of the stabilization policies may have been inevitable. At the time, however, nothing was clear. The policies were complex and the crisis was deep. Working in an atmosphere of vigilant frenzy, the team took a leap of faith that the free market and the power of prudent macroeconomic policy would prevail. In the end, because of the cohesiveness of the team and the essential correctness of their economic positions, the gamble paid off.

The Refocusing of the Military

Throughout its history as an independent nation, the Indonesian armed forces, known as Angkatan Bersenjata Republik Indonesia (ABRI), have had a significant role in Indonesia's nation-building process. In Indonesia, as in other countries, the participation by the military in political or civilian affairs, particularly in times of peace, is a matter of some controversy. In the early years of the New Order, however, Indonesia's military leadership was composed of men whose training had been in the struggle for independence, rather than those who chose the military as a career. The background, outlook, and experience of Indonesia's military leaders was much the same as the country's civilian leaders. In fact, because there were no formal military academies for Indonesians, both civilian and military élites had studied at the same or similar schools.

It was highly fortuitous that during the late 1950s and early 1960s, the forward-looking director of Indonesia's military staff college, General Soewarto, invited professors from the University of Indonesia to give lectures on the overall state of the nation's economy to selected senior officers, including General Soeharto. Among the lecturers were several from the economics faculty at the University of Indonesia including Widjojo Nitisastro, Mohammad Sadli, Emil Salim, and Subroto. This was part of the broadening of training for the military élite, which also included stints abroad at military academies and staff colleges in the United States, the Netherlands, and other European countries. Later, when many of the same economics scholars would hold ministerial portfolios, they were already known and respected by the military leadership. Perhaps more important, these lectures gave military leaders an appreciation and conceptual understanding of how important economic matters were to the future of the nation.

During the early months of the New Order, Cabinet ministers as well as the professors who were acting as Soeharto's special economic advisors conducted several such seminars. The purpose of these particular seminars was twofold: first, they were designed to give the country's military élite enough background in economics so that they could understand the sources of Indonesia's current economic difficulties; second, the economic team wanted to obtain the military's express support for the policies about to be launched. After listening to the lectures, the military leadership in attendance generally agreed with the problem analysis and the recommended solutions. When the stabilization programme was launched in October 1966, the backing of the country's armed forces was already largely assured.[5] The military leaders generally trusted Soeharto and wanted to assist in every effort necessary to heal and repair the country. The seminars had created a climate of respect and reinforced the positive relationship between Indonesia's economic policymakers and the military. As has already been made clear, many of the stabilization policies placed a great strain on the whole country. Without the confidence and continuing support of the military, the restoration of the economy would have been impossible. In this respect and others, the military showed themselves committed partners in the nation's economic development.

GUIDING VALUES IN CREATING
A NEW ECONOMIC ORDER

In one form or another, Indonesia's core technocratic team continued to manage or influence economic policy for some three decades. As the emphasis switched from stabilization to economic development, the team was able to maintain its focus and solidarity because of many shared values—values that transcended a particular political position or school of economics. The essence of these values grew out of the Indonesian culture, but they were adapted and refined to assist in guiding policy formation. The list of such values could be quite long, but three stand out, namely, *gotong royong*, the 'Development Trilogy', and pragmatism.

Gotong Royong

Gotong royong is an Indonesian term that means mutual assistance or mutual self-help. It may be the most fundamental principle in organizing Indonesian society from the village level to the central government in Jakarta.[6] *Gotong royong* grew over centuries of Indonesian history and cannot be attributed to any particular government or individual. If, for example, a villager finds himself in distress, be it financial, physical, or even emotional, according to *gotong royong* it is the duty of the other villagers to help solve the problem. If someone's house burns down, in the spirit of *gotong royong*, neighbours will help to reconstruct it. Similarly, if a child is orphaned, *gotong royong* will lead another family to take in the child and raise him as part of their own family. Indonesia's philosophy of *gotong royong* contrasts sharply with the 'individualism' so popular in the West. Quite literally, Indonesians are rarely alone. From birth to death, Indonesians are almost always in the company of their family, friends, or colleagues. In a very practical and tangible sense, Indonesians are part of an extended family that likely includes neighbours along with blood relatives. Membership in an Indonesian extended family implies service to the needy in one's community. It is part of the Indonesian character to share in both fortune and misfortune.[7]

There have been various ways in which *gotong royong* has been translated into political actions and policies. In times of distress, the government has called on citizens to support policies that it believed were in the best interest of the nation although such policies may have required individual sacrifice. Especially in the early days of the New Order, *gotong royong* had two practical meanings. First, it meant that there was a cultural alternative to communism. *Gotong royong* provided a 'home-grown' ideological basis for guiding economic policy that was socially responsible, solicitous of the welfare of each individual, and generally compatible with free market economics. Second, *gotong royong* has had a moderating effect on Indonesia's policymaking process. This is because *gotong royong* relates closely to two other Indonesian socializing concepts: *musyawarah*, which means dialogue and *mufakat*, which means consensus. To create national cohesion after the trauma of the mid-1960s the government took great pains to produce a policy agenda that grew out of dialogue and consensus. In developing its 'style' of governance, the New Order tried to avoid the two extremes that threatened the nation's fragile stability—the oppressiveness of dictatorial autocracy and the paralysis of dysfunctional factional democracy. The government regarded both as political dead ends. The New Order's method for achieving a 'middle-way' between the two extremes was dialogue and consensus, both within the government and in its relations with the Parliament. Generally, Indonesians have been culturally predisposed to seek consensus through dialogue rather than having to resort to a vote. In many cases, this commitment to dialogue and consensus meant that decisions were not always taken as expeditiously as policymakers would have liked. However, when policies were truly formulated in the spirit of *musyawarah* and *mufakat*, they have generally received wide public support and withstood the test of time.[8]

The Development Trilogy

There are many ways to define development. In the early days of the New Order, the essence of a vision of development began to take shape and this eventually became known as the 'Development Trilogy' consisting of

Stability, Growth, and Equity. This Trilogy epitomized Indonesia's vision of development. The Development Trilogy is a simple but powerful idea which, more than anything else, expresses the New Order's pragmatic and ideological standard against which all economic policies could be measured.

Given Indonesia's early experience of hyperinflation and political unrest, the value of *Stability* was emblazoned in the minds of the country's new leaders as an absolute necessity for maintaining national strength and cohesion. New Order leaders recognized that loss of stability shatters the normal functioning of markets and injures the basis for civil social exchange. Stability in the extreme—oppressive stability—can lead to social rigidity, economic stagnation, and national decline. The government's desire, therefore, was to achieve a 'dynamic stability' that fostered economic growth. This is a similar idea to market equilibrium, which is a kind of stability that is ever changing. Social stability is also ever changing and adaptive to contemporary needs, yet supportive of development.

Growth is the second element of the Development Trilogy. Especially for a poor country like Indonesia, growth is indispensable. Only through economic growth can the government have any chance to respond to the needs of its people. In those early days, the economic *status quo* was unthinkable. By way of head-to-head comparison, the 1966 level of per capita income of Indonesia was $60, while in India—one of the poorest countries in the world—the comparable level in the same year was nearly 50 per cent higher: it was $90. The fact was clear—Indonesia needed to grow rapidly if the country hoped to achieve an acceptable standard of living.

The third component of the Development Trilogy, *Equity*, is a necessary corollary to stability and growth. Indonesia entered its modern period acutely sensitive to the potential dangers of unfettered capitalism. Rightly or wrongly, the country tended to see colonialism as an example of capitalism at its worst. Huge income disparities and a disinterest in the welfare of other members in the community were characteristics commonly associated with 'free-fight' capitalism. These were antithetical to Indonesia's cultural norms. The government believed that equity was necessary to ensure that the fruits of growth did not benefit only a small élite. By committing itself to equity, Indonesia's New Order leaders hoped to avoid the dark side of capitalism and demonstrate that economic growth could benefit the society at large.

Pragmatism and Economic Policy

One of the most dramatic shifts in philosophy and style between the New Order and the Old Order was the relinquishing of the extreme, emotion-charged focus on ideology for a more detached, analytical, and flexible approach based on pragmatism. This was particularly true in the formulation of economic policy. In the thirty-year period under consideration in this book, the pendulum of economic policy swung in varying degrees between the left and right. Yet, ultimately, these labels were inconsequential and were of no interest to Indonesia's New Order policymakers. Their concern was for what worked. Economic policy formulation is an imprecise science executed in complex social environments. For every policy, there are winners and losers.[9] Economics is never politically neutral and therefore Indonesia was unable to create economic policy that was politically neutral. However, for the first time since independence, the country tried to formulate economic policy based on the best understanding of macro- and micro-economics, rather than political ideology. Through the Development Trilogy of stability, growth, and equity, Indonesia found a way of attempting to reconcile ideas of social good and economic good.

It was perhaps an odd blessing that the style of Indonesia's modern-day economic policymaking was formed during a period of crisis. The survival of the government and, perhaps, even the country depended on achieving an economic recovery. Just as necessity is often the mother of invention, in Indonesia, crisis seems to have been the mother of pragmatism. The focus of the economic team had to be on what worked, not on a particular school of thought. This is not to say that the government's pragmatism, and especially that of the economic team, stemmed from an ideological shallowness or a lack of any true convictions. Virtually every economic policy was geared to achieve one objective: that of *economic development*. The success or failure of a policy was judged by the extent it contributed to economic development, which in turn was further defined as the 'Development Trilogy'. Furthermore, the economic team members were generally strong believers in the neoclassical school of economics, which emphasized the efficiency of free markets. However, even with these convictions, the economic team's commitment to pragmatism left the door wide open to adopt whatever policies contributed to economic development.

In a 1991 report, the World Bank came to a conclusion supportive of Indonesia's position on pragmatism: 'Perhaps the clearest lesson from work on development during the past thirty years is that there is a premium on pragmatism and an open mind. Ideas that were once the conventional wisdom, and which guided governments and multilateral institutions in forming their approaches to development, have largely been set aside.... There is no magic cure for economic backwardness' (p. 49).

Pragmatism meant that in formulating economic policymaking, there were few taboos. Before the government adopted a policy, there were two basic criteria to be met: the policy had to support development and it had to be politically defensible. Experience taught the economic team that effective pragmatism was an art of astute compromise. Instead of economics in the service of politics, under the New Order, *politics was usually conducted in support of economics.* Earlier, it was mentioned that it was the custom under both Sukarno and Soeharto to give each Cabinet a name that epitomized the government's fundamental mission. Because of the government's unswerving and overwhelming commitment to economic development, since 1968 each successive five-year administration has been called simply a 'Development Cabinet' (with each one numbered in sequence), while Indonesia's economic plans are always called 'Five-Year Development Plans', or in Indonesian, 'Repelita' which is short for Rencana Pembangunan Lima Tahun.

OBSERVATIONS AT THE BIRTH OF A NEW ECONOMIC CULTURE

The stabilization period was a defining moment in the history of modern Indonesia. Indonesia emerged from this period of stress and trauma stronger and more confident than ever. The New Order won many political converts during this period, from the left and right, as well as those who had become politically disenfranchised, and those who had always operated outside the political process. During this period, the government leaders learned much and developed a more sophisticated and cohesive approach to economic management. Throughout this process, it became clear that in economic policymaking, non-economic factors often have a decisive role in determining whether a policy is successful. The following are a few of the conditions which we discovered were necessary if the New Order were to succeed in creating a new economic culture for Indonesia.

1. *Reconciling Political and Economic Time.* It is a great challenge for economic policymakers to reconcile the fact that the fields of economics and politics operate according to two different clocks. In economics, 'short-term' generally means less than a year and 'long-term' refers to five years or more. In politics, the 'short-term' is measured in days or hours, and in five years a political lifetime can be destroyed and reincarnated many times over. When the stabilization programme began in earnest in October 1966, the government knew it would take a minimum of two to three years to tame inflation. The pressing question was, would the country give the government that much time to achieve its goal? Many observers doubted the survivability of the new government. If the leadership made any serious misstep, that could easily have been its first step

toward the exit. By the summer of 1966, there were already predictions of the imminent demise of the New Order.[10]

2. *Building on a Foundation of Stability.* In the early days of the New Order, the terms 'stability' and 'stabilization' were used as shorthand for 'killing inflation'. Throughout the entire stabilization process, the government maintained a level of fiscal restraint and responsibility that was unprecedented for Indonesia. For the first time, the government balanced its budgets, reduced subsidies, and increased the supply of essential goods—especially rice and textiles. Over time, Indonesia's leadership became increasingly aware of the link between 'stabilization' and 'stability'. The government came to see the emerging stability not as an emergency economic measure, but as a prerequisite for long-term planning and sustainable economic growth. The commitment to stability became one of the government's basic economic and social tenets. This reinforced the importance of the Development Trilogy as the guiding philosophy for Indonesia's economic development.

3. *A New Role for Expertise.* Indonesia's stabilization effort required a high level of expertise in economic policy formulation. After the stabilization process was underway, the government retained its respect for expertise. For a country in which the notion of extended family is omnipresent, the new government placed a surprising emphasis on merit. The high representation of Ph.Ds in the upper circles of the New Order did not so much reflect an enrapturement with postgraduate degrees as a heightened appreciation for the value of expertise.

In selecting the economic team, Soeharto favoured competence over political connections. After the Cabinet was installed in 1968, the *Far Eastern Economic Review* reported:

The high percentage of intellectuals in the new Cabinet (11 out of 23) is one of its most remarkable characteristics. Seven Ministers are university professors. While half of the Ministers of the previous *Ampera* Cabinet came from the Armed Forces, the Development Cabinet has only six in uniform. The political parties and mass organizations have only eight representatives. This suggests that the composition of the new cabinet was not dictated by the need to maintain a balance of power or by political horse-trading. In short, the Development Cabinet is a 'cabinet of experts,' with few exceptions (Roeder, 1968: 591).

Equally important, after the economic team was in place, the government provided the economic team with favourable conditions for carrying out its job. A World Bank publication (1993a: 167) states that one of the traits necessary for economic growth is 'technocratic insulation', that is, 'the ability of economic technocrats to formulate and implement policies in keeping with politically formulated national goals with a minimum of lobbying for special favors from politicians and interest groups'. This aptly describes the conditions the government tried to create for the economic team.

4. *Political Courage*. If anything was tested during the stabilization period, it was the *character* of the Indonesian leadership. The stabilization process was, above all, a test of political courage. When Indonesia's leadership formulated and introduced economic policies, the only instruments it had were academic theories, six-month old statistics, and its faith in the resilience, intelligence, and initiative of the Indonesian people. The stabilization process was a gamble with the highest stakes, both personal and national. With less courage, the government would never have cut subsidies or controlled the money supply as it did. It held its ground on the policies of importance and this fact permitted the stabilization process to move forward quickly and efficiently. Courage may have been of greater importance to the recovery than all the economic theories the economic team used to guide policy decisions.

During the stabilization period, the New Order was born and with it, a new economic culture was founded. These early years set a new course for the country. People inside the government and out accorded greater respect and credibility to the field of economics. The political climate was more moderate and after more than a decade of 'living dangerously' Indonesia found a social stability that had been all but forgotten. There were, of course, many difficulties ahead, but as the country entered the 1970s, the conditions were ripe to launch a more ambitious programme for long-term economic growth.

1. The term MPRS is translated as 'Provisional People's Consultative Assembly' because in the 1950s Indonesia hoped to draft a new constitution. While work on the constitution was underway, the People's Consultative Assembly was called 'Provisional' because it was expected that the body would be significantly altered when the revised constitution was finished. Instead, Sukarno decided that the country should stay with the original 1945 Constitution. The New Order also agreed to retain the 1945 Constitution and thus, there was no need to consider the People's Consultative Assembly a 'provisional' body. The institution thereafter reassumed its original name of Majelis Permusyawaratan Rakyat or simply 'MPR'. Unlike the DPR, or Parliament, which operates continually to formulate and ratify the laws that govern the country, the MPR is assembled only periodically to elect the President and to approve the Garis-garis Besar Haluan Negara (GBHN or The Broad Outline of the Nation's Direction).

2. During the early years, I was Governor of Bank Indonesia. Perhaps because my office at the Bank was one of the few that had air-conditioning, or perhaps because the Bank had a good reputation as an environment for maintaining confidentiality, this location informally became the site for many strategy and planning meetings among the economic advisory

staff and the economic ministers. After the special economic advisers were given ministerial positions, the term 'technocrat' came into wider circulation and was broadly used to refer to the officials who were pragmatic, market-oriented, and usually trained economists.

3. I use the term 'economic team' to mean both economic Cabinet ministers and advisers during the early stabilization period. Later, when the early technocrats became ministers themselves, the 'economic team' refers simply to the senior officials, generally economic ministers, who worked together in the formulation of economic policy. This spirit of team-work was present among most of Indonesia's economic policymakers throughout my tenure in government, from 1965 to 1993.

4. I learned many important lessons from Widjojo; one of the most important was the value of maintaining a low profile. Throughout his career, his objective was to promote economic policies, not himself. I have tried to abide by this principle as well. By keeping policies in the foreground and personalities in the background, I believe that I was better able to manoeuvre in what was often a complex political environment and effect positive policy changes. However, the undisputed master of low profile but effective leadership has been Widjojo.

5. In August of 1966, the military staff college held a seminar for the nation's military élite at which Widjojo and I, together with other economists including Sadli, Subroto, Emil Salim, gave lectures. In these talks, we gave fairly thorough analyses of the current economic conditions and the measures we believed were needed to restore health to the economy. I concluded my lecture by saying, 'The duty we all face to overcome our difficulties is extremely heavy. The stabilization and rehabilitation programme planned by the government only will succeed if it receives the full support and understanding of all levels of society. What is needed most are discipline and self-restraint from us all, so that we obedi-ently follow the rules of the game, because in the economy, there are no magical shortcuts. Diligent work and discipline are still the best ingredients for success' (Radius Prawiro, 1966). Later, when the government was implementing painful economic policies, it was fortuitous that these seminars were held as they helped build solidarity between the government's economic leaders and military leaders.

6. Indonesia is a large country with many regional languages, ethnic groups, and local traditions. There is a risk, therefore, in referring to any attribute as representing 'Indonesian culture'. None the less, there are various norms and values, such as *gotong royong*, that are generally embraced throughout Indonesia and are at the heart of the nation's collective culture.

7. In recent years, there has been rapid urbanization in Indonesia and this has tested the mettle of *gotong royong*. The *gotong royong* spirit is still strong in Indonesia, but it may be inevitable that community ties weaken as more Indonesians live in large cities. One of the challenges of modern Indonesia is to find ways to adapt positive traditional norms such as *gotong royong* to a modern industrialized setting.

8. As mentioned in the Prologue, during the period 1946–57 Indonesia had a very liberal democratic system. *Gotong royong* notwithstanding, the country's initial experience with democracy was so divisive that Sukarno replaced it with a system that put virtually all government power in his hands. The New Order tried to avoid both extremes.

9. Pareto optimality—the idea that in negotiating, parties will find a point which is optimal for all parties—is a wonderful theory. However, no matter how well crafted a policy may be, there will always be those who feel that the policy has rendered them worse off than they could have been without the policy. Even in cases when everyone 'wins' or every-one is better off, some groups will argue that they are less well off than they could have been. This means even a hypothetically 'best' policy will still be rejected as deficient by

some. If, for example, a policy eliminates a monopoly, the monopolist will feel penalized. If a policy authorizes a monopoly, others will argue they are being deprived of economic opportunities. Pareto may be right that there is a point of optimal benefit for all, but the problem is, in reality, many people will seek maximum benefit for themselves, rather than optimal benefit for the collective.

10. See for example the 21 July 1966 issue of the *Far Eastern Economic Review* in which it reports, 'There are in Indonesia, plenty of people who do not believe in the ability of the new regime to survive'.

PART II

1969–1983
GROWTH AMID GLOBAL
TURMOIL

Introduction

THE 1970s were a period of widespread insecurity and disillusionment in world affairs, a time noteworthy for its lack of political or economic consensus. Indonesia entered the 1970s with a hard-won, but tenuous stability. As the next step, the government needed to guide the country along the road to economic development as it tried to integrate itself more closely into the world economy. The conditions of the time, however, were far from conducive.

The 1960s may have been the apex of the Pax Americana that had reigned for some quarter of a century following the Second World War. By the time the 1970s arrived, the United States was slipping badly, and to many around the world, these changes made the future increasingly uncertain. The tension in the superpower rivalry escalated, and the effects spread around the globe. The ambitious programmes that the United States launched with fanfare in the 1960s, such as President Lyndon Johnson's 'Great Society' and 'War on Poverty', ended with little progress and plenty of cynicism. Then, in 1972, the Watergate scandal occurred, forcing President Richard Nixon two years later to resign from office in disgrace. Even more shocking to those who believed in American military invincibility was the war in Vietnam—a fiasco for the Americans in which the communist faction of a small poor country, backed by the Soviet Union and China, was able to humble a superpower. The image of America's power, however, may have hit rock bottom when in November 1979, Iranian terrorists seized the American embassy in Tehran and then, with the backing of the Iranian leadership, held the diplomatic staff hostage for 444 days.

In many respects, America's decline was matched by Soviet gains. The communist doctrine was spreading. Among many developing countries, however, the trend was not just another intellectual fashion. In the name of Marx, Lenin, and Mao, nations were being re-engineered in the most unnatural ways. The 1973 cease-fire between the Americans and the North Vietnamese opened the door for a full-scale communist victory two years later. Cambodia and Laos soon followed. What then happened was terrifying. Everywhere communism spread, it left death and destruction in its wake; yet its appeal, especially among developing countries, continued undiminished. In Africa, the former Portuguese colonies of Mozambique and Angola became hotbeds of communist insurgence, with Cuban troops acting as Moscow's willing proxy. In Latin America, from Peru to Nicaragua, communist rebels kept much of the continent in a state of continual unrest. Communist parties were even strong in Western Europe, particularly in Italy and Portugal.

Indonesia had no interest in entangling itself in the web of cold war dualism. As a practical matter, however, Indonesia's leadership had staked the nation's future on the belief that the winning strategy for stable economic growth was market economics. For Indonesia, America's difficulties were as disconcerting as the Soviet Union's successes. Indonesia, like many other former colonies, was in its early and formative stages of nation building, and the course it would follow for economic development was not entirely certain. The superpower schism and the ways that the left–right competition was playing out among developing countries were disturbing. The existence of at least two very powerful and opposing camps in world affairs represented a serious disagreement about what worked best to help countries flourish.

The turmoil that marred the political sphere was also present and concentrated in the economic sphere. Weaknesses were appearing in many of the basic institutions of Western capitalist economies. Since the close of the Second World War, the cornerstone of the international economy was the fixed exchange rate system, according to which most national currencies varied little in relation to the dollar, which itself was fixed on a gold standard. For years, $35 bought one troy ounce of gold. The variation was nil. The dollar was firm, fixed, reliable, and secure; it served as the anchor for many other currencies. Then in August 1971, US President Nixon announced his 'New Economic Policy' according to which the gold standard was abandoned, the dollar was devalued, and a 10 per cent surcharge was placed on imports. The surcharge did not last long, but the gold standard and the relative stability it brought had become suddenly and permanently extinct. The next year, the Europeans devised the 'snake', which permitted a 2.25 per cent band of fluctuation in their currencies' values. Then in 1975, the IMF formally recognized the floating exchange rate system and this would soon be adopted by central banks in many countries.

The logic behind floating rates is unassailable. The risk that accompanies free exchange rates, however, is that currencies can become too volatile and subjected to speculative pressures. The reality of this risk soon became painfully evident to governments and private investors. In 1980, with a confrontation between Washington and Moscow looming over the Soviet invasion of Afghanistan, gold peaked over $850 an ounce.

Similarly, the dollar fell against the German mark from DM 3.48 in July 1971 to DM 1.75 in July 1980, convulsing unpredictably as it made its unsteady descent. The world currency system had become inherently unstable.

International economic insecurity was exacerbated when world oil markets were rocked by two related crises: first, the Arab oil embargo of 1973, and then the Iranian revolution in 1979. Oil prices soared and the impact on the international economy was immense. As an oil producing country, Indonesia gained from the substantial oil windfalls. The world economy, however, slid into a prolonged recession. Developing countries were particularly vulnerable to the gyrations in international economics. None of the rules or theories in economics provided a secure way to avoid these difficulties, or a means to react appropriately after they occurred. The disillusionment of this period ran deep.

The economic stabilization that Indonesia achieved during the late 1960s, though substantial, was insufficient to respond to the country's pervasive needs. Every sector of the economy needed to be overhauled. The country had virtually no roads and few ports. The nation's population was growing at 2.3 per cent per annum, yet farmers continued to rely on cultivation methods that had not changed for centuries. Indonesia's agriculture was inadequate, and industry offered little in terms of alternative employment opportunities. Consequently, food shortages and unemployment were chronic and extreme. The nation had virtually no industry. Its foreign trade was minute. Moreover, few children had the opportunity to attend school. Under these conditions, Indonesia set its course in 1969 with a modest five-year development plan, hoping to ratchet the economy up, one notch at a time. The country's plans were circumvented by the unanticipated oil boom. For Indonesia, this appeared to be a blessing, but only to a point. The volatility in commodity market and exchange rates renewed inflationary pressures while rising political and economic nationalism made this period a difficult one. None the less, Indonesia's Development Trilogy—Stability, Growth, and Equity—remained the nation's guiding principle. In this period of doubt, turmoil, and recession, the focus of the government's efforts was to deliver on the second pillar of development: economic growth.

4
The Promise and Peril of Oil Money

ALMOST every culture has a fable that goes something like this:

Once upon a time, there was an old farmer and his wife who lived honest and good lives. They had a warm household, with kind and respectful children, but they suffered from a lifetime of poverty. They toiled on their small plot of land and for years scraped out a meager living. Every day they prayed that their hardships would pass. Then one day, one of their prized ducks wandered away. After a long search, the farmer and his wife finally found the duck by a magic fountain from which poured an endless stream of gold. 'Do you know what this is, darling?' said the man. 'This is the answer to all our prayers!' said his wife. 'That's right. We're rich! From now on, all of our troubles are over!'

Of course, the fable tells us that in the end, there was a price to pay for the riches, and in light of the costs, their former lifestyle was not so bad after all.

In the 1970s, many Indonesians saw oil as such a fountain of gold. Although oil had been extracted from Indonesia's territories since the late nineteenth century, production had increased only slowly. Then suddenly, in less than a decade, Indonesia grew to be one of the world's major producers and exporters of oil and gas at a time when oil prices were reaching historic highs. When the full impact of this development was understood, there was widespread euphoria. It suddenly looked as if Indonesia's struggle with poverty might come to a relatively quick and easy end. In economics however—as in fables—life is never so simple. There is always a price to pay, even for easy money, and if one is not careful, what was once considered a blessing may one day be referred to as 'the devil's excrement'.[1]

There are many ways to view oil. On one level, oil is a simple mineral in the hydrocarbon family. On another level, oil is a fossil fuel that serves as the primary energy source for the modern economy. Oil is also the substance on which one of the most important industries in the world is based. Above all, however, oil is *money*. Just as the world was abandoning the gold standard, the black gold of petroleum moved into prominence as one of the most basic units of international currency. No matter how strict a foreign exchange regime may be, there is no country which is not interested in trading a barrel of oil. Especially in the 1970s, oil was power, both literally and figuratively. When such power finds itself suddenly highly concentrated in a particular point, a shift in the political and economic nexus is inevitable.

A shift in the power equation of world economics did take place in October 1973 when several Arab countries launched an oil embargo against the United States and the Netherlands. The panic trading that ensued led to a quadrupling of oil prices over the next two years.[2] The shock[3] subsided and price levels started to ease around 1977, leading to growing anxiety among the oil producing countries. Then in 1979, the revolution in Iran threw another round of chaos into the world oil markets and the second oil shock was born, again causing oil prices to soar. During the decade from 1970 to 1980, Indonesian oil prices appreciated seventeen-fold. By 1983, the law of 'economic gravity' began to catch up with the oil industry, and prices began to fall as drastically as they had risen.

The 1970s were Indonesia's oil decade. Never again is the price movement of a single commodity likely to so influence the Indonesian economy. In 1970, Indonesia's oil traded at $1.67 per barrel. The country produced some 0.89 million barrels per day, which constituted 29 per cent of the central government's revenues. Just over a decade later, in 1981, Indonesia produced about 1.6 million barrels per day, each of which fetched about $35 per barrel. This constituted about 70 per cent of the government's revenues. Indonesia's oil wealth changed the country forever. This wealth, however, was non-renewable and finite. Indonesia's known reserves are relatively small, and sometime early in the twenty-first century Indonesia is likely to become a net oil importer. For a decade, however, Indonesia saw a surge in revenues that exceeded all expectations.

The growth in oil revenues in the 1970s was extreme and the eventual decline was extreme. This was a period when all the knowledge, theories, and intuitions on macroeconomics were tested under fire. Managing the country's oil windfall proved to be one of the most complex and important acts of economic policymaking the country has ever faced. Information was limited and changes in markets were extreme and unpredictable. When the economy convulses, the political environment reverberates in unpredictable ways. Politics and economics can never be separated. Yet, while economic analysis alone can strain the capacity of the most advanced supercomputers, politics adds to the intricacy by an incalculable degree. Despite the complexity of this topic, this chapter reviews some of the salient political and economic issues associated with the rise and fall of Indonesia's oil economy during the 1970s and early 1980s. In the long run, these experiences had a crucial role in helping the economic team to refine its prudent and pragmatic approach to economic policy formulation.

A BRIEF SUMMARY OF THE LONG HISTORY OF INDONESIAN OIL

In 1985, Indonesia celebrated its centennial as an oil producing country, making Indonesia one of the oldest oil-producing countries in Asia.[4] The Dutch exploited the original fields in northern Sumatra. By the 1930s, three foreign oil companies, Royal Dutch Shell, Caltex, and Stanvac,[5] dominated the industry with a cluster of smaller companies operating mostly around Sumatra and Java. After Indonesia gained independence, it nationalized some small oil firms and placed heavy restrictions on the major foreign oil companies. Exploration declined and the industry stagnated, only producing around 150,000 barrels per day in the late 1950s.

In 1960, the government instituted Law No. 44 as the legal framework for managing natural resources with foreign-based companies. This stated that Indonesia could contract with other entities to do the work in exchange for royalties. The agreements formulated under this law were known as 'contracts of work'. These contracts gave the extractor what amounted to a concession from which monies were paid to the government based on the sales of oil, minus certain expenses. In granting these contracts, the government tended to favour certain companies, particularly Dutch-based ones such as Royal Dutch Shell. This is because the Indonesian government officials felt then that they could not adequately supervise the extraction operations, and that the Dutch, who had the longest experience in Indonesia, would be more likely than companies of other countries to operate in Indonesia's best interest. Indonesia was in a bad bargaining position. It could not adequately judge the costs of exploration and production or estimate the profits from this work. This made it impossible to negotiate appropriately contract of work agreements.

Things changed in the early 1960s when Indonesia created a new type of contractual arrangement with foreign oil contractors. Instead of the 'contract of work', the new agreements were called 'production sharing' contracts. In brief, the contractors financed the exploration, development, and production costs in a particular area, while Indonesia's state-owned oil company, Pertamina, would manage the operations. According to this arrangement, Indonesia and the foreign oil contractors would share the oil as it came out of the ground. The production company retained a portion of the crude oil to compensate for its exploration and other costs and the remainder of the crude was divided between the company and Indonesia at an agreed upon ratio. The 'production sharing' contract was the brain-child of Ibnu Sutowo, a central figure in the early development of Indonesia's oil industry. Ibnu had a gift for business and found himself at the centre of the most important industry in the early history of the Republic of Indonesia. In 1961, Indonesia had three small oil companies, PN Permina, PN Permigan, and PT Pertamin.[6] Ibnu became chairman of the board that oversaw these companies. In 1968, the firms were merged to form Pertamina under his direction.

Indonesia's oil output grew steadily from the late 1960s. In 1967, oil revenues started to appear as a separate line of revenues in the government's budgets. From 1967 to 1971 the country's oil revenues grew from Rp 7.4 billion to Rp 99.2 billion, that is, an increase of 1,230 per cent and constituted 42.9 per cent of Indonesia's total exports. In February 1971, the country's oil output for the first time reached one million barrels a day.

If things had levelled off there, oil would have continued to have a major role in the country's economic development. This was not to be. The oil embargo launched in 1973 sent prices skyward and with it came the incentive to increase exploration and production. Indonesia's oil output rose gradually, and its stature as an energy supplier grew when it developed the capacity to export liquefied natural gas (LNG). In 1971, President Soeharto gave me the responsibility to open discussions with the Japanese regarding the importation of LNG from Indonesia. This was a difficult struggle because no deal was possible between Indonesia and Japan without first getting approval from the Japanese Parliament and Cabinet. They were reluctant because at the time many considered the large-scale use of LNG to be risky. The skeptics pointed out that the associated technologies—such as liquefaction processes, building of special LNG tankers, and the construction of gasification plants—were relatively new technologies, extremely sophisticated, and required huge capital outlays. None the less, in 1973, Pertamina signed its first contracts with companies from Japan and the United States. In a matter of years Indonesia became the world's largest exporter of LNG, with sales going primarily to Japan, Korea, and Taiwan after the American company withdrew its purchase order.

During this period, Indonesia intensified its co-operation with various foreign contractors. Most of the money to build the industry came from foreign oil companies. This contribution was essential to the expansion of the industry, but by the mid-1970s production started to decline due to depleted resources and a decline in exploration.

Throughout the mid-1970s Indonesia's oil production hovered about 1.3 million barrels per day (bpd) as prices sank and rose erratically. Then in 1979, the second oil shock struck and over the course of the next couple of years, the government's oil revenues tripled. During the decade, oil came to dominate Indonesia's economy as no commodity had done before, except perhaps rice. In 1980, with some 70 per cent of fiscal revenues derived from oil, the government coffers relied on one taxpayer, the oil industry. Oil had come to exert a powerful influence over Indonesia's economy, and one that was fundamentally unstable and unreliable. The government's economic leaders knew that it was not in the country's long-term interest to become overdependent on a single commodity, but for the time being, the benefits from oil were enormous and irresistible.[7]

PERTAMINA: THE PRODIGAL ENTERPRISE

The insatiable appetite for energy among the world's industrialized nations created a huge demand for Indonesia's oil during the 1970s. Indonesia channelled this demand through Pertamina which grew rapidly until 1975 when troubles suddenly erupted at the state-owned enterprise. The events associated with the difficulties at Pertamina had a profound impact on Indonesia's development. The lessons were valuable, but the costs were high.

The Rapid Rise and Fall of an Oil Empire[8]

At the centre of Pertamina's tumultuous development was Ibnu Sutowo. He, more than anyone, helped to transform Pertamina from a collection of third world businesses to a multinational conglomerate that topped out in the mid-1970s as the two-hundreth largest international corporation. For Indonesia, this was an astonishing accomplishment. Despite its size and importance, Pertamina had only the veneer of a sophisticated multinational corporation. It was, however, a multibillion-dollar veneer, and that was enough to convey a very favourable impression. Beneath the surface, however, Pertamina lacked systems, controls, management, and experience. Pertamina was an accident waiting to happen. There were numerous signs. None, unfortunately, were sufficient to arrest the company's ominous momentum.

Pertamina grew so large so quickly that it became the focus of public concern. In early 1970, students held demonstrations at which they were particularly vocal in expressing their displeasure regarding the government's decision to reduce subsidies on kerosene and petrol—a move they saw as further enriching Pertamina. Newspapers openly questioned Pertamina's finances. President Soeharto acted by appointing a special panel, known as 'The Commission of Four', to investigate issues of corruption. Pertamina was the primary focus of their inquiry which lasted about five months. In June, the Commission submitted its report to

President Soeharto. The report was highly critical of Pertamina and its leadership. Based on its recommendations, the government passed a bill in 1971 that obliged Pertamina to give 60 per cent of its net income—based on its own production as well as funds collected from foreign contractors—to the central treasury. In January 1972, the government appointed a board of directors with the Minister of Mines as the chairman to supervise Pertamina.

Over the next few years, Pertamina continued to grow in size, power, and stature. The measures introduced to gain greater control over the company were unsuccessful. Pertamina was unapologetic. Under Ibnu's direction, Pertamina had become the country's primary engine of growth. Those who opposed it, even Cabinet ministers, were regarded by Pertamina and its supporters as meddlesome obstructers. By all outward appearances, Pertamina was a great success—a national treasure. Ibnu was attaining a status reserved for movie stars and other celebrities. He was the first indigenous Indonesian (*pribumi*)[9] to succeed on a grand scale as an entrepreneur—a builder of the nation's business infrastructure, an Indonesian Rockefeller. From the early 1960s to the early 1970s, the country's oil revenues grew through a combination of increased volume, higher prices, and new contracts that brought greater benefit to Indonesia. As the importance of the oil industry increased in Indonesia, so did Ibnu's personal dominance over a growing empire. Increasingly, Pertamina channelled its assets into ventures that had little or nothing to do with oil.

Pertamina's supporters touted the company as a new model of economic development, more dynamic and aggressive than that being proposed by the country's economic planning board. New names were used to describe Pertamina. It was frequently referred to as 'Indonesia's other development agency', an 'agent of development', and even, 'a state within a state'. Many of Pertamina's supporters pointed with pride to the company's success as proof that a quasi-independent state-owned enterprise could outperform the 'economic bureaucrats'. This idea, however, was fundamentally flawed: Pertamina lacked the economists, the planners, the engineers, and even the authority to act as a development agency. It could have hired such professionals, but it did not. What it did have though—which no other state-owned enterprise had—was money, oil money. For this reason, Pertamina had unimpeded access to the world financial community and to a host of loans that far exceeded what then was available to any other government enterprise. Rather than a 'development agency', there are two other terms that would better describe Pertamina's conduct: it assumed the role of a *quasi-national treasury*, collecting the majority of taxes and dispensing those funds in such volume that it had a direct impact on the money supply. Second, Pertamina acted as a *venture capitalist.* A growing economy needs venture capitalists, but, again, Pertamina was neither qualified nor authorized for this role.

The company branched out. Pertamina invested in a huge steel making facility, Krakatau Steel. It built hospitals, hotels and even drew up plans for a giant floating fertilizer factory. It also began work on the development of Batam Island, near Singapore. The costs of these projects were colossal and none of them was included in the Five Year Plan or even in any of the annual budgets. Pertamina, for all its apparent success, was undermining the country's economic plans by draining resources that should have been available to the government and by operating on such a scale that its mistakes affected the entire economy. This situation was of great concern to the nation's economic policymakers.

Yet, the company suffered from no shortage of supporters. Pertamina was the corporate equivalent of St Nicholas. It was excessively generous with its contractors, its suppliers, and its top employees. For this reason, and its brash, can-do spirit, the company was greatly admired. In 1972, the *Far Eastern Economic Review* reported:

Where a general has made a successful job of a public enterprise, the technocrats, and some other intellectuals, are inclined to pooh-pooh complaints.... Pertamina, the state oil enterprise, is another instance. 'Aren't we better off,' said one civilian minister, 'with an imaginative, go-ahead man like General Ibnu Sutowo than a conservative bureaucratic man always looking at the rule book? Five years go Pertamina was laughed at. Today it deals on equal terms with the international giants, is pulling in $500 million a year in oil exports, has got our crude output past the million-barrels-a-day mark and looks like saving Repelita'.... He added: 'A few irregularities pale into insignificance by comparison' (Wilson, 1972).

In an article published several years later, Ibnu himself was quoted as saying, 'Some people lay too much stress on control and not enough on building the country' (Bernard, 1978).

In March 1972, the Ministry of Finance and the IMF settled on terms for an important stand-by loan. The agreement, however, placed tight restrictions on Indonesia's medium-term borrowing. According to the agreement, all state-owned enterprises needed to obtain permission from the Ministry of Finance before borrowing overseas. Pertamina initially balked, but later agreed to the tight limits on all borrowing between one and fifteen years. Since this was the type of borrowing Pertamina generally relied on, the economic team saw the restrictions as a way of putting a cap on Pertamina's spending.

A power struggle was emerging in the Cabinet between the economic ministers and those who supported Pertamina and its approach to business and development. The struggle was not personal or acrimonious, but grew from incompatible views on how to foster the country's economic development. The economic ministers believed that the nation's finances had to be managed carefully and systematically to avoid inflation and to allocate funds for maximum long-term growth. Ibnu and his supporters felt that such an approach inhibited the freedom that entrepreneurship needed. The methods advocated by the economic team were too slow and calculated for their taste. Ibnu was prepared to take substantial risks based on the expected trends of the market. The restrictions on medium-term borrowing constrained the financial autonomy of Pertamina just as it did any other government agency, and in this, the two schools of thought collided.

Despite its wealth, in 1972 Pertamina began reducing its tax contribution to the government. Then in October 1974, it stopped paying taxes altogether, with the justification that it needed the funds to support its development projects. The resulting increase in funds was not enough. Pertamina chose to ignore the controls that were placed on it and continued to borrow heavily. However, instead of borrowing medium-term loans, it borrowed in the short-term and long-term markets, that is, loans repayable in less than one year or over fifteen years. It was a public secret that Pertamina was circumventing the restrictions placed on it. What the government did not know was the extent of the violations. Pertamina had become too powerful. No one in the Cabinet had the authority to rein it in.

The first clear signs of serious difficulties came in 1974 when Pertamina withheld its quarterly payment to the government on its own income as well as those from foreign contractors. Around this time, Pertamina started to look for loans from local banks. This was a sign of distress, because Pertamina had generally been doing its borrowing offshore. The local borrowing suggested that Pertamina was facing difficulties securing financing. Soon thereafter, in February 1975, Pertamina missed a payment on a $40 million loan from the Republic National Bank of Dallas. This was a relatively small bank that virtually no one in the government outside of Pertamina had heard of. A larger bank would probably not have called in the loan, preferring to work directly with the customer to settle the problem informally. For a big bank and a company the size of Pertamina, $40 million was not a large sum. This was not so for a smaller bank. It was courageous of the bank to call the loan. It created considerable difficulties, generated negative attention, and brought to light the extent of Pertamina's financial problems.

The difficulties were magnified because there was a cross-default clause in most of Indonesia's sovereign commercial loans. Accordingly, if the country defaulted on any of its loans, all other loans would be called in. The purpose of this condition was to protect the creditor, because if the country defaulted, then all its creditors would share the burden. The implications of default, therefore, were catastrophic.

Crisis Management

In the weeks that followed, the extent of Pertamina's problem became known. The company had accumulated about $10.5 billion in debt of which approximately $1.5 billion was short-term.[10] The magnitude of this debt was astonishing. Several members of the Cabinet were immediately organized into a team to take control of the situation.[11] Minister Widjojo and Central Bank Governor Rachmat Saleh focused on Pertamina's loan portfolio. Minister J. B. Sumarlin had responsibility for reviewing Pertamina's contracts with all its contractors and renegotiating them where they were deemed unacceptable. Gen. Hasnan Habib, assisted by Maj.-Gen. Piet Haryono and Brig.-Gen. Ismail Saleh, took responsibility for reviewing the Pertamina organization. I initially reviewed Pertamina contracts along with Minister Sumarlin and later took responsibility for resolving Pertamina's tanker deals.

Rachmat Saleh travelled around the world to renegotiate the terms of Pertamina's loans. Eventually, he arranged to have all short-term loans converted to medium-term and transferred directly to Bank Indonesia. The government passed regulations requiring that thereafter, all offshore borrowing by state-owned enterprises had to be done through the Ministry of Finance or Bank Indonesia. Minister Sumarlin poured over Pertamina's contracts and met with most of Pertamina's domestic and foreign contractors. He and his team found evidence of pervasive overcharging. On this, the local newspaper *Kompas* reported that Sumarlin said, 'There are three ways in which contractors can participate in settling the problem: They are to reduce the charges included in a contract, to extend the payment date and be prepared to revise the contract to lighten Pertamina's burden.'[12] Besides this, due to financial pressures, the government had to renegotiate its contracts with oil producing contractors to get a greater return per barrel of oil.

As the reorganization continued, the company was restructured to create a more logical and transparent organization. Further, Pertamina divested itself of many non-oil related projects. Other projects were simply cancelled. Most importantly, following the default, the government arranged for all oil contractors to make their payments from oil operations directly to the national treasury. Ibnu and seven other directors were honourably dismissed and Maj.-Gen. Piet Haryono, formerly the director general of budgeting of the Ministry of Finance, became the new head of Pertamina.

One problem remained—the tankers leased by Pertamina. This was a $3.3 billion problem, the largest of Pertamina's debts and it would take considerable time and effort to resolve. Several firms were involved. There were smaller contracts that were contested by firms from the United Kingdom, Norway, the United States, Japan, and Hong Kong, and a collection of firms connected with the tanker magnate Bruce Rappaport. The disputes with the smaller companies together amounted to over $1 billion. These contracts were settled without significant difficulties. The problem with Rappaport was another matter. At a time when the oil market had already peaked and there were projections of a significant oversupply in the tanker market, Ibnu had committed Indonesia to some $1.55 billion in tanker leases. The firms with which these obligations were made were all directly connected to Rappaport. As with the smaller firms, Indonesia tried to terminate the contract with Rappaport. He, however, preferred to manage this affair in the courts, probably expecting that Indonesia would back down. Indonesia was not so inclined, and in a matter of months the two were locked in legal battles in the United States, United Kingdom, the Netherlands, Belgium, France, Switzerland, Japan, and Singapore.

In his hand, Rappaport had a multitude of contracts with Pertamina, including 1,600 promissory notes all signed by Ibnu. The terms of these contracts were so flagrantly bad that they strained credulity.[13] The legal dispute shook the confidence of the consortium of banks with which Indonesia had arranged the settlement of the Pertamina loans. Pressure mounted on Indonesia to find a quick settlement. Indonesia's case looked progressively more grim.

Things improved when Ibnu was confronted with the weight of evidence. He then agreed to make an affidavit in which he implicated Rappaport of fraud. The case remained deadlocked, but Indonesia believed that the cost of stalemate was greater for Rappaport than for the country. The tankers could not be used while the various cases were pending. Therefore, while Rappaport was paying an expensive team of lawyers to execute his legal strategy, he was losing potential revenues that could have been gained by releasing the tankers. Furthermore, Indonesia believed that it was better prepared to fight a global battle than Rappaport, especially since it seemed that world opinion was turning against him. In August 1977, Pertamina and Rappaport reached a settlement. Pertamina agreed to pay $150 million to cover $1.55 billion in contracts with Rappaport—both those that had been fulfilled and those still pending. With the resolution of the tanker affair, the Pertamina debacle was technically brought to a close. In reality, however, the scandal had a lasting impact on the economy of Indonesia as well as the country's economic policies.

Through the efforts of the economic team, the final costs of the Pertamina affair were reduced from about $10.5 billion to about $6.2 billion. The debt was more than three times the level of Indonesia's international debt handled under the Abs settlement just five years earlier. In dollar terms, the entire national budget for 1974/5 was $3.8 billion. The cost of the Pertamina scandal—especially for a country at Indonesia's income level and stage of development—was immense.

The Aftermath

The Pertamina affair took place just as the first oil boom was reaching a peak. Under normal conditions, it would have been reasonable to expect continued expansion of the GDP of at least 8–9 per cent. Instead, the GDP grew only by 5 per cent in 1975. Similarly, the government was trying to develop its foreign exchange reserves. From 1972 to 1974, Indonesia's foreign exchange reserves grew from $576 million to $1.5 billion, an increase of over 160 per cent in two years. In 1975, because Pertamina was not contributing its share of revenues to the nation, Indonesia's reserves fell to $594 million, almost 1972 levels. Furthermore, Indonesia's indebtedness increased as the country was forced to seek commercial financing to cover Pertamina's debt and to safeguard the nation's liquidity. On this, President Soeharto stated in his 1976 budget address to Parliament, 'The difficulties experienced by Pertamina obviously have wide implications, especially since they involve huge amounts of money. In addition to affecting the company itself, these difficulties also have a series of serious consequences for efforts to step up national development activities in general.'

Some of the most significant costs from Pertamina's adventurism defy calculation.

• There were massive opportunity costs associated with channelling money to cover Pertamina debts that could have been better applied elsewhere;
• The attention of many of the government's senior officials was diverted from the urgent tasks of economic development to manage the crisis;
• The process fuelled inflation (this is discussed further below);
• National development was disrupted;
• Public confidence in governmental institutions was shaken.

It would take the country several years to recover from this crisis, but in the end the country matured from the experience. The most obvious benefit was that since restructuring, Pertamina has turned into a well-managed state-owned enterprise that has contributed considerable financial resources to national development.

It is most regrettable that it took a crisis before Indonesia took correct-ive measures to bring financial and managerial accountability to Pertamina. The Pertamina 'alternative' model of development was rejected in favour of the more pragmatic and prudent approach to economic devel-opment advocated by Bappenas. It would be, however, an error to reduce the Pertamina affair to a showdown between management styles. By overextending its reach, Pertamina tried to assume a role in the economy for which it was unqualified and ill-suited. This was not a dispute between technocrats and non-technocrats; this was a matter of good governance. Beyond this, the problem was deeper and more fundamental: Pertamina's most grave transgression was the pervasiveness and extremism of fraudu-lent activities that had become 'business as usual' within the company. Pertamina operated outside the law, the strictures of governmental regula-tions, and the conventions of acceptable business practices. The price of this misadventure was that it came perilously close to bankrupting the country.[14]

Indonesia was fortunate. If the crisis had not occurred relatively early in the growth of the oil industry, Pertamina could have run up far greater debts that could have resulted in even more severe consequences. The oil industry has been the ruin of many countries. Indonesia came close to being on the list of casualties who fell from mismanaged oil windfalls. The government attacked the crisis decisively and with determination and con-sequently Indonesia was able to regain its growth momentum within a year. The Pertamina affair, however, was a severe blow to the country. As the crisis was winding down, the Minister of Mines, Mohammad Sadli, stated in January 1976, 'We look upon Pertamina's losses as expensive tuition for a bitter lesson. There is no need to blame anyone. We are all at fault.'[15] Sadli was right. The question that needs to be asked two decades later is whether sufficient action has been taken so that similar crises can be avoided in the future. Until now, the answer is equivocal.

MONEY FROM THE SKY: OIL WINDFALLS

In just one year, between 1973 and 1974, Indonesia's oil and gas exports skyrocketed from $1.6 billion to $5.2 billion. Indonesia was drenched in a downpour of petrodollars. This astonishing increase exceeded everyone's wildest predictions. No one knew the boom was coming or how long it would last. The mood in the government was one of jubilant disbelief. The country's economic ministers had to remind themselves of what they already knew, that is, that the boom was probably a short-term phenomenon and that the sudden influx of money brought with it a whole array of economic problems for which there were no clear set of suitable policies.

The abrupt change in the oil markets rendered both Indonesia's Five-Year Development Plan and the annual budgets virtually useless. While long-term economic planning is at best scientific guesswork, the volatile oil market forced planners to consider all plans as being perpetually 'work in progress'. The government quickly had to develop a strategy for the optimal use of the unanticipated funds. This would seem to be the best kind of problem. However, experience would show that a sudden influx of wealth could have serious negative consequences on a country's economic development.

One of Indonesia's greatest concerns was the revival of inflation (Figure 4.1). After having just emerged from a tough and protracted battle with hyperinflation, in 1971, with an annual inflation rate of 2.5 per cent, a major battle had been won, but not the war; inflation revived. This time, however, like sicknesses resistant to antibiotics, the earlier methods could no longer be applied with the same results. Although the symptoms of inflation were essentially unchanged, the causes were different from those of the 1960s. In the 1970s, there were four prominent factors that fuelled inflation: rice shortages due to several unusually dry growing seasons; oil windfalls; 'imported inflation'; and the influence of Pertamina itself.

1. *Rice Shortages*. Indonesia experienced several rice shortages during the period 1969–83, but probably none worse than that of 1972. Although the National Logistics Board, Bulog, had made strides in stabilizing rice

FIGURE 4.1
Rate of Inflation, 1969–1982

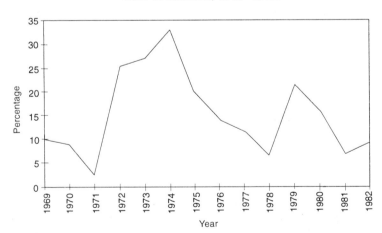

Source: Indonesia, Central Bureau of Statistics.

supplies and prices, in this instance, Bulog was caught completely off guard. The agency remedied the situation as best as it could, but took over a year before it was able to rebuild its strategic rice reserves. During 1972, rice prices rose over 100 per cent and this had a direct and almost immediate impact on the entire economy and was the primary cause of inflation.

2. *Oil windfalls.* Apart from the 1972 rice crisis, the most important cause of Indonesia's inflation in the 1970s was its oil windfall revenues. Instead of creating money by 'printing it', as happened in the Sukarno era, the oil windfall was similar to having money fall from the sky, with the important qualification that this money was in the form of foreign exchange. Banks were flush with cash and the readily available capital created inflationary pressure. In principle, there are ways to 'sterilize' such windfalls so that the influx does not result in higher inflation. As will be discussed later, this is what the government tried to do. The approach was generally successful, but only somewhat.

3. *Imported Inflation.* Especially following the oil shocks, world inflation rose sharply. The weighted average annual inflation of the OECD countries from 1970 to 1980 was 9.0 per cent. By contrast, from 1980 to 1991 the inflation rate fell to 4.3 per cent (World Bank, 1993b). Because Indonesia was receiving a growing percentage of its GDP from trade, it was, in effect, importing inflation. The price rises for imported goods were passed on to local customers and these added to domestic inflation.

4. *The Pertamina Factor.* Pertamina, in its own right, exercised a powerful impact on the economy and the country's inflation rate, especially during the period 1973–6. Pertamina's budgets were enormous and largely beyond government control. Unlike the government, however, which supported a large corps of civil servants, Pertamina's overhead was comparatively small. If the company channelled even a moderate portion of its revenues into domestic investment, it could have had a significant impact on the economy. Instead, Pertamina took out enormous loans to finance a long list of capital-intensive projects. Much of this was off-budget financing, and this injected large and unexpected funds to the money supply. Pertamina's borrowing was so extensive that it was discernible in Indonesia's balance of payment figures. Even to outside observers the transgression did not go unnoticed. In March 1973, the *Bulletin of Indonesian Economic Studies* reported:

Perhaps the most notable feature of the 1972–3 balance of payment figures is the very large balance item—an estimated $321 million—of 'unidentified capital inflows, errors and omission'.... An Australian newspaper reported in February that Pertamina 'has borrowed more than $350 million during the current financial year without the knowledge of Indonesian monetary authorities. . . . The borrowings are in breach of Indonesian arrangements with the IMF, which limits new and short-term foreign borrowing to a total of $140 million'.[16] If this report is correct, actual capital inflow was even larger than the figures show for identified and unidentified inflows (Grenville, 1973).

Pertamina's finances from oil revenues and commercial borrowings grew to the point that they rivalled those of the government. The introduction of these funds into the money supply was largely outside the control of the government. What this means is that from about 1973 to 1975, Pertamina was not only acting like a 'development agency', it was acting like the treasury and having a powerful influence on the money supply. This unexpected injection of funds into the money supply added fuel to the fire of inflation that was already growing due to monetary expansion and drought-caused rice shortages. By 1976, the government was gaining control over the crisis and was able to diminish gradually the infusion of funds into the money supply from Pertamina. This helped reduce inflationary pressures.

After the Pertamina rescue operation began, the government cut back drastically on Pertamina's investment spending. The government cancelled entire projects, others were scaled back, and virtually every contract was reviewed to bring down costs. This led to cut-backs in private consumption as many businesses found their revenues suddenly reduced. This served to dampen inflationary pressures. Perhaps the most important measure the government took to reduce inflation in the wake of the Pertamina crisis was to use revenues from the country's oil sales to cover Pertamina's commercial debts. This diverted foreign exchange out of the country, which contributed to the reduction in inflation that began in 1975 and continued through 1978. Therefore, while Pertamina was an important source of Indonesia's inflation in the early to mid-1970s, ironically, the crisis it created also helped to bring inflation under control. Unfortunately, the diversion of funds to the Pertamina rescue contributed to the slow-down in Indonesia's economy in 1975.

AN ECONOMY OUT OF BALANCE: THE DUTCH DISEASE AND THE 1978 DEVALUATION

When the Pertamina crisis had peaked, so had the first oil shock. Oil prices rose from about $12 a barrel in 1974 to $13.50 in 1978. Although the boom was over, the oil sector still dominated the Indonesian economy. From 1975 to 1978, oil comprised 69 per cent of Indonesia's exports and supplied on average some 46 per cent of government revenues. If one deducted timber from the calculations, the dominance of oil was even

greater still. There was a danger in this situation, and that danger eventually became known as the 'Dutch disease.'[17] This term and the ideas associated with it did not form a direct part of the policy formulation process
during the 1970s. This is regrettable since the theoretical framework of the
Dutch disease may have been put to profitable use in policy planning,
especially during the oil boom. None the less, it was clear to the economic
team that Indonesia's oil wealth was creating distortions and disequilib-
rium in the economy and policy responses were needed. As we look back,
the analytic tools provided from Dutch disease models provide a valuable
framework for assessing the policies of the period.

The term 'Dutch disease' seems to trace its origin to an article that
appeared in the *Economist* on 26 November 1977. During this period, the
Dutch economy bore some striking similarities to that of Indonesia. The
article notes that the Dutch economy had become enriched by its natural
gas holdings, but while the country's external economy appeared strong
and healthy, internally the country was struck by growing unemployment
and stagnation. Furthermore, the *Economist* states that the guilder 'is now
significantly less competitive... than it was five years ago, because gas
buoying up the current account has prevented the exchange rate from con-
forming to the country's underlying inflationary position'. In sum, the
Economist states, 'This contrast—between external health and internal
ailments—is the symptom of "the Dutch disease".'

In practice, the Dutch disease occurs when a government fails to undertake the necessary economic steps to best accommodate the temporary
windfall from a booming sector. This tends to lead to rising prices of non-
tradables relative to tradables.[18] This was true for Indonesia. During the
1970s, Indonesia's oil sector was booming and investment in that sector
was intense. The boom brought a sudden surge in foreign exchange.
Inevitably, a portion of this foreign exchange was converted into local currency that was used to buy non-tradables (local products and services),
which contributed to an increase in domestic inflation. Indonesia's
exchange rate, however, was fixed at Rp 415 to the dollar. Since the
exchange rate stayed constant despite the rise in domestic prices,
Indonesia's exports (that is, the tradables) became less competitive.

Because the domestic market is small compared to the export market,
prices for tradables are set by the international market. However, since
non-tradables by definition are only sold within the local market, those
prices are set by local supply, demand, and whatever economic policies
will influence prices. Rising inflation reduced the competitiveness of economic sectors outside the booming oil sector. To put this more simply,
when there is a booming export market, such as the oil sector in Indonesia
in the 1970s, this sector grows much faster than other sectors. And like a

child growing up very quickly, the booming sector demands a lot of attention. Investment increases in the sector. Wages and salaries in the sector go
up. More companies are attracted to work in that sector. The boom in one
sector, however, can be detrimental to another. While everything associated with the booming sectors seems to be flourishing, the scrawny non-
booming sectors are neglected because of declining profits due to rising
costs. Businesses leave the weak sector because it is not in their financial
interest to work there since domestic costs have risen and profits declined.
They are more inclined to invest in the booming sector. The weak sectors
stagnate, and this can lead to decline and even de-industrialization in the
weak sectors unless steps are taken to protect them.

In Indonesia's case, rather than preside over a decline in sectors outside
the booming sector, the government channelled money to build domestic
industries and to achieve rice self-sufficiency. This helped to limit the
affects of the Dutch disease in Indonesia. There was, however, a price to
pay. Because Indonesia's currency had become overvalued, it meant that
Indonesia's exports were relatively expensive, and imports were relatively
cheap. So long as the government kept the exchange rate pegged at
an unrealistic level, then there was a risk that Indonesia's products would
be grossly uncompetitive against imports. Under these circumstances,
Indonesia needed to erect tariff and non-tariff barriers to protect
Indonesia's local industry.

The method for 'treating' the Dutch disease lies in the utilization of the
windfalls of the booming sector. To avoid the Dutch disease in an economy with a booming sector the benefits of the boom must be distributed
across the economy. In this way, the boom in one sector does not work to
the detriment of other sectors. If the windfalls are not 'sterilized' then the
boom will fuel inflation and this will exacerbate the imbalances caused by
the booming sector.

The tools with which the government of Indonesia dealt with this problem embraced the full spectrum of macroeconomic techniques. In reviewing this topic, we will first focus on exchange rate policy after which we
will consider other aspects of monetary and fiscal policy.

During most of the 1970s, the government tried to maintain a stable
monetary environment as a way to foster business development. For this
reason, from August 1971 until October 1978, Indonesia pegged the currency at Rp 415 to the dollar. During this seven-year period, however,
Indonesia experienced cumulative inflation of 141 per cent while in the
United States inflation during the same period was 54 per cent. In 1978,
despite the prolonged period in which the rupiah was pegged to the dollar,
and the chronically high level of inflation, the prevailing wisdom inside
the country and out was there was no need to devalue the currency. The

strongest argument against devaluation was that the country's foreign exchange reserves had grown steadily, surpassing $2.4 billion in 1978, sufficient for five months of imports. Indonesia's balance of payment position was strong, and showed no sign of serious deterioration, especially given the strength in the oil market. Finally, inflation in 1978 had dropped to 6.7 per cent, and a devaluation would certainly stimulate inflation. For these reasons, most analysts deemed that a devaluation was best postponed until such a time when it was more obviously needed.

After exhaustive economic analysis and political soul-searching, the government decided otherwise. On 15 November 1978, the government devalued the rupiah by 50 per cent. Devaluations are among the most painful policy a government can implement. They inevitably lead to brutal criticisms, and this time was certainly no exception. However, the government reasoned that the oil boom was over and Indonesia had been left with an economy facing serious structural problems. Despite the government's best efforts, with the notable exception of timber, much of the non-oil traded sector had suffered. For the previous five years, the country could afford to overlook the modest growth or decline in its non-oil tradable sector. It was the conviction of Indonesia's economic ministers that a devaluation was necessary to help in the revival of this weakened sector.

The government recognized that the benefit from devaluation, if any, would be temporary. In 1978, however, the government believed that virtually all Indonesian traded goods except oil (a product for which the country essentially collected taxes) were at a competitive disadvantage because of the overvalued rupiah and the dominance of the oil sector. The government expected that the devaluation would not only remove this disadvantage but would also provide a temporary price advantage while an undervalued rupiah gradually rose to a new equilibrium against the dollar and other currencies. While the exchange rate advantage would not last, the government hoped that this would be enough to reactivate industries that had been stagnating or declining over several years.

The immediate reaction of many local businesses was to raise prices. The government imposed a price freeze that stood for about two months. Indonesia's economic policymakers were well aware that price controls are generally exercises in futility. In this case, however, the government implemented the measure to provide a kind of 'cooling-off' period, to prevent impulsive across-the-board price rises. When the freeze ended, price increases were moderate. In 1979 the inflation rate jumped to 21.8 per cent, about 10 to 12 per cent higher than it would have been without the devaluation. This was roughly in keeping with the expectation of the economic planners. As hoped, there was an immediate and sizeable growth in non-oil exports. The expansion, however, only lasted for two years and then declined. None the less, this was the beginning of a longer-term effort to turn the country away from an overdependence on oil and to assist in the process of building a more diversified, export-oriented economy.[19] Although the term 'Dutch disease' was never invoked to explain the devaluation, by realigning the currency the government was attempting to remedy the developmental imbalances brought on by the boom in the nation's oil sector.

TWO BOOMS: HARMONIZING MONETARY AND FISCAL POLICY

By 1978, most observers already saw Indonesia's oil boom as an anomaly in the ebb and flow of world economic events. The government accepted the advance in oil revenues for what they were—a windfall. The November 1978 devaluation was a sign that the government had begun a process of shifting policy gears to adjust to a period when oil would play a greatly diminished role in the economic life of the country. And then, less than two months after Indonesia's devaluation, on 5 January 1979 the Shah of Iran fled his country, and the exiled Islamic leader, Ayatollah Ruhollah Khomeini, returned to Teheran. In November 1979, diplomatic staff of the United States embassy in Teheran was taken hostage, and ten months later, Iran and Iraq were at war. Again, the slippery world of petroleum was suddenly turned on its head. The second oil shock had erupted. With the memory of the previous shock still painfully present in the minds of consumers and traders alike, panic hit world oil markets. Within a year, the price of Indonesia's oil almost doubled, rising from $15.65 per barrel in 1979 to $29.50 in 1980. Indonesia again faced the benefits and problems of how best to manage huge oil windfalls.

The second oil boom raised the specter of new infusions of oil money and along with it inflation and an economy generally out of balance. The government tried to 'sterilize' the oil windfalls to reduce the inflationary impact on the economy. The method of sterilization did not change substantially from Indonesia's first oil boom to the second. The government was, however, somewhat more successful during the second. In general, the essential methods for sterilizing the foreign exchange earnings from oil exports are:

- Hold the money offshore either in liquid form or as foreign investments;
- Use the foreign exchange to purchase imports and then introduce those imports into the economy with a minimal increase in the domestic money supply;

- Use the foreign exchange to pay off foreign debts;
- Build the nation's foreign exchange reserves.

Indonesia's objectives in using the oil windfalls were to maximize the developmental impact of the windfalls while at the same time endeavouring to minimize inflation. Adherence to these objectives influenced Indonesia's method of managing its oil revenues.

If the prevention of inflation was the only objective of the nation's economic policymakers, then they could have easily collected the oil money and placed it in a vault in the sea and forgotten about it. Similar to this, but not as extreme, the government could have used the windfalls to make overseas investments. The government's intention, however, was to employ the oil windfalls to respond to the country's urgent need for economic development.[20] In the 1970s, Indonesia was still one of the world's poorest countries. In view of the size of the country's population and development challenges, the oil windfall was relatively small.[21] The government, therefore, felt an overwhelming need to draw aggressively on the windfall for investments that would advance Indonesia's development.

The windfall utilization strategy focused on both the objects of investment and the method for employing the windfalls. The objects of investment comprised the industries or projects identified in the country's five-year economic development plans (Repelitas) and annual budgets. The Repelitas laid out a complex matrix of investment goals for the plan period. The government allocated revenues for these projects and, in some cases, oil windfalls provided the additional revenues that permitted the government to reach beyond plan targets or achieve them more quickly than projected.

The government's method for windfall utilization was import-intensive, with imports concentrated in social and economic infrastructure development. The government emphasized infrastructure because it served all sectors of the economy although the agrarian sector was expected to reap the greatest benefits. The nation's planners felt that it was appropriate to emphasize agricultural development because this sector employed the majority of Indonesians and was vital for the achievement of food security. Except for rice purchases, Indonesia's oil windfall strategy directed a minimum of revenues to consumption. There were years, however, when the government's rupiah expenditures exceeded its rupiah revenues by a substantial margin, such as in 1974. This exacerbated inflation.

When the government found itself with a large influx of petrodollars, it adjusted trade policy to accommodate the monetary sterilization policy. The method relied on two simple and related ideas; that is, in large volume, imports tend to be deflationary, while exports tend to be inflationary. Exports feed inflation because upon sale they bring in foreign exchange. When this is converted into the local currency, the money supply expands, and that expansion adds inflationary pressure. Imports, on the other hand, are deflationary. Imports 'absorb' liquidity because to buy imports, traders sell rupiah to the bank for foreign exchange. This is then sent overseas in exchange for the imported goods.

To minimize the inflationary impact of the investment of oil windfalls, where possible, the government would increase the imported component in projects. Bridges, for example, use a greater portion of imported components than roads, so the government would prefer to invest in a bridge rather than a road. A bridge without a road, however, is useless. Inevitably, a considerable portion of the windfall had to be channelled into domestic products and services as well. This was unavoidable and added to the difficulty of the sterilization process. The key to sterilization, therefore, was to apply the oil money to the right purchase in the right places and, above all, to keep it in the central bank and portion it out under very controlled conditions.

The government also balanced this inflation-guided trade strategy with a systematic long-term effort to build reserves. Following the Pertamina crisis, Indonesia's foreign exchange reserves stood at $594 million. By 1980, they had grown to a comfortable level of $5.4 billion. These proved indispensable when Indonesia needed to maintain relative financial stability in the face of the adverse economic conditions of the mid-1980s.

Throughout the 1970s, one of the primary methods for using oil windfalls was in an extensive programme of social and economic infrastructure development.[22] Although not an ideal method for sterilization of oil money, its long-term benefit to the country cannot be overstated. There were some instances when the government invested oil windfall for consumption purposes, notably for rice, fertilizer subsidies, and fuel subsidies. Throughout the 1970s, the agrarian sector progressed fitfully. Progress in agriculture was uneven, but at least the growth in rice production was impressive. However, during several years in the 1970s, Indonesia suffered from severe weather conditions which resulted in exceptionally poor harvests. The government had to make major rice purchases in those years. These purchases were anti-inflationary not only because they channelled Indonesia's foreign exchange for non-domestic purchases but also because the imported supplies responded to a shortage in domestic production. Without the imports, the ensuing shortages would have placed considerable upward pressure on rice prices, and this would have had an impact on the entire economy. While the use of the oil windfall in this case did not contribute to the country's long-term development, it did meet an urgent need and helped in the effort to hold down inflation.

There is one measure that the government did not undertake to sterilize the oil windfalls that may have been advisable, that is, the early repayment of Indonesia's foreign debt. This would have been both beneficial and non-inflationary. The government did not choose this option, however, because it was concerned that in so doing, the IGGI donors might misconstrue early payment as a sign that Indonesia's need for aid had significantly diminished. This, the government feared, would result in a reduction in future aid commitments. Given the soft terms of the loans, the government decided it was better to channel the oil windfalls into other development projects and repay the country's loans according to the original schedule.

If we compare the sterilization policies during the two oil boom periods, there were no significant changes in the theory. The government, however, did become more adept with practice. The two periods were very different, and this makes the economic comparisons more difficult. The first boom was marred by the Pertamina crisis. The second boom immediately followed a major devaluation. Both of these events coloured the behaviour of the economy. Government consumption expenditures were predominantly for rice during the first boom, whereas the largest subsidies during the second boom were for petroleum products. During the second boom, the government continued to emphasize similar approaches to sterilization, however it was far more restrained in its expenditures. Instead, it allocated more funds and effort to boost foreign exchange reserves. In support of this, the government also undertook a programme of gold purchases as a way of diversifying the nation's reserve portfolio.

THE BOOM FADES: REFLECTIONS AFTER THE PARTY

As with the first, the second oil shock again caught Indonesia and the world by surprise. Before the second oil shock, most analysts had predicted relatively low prices until the late-1980s. Once the second shock occurred, many analysts then predicted a period of prolonged high prices. Repeatedly the analysts were wrong. The oil market was so unstable that it defied prediction. By 1983, oil prices were already on the decline, and this would lead to a full scale avalanche in 1986 (Figure 4.2). This, in turn, created a very difficult environment for Indonesia's planners as well as for economies around the world. Especially during the second oil boom, the government's delight in the increased revenues was tempered by cautious skepticism. The oil-revenue projections for Repelita III, which went into effect on 1 April 1979, were almost immediately superseded by the wholly unexpected boom. The principles of the five-year economic development

FIGURE 4.2
Price per Barrel of Indonesian Oil, 1970–1989

Source: Nota Keuangan dan Rancangan Anggaran Pendapatan & Belanja Negara.

plan, however, continued to serve as a guideline for development policy. The operative attitude in the government was to treat the boom as temporary windfall and to try to employ the funds in a way that would sustain the country after the boom had passed. For this reason, there was a deliberate effort to diversify the economy to decrease the dependence on oil. While this was an appropriate attitude, the renewed flow of oil money had a way of engendering economic dependence. Government projects, both routine and developmental, all relied to some extent on oil money. Kicking the oil habit would prove to be near impossible so long as the large sums of oil money poured into the country. When the second boom did finally end, what remained was a multitude of questions. What did the country learn? Was the boom good or bad? What did the government do right and what did it do wrong?

In *Oil Windfalls: Blessing or Curse?*, Alan Gelb (1988) and associates compare the manner in which six developing oil exporters managed the growth in national income derived from the oil shocks of 1973 and 1979, when oil prices rose, and 1984, when prices dropped. He suggests that endowment with mineral resources generally encourages countries to adopt highly leveraged, overextended strategies that render them more vulnerable to shocks. Among the countries covered in Gelb's study, Indonesia was the poorest and most populous to receive an oil windfall. Furthermore, the other six countries had average per capita oil exports that were about twelve times those of Indonesia. Despite Indonesia's economic difficulties, the authors concluded, 'To a surprising extent, the poorest country in the sample has managed to avoid the most serious problems of the Dutch disease, and its economic performance stands out as being relatively successful' (Gelb, 1988: 224).

Whatever the country's achievement, in the wake of two booms, the blessings were decidedly mixed. Some of the worst experiences of Indonesia's oil booms proved the most beneficial. The Pertamina debacle was not a coincidence. The crisis was almost inevitable, given the country's inadequate understanding about the dynamics of economic development and the prevalence of business practices that violated basic standards of acceptable commerce. However, because of the Pertamina crisis, Indonesia suddenly woke up from the illusion that it could translate oil money into quick and easy economic development. The government became more rigorous in scrutinizing its investments, and stricter controls were generally placed on state-owned enterprises. Of more direct benefit, the booms financed massive infrastructure development, and progress in this area permanently altered the basic structure of the Indonesian economy. The booms also permitted Indonesia to build its foreign exchange reserves which were necessary for the country to expand its trading capacity. Finally, the government became more skilful in sterilizing large influxes of foreign exchange, and this was an important step in internationalizing the Indonesian economy and in controlling inflation.

Indonesia's oil boom money had many adverse consequences that economic theory at that time could not have predicted or helped to manage. One issue could be described as a change in 'climate'. Specifically, the expansion in oil money caused by the two oil booms allowed Indonesia to gloss over pervasive weaknesses in the economy. Inefficiencies were perpetuated, and waste increased. Most aspects of the micro-economy, from the operations of private businesses and state-owned enterprises to the government bureaucracy, tended to be poorly managed. The oil boom, in many cases, permitted already bloated staffs to swell, while many impractical, dysfunctional, or corrupt business practices grew worse.

Oil money skewed markets towards the oil sector in ways that created structural imbalances in the economy. The surge in oil money made it more difficult for the government to control the growth in the money supply. This, along with other factors, greatly contributed to Indonesia's rise in inflation during this period. Foreign investment became highly politicized, and the trade regime became more distorted as the government erected tariff and non-tariff barriers. Most significantly, oil money gave Indonesia a false sense of security, and this, in turn, served to fuel the autarky-oriented economic nationalism that favoured inward looking policies.

The Pertamina affair should be seen as more than a dramatic story. The affair had much to teach Indonesia. One of the most painful and important lessons of the Pertamina debacle is that through inaction, the government permitted a crisis to occur. It should have been apparent to any informed observer that Pertamina was engaging in dangerous business practices. The Pertamina leadership and its supporters, however, believed that they could 'bend the rules'. The problem is that they bent the rules past the breaking point. One of the lessons from this affair is that there is an important difference between pragmatism and opportunism. According to Indonesia's economic pragmatism, economic policies should be based on a deep and thorough knowledge of the principles of economics. Based thereon, pragmatism led Indonesia's leaders to address problems with imagination, flexibility, and creativity. Under the opportunistic approach to policymaking, on the other hand, the end justified the means. The Pertamina affair illustrated the risks of economic opportunism. It was a stark reminder that good governance requires continuous vigilance as well as checks and balances to ensure that the collective wisdom of the people can have a tempering effect on the grandiose or misguided plans of public figures. By remaining impassive as the Pertamina empire expanded, the government created conditions ripe for a crisis. Perhaps history can be somewhat forgiving in this case, as the government was young and inexperienced. Many believed that the Pertamina model did indeed offer an effective route to economic development. Today we know better.

Despite the set-backs, between 1970 and 1980, the average income of Indonesians rose from $80 to $490. In the process, the government's understanding of the development process became deeper and broader. Indonesia learned that there is no easy money, not even oil money, and that when wealth comes to a country through whatever form, the fundamental task of the nation's leadership is to devise an investment strategy to achieve maximum long-term economic benefit with minimal social and economic dislocations. There is no set methodology for this challenging task. In Indonesia's case, monetary sterilization efforts and the emphasis on infrastructure developments were perhaps the most effective policies for the effective utilization of the sudden surge in oil money.

1. These were the words of one deeply disillusioned Indonesian official, although I cannot remember who said them or where I read them.
2. The embargo was linked with the Organization of Petroleum Exporting Countries (OPEC) because most of the participants were OPEC countries. The embargo was not, however, an OPEC policy. Indonesia is a member of OPEC and never participated in the embargo.

3. Since the 1970s there have been three 'oil shocks': the first in 1973, when prices rose, the second in 1979, when prices rose again, and the third in 1984–6, when they fell. For Indonesia, the first two shocks brought a great influx in money, while the third brought a decline. For this reason, the first two shocks, from the Indonesian perspective, were called 'booms' and the decline in oil prices was a 'bust' or more aptly, a financial catastrophe.

4. This section draws on information from Bartlett (1972) and Kong (1986).

5. Caltex was formed by the Standard Oil of California and Texaco, and Stanvac was formed when the Standard Oil of New Jersey merged with Socony-Vacuum.

6. The term PT is an abbreviation for Perseroan Terbatas, Indonesian for a limited liability company. PN is an abbreviation for Perusahan Negara, that is, a state-owned company.

7. For more on Indonesian oil exploration and mining efforts see Prijono (1983).

8. One of the best and most complete descriptions of the Pertamina crisis appears in Lipsky (1978). This section refers to that work along with archival documents and my own personal experience in managing the crisis.

9. The term *pribumi* refers to an indigenous Indonesian. The term generally is used to distinguish an indigenous Indonesian from other Indonesian citizens of foreign origin or ancestry. The Indonesian Chinese are the country's most prominent non-*pribumi* group.

10. For more information on this, see *Sinar Harapan*, 20 May 1976.

11. In my twenty-eight years as a Cabinet official, I never saw the Cabinet so mobilized. The Pertamina default was an emergency that briefly put the financial stability of the nation at serious risk. This matter was treated with the attention reserved for a war or extreme national calamity.

12. Reported in *Kompas*, 14 November 1975, p. 2.

13. The ships were even too large to use in Indonesian waters. They did not have the heating coils needed for Indonesian oil. Beyond that, the contract prices were grossly inflated beyond market costs. For more information, see *Kompas*, 29 November 1976.

14. Ibnu provided revealing details himself in an interview: 'Some time earlier,' he stated, 'we had already found the situation difficult because there was a provision that permitted us to borrow money for less than one year and more than fifteen years. For a national company like Pertamina, the imposition of a condition that forces us to look for loans of over fifteen years is quite impractical. The credits that we need are precisely those of between about five and eight years. At the time [that the condition was imposed], I told the President and the Board of Commissioners that such a provision was tantamount to forbidding Pertamina from seeking credits. We were virtually forbidden to undertake investments. They told me that it was a condition imposed by the International Monetary Fund.... [Earlier in the interview Ibnu reported] The problem was that in 1974 we made an agreement for a twenty-one year loan. The total involved was $1.7 billion.... We obtained short-term loans which were essentially bridging finance. Well, the long-term credit did not come, and that was the problem.' Here Ibnu is mistaken. The problem was not that the long-term loan did not come through. The problem was that constraints on credit were bypassed when the intent of the credit restrictions was clear. (Quote taken from *Tempo*, 17 January 1976, cited in a article by Peter McCawley (1978: 14)).

15. This statement appeared in *Kompas*, 13 January 1976.

16. This quote is from the *National Times*, 12 February 1973.

17. This topic has received quite a bit of discussion by a number of distinguished scholars. A few relevant works that have been reviewed for this section are Corden (1984), Gelb (1988), Neary (1986), Warr (1992), and Woo, Glassburner, and Nasution (1994).

The purpose of this section is not to duplicate what these and other authors have already covered quite ably. However, it is my hope to provide some insight into the factors behind the policies of that time—decisions made without the benefit of subsequent scholarship on the Dutch disease phenomenon.

18. By tradables is meant those things that are traded internationally. This is essentially a synonym for 'exports'. Non-tradable refer to things that generally are not exported, such as services, or those produced from local components and sold locally. Indonesia's difficulties among tradables were confined to non-oil exports, since oil was itself the 'booming sector'. During this period, Indonesia's primary 'tradable' products were agricultural commodities, such as rubber, coffee, tea, and palm oil, as well as timber.

19. In their discussion of the Dutch disease, Woo, Glassburner, and Nasution (1994: 93) refer to Mari Elka Pangestu's 1986 Ph.D. dissertation wherein Pangestu concluded that 'without a devaluation the supply of tradables would have been 30 per cent lower per quarter between the third quarter of 1980 and the fourth quarter of 1982'.

20. The Netherlands employed a strategy of investing much of their windfalls from the gas sector into overseas investment. The Dutch disease, therefore, manifested itself in the Netherlands with a sharp contrast between the booming external sector and a declining domestic economy. Indonesia's experience of the Dutch disease was somewhat different in that in Indonesia's case, the boom was experienced in the oil sector, while the non-oil tradable sector was in relative decline.

21. Indeed, on this matter, the *Bulletin of Indonesian Economic Studies* states: 'Because of Indonesia's large population, the fourfold increase in the price of oil, although it has more than doubled Indonesia's export earnings and government revenues, has added only $20 to Indonesia's average income per head in nominal terms and, if allowance is made for the effect of the steep rise in import prices over the past two years on Indonesia's terms of trade and on the real value of capital inflow, only $6 at 1972/3 prices' (Arndt, 1975: 9–10).

22. Social infrastructure development is discussed in Chapter 7 and will not be further addressed here.

5
Agriculture: Cultivating the Soul of Indonesia

THE soul of Indonesia is its land. Indonesians have been cultivating these lands for millennia. The country's farm communities have not only provided the nation with food and a host of export crops, they have been caretakers of many of the nation's traditions and customs. Above all, however, Indonesia's farms have supplied the people with rice, which since time immemorial, has been the country's prime staple, its 'staff of life'. There have been many periods in Indonesian history when rice harvests were poor. When this happened, the resulting hunger could be calamitous to the hardest hit and destabilizing to the society as a whole. That is why, in 1968, as work began on Repelita I, Indonesia's economic policymakers made one of the most important decisions in Indonesia's modern history: to follow a route to economic development based above all on agricultural development. At that time, the typical approach to economic development for a less developed country emphasized exploiting agriculture to make a fast transition to industrialization. For most countries, development planning was essentially synonymous with industrial planning. Of course, the government understood that the nation needed to industrialize. However, what was unusual in Indonesia's strategy was that the country gave first priority to agricultural development for its own sake.

For many years thereafter, Indonesia's agriculture development policies were implemented almost single-mindedly in the service of one overarching goal: that of achieving self-sufficiency in rice. Although it took fifteen years to reach this goal, along the way, the economic team learned many lessons about when to hold firmly to the principles of classical economics and when it was more pragmatic to innovate, if only through temporary measures. For example, the government developed Bulog, an agency designed to moderate the supplies and prices of rice. Although Bulog's intervention ran counter to free market orthodoxy, it helped to safeguard the nation's food supply and maintain political stability. The country also undertook a programme of massive public investment in infrastructure. In so doing, supplies could reach the villages, and agriculture products could easily make it to markets. These policies ended by serving two essential objectives: the people's nutritional needs were met, and the rural exodus to the cities was slowed by providing gainful employment in the countryside.

In its approach to agricultural development, Indonesia did not focus on one facet only. Instead, the government initiated an across-the-board set of interlocking policies that included technological innovations, infrastructure improvements, the development of a nationwide logistics system, and—the most fundamental economic tactic of all—the monetization of the rural sector. This chapter will examine each of these building blocks.

NOTES ON THE GEOGRAPHY AND HISTORY OF INDONESIAN AGRICULTURE

Indonesia straddles the equator as the world's largest chain of islands. With temperatures averaging about 26–32 °C, Indonesia's climate is warm without being oppressively so, thanks to cool ocean breezes. The bulk of the country's precipitation falls during the rainy season from October to March, with the rain concentrated in the monsoons of December and January. The dry season lasts roughly from April to September.

Indonesia lies along the 'Ring of Fire', a volcanic area in the Pacific Ocean in which most of the world's active volcanoes are concentrated. Centuries of volcanic activity has enriched the soil of many of Indonesia's islands, particularly those of Java and Bali, and traditionally this enabled the farmers there to cultivate their crops with little or no fertilizer. Neither land fertility nor rainfall, however, is evenly distributed across the 5,000 kilometres of the archipelago and some parts of the country, particularly in the eastern region, are relatively arid and have poor soil. In the country's main rice growing areas—Java, Bali, Madura, and South Sulawesi—farmers have traditionally harvested two crops of rice per year. Through advances in agrarian technologies, this has been raised in these productive areas to five harvests every two years.

Traditions have both helped and hindered Indonesia's farmers. Many aspects of Indonesia's farming, especially rice farming, have been carried out according to age-old practices. Before the establishment of the New Order, little of Indonesia's agriculture had been integrated into the modern economy, with its high-volume trade, technical advances, and its diversity of crop types and marketing methods. Agriculture in Indonesia was largely a village affair. It worked by ensuring survival, but little beyond that.

A relatively small portion of the people moved to cities or chose to engage in commerce or the civil service. Indonesia's population remained overwhelmingly rural. As the population expanded, especially on Java, there was little new land for agricultural development. Consequently, the existing plots were subdivided within a family from one generation to the next, until finally Indonesian farms were among the smallest in the world.[1] In the later half of this century, when plots could no longer be subdivided, there emerged a new class of rural worker, the landless farmer.

Two scholars have done particularly influential studies on Indonesia's agriculture conditions in the pre-New Order period: the Dutch economist, Jan Boeke, and the American anthropologist, Clifford Geertz. Looking to explain the reasons for the failure of Dutch colonial policy in Indonesia, Boeke (1946) argued that there was a fundamental distinction between the objectives of economic activities in Western and Eastern society. While Westerners acted out of economic needs, Boeke believed Easterners such as Indonesians acted primarily by social needs. He argued that because of the social (rather than economic) orientation of Indonesian farmers and villages, it would be futile to introduce Western technology and institutions. These, he suggested, would not produce any change in the way agriculture was structured, and thus, would not generate capital. The Dutch, he pointed out, had become alarmed at population growth outstripping rice production in the early days of the twentieth century, and had introduced irrigation systems, fertilizers, new schemes of crop rotation, and other innovations, in an attempt to make rice production grow faster. Their efforts, however, could not reverse generations of traditions no matter how dysfunctional they had become.

In this, Boeke was prefiguring the views of Clifford Geertz who wrote on Indonesian farm practices in the early 1960s. Geertz's research led him to the idea of 'shared poverty', in which agricultural sector jobs and income are all shared by members of a family, or clan, or village, so that all worked and had food, but remained poor. Geertz (1963: 146) glumly concluded that it was probably impossible to significantly improve Indonesian agriculture because without enormously changing the social structure, 'any alteration of the persisting direction of its development, pouring fertilizer onto Java's Lilliputian fields is likely, as modern irrigation, labour-intensive cultivation and crop diversification before it, to make only one thing grow: paralysis'.

Boeke's and Geertz's pessimism were too extreme. To be sure, Javanese farm plots were too small. Despite these limitations, however, Peter Timmer (1975: 199) notes, 'Within the constraints of farm size, input availability, and capital resources, the Indonesian is a remarkably able agriculturist. The available econometric evidence, while not strong, indicates a market awareness, sense of economic calculation, and a willingness to innovate (subject to fairly obvious constraints).' Moreover, the idea of 'shared poverty' is better looked upon as a manifestation of what happens when the spirit of *gotong royong* confronts communal poverty. As earlier noted, *gotong royong* is a way of tightly linking the people of a community. There are drawbacks to such links in a traditional society, but there are also benefits. The method of harvesting provides a good example. According to Indonesia's traditional *bawon* system, essentially anyone who wanted to help in the harvesting of a farmer's crop was permitted. Upon completion, the farmer would give each worker a portion of the harvest. The following day, the owner of a field might also join in the harvesting of his neighbour's field. This system ensured that no one in a community went without food if he was able to work. It also meant that rarely did anyone become much richer or poorer than his neighbours did. To Geertz, this was a form of shared poverty. The Indonesian view, however was that no one in a village community should grow rich while his neighbours risked starvation. Communities moved together through periods of critical poverty and relative plenty. Rather than shared poverty, *gotong royong* represented a kind of spontaneous communal social security.

RICE IN INDONESIA'S AGRARIAN DEVELOPMENT

Despite the collective involvement in agriculture, Indonesia's farm land was overburdened and the majority of the rural countryside lived so close to subsistence that a period of bad weather or political turmoil could have disastrous consequences for millions of people. According to Leon Mears and Sidik Moeljono (1981: 25), 'the rice production on Java in 1965 was only 2 per cent greater than the 1954 level which had represented a recovery only to pre-World War II output. Rice yields throughout Indonesia had remained constant for over a decade. . . . This still left a growing deficit as population expanded by over 2 per cent yearly. And what was worse, per capita availability of rice for consumption had dropped from 107 kg in 1960 to 92 kg in 1965.' When the New Order came to power in March 1966, one of the most disturbing findings was that there was virtually no rice in any of the government's storage facilities. Rice output levels had fallen so low that there was a risk of severe food shortages, which undoubtedly could have led to civil unrest.[2]

During the first years of the post-Sukarno era, Indonesia's economic team was almost entirely preoccupied with controlling inflation. Besides the previous mismanagement of the country's monetary and fiscal policy which the new government had inherited, the other primary contributor to the inflation at that time were shortages in the nation's rice supplies. In late 1967, Indonesia again experienced a poor rice harvest. Speculators stepped in and over the course of fourteen months rice prices rose 600 per cent. This experience was shocking and sent a strong message to the economic policymakers: 'Neglect agriculture at your peril.'

Indonesia's Mission: Rice Self-sufficiency

The general focus on agriculture in Repelita I only communicated half the story: the other half was rice. When Repelita I began in 1969, the government had the averred goal of achieving rice self-sufficiency within five years. The country did not achieve this goal, but rice self-sufficiency became the explicit and implicit objective of all Indonesian agricultural policy until the goal was realized fifteen years later in 1984. As a national goal, rice self-sufficiency became Indonesia's equivalent of America's Apollo mission to the moon. Rice self-sufficiency, however, was in many ways more complex and difficult to achieve. It necessitated not only money and research but also the support of millions of farmers, traders, suppliers, and educators. Indonesia's rice mission also required addressing subtle yet complex social and cultural issues. According to agrarian traditions, for example, farmers relied on complicated astrological calculations to identify when plantings should be done to coincide with the return of the monsoon season. With the introduction of irrigation systems, however, such approaches were no longer applicable. Still, while encouraging the application of modern methodologies to rice cultivation, the government had to respect those traditions and practices that had been part of Indonesia's agrarian life for centuries. If the government trod roughly on local culture and customs, not only would the programme fail, but there could be adverse political consequences as well.

To understand the importance of achieving rice self-sufficiency, it is necessary to recognize the special significance of rice in the Indonesian diet, culture, and politics. Foremost, rice is the dominant staple in the Indonesian diet. In the late 1960s and early 1970s not only did rice supply more than three-fifths of the carbohydrates in the Indonesian diet (Timmer, 1975: 205), it was also the major source of protein. The government frequently encouraged the people to eat other staples, such as bread, corn, sago, wheat kasha, and even a kind of imitation rice made from wheat flour. The people, however, rejected them all (especially the imitation rice). When rice prices rose to the point where people had to cut back, the result was a more poorly nourished population, a people struck with hunger.

Rice has always had the undisputed pride of place in the Indonesian diet. So central is rice that it is conceptually interchangeable with the idea of 'food'. Rice is more than the basis of Indonesian agriculture, it is the centre of most important social intercourse. It is eaten for breakfast, lunch, and dinner. Typically, when people work together, it is over rice. When a serious communal conflict is resolved, reconciliation is frequently over rice. When they celebrate together, mourn together, or simply come together as family and friends, rice is the constant that is at the centre of many daily human interactions, rituals, and rites of passage in Indonesia's traditional life.

At the level of economics, rice has also long served as the primary medium of exchange. Rice was the traditional substance of barter. It was convertible into meat, clothing, or household items. For all practical purposes, rice was money and Indonesia's economy was a rice economy. The role of rice as a kind of quasi-money was reinforced by both the Sukarno government and the early years of the Soeharto government, when rice was distributed as a regular portion of the payment to civil servants.

For these reasons, whenever rice is scarce, it is a profoundly troubling experience for Indonesians. It portends that the world, in some way, is falling apart. So when the New Order government made agriculture the centre of its development strategy, this decision was not so much an example of radical thinking, but another sign of the practical and insightful thinking that was behind most of the country's successful economic policies. Later, in the 1970s, as the rise in oil prices drastically altered Indonesia's economic landscape, agriculture continued to be one of the primary focuses of the New Order efforts. Although the oil-induced surge in foreign exchange holdings permitted the government to direct more attention to other aspects of the economy, the goal of achieving rice self-sufficiency was never abandoned. The commitment to agriculture prevented the government from being seduced into squandering the surge of oil revenues on capital intensive projects that yielded little in terms of employment or the many other urgent needs of the society.

Building Blocks to Rice Self-sufficiency

The obstacles to achieving rice self-sufficiency were formidable. From the time that the goal was set in 1969 to the time when it was accomplished in 1984, Indonesia had harvests that were alternately exceptionally good and bad. The developmental process that led to rice self-sufficiency was not linear and formulaic. It required steady long-term vigilance over a decade and a half, and it required an experimental attitude. When something worked, the government stayed with it. When it did not, alternatives were sought. The effort required an unwavering national commitment that was embraced on all levels of society, from the President, to every branch of government, to industry, and right into the rice fields. The following paragraphs summarize some of the essential steps taken in the march toward rice self-sufficiency:

Bulog and Rice Prices

Several government agencies were deeply involved in the issue of food security, most notably the Co-ordinating Ministry for the Economy, Industry, Finance, and Development Supervision, the Ministry of Agriculture, Bulog, Bappenas, the Ministry of Trade, the Ministry of Co-operatives, the Ministry of Finance, and Bank Indonesia. Each of these agencies was acutely aware of the high stakes for the government in achieving agricultural advancement; to this end, they all contributed to policy formulation and the provision of manpower. If, however, there is any institution that should be singled out in the achievement of rice self-sufficiency, it is Bulog, the Food Logistics Board. What is noteworthy about Bulog's contribution in support of the effort to achieve rice self-sufficiency is that Bulog achieved its goal not through direct involvement in the business of farming but in the business of managing supplies and prices. Bulog was again proof of the synergy between macro- and micro-economic management. Bulog intervened in the supply and price of rice on a national level, and this had a powerful impact on economic behaviour at the micro level. One could say, Bulog represented a perverse victory; Bulog was deliberately created to distort the price mechanism for rice. It violated a basic economic tenet held dear by all the county's economic policymakers, that is, that the markets themselves should be free to set prices. Yet, Indonesia's economic team supported the creation and ongoing operations of Bulog as a cornerstone of the country's agricultural policy.

Bulog constituted an economic paradox: it manipulated markets to help foster stronger markets. The economic team (here including the Minister of Agriculture and Chairman of Bulog) held that Indonesia's agricultural economy had become so impoverished that it forced farmers into behaviour patterns that were logical for a subsistence economy but not for a modern market economy. The goal of Bulog was to help draw farmers into the formal market economy. To do this, the most important thing was to create functioning markets for agricultural products, and rice in particular.[3]

Bulog is Indonesia's middleman par excellence. As such, it tried to satisfy the sometimes conflicting objectives of three constituencies, in this case, Indonesia's rice farmers, the consumers, and the rice retailers and traders. Bulog's goal was to create reliable, steady markets for the country's most important commodity, rice. Bulog's main tools to achieve this goal were the creation of a buffer stock through the construction of nation-wide storage facilities and the ability to set two key prices: a floor price that represented the minimum a farmer would receive in selling his rice, and a ceiling price that was the maximum consumers would be charged for rice. The margin between these two prices represented the amount wholesalers and retailers could earn by trading rice.

Setting floor and ceiling prices was as important as it was complex. If the ceiling price was too high, it could provoke inflation and consumer outrage. If the ceiling price was too low, there would be no incentive for traders to sell rice. Similarly, if the floor price for rice was too high, traders would have little incentive to buy it since their profit margin would be too narrow. However, if the floor price was too low, farmers would have no incentive to grow rice (at least, beyond what they would consume themselves). Bulog set the floor price at which co-operatives, acting on Bulog's behalf, would pay for rice. If farmers chose to sell directly to wholesalers, the price would generally be about the same as the Bulog price. Bulog's main tool in stabilizing the market was the storage network it set up across the country. When supplies in the market began to fall and upward pressure on prices appeared, Bulog would draw down its buffer stock by injecting rice into the market to hold down prices. Conversely, when prices began to fall due to oversupply, Bulog would engage in purchasing operations to build its buffer stock. In all this, Bulog relied on international markets to apply exogenous forces to influence the country's internal markets. For example, if domestic rice supplies fell below required levels, Bulog bought rice in international markets. If imported rice was more expensive than local rice, Bulog sold it at subsidized prices.

In its early years, during the 1970s, Bulog gradually raised the floor price offered to farmers for rice. In the mid-1980s, when Indonesia produced rice surpluses, rather than let prices fall, Bulog exported rice internationally. These measures added stability to the market. Besides increasing the income of rice farmers, they were given a sense of security that had never been part of the agrarian experience. A welcomed side-effect of Bulog's operations was that it effectively put rice speculators out of business. Farmers could see that it was to their interest to produce rice instead of other crops whose prices could vary widely depending on international markets. Since Bulog was founded on 10 May 1967, farmers became increasingly confident in the reliability and profitability of the rice market. This confidence was vital to sustained growth in Indonesia's rice crops that ultimately led to the achievement of rice self-sufficiency.

Technology and Education
At the heart of the government's agricultural support services were technology and education. Since 1963, Indonesia initiated a number of programmes to introduce the nation's farmers to practices that would improve

farm productivity. Especially in the early years of the New Order, the Faculty of Agriculture at the University of Indonesia, which later became the Institut Pertanian Bogor (IPB or Agriculture Institute of Bogor), had a leading role in the development of policies, seed strains, and techniques for crop cultivation. The original programme was based upon the *Panca Usaha*, that is, the fivefold method to better farming, consisting of: a) improved water control; b) use of selected seeds; c) use of fertilizer and pesticides; d) better cultivation methods; and e) stronger co-operatives.

There were many breakthroughs and problems associated with these extension programmes. The most enduring programme was called Bimas for Bimbingan masal, that is, Mass Guidance. In its early days, the basic method used under Bimas was to have students trained at the IPB, live in the villages, and work alongside the farmers as a way of imparting skills. This method was quite effective; however, to expand the programme to the national scale, it employed a corps of professionals who were well-trained and committed to teaching people about applicable agrarian technology. After launching various agricultural extension services in Java, they were soon spread throughout the country. Over the years, the government relied on these extension services to introduce new seeds, techniques, and other inputs that promised to improve crop yields.

While the government endeavoured to introduce farmers to the latest in agrarian technologies, it emphasized education to ensure that new techniques and technologies were understood and properly employed. The educational efforts were carried out through the co-operatives, by Ministry of Agriculture field workers, and through demonstration fields. The government especially emphasized four 'technologies': irrigation techniques, high yielding rice varieties, fertilizers, and pesticides.

The improvement in rice yields depended, above all, on improved strains of rice. These high yielding varieties were developed by the International Rice Research Institute (IRRI) in Los Baños, Philippines, with financial and technical support from various countries, most notably the United States and Japan. For many years, researchers in Indonesia have worked closely with IRRI by drawing on new experimental strains and by giving feedback to the Institute on the results of field tests in experimental plots as well as large scale plantings. In the 1970s, Indonesia introduced several revolutionary new strains of rice, including PB-5 and PB-8 (that is, *Padi Baru* or 'New Rice' Nos. 5 and 8). These varieties were more disease resistant than the older one; they were high yielding plants, and because they grew more quickly, they permitted the farmer to obtain more harvests per year. Previous rice strains produced an average of 1.25 tonnes per hectare; used properly, PB-5 and PB-8 could produce between 3 and 4 tonnes per hectare.

The other major contributor to improved rice yields was the increased use of chemical fertilizers. To this end, the government invested in fertilizer factories that drew on the country's abundant supply of natural gas, the essential petrochemical ingredient in the fertilizer production process. Responding to growing demand and industrial capacity, from 1969 until 1984 Indonesia's fertilizer production increased 49 times. As the price for rice increased over time, the price of fertilizer during this period increased little, thus making it more economical for farmers to use fertilizers.

The government had other options it chose not to pursue. Instead of subsidizing fertilizer, the government could have simply bought more rice imports. However, in the early 1970s there was already sufficient evidence to demonstrate a positive correlation between fertilizer use and farm output. The government was convinced that what it spent on fertilizer would be more than offset by productivity gains. For this reason, for many years, fertilizer constituted the biggest subsidy in the government budget. While the expense was great, the investment yielded big pay-offs as it resulted not only in increased agricultural outputs, but also influenced the way farmers cultivated their crops.

Pesticide use was also considered important to agricultural development. However, by the mid-1980s the government better understood the potential hazards from frequent application of pesticides. For this reason, the government reversed its former policy that encouraged the widespread use of broad-band pesticides. To encourage an effective yet ecologically sustainable approach to pest control, Indonesia eventually adopted a programme known as Integrated Pest Management (IPM) as its official policy for pest control.

Without the contributions of these advances in seed varieties and the availability of fertilizer, rice self-sufficiency would never have been possible no matter how motivated the farm population.

Village Co-operatives

Although the idea of the co-operative is written into Indonesia's 1945 Constitution, the co-operative movement did not take off on a large scale until 1972. It was in that year that Indonesia was struck with another disastrous rice harvest, and the government encouraged the formation of co-operatives as a way of strengthening the institutional framework needed to support greater efficiency in rice production. There are two basic forms of co-operatives, at the village level there is the Badan Usaha Unit Desa (BUUD). At the level of the *kabupaten* (district or regency), there are full-scale co-operatives, called Koperasi Unit Desa (KUD). Writing in 1981, Ruth Daroesman (1981: 24) stated that membership averaged about 350 farmers per KUD, although there could be as few as 20 or as many as 3,000 members. The co-operatives acted as distribution centres for agricultural supplies, such as seed and fertilizers. In some cases, rice processing facilities were located at co-operatives. It was also through the intermediary of the BUUDs and KUDs that Bulog carried out its rice procurement activities. The co-operatives also acted as centres for disseminating information or for organizing meetings. In some cases, the government made credit available to farmers through co-operatives. In more general terms, the co-operatives served two essential functions: first, they were practical functioning units that created a direct link between Bulog and the farmers. Without this link, it would have been impossible to administer the Bimas programme or Bulog's rice procurement activities. Second, the co-operatives became a grass roots means for communicating to and mobilizing farmers on a nation-wide basis.

Infrastructure

Infrastructure development was one of the key elements of the New Order development effort. Many aspects of infrastructure development were directly geared toward agricultural development, all of which directly contributed to the achievement of rice self-sufficiency. Irrigation systems were an essential area for agrarian infrastructure development. The government classified irrigation systems as primary, secondary, and tertiary, the latter being those systems that brought water directly to the fields. The government worked only on primary and secondary systems, but left the tertiary systems to the farmers themselves. During the period from 1969 to 1984 the government rehabilitated or newly constructed irrigation systems for over 2,700,000 hectares of farm land.[4] Other infrastructure work that would have a direct impact on achieving the country's goal of rice self-sufficiency was a massive programme for the construction or rehabilitation of roads and ports.

Another area that could loosely be considered agrarian infrastructure was the development of rice milling facilities. At the outset of the New Order, there were several large rice mills most of which were located on Java. Due to their size, these tended to dominate the sector. In 1969, the government introduced some three hundred smaller mills that contained rice dryers, and it encouraged farmers to take their harvest to these. These mills were generally very successful, due in large part to their proximity to the farms. The private sector quickly became interested in these smaller mills and began to establish their own; by 1973, the total rice milling capacity on Java had jumped six times (Sapuan, 1989: 89).

All of these policies worked together and contributed to the progressive development of Indonesia's agricultural sector. The progress toward rice self-sufficiency, however, was rough. After a very good harvest in 1971 and experiences that seemed to prove that the Bulog formula worked, Indonesia was struck with the 1972 drought. The ensuing rice shortage caught the government completely off guard. It was not until well after mid-year that the government realized that rice supplies would probably be insufficient. Unfortunately, world rice supplies were exceptionally low that year, and it was very difficult for Indonesia to obtain an emergency quota. Prices of rice in Jakarta doubled, from Rp 48.5 per kilogram in January 1972 to Rp 84.4 in January 1974. The shortage fuelled a rapid burst of inflation and sent a shock wave throughout the economy. The crisis alarmed the economic policymakers. As a result, the process of building and maintaining rice supplies was expanded. Using windfall profits from oil revenues, the government launched an intensified programme of building a nationwide network of storage and warehouse facilities for rice and agricultural supplies. This, in turn, stimulated the growth of Indonesia's rural co-operatives.

Throughout the 1970s, rice production grew unevenly, but in most years, it did continue to grow. During those years when Indonesia's rice production was low, Bulog raised imports. In the process, for a few years Indonesia ranked as one of the world's largest importers of rice. This unfortunate distinction was not as bad as it would seem. As mentioned, the imports were used as a way to sterilize the oil windfalls that were streaming into the country. They kept the retail price of rice low, and yet the floor price offered to local farmers was maintained at its planned level. Therefore, the incentive for local farmers to continue expanding rice production was never diminished.

A turning point in the effort to achieve rice self-sufficiency occurred in 1983. Similar to 1972, severe drought conditions prevailed in Indonesia and many analysts predicted rice shortages and rising prices. Despite the troubles, however, the 1983 rice crop was very good and prices remained steady. Then, in 1984, for the first time on record, Indonesia achieved a rice surplus. After fifteen years of struggle, Indonesia accomplished its long-sought goal of rice self-sufficiency. A historic landmark had been reached that was emblematic of the restructuring of Indonesia's agrarian sector (see Figure 5.1 for a graph depicting the changes in rice production between 1969 and 1984). Indonesia's farms showed that sustainable high outputs were possible, even in years with unusually poor weather. In 1985, the Food and Agriculture Organization (FAO) of the United Nations recognized this accomplishment by bestowing a special award on President Soeharto at a ceremony held in Rome, Italy.

Since 1984, there have been years of rice surplus and years of rice deficit, but in every year Indonesia's productivity has been sufficiently high to keep the country in a comfortable position in terms of rice supplies.

FIGURE 5.1
Rice Production, 1969–1984

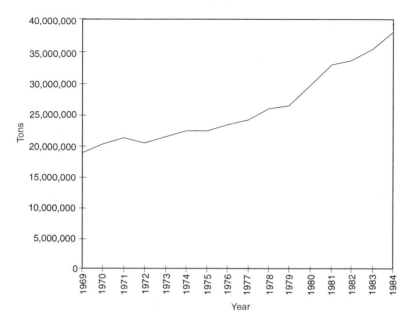

Source: Statistics supplied by Bulog.

MONETIZATION OF THE RURAL SECTOR

In 1964, the *Far Eastern Economic Review* reported, 'Indonesian politicians take pride in reminding foreign correspondents and diplomats that racing inflation does not spell doom to the Indonesian economy because the great majority of Indonesians are independent of the monetary system' (Wilson, 1964: 70). Until the early 1970s, Indonesian farmers, as a rule, had never been integrated into the formal economy. The typical farmer lived in a modest house constructed from local materials. Whatever wealth he had was in real products. According to the agrarian logic of this time, this was safest since money was so unstable. When a family was living at the subsistence level, money was a risk best avoided.

Improved seed strains, ample supplies of fertilizer, rural co-operatives, irrigation, and roads were the bricks and mortar of agricultural development. However, a building—no matter how well constructed—will not stand long unless its foundation is solid and strong. Indonesian agricultural was founded on barter, and this was a weak base for development. To bring economic advancement to Indonesia's rural economy, it had to share the same economic foundation as the rest of the economy: the rural sector needed to be brought into the monetary economy. To do so, however, would require extracting the economy from the patterns of subsistence that were virtually synonymous with rural living. Subsistence and barter were inextricably linked. To raise living standards the barter economy had to be replaced with commerce based on money, that is, the rural sector had to be 'monetized'.

The significance of this fact cannot be overstated: the non-monetary nature of the rural sector exerted a powerful influence over not just Indonesia's farmers, but the entire national economy. There were many serious implications of having most of the nation's farmers operating out-side the monetary economy. First, Indonesia's farmers were living with no savings or insurance to serve as a buffer in the case of a calamity, an eco-nomic downturn, or a failed crop. Were it not for the communal spirit of *gotong royong*, farm life would have been unbearably insecure. Second, Indonesia's farmers were not engaging in capital formation that could be directed to the improvement of their farms. With no capital whatsoever, the rural population was condemning itself to perpetuating the same farming practices year after year regardless of the opportunities that might be available. Thirdly, because Indonesia's agrarian population—the largest sector of the economy—was not holding its wealth in banks, then banks had fewer funds that could be lent to others. Potential savings from the rural sector that could have been reinvested to build the local economy, were lost. This meant that the minority of the population who operated within the monetary economy carried the full burden of capital formation for all of Indonesia. This was a serious impediment to development.

When Indonesia's economic stabilization was starting to take hold in the late 1960s, the government undertook a long-term effort to bring gradually the nation's agricultural sector into the monetary economy. To achieve these objectives, two basic methods were used: a) the government tried to persuade farmers to trade their products for money, rather than for bartered goods; b) by creating a network of rural banks, the government made credit available to farmers both as a means to get them to deal in money and to help them improve their farm operations.

The government's main 'persuaders' for farmers to use money rather than barter were Bulog and the co-operatives. Bulog's market operation was its principal method for getting farmers to trade their production for money.[5] If the farmers opted to sell their production to a co-operative, they had no choice but to accept money for their goods. The use of money was reinforced when farmers wanted to buy fertilizer or other goods sponsored by the Bimas or related government programmes. In some cases, the goods were given to farmers freely to use on a trial basis in demonstration plots. In such cases, the government would require that the inputs be used in fields that were located along a roadside, or preferably at the junction of a crossroad. In this way, the positive effects of the inputs could be readily seen by all who passed by the field. In most cases, however, farmers paid in cash or had to seek credit.

The government could have easily minimized the monetary dimension in its agriculture development efforts. The government already had a well-established precedent of supplying quotas of rice to the country's civil servants in place of cash salaries. With the farmers, the government, for example, could have opted to trade fertilizer for rice. It chose not to pursue this option because this would have strengthened the barter approach to marketing that the government was trying to uproot.

The methods for supplying credit to rural borrowers were complex. There already existed an informal system for providing credit to farmers through moneylenders. Moneylenders usually did not reside in the villages. They generally lent at usurious terms, and for that they were reviled. However, the moneylenders did respond to a need that was not being satisfied by more formal institutions, such as banks. They took initiative to make themselves available to farmers. They also showed some creativity by having the terms of loans negotiable. The moneylenders, however, exploited the plight of farmers. They used their unequal negotiating position to wring exorbitant returns. With no competition, farmers often had no alternative but to work with the moneylenders. To end this racket, the government had to offer farmers something better.

As a way of responding to the need for credit in the countryside and monetizing the rural sector, the government formalized and improved the credit elements of the extension programme. The programme made credit available through institutions such as the Ministry of Agriculture, co-operatives, and banks. One of the principal vehicles through which the government channelled credit to farmers was the branch network of Bank Rakyat Indonesia (BRI). Although the programme was successful, it was constrained early on by the relatively small number of BRI branches. This forced many farmers to travel great distances to obtain small loans. The expense and inconvenience made it impractical for many farmers to seek credit. For this reason, another step taken to monetize the rural sector was a programme to expand the network of village banks (*bank desa*) across the country.

The village banks were owned by the villagers themselves and frequently had the village head as the manager of the bank, with a local teacher serving as the bookkeeper. They used the simplest accounting methods. For example, the primary lending technique they employed was called Sepuluh Kembali Duablas ('Ten Against Twelve'). This meant that if a villager borrowed Rp 10,000 he would have to pay back Rp 12,000. Whether the villager repaid his loan after two weeks or one month, he would still have to repay Rp 12,000. This system was adopted because it required very little mathematical skills to understand and the book-keeping was extremely simple. All loans were short term. There were rarely examples of malfeasance because if a villager was caught abusing the system, he could find himself shunned by the bank and the village at large. If a villager was denied credit from his local village bank, it was virtually impossible that he could expect to obtain credit from the bank in another village. The village banks, therefore, soon became important institutions in the effort to monetize the rural sector. The government supplemented these banks with other credit co-operatives and other programmes and institutions authorized to lend to the rural population.[6] Some of these other programmes are described in the next few paragraphs.

Annual credit provisions provided through Bimas peaked in 1980 at $130 million and thereafter declined considerably (Tabor, 1992: 178). By the mid-1980s, after Indonesia had achieved rice self-sufficiency, the government continued to provide credits for the development of the rural sector, but those credits were no longer specifically targeted to support rice production.

Another programme, the Badan Kredit Kecamatan (BKK or Subdistrict Credit Agency),[7] was introduced in 1970 in the province of Central Java. The credit was designed to meet the needs of individual small rural entrepreneurs, engaged primarily in small scale trading, handicrafts, and food services. The average loan size was initially around Rp 10,000, about $16 at the exchange rate of the time. Loans could be higher, however, and in 1988, the loan ceiling reached Rp 1 million, or about $590. An innovative dimension to this programme was that borrowers were required to participate in a mandatory savings plan. Experience showed that borrowers were willing to pay interest rates—directly and indirectly, through the mandatory savings programme—that were higher than those prevailing for other government-sponsored programmes but less than those typically charged by local moneylenders. The BKK programme grew dramatically, comprising over half a million loans outstanding by 1987. By 1992, total loans outstanding amounted to almost Rp 50 billion, and the savings mobilized was over Rp 6 billion.

Two other important programmes the government initiated in 1974 to bring credit to farmers and small traders and craftsmen were the Kredit Investasi Kecil (KIK or Small Investment Credit), and the Kredit Modal Kerja Permanen (KMKP or Working Capital Credit Scheme). The small investment loans were primarily for start up ventures whereas the working capital was intended to provide working capital for ongoing projects. The subsidized interest rates were between 10.5 per cent and 12.0 per cent per year, substantially lower than commercial loans at that time. The government was aware that there was a risk that individuals would borrow money and use it for purposes other than those for which the loans were approved. For this reason, the banks made spot checks to ensure that farmers were using the loans appropriately. Unlike the BKK, which provided very small loans, the small investment credits and working capital loans were on average between Rp 2–Rp 3 million. These various programmes served three purposes: they subsidized farmers who were willing to participate in the government programme; they brought farmers directly into the monetary economy; and they indirectly encouraged farmers to keep farming rather than leave the land in search of other ways to make a living.

Although this part of the book focuses on the period 1969–83, we should mention that later in the 1980s there were very important developments in the extension of credit to the rural sector through two programmes known as Kupedes and Simpedes. The Kredit Umum Pedesaan (Kupedes or General Rural Credit) programme, begun in 1984, introduced general rural credit offered at commercial interest rates. Simpanan Pedesaan (Simpedes or General Rural Savings Accounts) was introduced as a pilot project in November 1984, and in 1986 the programme was launched throughout the country. Both programmes were offered nationwide through the branches of the BRI.[8]

Simpedes paid up to 12 per cent on savings balances, depending on the amount. Unlike the Tabanas savings programme,[9] under Simpedes, savers were permitted unlimited withdrawals, a feature that helped make Simpedes the preferred savings instrument among village customers. A further incentive to save was provided by semi-annual drawings in which savers were eligible to win prizes.

The Kupedes/Simpedes (K/S) system was profitable in the year it was introduced. The spread between loan and deposit interest rates was set to enable institutional profitability. By 1991, the Kupedes programme supplied over two-thirds of BRI's total profits. The result of the new programme was that village bank deposits increased from $17.6 million in June 1983 to $1.30 billion in December 1991. In 1989, BRI began to open unit banks in urban areas; these, too, rapidly became profitable.

Seven months after Simpedes went national, its balances passed the total for Tabanas funds held in the village units. By the end of 1988, balances had grown to Rp 334 billion ($190 million) compared to Rp 88 billion ($50 million) in Tabanas. Furthermore, most of the individual village units were operating at a profit. In contrast to the earlier period when Bimas losses were cross-subsidized from profits made in other BRI operations, the village units not only paid for themselves but also helped to cover losses incurred in BRI's regular commercial banking business.

Indonesia's rural lending programmes were among the most successful implemented in any developing country. On the credit side, they showed that rural Indonesians were willing to borrow at market rates. The other complementary point that should be made is that rural Indonesians were willing and able savers. When Indonesia's rural population was provided with effective financial programmes through the BRI village banks, the BKK, and other legitimate channels, rapid progress was made in integrating the countryside into the regional and national financial markets. What was needed were the institutions to respond to the demand for financial services in the countryside.

Probably the most important advances in rural credit occurred when bank deregulation took place first in 1983 and later in 1988. The changes in policy led to an explosion of bank branches in towns and villages across the country all of which were eager to lend to farmers and other small businesses. This financial deregulation greatly advanced efforts to deepen financial institutions and practices throughout the Indonesian countryside. The rapid proliferation of banks in the rural areas of Indonesia was possible in large part because of the earlier efforts of the government to bring farmers into the monetary economy during the 1970s and early 1980s.

Through BRI, BKK, Simpedes, and others such institutions and programmes, the government succeeded in its objective of monetizing the rural sector. Not only did this permit Indonesia's farmers to improve their welfare by integrating their work into the modern economy, the monetized rural sector also generated vast sums of investment funds that were essential to the nation's development efforts.

TENDING THE GARDEN: LESSONS FROM THE ROAD TO RICE SELF-SUFFICIENCY

Indonesia's agriculture by no means can be reduced to the cultivation of rice or even food crops. None the less, we have focused on the quest for rice self-sufficiency in this chapter because it represented the greatest challenge faced by Indonesia's agricultural sector as well as for the country's economic team. Economists usually consider agriculture a field that is best studied using the tools of micro-economics since the same kind of analysis that applies to the firm or corporation can also be applied to individual farmers. In the case of achieving rice self-sufficiency, however, the issues were equally macroeconomic and micro-economic, and this was clearly reflected in many of the country's economic and agricultural policies. Indonesia's money supply, its exports and imports, its inflation rate, and unemployment level were all directly influenced by the agrarian sector, and, more specifically, its rice supplies. From the very early days of the New Order, Indonesia's economic policymakers recognized the tight and powerful linkages between the rural sector and the economic health of the country as a whole. Even in the most intoxicating moments of the oil boom, the government never lost sight of the importance of agriculture. The economic policymakers never forgot that Indonesia's roots were in the land, and will stay there for many generations to come. It would be an omission, however, if we did not recognize that, besides the success in rice production, much of Indonesia's agricultural sector floundered during the 1970s and early 1980s. As discussed in the earlier chapter, until 1978 Indonesia had maintained a fixed exchange rate and the rupiah grew steadily overvalued. Indonesia's primary non-oil exports were agricultural commodities, all of which suffered from the currency misalignment. Therefore, while the entire agrarian sector benefited from the development of infrastructure, especially through roads and ports, the export-oriented estate crop sector was handicapped. In this respect, Indonesia's economic policies were not equally beneficial to all sectors of agriculture. The following paragraphs summarize a few of the salient lessons that emerged during Indonesia's fifteen-year quest to achieve self-sufficiency in rice.

1. *The Developmental Challenge to Macroeconomic Orthodoxy.* The economists who were guiding Indonesia's economic policy were all firm believers in the wisdom and validity of prudent economic policies. And yet, logic and intuition led the team to believe that there were times in which the conditions in developing economies require policies that run counter to economic orthodoxy. There were two striking examples where the government adopted policies that it believed were appropriate as temporary measures until such time when the economy had matured enough to permit the market to rule on its own.

i) *Subsidies as an Appropriate Intervention.* Subsidies are pervasive in almost all economies. Some countries subsidize the poor, some subsidize medicine, while others subsidize strategic businesses. Undoubtedly, across all nations, the sector that is accorded the greatest amount of trade protection and subsidies is agriculture. Governments frequently pay farmers *not* to grow certain products, or to grow products no one wants to buy. Typically, subsidies are a form of negative tax. They facilitate or encourage consumption. The recipients of subsidies are always happy to receive them. However, it is always easier for a government to give a subsidy than to remove it. When subsidies are maintained beyond their usefulness, for fear of the political consequences of termination, they are stripped of their value as a tool for assisting economic development. Under these circumstances, the subsidy is a market distorter that should be eschewed by economic policymakers.

Indonesia's food and seed subsidy merits special reflection. During the 1970s, Indonesia gave very high subsidies to two commodities, petrol and fertilizer. Yet, the significance of the two could not be more different. For petrol, Indonesia's subsidy was a consumption facilitator (that had the associated benefit of reducing the consumption of wood as a source of energy). It was a politically popular move, but from a purely economic perspective, after a certain point the subsidy was no longer justifiable. The fertilizer subsidy (as with the seed subsidy) was another matter altogether. The fertilizer subsidy constituted what I would call a 'structural adjustment subsidy'. The intent of the subsidy was not so much to facilitate consumption (although, of course, that is what it did), but to encourage a particular behaviour that the government hoped would become habit forming, that is, the use of modern farming technologies, such as advanced seed strains and fertilizers. The subsidy was a form of drawn-out inducement for the nation's farmers. The government believed that when Indonesia's farmers had become 'married' to modern farming techniques, they would never get divorced. The government could then remove the subsidy. This proved to be correct. Over time, the income of farmers grew to a level that it became impossible for them to return to their former practices without inflicting penalties upon themselves. Rather than a consumption facilitator, the fertilizer subsidy would be better compared to government investment in education. Instead of expenditures on textbooks and teachers, the government supplied bags of chemicals and agricultural extension agents. When the lessons were well learned, the government withdrew the subsidy, confident that the market would take off.[10] The subsidy had become superfluous. In effect, the government had used subsidies to engineer a structural change in the most important sector of the economy, agriculture.

ii) *Special Case for Price Management.* Only in extremely exceptional circumstances did Indonesia's economic team favour price controls. However, the efforts of Bulog have demonstrated that in some instances price management can be successful and appropriate. Bulog did not engage in arbitrary price-setting. Over the years, Bulog has tried to maintain adequate rice supplies while responding to the interest of its three main constituencies: farmers, consumers, and retailers. Conscious of these competing interests, it has tried to calculate what approximately would be the prices in an optimal market. A classical economist would argue that the free market could do this more efficiently. While this argument has merit, at Indonesia's stage of development, the free market would never have led to the stability in price and supply that the country needed. The volatility in price and supply that would have occurred had Bulog not intervened could have had serious consequences for Indonesia's political stability.

If, however, we agree that in a developing country there are instances when some form of price control is advisable, we must also ask, *for how long*? The probable answer is, 'As long as the control is required to launch the development process; otherwise, it should be abandoned.' In the near future, Indonesia's capacity to grow and market rice may soon develop to the point that Bulog can leave price determination to the free market. In such a case, there would still be a critical role for Bulog as the maintainer of strategic reserves of food supplies, especially rice. As before, when national markets are scarce, Bulog would sell from its reserves. When national markets are abundant, Bulog would build reserves. Its role would then switch from *price setter* to *supply stabilizer*. This, it could be argued, is an appropriate and responsible long-term role for any government for commodities of such vital importance as rice is to the Indonesian economy.

2. *Social Engineering through Economics*. The trend toward urbanization has been well documented in developing countries for many decades. Governments have unwittingly encouraged this trend through policies that favoured industry over agriculture. In the early days of the New Order, some critics felt that the emphasis on agriculture was a way of maintaining the *status quo* and would condemn Indonesia to a state of permanent underdevelopment. In fact, just the opposite was true. *Status quo* policies would have remained impassive in the face of the rural exodus, and this would have accelerated the population growth in the cities. Without Indonesia's pro-agriculture policies, instead of having a 9 million population in Jakarta, there might be as many as twice that amount, and likewise for all of Indonesia's major cities.[11] The country's agriculture policies were only partly designed with food production in mind. They were also created to counter the trend toward rampant hyper-urbanization that is so common among developing countries. Indonesia's economic team saw agriculture as the most viable option for providing employment opportunities for the majority of Indonesians. The migration to the cities is unstoppable. However, Indonesia's agrarian policies have slowed that trend, and this has permitted the steady build-up of industry while keeping in check the problem of urban unemployment.

3. *The Power of Money*. Indonesia's experience in the monetization of the rural sector gives convincing evidence of the value of bringing all

segments of society into the monetary economy. Especially in developing countries, there tend to be large segments of the population that operate outside the formal, monetized economy. Money is the most efficient means for building the capital needed for economic development. By monetizing the agrarian sector, Indonesia took a major step in transforming the economy from one that was geared toward subsistence to one geared toward capital formation. This was one of the most important steps taken to create self-sustainable development.

4. *The Value of Great Goals*. For some time the word 'vision' has figured prominently in the literature of management and leadership. 'Vision' is equally important for nations. A nation's vision is expressed through its commitment to great goals. Indonesia's commitment to rice self-sufficiency served as the rallying cry for agricultural development for a decade and a half. Throughout this period, Indonesia progressed on many fronts, but the goal of rice self-sufficiency kept the pressure on the government and the farming community to maintain the effort for continued growth. Indonesia was able to achieve rice self-sufficiency because it maintained political stability and kept its focus on the achievement of its long-term goals. When such goals are accomplished, a country must take stock and ask itself what should be its future goals and aspirations. Today, when Indonesia considers agrarian policy issues, the nation must commit itself to raising the incomes of the rural sector, crop diversification, and the provision of a more nutritious diet for all Indonesians. These goals may lack the grandeur of the attainment of rice self-sufficiency, but they are great none the less. There may be other agricultural goals that are even more important. What is essential is that the goals truly support development and are based on sound economic principles. Otherwise, economic policy can become hostage to political factions and special interest groups and economic development will be sacrificed in the name of slogans and propaganda.

5. *Addressing Educational and Institutional 'Thinness'*. One of the most serious problems Indonesia faced in its efforts to achieve rice self-sufficiency was the lack of qualified personnel to carry out the tasks of development. This is common among developing countries. For example, in the early 1970s the government was too ambitious in its efforts to expand the KUDs and BUUDs. As a result, initially many of these organizations were unprepared and unqualified to assist in the widespread credit programmes that the government had planned. Governments hoping to achieve rapid economic development must be prepared to devote a considerable amount of time, effort, and resources to cultivating the human resources needed to execute development programmes. The investment, though considerable, can deliver yields that exceed those of the most bullish of markets.

1. According to a study by Peter Timmer (1975: 198), 'although very wide variations in both land tenure and land quality make "average land ownership" a dubious concept at the micro level, the pressing fact is that over two thirds of the farm population have less than half a hectare to cultivate, and probably less than a third'.

2. Rice supplies grew again in 1966, but at the beginning of the year, the situation was grave. Had the situation been permitted to deteriorate further, the outcome would have been disastrous, especially since Indonesia did not have the foreign exchange to finance large-scale imports.

3. The importance of rice prices was emphasized in Repelita I, wherein it states: 'Rice constitutes the Indonesian's most important food-grain in its contribution to total calories consumed and to his wages and salary structure. Besides, the larger part of the Indonesian agricultural population participates in rice production. Therefore, every movement of the price of rice will influence the welfare of the major part of the Indonesian nation' (Indonesia, Department of Information, 1969: Vol. 2a, p. 10).

4. Estimate based on table 'Addition to irrigated areas from public investment' in Pearson (1991: 18).

5. Naturally, farmers continued to keep a portion of their produce for their own consumption.

6. For more information, see the discussion on credit in the agriculture section of Repelita I.

7. The discussion on the BKK programme draws on the study by Reidinger (1994).

8. The discussion of Simpedes and Kupedes draws on a very good review of the programme that appears in Snodgrass (1991).

9. Tabanas was introduced during Indonesia's stabilization period and is discussed in Chapter 1.

10. That the subsidies achieved their objective should put to rest the ideas of scholars such as Boeke, Geertz, Penny (1966a) and others who suggested that Indonesia's culture somehow renders our farmers immune to market forces. However, when markets fail, as they often can, Indonesia's culture offers some security in the collective action of *gotong royong*.

11. In the mid-1990s, the population of Mexico City, for example, was about the same as that of Jakarta, although Mexico's population is about half that of Indonesia.

6
Industrialization and Trade: Twists and Turns on the Road of Economic Pragmatism

WHILE Indonesia's decision to make agriculture the foundation of the country's development plans was a departure from conventional wisdom, it was none the less clear from the outset that the country could not progress as a modern nation if the economy depended entirely on tilling the soil. In the late 1960s, when the New Order government was launching its plans for economic development, much of the current economic literature equated development with industrialization. Indeed, industrialization and development are so tightly linked that the term 'industrialized country' is used to mean a country that has achieved a sustained high standard of living for its population. Although Indonesia had adopted an 'agriculture first' policy, the country's economic team was also deeply committed to progressive industrialization as a cornerstone of the country's economic development strategy. They also knew that ill-conceived programmes to achieve rapid industrialization could result in economic dislocations, wasted investments, and the depletion of the country's minuscule wealth.

The statistical evidence from the Sukarno period was so slim and unreliable that it is difficult to assess the state of Indonesia's industrialization during those years. However, the available evidence suggests that at the outset of the New Order, Indonesia was the least industrialized of any of the large developing countries throughout the world.[1] In 1969, with the launch of Repelita I, Indonesia set its course for industrial development. The plan lacked grand projects and campaigns. Instead, the country determined to take a gradual route that would lay the foundation for industrialization over a period of about twenty-five years. Its virtue lay in the fact that it was realistic and feasible.

From the vantage point of the late-1990s, with Indonesia having become a newly industrialized country (NIC), it might be tempting to say we succeeded. However, along the way country sometimes took wrong turns and at other times reached dead ends, and the experience gained, especially in the early years can be boiled down to some important lessons. Here is a sampling of these lessons:

- Protectionism—whether it is used to cultivate infant industries or to promote equity by assisting economically disadvantaged groups—can play an important role in economic development, but only if it serves clearly defined goals and has a limited time line for its application;
- The success of an industrial policy is linked to the maintenance of a realistic exchange rate;
- Economic strategies have to be flexible and realistic so that they can change in response to shifting circumstances and, if necessary, can be rescinded when they have outlived their usefulness.

This chapter will sketch the theoretical framework within which Indonesia's policymakers made their decisions and will trace some of the historical developments—those moments in time when theory and reality collided and adjustments were made—that led to these lessons.

CHARACTERISTICS OF INDONESIA'S INDUSTRY

The Indonesian industrial sector[2] is divided into four classifications: cottage industries, small industries, medium industries, and large industries.[3] Two features common to most of Indonesia's industry through the early 1980s were that it was *small* and *rural.* According to a World Bank report (1979: 7), manufacturing in Indonesia was conducted by 1.3 million establishments, 1.2 million of which were cottage industries. Of these, 94 per cent were located in the countryside. Cottage industries consisted primarily of the manufacture of handicrafts and food products. This was conducted generally by women working alone, with family members or with neighbours. This work was unsalaried and earnings for goods sold went to the general support of the family. There was little certainty regarding the price or volume of goods sold. As deficient as the revenues were for this type of work, it did provide an important source of rural income and the products manufactured were valued by consumers. Typical examples of cottage industry products are handicrafts such as handwoven baskets or food products such as rice cakes in palm-leaf wrappings. A shop employing five to ninety-nine people to produce batik textiles is an example of a typical small- or medium-size industry. Besides the few very large foreign investments then operating in the country, such as Unilever, the Anglo-Dutch soaps and toiletries giant, the typical large-scale industry in Indonesia was a mechanized textile factory.

With most cottage and small-scale industries located in the countryside, output was highly seasonal. During the harvest and planting periods, work in the cottage and small-scale industries all but came to a halt. There were other linkages with agriculture as well: the goods produced in the cottage and small-scale industrial sector were sold primarily in rural markets. Furthermore, agricultural programmes, credit facilities, and co-operatives that were specifically geared toward improving the farm economy also served to boost the cottage and small-scale industrial sector.

Because Indonesia's infrastructure was extremely undeveloped, it was impractical for most cottage and small-scale industries to sell their goods outside the local market. Cottage and small-scale industries usually transported their goods on foot or by cart. Sometimes cottage and small-scale industries sold their products to traders or to the local co-operatives as a way to reach wider markets. Only medium- and large-scale industries routinely distributed their goods using motorized vehicles or ships. In the early 1970s, virtually all of Indonesia's medium- and large-scale industries were located in Java, Bali, and Sumatra. With the spread of mining and oil-related industries to other islands, supporting industries followed. Soon thereafter, industrial development evolved in these areas independent of the oil and gas sector. Yet, even as industry gradually spread throughout the archipelago, in the late 1960s, provincial barriers inhibited the trade of goods among provinces. These barriers were erected erratically. Sometimes a provincial governor would set up local tariffs and quotas to raise revenues and to regulate the flow of goods in and out of their provinces. Sometimes levies were even imposed at the *kabupaten* level.[4]

One of the most important constraining factors in the country's industrial development in the early 1970s was the country's limited foreign exchange. Since there was little indigenous industry, machinery of almost every variety had to be imported. With foreign exchange scarce, Indonesia had to maintain strict controls over its imports.[5] This restriction impeded the nation in its ability to build the industries that would increase the nation's foreign exchange reserves.

Industry, and manufacturing in particular, made a relatively minor contribution to employment generation in the early years of the New Order. During the turbulent 1960s, Indonesians in large numbers abandoned the cities and the industrial sector to return to the relative security of the countryside. Indonesia's villagers lived in houses without water or electricity, and measured their wealth in bags of rice. Yet, when the shops and factories in the cities closed their doors and the urban streets were teeming with the unemployed, Indonesia's farms offered the respite and relief of *gotong royong*. Indonesia's emaciated industry had grown weaker under the influence of years of political upheaval. By the end of the 1960s, the country was ready to begin the long process of reconstruction.

THEORETICAL DIMENSIONS OF INDUSTRIAL AND TRADE DEVELOPMENT

Economists frequently evaluate economic development in terms of the extent to which a country is 'inward looking' or 'outward looking'. Typically, an 'inward looking' country is one that seeks to promote industrialization through import substitution, often guided by economic planning and state ownership of industry. Inward looking economies are generally inhospitable to foreign investment and tend to maintain highly restrictive trade regimes. On the other hand, the archetypal 'outward looking' country seeks to expand foreign trade by keeping an open door to imports, exports, and foreign investment. Certainly, Indonesia during the Old Order was squarely classified among the 'inward looking countries'[6] and this attitude was sustained during the oil boom years of the 1970s.[7]

The 'inward looking' and 'outward looking' characterizations are closely related to two other ideas, namely the import substitution and export promotion policies. These two strategies represented the two fundamental schools of thought on the role of trade in economic development. From the perspective of the 1990s, the debate evokes little passion. Export orientation is the king of development models and import substitution has been largely discredited. In the 1960s, however, import substitution was as securely established in the economic orthodoxy as the alleged correspondence between inflation and unemployment. In his 1958 article, 'An Economic Justification of Protectionism', the MIT professor, Everett Hagen (1958: 513) offered a convincing defence:

The broad historical record suggests that protectionism may have accelerated development. A number of countries that have entered upon economic development since the original industrial revolution in England have done so behind a protectionist wall....

It is possible that if industrial protection had not existed, the entrepreneurs who started industrial ventures would have devoted their energies to other ventures, and would have drawn capital and labour so effectively into other ventures that real per capita income would have increased even faster than it did under protectionism. It is possible, but it does not seem probable.

By the early 1970s, although past its peak, the philosophy of import substitution was still widely embraced and used to justify protection of infant industries. Henry Bruton (1970: 126), for example, writing on import substitution in 1970, provides a classic argument for import substitution: 'To a very large extent it [i.e., import substitution or 'IS'] was arrived at by default, and is not only the most common (frequently observed) strategy in practice, but it is indeed perhaps the only one....

Even if it is assumed that a number of strategies are examined, the IS strategy is likely to be selected because it apparently calls merely for keeping out imports, a task most governments can be expected to accomplish.' Bruton acknowledges that there are problems with import substitution, but these, he suggests, are not deficiencies in the strategy per se, but in the implementation. '[T]o implement their IS policy, countries have chosen instruments and techniques that seem, in effect, to prevent that very policy from being successful.... What appears needed, then, is a way to achieve these advantages of IS without creating the distortions and misallocations that to-date appear so ubiquitous, and that appear responsible for its failure' (p. 124).

Defenders of import substitution—and they were legion—enumerate many advantages it accrued to the developing economy: it conserved foreign exchange; it created employment; it contributed to the growing industrialization of an economy; and it accelerated the technological advancement of an economy. In varying degrees, Indonesia's economic and political leaders accepted all of these arguments and adopted many protectionist policies, especially during the 1970s. In some cases, these policies were of genuine value; in most cases, however, the policies perpetuated inefficiencies.

As the decade progressed, scholars and policymakers grew more skeptical. However, instead of abandoning import substitution altogether, many economists and policymakers sought modifications that would compensate for its inherent shortcomings. Some argued, for example, that import substitution was an effective methodology that could assist countries making the transition from a colonial economy to a mature, industrialized economy. They held that it should not be a permanent feature of the economy, but a phase that would last one or at most two decades. During this phase, they maintained manufacturing for export was desirable, but not as important to the country's economic development as manufacturing for domestic consumption.[8]

In economics, as in life, actions speak louder than words. By the mid-1970s, Asia had produced three economies that gave strong support to a model that combined export promotion and selective industrial protection. First, there was Japan, which, by the 1960s had already established itself as Asia's leading industrialized nation, due largely to export promotion. Taiwan and South Korea were the next two major economies that demonstrated that the export promotion approach to development could be a powerful strategy. By the late-1970s, Indonesia would be looking toward these economies as vivid examples of the power of export-oriented economic policies. Before then, however, the country would test its own approaches to development.

BUILDING AN INDUSTRIAL FOUNDATION

Presuppositions of the New Order Industrial Policy

Repelita I is one of the first formal manifestations of Indonesia's industrial policy under the New Order. While asserting a commitment to agriculture, the plan also affirms the central position of industrialization in the country's development.

Indonesia's economic structure has been imbalanced toward agriculture for too long. Industry provided only a small contribution to national production, and industrial activities have been declining for years.... Our long-term objective is to build an economic structure in which agriculture, industry and services are balanced. To attain this long-term objective, the process of development must take place gradually. At present emphasis is placed primarily on agriculture. This means that the industrial sector must become the supporting sector and a stimulant to agricultural development. At the same time preparations are being made to develop industry more extensively in the future (Department of Information, 1969: Vol. 2B, p. 1).

Repelita I set the ambitious target of increasing the value of industrial production by at least 90 per cent over the five-year period. To accomplish this goal, the government planned to emphasize the rehabilitation of existing industrial investments as well as new investments to build on existing industrial capacity. With this in mind, plans called for developing industries with the following characteristics:

1. Industries supporting agricultural development or the processing of agricultural products;
2. Industries generating foreign exchange or saving foreign exchange by producing import-substituting commodities;
3. Industries processing large quantities of domestic raw materials;
4. Labour-intensive industries;
5. Industries promoting regional development.

Interestingly, these criteria, especially the last four, have continued to guide industrial policies throughout the duration of the New Order government. The primary divergences occurred when Indonesia experienced the sharp price increases that accompanied the two oil booms in 1973 and 1979.

The Government as Investor

From its early days as an independent country, the Indonesian government assumed an active and often dominant position in the nation's industry. The creation of the state banks and various state-owned enterprises are early manifestation of the government's role in industry. The nationalization of foreign companies under Sukarno was another. When the New Order came to power in 1966, it needed quickly to find ways to promote development. Its answer was to create an economic environment that was welcoming to investment, both public and private. To this end, less than nine months after Sukarno transferred executive authority to Soeharto, the new government established laws to govern private investment and state-owned enterprises.

From the start, the New Order government expected to play a significant role in the development of the economy. It never, however, attempted or desired to control the economy in the mould of the planned economies in the socialist bloc. Especially in the early years of the New Order, Indonesia's policies toward industrialization were guided more by economic pragmatism than extreme nationalism or other ideological motivations. The government tried to encourage a two-track approach to industrialization: on one hand, for the first time, the government welcomed and encouraged the development of a vigorous private sector; on the other hand, the government saw itself as the chief architect of the nation's development, and it was prepared to take whatever steps necessary to foster economic growth. The justifications for a strong state sector were essentially six:

1. State-owned enterprises could generate revenues that supported government operations;

2. The state could put its resources to use to create those economic entities that would satisfy the strategic economic objectives laid out in the country's five year plans, such as infrastructure development;

3. The state could venture into areas that were beyond the financial resources of most local entrepreneurs;

4. In an economy where participation by indigenous Indonesians was concentrated in agriculture, the state could put its resources to use to create previously unavailable employment opportunities in business and industry;

5. In some instances state-owned enterprises introduced industrial development into remote areas;

6. In some instances state involvement in the private sector was intended to eliminate speculation.

With the backing of the government, state-owned enterprises grew quickly in number and size. Although the new government was committed to a robust state commercial sector, it eliminated much of the preferential treatment that previously had been accorded on state-owned enterprises. Except in the case of acceptable government monopolies, such as public utilities, it did not attempt to interfere with the market in ways that put private companies at a competitive disadvantage. None the less, the 'playing field' was not level either: state-owned enterprises were often run by senior military officers, which conferred political advantage. They served a political mission to encourage industrial participation among indigenous Indonesians (*pribumis*). And no matter how poor their performance may have been, no state-owned enterprises ever filed for bankruptcy.

In the late 1960s and early 1970s, the new government's policy toward state-owned enterprises reflected its number one priority, to stabilize the economy and encourage growth. To remove real or perceived favouritism, in 1969 the government enacted new legislation (Law No. 12) under which most state firms became limited liability corporations and subject to the same laws and taxation requirements as private companies. It was not simply a spirit of fair play that led the government to treat state-owned enterprises and private enterprises equally. During the stabilization period, when these policies were first formulated, the government was broke. It could hardly afford to subsidize wasteful and inefficient businesses. The government, therefore, showed little favouritism to state firms over private, or *pribumi* over non-*pribumi*, domestic over foreign.

There is no doubt that state-owned enterprises performed an important function. They produced many important goods that responded to the demand in local and international markets and, in some cases, they generated profits for the government. According to the 1974–5 census of industry, about 20 per cent of the work-force in medium and large-scale industries was employed in state-owned enterprises (McCawley, 1981: 74). By the mid-1980s, Indonesia had over 200 state-owned enterprises in industries ranging from tea plantations to steel manufacturing. In general, however, the economic performance of most state-owned enterprises was substandard, and their survival depended on sustained government subsidy.

Direct Foreign Investment

On 1 January 1967, Indonesia took one of its most important steps in building a modern economy: it enacted far-reaching new laws governing foreign and domestic investment. For the first time, Indonesia introduced a body of law that clearly articulated the rights and restrictions on foreign investment, while also providing investors with the protection they needed to invest with security. Among other things, these laws guaranteed foreign investments would not be nationalized without appropriate compensation. The importance in the law was as much in its symbolism as its legal weight. As proof of the country's sincerity, a group of foreign firms that had previously been nationalized were returned to their former owners. In

other instances, the owners of nationalized firms were given financial compensation. The message: after an extended period of economic xenophobia
under the Old Order government, Indonesia openly welcomed active participation in its economy by foreign as well as domestic investors.
Moreover, this message was law. The results were striking. No sooner was
the new law inaugurated than in April 1967 the American company
Freeport Sulfur committed $75 million to explore and mine copper in
Irian Jaya. A steady and unprecedented stream of investment began to
flow into the country. The procession of investors was initially led by the
Americans, but before long, the Japanese seized the lead.[9] The changes
spoke volumes about enormous economic potential that had been stymied
under the heavy clouds of prolonged political turbulence. During the six
years from 1967 to 1972, Indonesia's Badan Koordinasi Penanaman
Modal (BKPM or Investment Co-ordinating Board) approved $2.3 bil-
lion in foreign investment. Domestic investment showed a comparable
expansion, with over Rp 667 billion approved between November 1969
and January 1972. The data are not available to make meaningful comparisons with pre-New Order years, but there is no doubt that the increase
was tremendous.

With its early concentration of investment in the textile sector,
Indonesia followed a pattern that has been typical of many countries in
the early stages of industrial development. Indeed, the rise of this sector
served as a microcosm of Indonesia's early stages of industrial development. At the outset of the New Order, the textile industry was suffering
from extreme underutilization. The fledgling industry was in decline
because consumers were too impoverished to buy clothes. Moreover, manufacturers could not obtain the foreign exchange needed to import
machinery or yarn. When the industry started to take off in the early
1970s, the growth was spectacular. Not only was there an explosion in
new investment, but existing factories that had been idled were suddenly
operating at capacity, and owners took steps to expand output. Several factors contributed to the growth, such as availability of credit and foreign
exchange, infrastructure development, and the contribution of well-
targeted foreign aid, such as US PL 480 yarns that were used to get stalled
factories up and running. Textile production grew from 317 million
metres in 1968 to 816 million metres in 1972. The growth in this industry was illustrative of the pent-up demand in the Indonesian market and
entrepreneurial capacity that was eager to respond if given the opportunity.

Industrial growth was not confined to the textile industry. From the
launching of the investment laws in 1967 to the end of 1973, output in
the manufacturing sector grew by 62 per cent. Largely, the growth in this
sector reflected the guidelines of Repelita I. In keeping with the import

substitution orientation of this period, most of the investment was geared toward satisfying local demand for consumer goods. Domestic investment tended to be in more labour-intensive enterprises than was seen in foreign investment, but both provided employment, albeit on a much smaller scale than agriculture.

Converging Difficulties in the Early Stages of Industrialization

During the 1970s, Indonesia laid the groundwork for the transition from an agrarian economy to industrialization. It was not an easy transition. Many forces converged to make this a difficult period, not so much in terms of meeting growth targets, but in terms of finding an acceptable means to accommodate the nation's rapid economic development with many converging and often conflicting political and emotional forces. Some of the problems Indonesia faced were unexpected and unique to the country and the times. Others were almost predictable for a country making the transition from a very low level of economic development to one in the early stages of industrialization. The most unexpected and important influence on Indonesia's development during this period was the surge in oil wealth, which permitted the country to accelerate its industrial expansion. That same oil boom sparked a protracted recession among the industrialized countries. The recession dampened the flows of both international trade and investment. More countries adopted increasingly protectionist policies, a trend that hurt Indonesia. Worldwide transnational investment flows slowed, and Indonesia was among those who lost out.

Domestically, however, Indonesia found itself at a different kind of crossroad. In the early to mid-1970s, the trauma of the stabilization period was receding and optimism, self-confidence, and a desire for self-determination were emerging in the national mood. Oil prices began to soar in 1973 and suddenly Indonesians began to give vent to a side of nationalism that previously lay dormant, just below the surface. It was suddenly commonplace to ask the question openly, 'Would it not be better to build our country by ourselves, rather than depending on foreign investment?' As with most countries that made the transition from colony-status to independence, many Indonesians regarded the country's newly emerging wealth as the best opportunity to assert greater autarky.

On 29 December 1973, the Indonesian newspaper *Kompas* published an article entitled, 'The Economy in 1973: Teetering Between Brightness and Gloom'. On the subject of investment the article stated:

The issue has been further complicated by the *pribumi*–non-*pribumi* problem.... Foreign capital is being attacked mainly because of the rapid growth of Japanese capital and Japanese domination of the markets, which can be seen every day.

Some groups in society do not approve of the influx of foreign capital and want to see this current reduced. However, the government, which has promised facilities and peaceful working conditions to foreign capital in order to promote the domestic economy, cannot agree with this view.

Speaking in a similar vein several months later, Mohammad Sadli (1974: 18), the first Chairman of BKPM, stated:

In the mind of the political public in Jakarta, the honeymoon with foreign invest-ment and foreign aid is apparently over. The economic progress of the last five years has produced the not so palatable social by-product of conspicuous con-sumption, a widening gap between the rich and poor, charges of corruption, etc. Since foreign aid and foreign investment have been important elements in the policies of the government, these are now blamed for accentuating the distortions. The criticism is unfair but the mood is there ... [and] the mood in Jakarta is also present in other capital cities in Asia.

Within a few weeks of this statement, the government decreed the follow-ing changes in economic policy:[10]

1. All foreign investment had to be in the form of joint ventures with *pribumi* partners;

2. Foreign investors were required to transfer 51 per cent of project equity to Indonesian partners within ten years;

3. Where the Indonesian partner is not *pribumi*, the 51 per cent of local equity should be achieved through the stock market with at least 50 per cent of the shares sold to *pribumi*;

4. To protect existing investments, a large number of sectors were closed to new investment;

5. State banks were instructed to limit their investment loans to *pribumi* only.

The general objective of these policies was summed up in the term 'Indonesianization', which suggested the progressive increase in participa-tion of indigenous Indonesians in all aspects of the economy and particu-larly in business.

To understand why the government decided to implement heavily interventionist policies, it is important to consider the broader political conditions of the moment. As with virtually all important issues of this period, oil money played a leading role. In 1974, Indonesian economic nationalism was particularly strong. Backed by a thousand oil wells, these policies seem unassailable. The 'bottom line' was Indonesia felt it could afford a decline in foreign investment since oil provided a comfortable cushion to keep the overall economy buoyant and strong.

Economists and political scientists could spend decades debating the pros and cons of Indonesia's policies and the influence of the global economy on Indonesia's internal policies. Investors, however, vote with their feet and many of the foreign investors in Indonesia at that time did precisely that: they chose to walk. Some scaled back or shut down their operations. Some removed their money from Indonesian banks. There was a sudden and marked decline in the stream of new foreign investment. Total foreign investment approvals dropped from $1.76 billion in 1975 to $449 million in 1976. A *Wall Street Journal* article pointed out that if the investment from the Asahan aluminum smelting project was excluded, investment approvals fell 61 per cent in 1975–9 from the 1970–4 period (Lachica, 1981). Commenting on the trend, the *Far Eastern Economic Review* quoted a report from an unidentified Western embassy in Jakarta: 'Facing most new investments are high and rising costs, increased bureaucratic hazards, and continuing uncertainties about investment groundrules and taxation policies, which have all become more important during 1974. Most evident has been the emergence of economic nationalism as perhaps the dominant force shaping government investment policies, overshadowing somewhat the pragmatic philosophy of 1967–73' (Coggin, 1975). This trend was particularly disturbing because investment was not keeping pace with the growing economy or the expanding workforce. The high oil prices did not last forever and by the early 1980s, the boom was over. Indonesia could no longer count on easy oil money to finance its economic growth. Without the buffer of oil money, the country could no longer afford to have an investment climate that was significantly less attractive than many other developing countries competing for the same investment funds. To regain its competitiveness as a site for foreign investment, the economy, and investment policies in general, would have to be completely overhauled.

TRADE, INDUSTRY, AND FINANCE: THE DEVELOPMENT TROIKA

Industry, trade, and finance are a tightly linked 'troika' in the development process. The three depend on each other, with trade acting as the bridge to the external economy. The link between industry and trade is obvious. Industry depends on trade for commercial viability and without industry, trade will be confined to the highly volatile trade in commodities. Equally important, but less direct, is the link between finance (or monetary policy) and trade. The availability of foreign exchange through the banking system and the management of the exchange rate are two of the most important factors in determining a country's ability to operate in international markets. Trade, therefore, depends above all on three things: first, having goods or services to sell (for the Indonesian government, the domain of the Ministry of Industry); second, a trade regime that is conducive to trade (the domain of the Ministry of Trade); and third, available foreign exchange reserves as a medium of exchange and an exchange rate that does not add undue distortions to the trading process (the domain of the Ministry of Finance and the central bank). From the early 1970s until the mid-1980s, Indonesia's trade policy attempted to manage a difficult balancing act between the country's industrial and monetary policies and volatile world markets gyrating under recession and highly unstable money markets.

Although Indonesia's early industrial policy favoured import substitution, the government tried to find an acceptable compromise between import substitution to conserve foreign exchange, and export promotion to generate foreign exchange. Indeed, Repelita I states: 'Our supply of foreign exchange at this moment is precarious. . . . This makes it imperative to exert all efforts to alleviate the burden through investments that yield foreign currency and attempts to use foreign currency efficiently. Thus the promotion of exports and import substitution are emphasized' (Department of Information, 1969 : Vol. 1, p. 14). Repelita I also stated that priority will be given to investment in export-oriented industries based on their productivity and foreign exchange earning potential. This was a challenging task. In 1969, after a decade of decline, Indonesia's exports were only just approaching the levels achieved in 1957. During the intervening twelve years, however, the population had grown by 29 per cent. Indonesia was in the initial stages of recovery from a prolonged period in which trade had atrophied.

Trade policy was formulated to a large extent to support industrial objectives. The 1970s was a period of considerable growth in Indonesia's industry. Measured in constant 1973 rupiah, Indonesia's industry in 1969 comprised 8.8 per cent of the country's GDP. By 1983, industry's share of the GDP had nearly doubled, rising to 15.1 per cent. This happened while the economy was expanding rapidly. That growth, however, did not come unencumbered. With every new factory, every new mill, and every new workshop, a new voice was added to the chorus demanding protection from cheaper imports. As industry grew, so did the pressure for protection. Every sector potentially affected by imports vigorously campaigned for the strong protection. Their arguments were vociferous and persuasive. The following summarizes some of the arguments advanced by specific interest groups:

1. *State-owned Enterprises and Government Ministries.* With the increase in oil revenues, state-owned enterprises proliferated. These enterprises were placed under the responsibility of the most relevant ministries. Suddenly,

a plethora of government ministries found themselves accountable for industrial enterprises. Government ministries, led by the Ministry of Industry, were suddenly transformed into a powerful force for lobbying for the special needs of these state enterprises. The state-owned enterprises frequently operated at a loss. Rather than this being a sign that the enterprise was in need of reform, the loss was used to justify continued protection.

2. *Indonesia's Infant Industries.* Indonesia's private sector urged the government to adopt strongly protective measures as a means to permit their young businesses to develop to a point where they would be better equipped to take on foreign industrial giants.

3. *Pribumis.* As latecomers to industry and commerce, indigenous Indonesians insisted they needed special assistance to help them catch up with their more established foreign and domestic competitors.

4. *Industries Small and Large.* Big domestic companies claimed that if not protected, they would be put out of business by foreign competitors. The small-scale industries were concentrated in labour-intensive sectors such as textile production and generally relied on simple technologies, such as hand looms and spinning-wheels. Representatives from these industries demanded preferential credits and subsidies, which in some cases were given as a way to ease the transition to more capital-intensive operations.

5. *Foreign Investors.* Some of the strongest pressure on the government came from foreign investors. Many of them were originally induced to invest in Indonesia with incentives such as tax holidays and preferential treatment regarding import and export controls. After building their operations in Indonesia, they often insisted that they could survive only if they were accorded protection from other possible entrants to the market.[11]

Protection came in two basic forms: trade restrictions that limited the influx of goods competitive with those produced domestically; and investment restrictions that limited competition to a select number of companies in a specific sector. Throughout the 1970s and early 1980s, trade and investment restrictions were broadly applied in Indonesia. BKPM routinely declared industries closed for further investment. Every year BKPM published its Daftar Skala Prioritas (DSP or investment priority list) in which it itemized those sectors open for domestic or foreign investment. Unless a sector was explicitly identified as open, it was closed by default. Industries such as pharmaceuticals, food processing, and aircraft assembly were made off limits for further investment. Foreigners were prohibited from engaging in trading and distribution services. The Ministry of Trade likewise introduced a host of regulations to limit competition. Such regulations were uniformly applauded by those receiving the protection and decried by those who were shut out.

A Step Backwards

As discussed in Chapter 4, Indonesia's exchange rate was set at Rp 415 to the dollar in August 1971 and remained at this level until November 1978. During this period, the average annual rate of inflation in Indonesia was 15.7 per cent. The rupiah grew grossly overvalued and this rendered Indonesia's exports less competitive.[12] Indonesia's overvalued exchange rate was a *de facto* trade policy, the gist of which was that Indonesia, at that time, gave higher priority to monetary stability than to trade development. Manufacturers or farmers had little incentive to gear their production toward the export market since there were little or no profits to be made.

With its oil-financed economic nationalism, from 1974 until 1978 Indonesia's trade, industry, investment, and financial policies all worked in harmony with each other—in an unholy alliance—to support the most inward looking economic policies in the history of the New Order. Indonesia's industrial and trade policies not only provided protection to inefficient businesses catering to the domestic market, the country's foreign investment policies discouraged all but the most determined new investors, and the country's exchange rate policy served as a disincentive to export. Oil was the sole important sector of the economy through which Indonesia had a relatively strong and balanced engagement with the international economy. In almost all other aspects, the country's policies were uncharacteristically inward looking. The economic pragmatism that was the hallmark of Indonesia's economic management was at its low point. When the oil money began to dry up, Indonesia was left with a weak base in export industries and underdeveloped trade relations with the rest of the world. It was at this point, in 1978, that the government took the decisive step and devalued the currency. Whatever shortcomings that policy may have had, the decision had the symbolic weight of signalling a change in outlook. Indonesia was endeavouring to return to a more outward looking philosophy.

It is important to emphasize that despite the difficulties during this period, Indonesia's non-oil exports did grow at a respectable pace. In 1974, Indonesia's non-oil exports were valued at $2.21 billion. By the time Indonesia devalued the rupiah in 1978, exports reached $3.66 billion. This represents an average increase of 13 per cent per year. During the same period, Indonesia's total imports increased from $3.84 billion to

$6.69 billion, an average of 15 per cent per year. According to a World Bank survey (1979: 24), the number of people engaged in the trade sector expanded from 4.7 million in 1971 to 7.1 million in 1976. Trade and industry grew considerably. The growth was imbalanced: Indonesia's exports were dominated by oil, and its imports grew faster than non-oil exports.

The second oil boom took place in 1979. Once again Indonesia was able to ride the wave of petroleum based wealth. However, the country entered the second boom with more understanding than the first. The economic planners in the early 1980s were laying the groundwork for the next major upheaval in the country's economic development, that is, managing the economy without the benefit of a booming oil sector.

ASSESSMENT AND LESSONS FROM THE EARLY YEARS OF INDONESIA'S INDUSTRIAL AND TRADE DEVELOPMENT

In 1969, the value of Indonesia's manufacturing output[13] was $1.42 billion and its non-oil exports were valued at $471 million. Fifteen years later at the end of the 1983, manufacturing had grown to $7.84 billion and non-oil exports had risen to $5.01 billion. On average manufacturing output rose at an annual rate of 13 per cent and non-oil exports rose by 18 per cent. Indonesia's growth in manufacturing and trade during this period was among the fastest in the world.[14] Of course, Indonesia began from such a low base for a country of its size, that rapid growth was necessary but insufficient. If the government had not adopted such inward looking policies during the 1974–8 period, the growth would have been more substantial. None the less, by any measure, the growth was impressive.

Indonesia's manufacturing was heavily concentrated in a few industries with rubber, coffee, and timber constituting 35.6 per cent of Indonesia's non-oil exports. This concentration revealed structural weaknesses in Indonesia's manufacturing and export sectors and a narrowness and vulnerability in the nation's economic development in general. The country's options were limited. A downturn in a sector or industry, recession abroad, or the imposition of a trade restriction could have grave consequences. During the 1970s, Indonesia's economy grew considerably, but there remained fundamental weaknesses both in terms of its manufacturing and export capacity.

In 1982, just over 10 per cent of Indonesia's work-force was in the industrial sector. By contrast, nearly 55 per cent worked in the agriculture sector. This concentration of the work-force in the agricultural sector was appropriate for Indonesia's economy at that stage of development.

Indonesia's development policies had been built on a principle of 'agriculture first'. This strategy created a situation that permitted most Indonesians to find work in the countryside while the industrial base was gradually expanded. With the building of new workshops, factories, and other industrial workplaces, there was an ample supply of labour that could be drawn from the cottage industry sector as well as from the landless agrarian labour force. In the meantime, however, agriculture continued to be the steadiest source of employment even as the labour force increased.

During the 1970s and early 1980s, Indonesia's industrial and trade strategy evolved gradually. This was Indonesia's period of apprenticeship, the origin of an industrial economy that was still more than a decade away. Some of the salient lessons of the period were as follows:

1. *Industrial Incubation and the Dangers of Benign Protectionism.* The desire to protect and cultivate infant industries is not entirely without merit, but easily misdirected. Protection frequently weakens the industries that are the intended beneficiaries. This should not be construed to mean that there is no effective method for a government to assist young companies. In the industrialized countries, a similar function is achieved through venture capital, government research grants, and defence contracts. Many of today's wealthiest countries have elaborate and sophisticated industrial policies that channel billions of dollars to local businesses. Developing countries do not have the resources to finance such programmes. What they can do, however, is to try to create an environment that is conducive to growth for young industries. The *easiest*—though probably not the best—way to achieve this is by offering protection to 'infant industry' since this approach requires no capital expenditure from the government. Indonesia's experience with this, however, has been mixed at best and generally negative. The most frequently cited criticism of this approach to industrial development is that infant industries become so dependent on protection, they are ready for retirement before they can stand on their own two feet. Protectionism hinders competition; consumer choice is reduced; prices rise; and in the end, the consumer bears the burden of inflated costs and poor quality. None the less, there are numerous examples where industries have grown to be strong competitors under the umbrella of protectionism. In Indonesia, Krakatau Steel is one such example. The company was given many years of protection, but today, it is competitive and profitable in international markets.[15]

Indonesia's efforts to cultivate infant industries probably would have been more successful and less burdensome to consumers if the government had confined its assistance to certain tax exemptions and in some instances, grants to young or pioneering enterprises. Perhaps the only way for protection to work successfully is if the government tells the protected industries exactly how long that protection will last. After the period is over, the protection should be removed with no exceptions. Otherwise, protectionism fosters dependency and inefficiency, and the entire economy suffers.

2. *Protectionism is Habit Forming*. Protectionism has a way of spreading gradually and accumulating over time. Once a protectionist policy is implemented, the protected industries will fiercely oppose its removal. Furthermore, representatives from other industries will clamour for similar levels of protection. The situation is reinforced when one's trading partners also engage in protectionism. Protectionism then tends to beget protectionism. Once protectionist policies are adopted, new layers of protectionism are added one on top of the other. Over time, the economy becomes increasingly distorted as protectionism grows. With every layer of protectionism, the level of dependence deepens. It takes little effort to implement a new protectionist policy. It takes colossal strength, however, to remove protectionist policies.

3. *The Need for a Realistic Exchange Rate*. In the 1970s, Indonesia operated under the assumption that it could afford to maintain an unrealistic exchange rate. Year after year, total exports exceeded imports. The Indonesian economy was running with the steroids of oil money. If oil and gas were removed from the calculations, Indonesia's trade deficit actually grew from $325 million in 1969 to over $9.36 billion in 1982.

In 1972, Indonesia removed all restrictions on the movement of foreign exchange. Since then, people have been free to move money in and out of the country without restrictions. This daring policy was more liberal than many of the world's richest countries. The policy gave foreign investors the confidence that they would be able to repatriate profits. Local depositors were assured that they had control over their money, and therefore, there was no need to hold funds offshore. This policy was deficient, however, so long as the rupiah was maintained at a fixed exchange rate. The fixed exchange rate provided the illusion of monetary stability. In reality, the rupiah was losing value because of high inflation, and the country's exporters had to suffer the consequences. It would not be until 1986 when Indonesia would move to a floating exchange rate. By this time, it was clear that a floating rate was essential for the maintenance of a healthy trade regime. The difficulty caused by an unrealistic exchange rate was probably—after the Pertamina affair—Indonesia's most costly and valuable economic lesson of the 1970s.

4. *Early Efforts to Assist the Economically Weak Groups*. The government's Indonesianization policies were among the most difficult policies to administer effectively. Governments in many countries have developed

programmes aimed at assisting the economically disadvantaged. Whenever there is an extreme concentration of wealth within a few distinct groups in any society, the inequality can cause tensions that can polarize the society and sometimes even erupt in violence. It was the government's duty to ensure that all Indonesians received equal rights and protection under the law. None the less, the government also had a duty to try to promote economic equity without stifling economic development. The modifications in investment policy enacted in the 1970s were an effort to correct specific perceived imbalances in Indonesia's economy. Unfortunately, the government faced a major difficulty in reconciling the national objective for rapid development with the relatively slow process of cultivating a strong class of indigenous entrepreneurs. Ultimately, Indonesia found no satisfactory solution and no consensus has been reached on this subject. However, short of an 'ultimate solution', the most practical and least divisive approach to promoting equity may be to provide the business community with indirect support through a sound educational system for Indonesian youths and a pro-business economic environment. Such policies require long-term patience and a sincere commitment to achieving a level playing field. Such methods may prove to be the most effective and enduring.

5. *Redefining State-owned Enterprises*. Over the years, the Indonesian government has invested heavily in state-owned enterprises. In too many instances, these enterprises have suffered from inefficiency and a lack of management expertise. The results have been a state-enterprise sector, which, rather than adding to the nation's wealth, has been a drain on government finances.[16] It would be preferable to apply provisions to state-owned enterprises similar to those recommended for 'infant industries'. Namely, a strict limit should be placed on the time during which trade protection or subsidies are offered. When this period is over, the protection should be removed no matter what. If the enterprises cannot survive, they should either be sold to the private sector or shut down. Alternatively, those with market potential could be listed on the stock exchange. Economist Arnold Harberger (1984: 434) provides the following comments on state-owned enterprises: 'Let the public and private sectors compete freely, under the same tax laws, the same regulations, and the same rules. And ... if the public-sector enterprise cannot compete (a) let it go under, (b) bail it out by just enough to keep it alive, but (c) never let it out-compete legitimate private enterprises simply by undercutting prices and making losses that are financed out of the public treasury.' These are sound recommendations.

6. *Fostering Industrial Development*. Indonesia must continue to dedicate its efforts and resources to industrial development. In so doing, the country

would do well to consider what lessons from its successful agricultural programme could be applied to industry. A country in its early stages of development may be able to apply creative approaches to industrial development without involving direct state intervention in the market. For example, as mentioned, Indonesia's cottage and small-scale industry sectors were—and continue to be—extremely large. The small credit programmes were examples of positive measures to develop small-scale industries. Despite the problem loans, these programmes helped foster entrepreneurship and raise the level of sophistication at the entry level of the industrial chain. The loans were an important step in creating a wide and diversified industrial base. To help this process of spreading industrial diversification, the time may be ripe for the government to consider the creation of the industrial equivalent of agricultural extension services. There are many potential programmes that could be considered, from providing instruction to small-scale and cottage industries on how to improve their capital investments, how to manage money and personnel, and how to apply new technologies in small-scale industries. These services might accelerate the transition from cottage and small-scale industries to medium and large-scale industries and in the process deepen the class of Indonesian entrepreneurs.

7. *Recognizing When the Usefulness of an Economic Strategy Has Ended.* During the late 1960s and early 1970s, the selective credit programme was one of the government's most effective tools for channelling scarce financial resources to projects that promised to deliver the maximum benefit. During the 1970s, Indonesia was still employing the selective credit policy. However, by the mid-1970s, the market had already become sufficiently complex and the banking system sufficiently sophisticated, that this form of credit management was no longer appropriate. The government was slow to recognize this change and continued to manipulate the credit market longer than was needed. This is a typical example of the kind of problems that can arise when a government holds on for too long to a successful intervention. Successful policymaking requires that governments know when to retire policies that have outlived their usefulness. One of the dangers in developmental economics is keeping policies in place too long due to bureaucratic inertia.

In many ways, the period from 1969 to 1983—the consolidation period in Indonesia's economic development—was one of the nation's periods of greatest struggle, particularly in the field of trade and industrial development. These sectors grew at impressive rates. However, growth statistics only tell a small part of the story. This was a period of deep economic 'soul-searching' for Indonesia. The country's economic planners struggled to keep up the momentum of economic development while balancing caution with innovation, and inward looking policies with outward look-ing policies. They moved with the flow of domestic politics, and when the country was ready, they guided the economy back to more market oriented policies. Indonesia created the economic foundation that would permit the future transformation of the economy. In the process, Indonesia's eco-nomic planners were given a wealth of experience that confirmed the value of economic pragmatism based on sound macroeconomic principles. During the 1970s, Indonesia made great progress in its efforts to develop as an industrial and trading nation. The long journey had just begun. The stage was set, however, for the next revolution in Indonesia's economic development, the period of deregulation, which took place in the 1980s.

1. According to McCawley (1981: 62–3), Burma was perhaps the only Asian country that was less industrialized than Indonesia. The countries of Indo-China were not included in this study.

2. Throughout this chapter, the term 'industrial sector' refers to light and heavy indus-try. While the petroleum and other extractive industries are included in formal definitions of industry, unless specified, the focus of this chapter is on industrial development outside the extractive industries.

3. Definitions of industrialization are based on those used by the Central Bureau of Statistics. The old and new definitions for industrial classifications are as follows:

Old and New Definitions of Industrial Establishments

	Old Definition	New Definition
Large-scale	100 or more employees without power, or 50 or more with power	100 or more employees
Medium-scale	10–99 employees without power, or 5–49 with power	20–99 employees
Small-scale	1–4 employees with power, or 1–9 employees without power	5–19 employees
Cottage	Establishment without paid workers	Establishment with less than 5 workers (including unpaid workers)

Sources: These definitions appear in various issues of the Central Bureau of Statistics' *Statistik Industri*.

4. In the early 1970s, Widjojo, officials from Bulog and the Ministry of Trade, and I visited the Governor of East Java. For some time, the local government had tried to restrict the sale of rice leaving the province. His motivation was to ensure that there were adequate supplies of rice for his constituency. During a meeting we pressed the Governor on this, noting that if we used the same logic each province should establish its own army, Indonesians should use visas to travel from one province to another, and other provinces should also place trade restrictions on goods to East Java. This would certainly lead to the

dissolution of the nation. After extensive discussions, he agreed that his policy was, in effect, creating a separate republic within Indonesia and this was untenable if we wanted the country to grow in strength and stability. The restrictions were removed and during this period, the government managed to eliminate most of the tariffs, quotas, and other types of barriers to the free flow of goods among provinces.

5. As will be discussed in Chapter 10, the sequence of Indonesia's deregulation was the reverse of most countries. Starting in the early 1970s, Indonesia deregulated the capital account, thereby allowing foreign exchange to enter and exit the country without government restrictions. The problem, of course, was that Indonesia's foreign exchange reserves were very limited. To preserve adequate levels of foreign exchange reserves, rather than impose direct controls on the movement of foreign exchange itself, Indonesia instead tried to restrict, or at least influence, the purchase of imports.

6. See Myint (1971) who places Indonesia along with Burma as examples of the most inward looking countries in Asia during the 1950s to mid-1960s.

7. During the 1970s, Indonesia was fortunate due to the oil boom to be able to expand its industrial capacity. Then, from the mid-1980, with its deregulation policy the country's policies became very outward looking.

8. For more on this subject, see the discussion in Paauw and Fei (1973).

9. Among the many investors in Indonesia, the Japanese investors tended to take a long-term view. After so many years, Japan remains the largest investor in Indonesia. Freeport, the original investor, has also remained in Indonesia and has greatly expanded its operations over the years.

10. For a thorough review of these policies, see the 'Resolution of the National Economic Stabilization Board (Dewan Stabilisasi Ekonomi Nasional)' of 22 January 1974 and the presidential directives of 21 September 1974.

11. The early foreign investors in Indonesia insisted on a tax holiday, exemption from import duties, and protection from foreign and domestic competition. In 1983, while I was Minister of Finance, over the vehement objections of the foreign investment community, the government rescinded the tax holiday and other forms of protection for foreign investments. Instead, we offered incentives to encourage exports (for example, exemption from import duties to manufacturers producing entirely for export) and an investment climate that was decidedly pro-business. The results, as will be discussed in Chapter 8, were generally positive. For more on financial reform, see Chapter 9.

12. For readers who are not familiar with these ideas let me offer a simplified illustration: First, let us assume that we are living in a world with only two currencies, the rupiah and the dollar. Imagine that the current exchange rate is Rp 100 to $1.00. Let us suppose that this exchange rate was fixed five years ago in Year 1 and that during this period the domestic rate of inflation has been running at about 11 per cent per year, whereas the dollar has experienced zero inflation during this period. If the two currencies had been allowed to float freely, after five years of inflation, the exchange rate would be roughly Rp 150 to $1.00. (Of course, in reality, there are other factors influencing an exchange rate other than inflation but in this simplified case let us limit the factors determining exchange equilibrium to inflation.) If the government kept the exchange rate at Rp 100 to US$1.00, we could say that there is a 50 per cent gap between the 'natural exchange rate' and the official exchange rate.

Let us now assume that in this model many countries produce and sell rubber, and therefore, Indonesia cannot be a 'price maker'. It is a 'price taker'. If the international price for rubber has stayed constant for the last five years at $4.00 for one unit, this would mean that an Indonesian farmer would get Rp 400 for his unit of rubber. Five years ago, when the natural exchange rate and actual exchange rate were the same, the Rp 400 may have been fine compensation for the farmer. In the last five years, however, inflation has eroded 50 per cent of the value of the rupiah. To get an equivalent value for the unit of rubber the farmer needs to obtain Rp 400 $\times$ 1.5 = Rp 600 (where the 1.5 represents the adjustment for inflation). In other words, the Indonesian farmer needs to get $6.00 for a unit of rubber not $4.00. Since the Indonesian farmer cannot set international prices, he must accept the $4.00, although it means he will get little or no profit from the sale. Alternatively, he could ask for a higher price, say $5.00 or $6.00 for his rubber. Yet, there is no incentive for international buyers to pay more than the $4.00 per unit since there are other producers who are willing to sell for $4.00. If the Indonesian farmer asks for more than $4.00 per unit, he will find it difficult to sell his product. In either case, the overvalued currency serves as strong disincentive to the farmer to engage in the export market.

13. In constant 1987 US dollar prices.

14. According to the World Bank, only South Korea and Singapore grew faster than Indonesia. Taiwan and Hong Kong are not included in these statistics, and they probably also grew faster than Indonesia. Still that would mean that during the period under question, Indonesia was within the top five countries in terms of growth in manufacturing development. This accomplishment is particularly noteworthy when the size and diversity of Indonesia are taken into account.

15. Krakatau Steel was transformed from a heavily subsidized state-owned enterprise to a profitable firm about to be privatized. The key to the transformation was the restructuring of the company's capital and management. When these changes were made, the market was opened for competition and Krakatau Steel showed it could stand on its own feet. For more on Krakatau Steel see the discussion in Chapter 10.

16. For a discussion of the privatization of Indonesia's state-owned enterprises, see Pangestu (1996).

7
Social Infrastructure: Indonesia's Quiet Cultural Revolution

ONE of the risks facing economic planners is to confuse 'development' with an increase in gross domestic product (GDP), per capita income, or such things as the number of kilometres of roads constructed or kilowatts of power generated. These are very important, of course, but they are analogous to structure without content. They are like houses without families or cities without community. Development is most easily described, understood, and evaluated in terms of the measurable components of an economy. In this way, economic development is amenable to the same empirical scrutiny as any other branch of economics. Yet, despite the fundamental importance of numerical analysis, economic development must continually go a step further to address issues pertaining to the quality of life. Economic development should respond to the essential question, *'How can we make life better?'* Put another way, in the attempt to promote development, if economists and planners confine their focus strictly to the 'hard' data of macroeconomics—changes in GDP or inflation rates, for example—the analysis will be so sterile that it will miss the essential human dimension of economic development. As a result, any ensuing policies will risk being fundamentally flawed.

It is the concern with quality of life that leads development economists to focus on what is called 'social infrastructure'. While 'physical infrastructure' consists of the material facilities needed for an economy to function, such as roads, bridges, and electricity, 'social infrastructure' refers to the essential social services including education, health care, family planning, and the provision of clean water, that are equally needed for a well-functioning community. Since the beginning of the New Order, Indonesia's policymakers have been acutely aware of the critical importance of social infrastructure to the nation's economic development. This chapter will focus on three aspects of this development that have been particularly important to Indonesia's development efforts: education, health care, and family planning.

In Chapter 3, we described the Development Trilogy—consisting of

Stability, Growth, and Equity—and explained that it has served as the guiding philosophy behind Indonesia's economic development efforts since the early days of the New Order. Economic stability was achieved during the stabilization period and has been maintained within reasonable margins ever since. Growth has also been a prominent characteristic of Indonesia's economic development, even during the turbulence of the oil decline in the mid-1980s. The third component—the pursuit of equitable economic development—has been a deep and abiding concern of the government. Although equity is difficult to measure, it has been a primary concern of the government in the formulation of many economic policies, and especially those concerned with social infrastructure. The purpose of equity within Indonesia's Development Trilogy is to ensure that the fruits of growth and stability are shared by all the nation, and particularly by those most in need.

From the beginning, the central problem Indonesia faced was poverty. The nation as a whole was poor. In these circumstances, the government did not have the means to finance welfare and social security programmes. Instead, it determined to concentrate its very limited resources in those areas where they were most urgently needed and where they promised the greatest economic return. In essence, the government applied the same strategy to social welfare as it did to other aspects of economic development: it focused on infrastructure development rather than consumption. By focusing on social infrastructure, the government hoped to respond to the most needy in ways that would permanently eradicate the root causes of poverty. This goal was sound. Behind this seemingly simple idea, however, was a radical assumption. The economic team held that Indonesia's poverty could not be eliminated simply by providing people with food, clothing, or even an increase in their disposable income. To spread the benefits of economic development to all segments of society, the government had to direct its attention to economic factors as well as to cultural factors that had a significant impact on the economy. Customs and conventions that made sense when Indonesia's economy was at a subsistence level could be impediments to the development of a modern economy. In other words, to reduce poverty and to increase equity, some of the everyday practices that for centuries had served Indonesians well had to give way to new ways suitable for a modern economy.

FINANCING CHANGE

As Indonesia began Repelita I in 1969, the urgent need for investment in social infrastructure was evident in countless examples of life made miserable through sickness, overcrowding, and ignorance. Despite the magnitude of Indonesia's need, the country's poverty was so deep that the government was forced to limit its efforts to the rehabilitation of existing facilities, including schools, hospitals, and health care facilities. From a total of just over Rp 1 trillion designated for the period, only about 9 per cent of the government's development fund for Repelita I were projected to be allocated to the three vital areas of education, health care, and family planning, with well over half going to education.

What was significant, however, is the manner in which Indonesia tried to maximize the impact of its investment and the extent to which the government increased social infrastructure spending as its income increased with the oil boom. Once the government succeeded in bringing relative stability to the economy, it turned its attention to the development of the country's social infrastructure and increased social spending beyond the original estimates. Comparing Repelita I (1969/70–1973/4), Repelita II (1974/5–1978/9), and Repelita III (1979/80–1983/4), Indonesia's actual spending on education, health care, and family planning rose from 10.9 per cent of the development budget to 19.1 per cent. The strong commitment to social infrastructure development persisted even after the oil boom had faded (Table 7.1).

As part of the goal to achieve a more equitable distribution of income, in 1970 President Soeharto initiated the Inpres programme (Instruksi Presiden, that is, 'Presidential Instruction') as a way of allocating additional funds to lower levels of government primarily for use in physical and social infrastructure projects. When the programme began, a total of Rp 4.6 billion was allocated for rural infrastructure development. The allocations grew in step with Indonesia's increase in oil revenues, peaking in 1983/84 with an allocation of Rp 1.4 trillion, comprising some 14 per cent of the development budget.[1] Inpres funds were disbursed in two ways: first, general Inpres funds were transferred directly to the three tiers of local government—the province, the district, and the subdistrict—and applied to projects identified locally as deserving priority; second, sectoral

TABLE 7.1

Government Expenditure on Education, Health Care, and Family Planning, Repelita I–III (Rp billion)

	Repelita I	Repelita II	Repelita III
Education	77.7	672.9	3,757.1
Health Care and Family Planning	25.0	205.3	1,061.4
Total Expenditure	944.6	5,960.6	25,272.2
Percentage of Development Budget	10.9	14.7	19.1

Source: *Lampiran Pidato Presiden/Mandataris MPR RI*, various years.

Inpres funds were allocated by the central government in the areas of health care, school development, road construction, reforestation and regreening, and market development. Some characteristics of the Inpres programme are as follows:

- Inpres programmes tended to be labour-intensive. This was particularly true of the rural infrastructure programmes;
- Inpres programmes were often used to help stabilize rural incomes by providing work and income in periods of low farm activity. Furthermore, over the long-term, Inpres programmes have been maintained at fairly constant levels even in periods of economic downturn;
- Inpres programmes have been aimed at equalizing development throughout the country, especially those areas that are least developed and most needy;
- The Inpres programmes were highly decentralized in that the way in which the Inpres funds were used was largely determined at the local level.

Of all the sectors that have received Inpres support, none benefited more dramatically than education.

HUMAN DEVELOPMENT THROUGH EDUCATION

Sound economic development requires growth across the spectrum of economic activities that together comprise the total economy. In the development process, however, a special position is reserved for education. Education is a country's investment in its children who, more than any anything else, are the future of a nation. Sustainable development requires a population with the skills to thrive in a complex and rigorous international market-place. Without a sound educational system, Indonesia could not hope to create a modern economy. The nation's workers would remain confined to unskilled labour, and farmers would have no alternative but to practice traditional agrarian methods. Economic progress would be all but impossible.

Background

Article 31 of Indonesia's 1945 Constitution guarantees all Indonesians the right to an education. This Article represented a noble sentiment, but the country had no way of fulfilling the duties it implied. The declaration in the Constitution represented, above all, the country's aspiration and a formal recognition of the vital importance of education to the nation's development. This constitutional clause set a legal and moral standard against which future governments and leaders would be judged. Living up to this proviso would be one of Indonesia's greatest challenges, and one it would approach in stages, over several decades.

One of the unfortunate characteristics of Indonesian society under colonial rule was that only a very small minority of children, usually in urban areas, received any formal academic training. According to a study by Ruth Daroesman (1971), under Dutch rule, there were only about 806,000 Indonesian students enrolled in three-year primary schools. Until the 1970s, the typical education of Indonesian children consisted of learning the trades, customs, and wisdom of their parents. This was applied to traditional farming and the management of household affairs. Some youths trained with local experts in fields such as carpentry, dance, the production of medicines, midwifery, and spiritual practices. This lifestyle did not require a formal education, and from the agrarian social perspective, the time children spent in school deprived parents of one of the principal benefits of having a child—to help with the work at home or on the farm.

When the New Order came to power in the mid-1960s, the nation's school system was in disarray. First, a very high percentage of students withdrew from school before finishing. According to Repelita I, less than 50 per cent of the children who entered primary schools finished all six grades. While there were 3.2 million students in the first year of primary school in 1967, there were only 978,000 in the sixth. The performance at higher levels was even more dismal. Not only were students leaving schools prematurely, but instruction was substandard. Again, according to Repelita I, 24 per cent of the teachers in the primary school were unqualified to teach and more than 54 per cent were only partly qualified (Department of Information, 1969: Vol. 2C, pp. 11–12).

Finally, in every respect, finances were a problem. School buildings were in disrepair and the most basic supplies, such as chalk, paper, writing instruments, and books, were lacking. Because of funding constraints, teacher salaries were abysmally low, which usually forced teachers to hold a second and even a third job. Despite these deficiencies, in the early years of the New Order, because of the shortage in funds, the government instituted a hiring freeze on all civil servants and this applied to teachers as well. In light of these conditions, Bachtiar Rifai, the Director-General for Education, described Indonesia's educational system in 1971 as being in a state of crisis. The system, he said, was capable of accommodating only a small fraction of Indonesia's youths who should be eligible for schooling.[2]

Under these circumstances, public schools had no choice but to charge tuition and other fees to students. Often these fees were exorbitant by local standards. In her 1972 study, Daroesman (p. 67) reports, for example, that typical annual school fees could cost a parent as much as

Rp 15,000 per student. And in those rare instances when a child was sent to a school providing board or lodging, the costs roughly doubled. By comparison, the annual salary of a teacher at that time was approximately Rp 60,000. These fees were an enormous burden for most Indonesians, and this explains, in large part, why education was limited to such a small percentage of the population and why so many students withdrew from their studies before they were completed.

Educational Equity and Culture

Given Indonesia's extremely tight finances, the government had to address two fundamental questions: first, what is the purpose of education; and, second, what is the most effective and equitable way of delivering educational services to the people of Indonesia?

From the broad perspective of the government, through the Ministry of Education, the purpose of education was manifold, and included not only developing intellectual skills but also inculcating a sense of civic duty and devotion to God. For the economic team, there were very important economic implications to education. Education was needed to impart to students the ability to read, write, and perform basic arithmetic. Without these skills, participation in the modern economy is impossible. This was true not only for those working in business and industry, but even agriculture as well. Without these essential abilities, the employment opportunities of the illiterate were restricted to unskilled labour and traditional farming. Illiteracy consolidated underdevelopment, because without education, most Indonesians would find themselves unqualified for any but the most menial of work.

The equity implications of education go even deeper than access to employment. The illiterate and uneducated have very limited access to information sources. An illiterate farmer cannot read directions for the proper use of pesticides or fertilizers. An illiterate mother cannot read what is the proper dosage of medicines to give to her child. An illiterate man will always feel himself to be intellectually and socially inferior to his educated peers. The uneducated are cut off from a world of culture and information, and this reduces their options for personal fulfilment. The lack of education also produces a sinister economic by-product: the uneducated become locked into a class of the economically disadvantaged. In a modern society, the illiterate tend to be treated as the eternal outsiders with fewer rights, uncounted voices, and meager opportunities. The illiterate are those the information age left behind.

Indonesia's leadership recognized that the nation's long-term development required an aggressive attack on illiteracy and innumeracy. What was less clear was what strategy the government should adopt. Should the country, for example, concentrate its school construction programme in the urban areas and gradually spread to the rural areas, or should construction be spread broadly throughout the country? Some argued that an urban focus would be appropriate as this would allow the government to achieve economies of scale by building fewer but larger schools of better quality in the city. Urban youths, they suggested, needed education more than their counterparts in the rural areas since farm communities were better able to absorb uneducated workers than the cities. Furthermore, the logistics of constructing and staffing schools in remote regions across Indonesia's vast archipelago were formidable. Given the country's very tight financial resources, any attempt at universal education, even at the primary level, might result in a uniform level of inadequacy, benefiting no one. Another question was whether Indonesia's educational expansion should focus on primary school expansion or whether it might not be preferable to expand the secondary schools and institutions of higher education.

In 1973, the government decided to commit itself to the ambitious goal that would serve as one of the corner-stones of Indonesia's development policy: to make six years of primary education available for every child in Indonesia. This decision was based above all on equity considerations. Indonesia's planners recognized that primary school education would be insufficient for many. However, if the country did not commit itself to universal education, it would be then formally supporting the creation of a segmented society in which literacy—and the attendant economic benefits—would be determined by geography, gender, income group, or some other arbitrary criteria.

Indonesia did not suffer from lack of ambition or vision. As the country set out Repelita I, the government did, however, lack money. The oil boom changed this, and once the oil money started to flow into the government treasury, Indonesia undertook a massive programme of investment in education. In 1974, President Soeharto launched a programme of school construction and teacher training. The government informed selected villages throughout the country that if they would allocate the land, the government would finance the construction of the school on it. During Repelita II, ending in 1979, 25,000 schools were constructed. Villages were designated as sites for school construction based on demographic need. The objective was to spread the benefits of education widely, with special measures to compensate for some of the economic disadvantages in Indonesia's more remote areas. In addition to school construction, the government invested heavily to increase the number of teachers and improve the quality of instruction.

Between 1969 and 1984 the number of children enrolled in Indonesian schools rose from 16.8 million to 33.2 million. The number of books purchased rose from 57 million during Repelita I to 246 million in Repelita III. Training for teachers increased as did salaries and the number of institutes dedicated to teacher training. Since all public school teachers are government employees, the Ministry of Education grew to be the largest employer in the nation. Indeed, in 1986, the Ministry of Education employed 48 per cent of Indonesia's civil servants.[3]

On 2 May 1984, in the presence of 110,000 people, President Soeharto held a ceremony at the Senayan sports stadium in Jakarta. There he announced to the nation that after ten years of school construction, teacher training, textbook production, and community outreach programmes, the government had succeeded in reaching its goal—universal primary education had been achieved.[4] Henceforward, the President declared, there would be compulsory primary education for all Indonesians. Furthermore, the government decreed that thereafter the school entrance fee would be abolished. In so doing, the government eliminated the principal remaining financial obstacle to public education.

Through the achievement of universal primary education, Indonesia accomplished its first important goal in the development of the nation's educational system. This accomplishment was a landmark in the long effort to build the nation's educational infrastructure. This permitted the government to begin an effort to advance further the nation's educational system. Three years later, in 1987, the government announced its next educational challenge, and committed itself to achieving nine years of universal education instead of the six years that had previously been the standard.

Although there are many important implications of universal primary education, there is probably none more significant than the impact on illiteracy. The illiteracy rate is defined by the World Bank as the portion of the population 15 years of age or older who cannot read, comprehend, and write a short statement on everyday life. In 1971, 43 per cent of Indonesia's population was illiterate. In 1990 the number had dropped to 23 per cent. This is still high, but given that the statistic covers all people, aged 15 and above, it does demonstrate a very large order of improvement. Indonesia's youths are much better prepared today for the modern workplace than were their parents. This accomplishment was possible because the government concentrated its resources at the primary school level, rather than diffusely on all levels of education. When that was accomplished, the government wasted no time in setting a new goal for the country's educational system.

By providing Indonesia's youths with an education, they could develop the intellectual capacity to better participate in and benefit from the nation's economic development. Because educational opportunities were universal, that meant that no child was left out. This approach resulted in an educational system that permitted the entire nation to move forward together.

DEVELOPMENT AND PUBLIC HEALTH

During the turbulent 1960s, Indonesia's rudimentary health care services deteriorated rapidly. With the economy ravaged by hyperinflation, the nation's health care facilities had become almost completely dysfunctional. Staff could not be paid, medicines could not be bought, and the health of the nation was deteriorating. Yet, medicine and hospitals are very expensive and health care professionals were in short supply. In the medical faculty, fewer than 1 per cent of those who entered the programme completed their degree.[5] In planning the assault on poverty, Indonesia's economic team began their policy deliberations with the assumption that economic development could not proceed without addressing the nation's health care needs. The problem the team faced was to devise a system that could respond to such massive needs within the confines of a very small national budget and many competing demands.

In 1969, infant mortality in Indonesia was 132 per 1,000 live births, and average life expectancy for Indonesians was 47 years. The predominant causes of such abbreviated life spans were inadequate nutrition, poor hygiene, and untreated sickness. Diarrhoea was a frequent though often unreported killer of young children. In 1970 smallpox claimed 1,714 lives, and 97,814 people were infected with malaria. To combat this health scourge, Indonesia had a small, poorly trained, and underpaid corps of doctors and nurses. The average ratio of doctors to population was 1:23,000. In the rural areas, the ratio was closer to 1 to 100,000–120,000 versus 1 to 5,000–6,000 in the cities. By comparison, in the United States the ratio of doctors to population was 1:634. Indonesia's health care was poor even in comparison to other very poor developing countries. India's doctor to population ratio, for example, was 1:4,955, almost five times that of Indonesia.[6]

Indonesia's health crisis was chronic and pervasive. As Indonesia's government tried to devise methods to contend with the nation's health needs, it was faced with some of its most difficult policy questions. Should, for example, a government accept any role in the provision of health care services or could this be left to the private sector? If one accepts that the government should have a role, who then should be the recipients of health care services? With what aspects of health should a government concern itself? Should the government define health care broadly to include diet and fitness or should it restrict the definition narrowly, to include only life-threatening diseases and injuries? Should the government step in only in cases of disaster or should citizens look to the government to treat the common cold? These are among the most difficult questions a government can face—questions for which there is little consensus from one country to another. There were compelling reasons for government intervention in health care. A nation whose population is unhealthy and malnourished will find it difficult to work effectively. Sickness and premature death rob a society of its productivity and detract from its general well-being. When farmers, workers, and others are struggling under the burden of ill health, they are unable to effectively earn their own livelihood. However, besides economics, in matters of health care economic planners must face fundamental issues of equity. There is an indisputable link between wealth and health. In every country, the poor die younger than the rich. For many, especially the poor, government health services may make the difference between life and death. Indonesia's commitment to equity as an intrinsic part of the development process meant that the government accepted the obligation to intervene in this important economic and social issue.

Methods for Delivering Health Care Services to a Poor Nation

Indonesia's very limited financial resources required that the country approach the colossal problem of health care with realism and creativity. The government had to try to improve the nation's health overall, but especially among the poor who were suffering the most. The programmes the government devised were far from Utopian, but they represented a milestone among efforts to deliver health care services to the population of a large developing country.

Consistent with its strategy of coping with tight funding, during Repelita I, the government focused its efforts on rehabilitating existing health care facilities. This was essentially a period for assessment, organization, and regrouping of resources. When the government's financial resources grew in the mid-1970s, funding for health care grew in step. The essence of Indonesia's health care strategy rested on three simple ideas:

1. Since the majority of Indonesians lived in the countryside, the government chose to focus most of its health care efforts in the rural areas rather than in urban centres. The idea was to bring health care to the people, rather than have the people travel to seek health care services;

2. The government would maximize its resources by investing in sev-

eral low cost programmes that promoted health care rather than more sophisticated treatment facilities that relied on expensive medical technology and medicines;

3. Rather than focus on curative medicine, the efforts would emphasize preventive medicine that would help people avoid the causes of ill health. This approach relied heavily on educational services that sought to offer Indonesians new options for personal and family health maintenance.

The methodology for delivering on this strategy relied on three basic elements: better nutrition, improved sanitation, and popular participation in health care programmes.

Improved Nutrition

When Indonesia entered the 1970s, the population was widely undernourished. According to one study, in 1969, the average caloric intake of Indonesians was 2,132 per day—below the *minimum* recommended level of 2,169. The effort to improve nutrition was directly tied to the overall effort to achieve rice self-sufficiency and stable rice prices. The undernourishment most Indonesians experienced was a daily assault on their health. The simple act of getting more rice into Indonesian rice bowls may have been the most important factor in improving the country's health. Through Bulog, the Ministry of Agriculture, and a number of other supporting organizations, the government sought to deliver reasonably priced food in a steady and reliable manner. By 1983, Indonesia's average daily per capita consumption had risen to 2,565 calories and by 1996 it had reached 3,151.[7] When Indonesian consumers felt secure that food would be consistently available in sufficient quantities, they developed healthier diets and more rational consumption habits.

Besides deficiencies in carbohydrates, there were many other deficiencies in the Indonesian diet. Large numbers of Indonesians suffered from deficiencies in vitamins and minerals, such as vitamin A, iron, and iodine. Additionally, many women were endangering the health of their babies by switching from breast-feeding to bottle feeding under the mistaken belief that the latter was 'modern' and better. There was ample evidence that from both nutritional and hygienic perspectives, Indonesians babies fared much better when breast-fed.

The main but not sole method for combating these nutritional problems was through education and the provision of dietary supplements. The principal educators were volunteers and nurses and other health care professionals. Several organizations focused on promoting better nutrition among Indonesia's families. One of the most prominent was the

Pendidikan Kesejahtraan Keluarga (PKK or Family Welfare Movement). The PKK was begun in late 1967 by a small group of volunteer women who believed that ultimately a better society would result from securing the well-being of the family. The members of the PKK were women whose objective was to educate other women in several essential skills, including education, nutrition and health care, environmental preservation, and home economics. The PKK has grown to become one of the most important volunteer agencies in Indonesia with some 4 million members.[8] As will be discussed below, Indonesia developed a nation-wide network of health centres. These centres also served as meeting places at which the Ministry of Health frequently held seminars to explain to communities concepts pertaining to nutrition and health. During Repelita III, (1978/9–1983/4) the PKK joined the effort to promote better nutrition by organizing a programme called the Taman Gizi ('Nutrition Garden'; also referred to as 'Weighing Posts'). Mothers were asked to bring their children to the local health care facility. There the babies were weighed and when it was considered appropriate the nurse or nutritional expert supplied mothers with vitamins and dietary supplements intended to help the baby grow.[9]

In these ways—by providing access to basic foods at reasonable prices, educational programmes that drew on a huge corps of volunteers, baby weighing, and the provision of dietary supplements—the government was able to improve the nation's dietary practices, and this had a profound impact on improving the nation's health. With the extensive participation of volunteers and active community involvement, knowledge and information about nutrition spread rapidly and widely across the country and helped make better nutritional practices part of the daily life of most Indonesians.

Water and Sanitation

The second general area of endeavour in the nation's health care programme was improved water supply and sanitation. As with other aspects of Indonesia's social infrastructure, little funding was available for new investments until 1974 when appropriations were made through the Inpres programme. Clean water is one of the vital necessities for healthful living. This, regrettably, was in short supply for many Indonesians and had been at the source of many health problems. Since the founding of the New Order, the government has made considerable effort to improve access to clean water and to educate the communities on ecologically sound ways to manage personal hygiene.

In Indonesia, most villages are situated near rivers. The rivers served not only as sources of irrigation, but also as places for washing the body and clothes and in some cases, as a substitute for toilets. Besides being unhygienic, these practices polluted the rivers. In so doing, communities sometimes unwittingly harmed themselves and their downstream neighbours by contaminating the river and even the water-table from which they drew well water. The government worked with communities throughout Indonesia, both in the countryside and in the cities to encourage people to adopt hygienic practices that contribute to the health of the community. Although responsibility for water and sanitation generally falls under the provincial governments, the largest source of funding came from Inpres funding. Indonesia had programmes to improve water supply and sanitation in both the cities and the countryside. The most extensive services, however, were needed in Indonesia's rural villages. The government backed programmes for digging wells, supplying hand pumps, and even developing rain catchment facilities.

In the 1970s, the government launched a programme to construct public sanitation facilities. These facilities, known as MCK (which stand for Mandi, Cuci, Kakus, or bathing, cleaning, toilet), were multifunctional units constructed for collective use by the villages, usually in the rural areas. MCKs were also constructed for use in many of Indonesia's 'urban villages',[10] as well. Rather than using a river for these sanitation functions, the MCKs served the same purpose. At the MCK, members of the community could obtain water, bathe themselves, wash their clothes, and use the toilets. Subsidies and direct assistance were given to individuals to build MCKs by their homes. By the end of 1992, the PKK was credited with the construction of 673,000 MCKs in villages across the country.[11]

The government also taught villagers where to dig wells so that they could have access to relatively fresh water. Water would still need to be boiled before consumption, but otherwise it was potable. As more people in the cities obtained access to flush toilets and tap water for bathing and drinking, the use of the urban MCKs declined. For those who do not have access to flush toilets or tap water, however, the MCKs continue to serve a valuable function.

An important characteristic of these water and sanitation programmes— MCK construction programmes, distribution of hand pumps for water supply, and hygiene education—is that on a per capita basis these programmes reduced pollution and improved hygiene and health at minimal per unit cost. More progress is still needed. These developments, however, were an important initial step in creating a culture that responded to the need for maintaining personal hygiene in an environmentally sensitive manner.

Health Centres

In Indonesia, as everywhere, the most sophisticated health care facilities are the hospitals. Hospitals, however, are extremely costly to construct and equip. For this reason, most hospitals in Indonesia are usually located at the *kabupaten* level or in the provincial capitals. Due to high costs and shortages of specialized personnel, hospitals were generally reserved for serious medical matters. However, Indonesia's most noteworthy innovation in delivering health care services in the context of a developing economy was its system of community health centres. Three institutions were created to deliver health care services to all Indonesian citizens:[12]

1. Pusat Kesehatan Masyarakat (Puskesmas or the Community Health Centres), offer both curative and preventive medical treatments. They are staffed by a trained medical professional, usually a doctor or a nurse, while maternal care is supplied by midwives or nurses. The Puskesmas are located mostly at the *kecamatan* (subdistrict) level.

2. Puskesmas Pembantu (Auxiliary Puskesmas or Health Subcentres) are usually staffed with two to three employees, with a nurse being the primary health care provider. These centres provide curative as well as preventive medicine and place particularly strong emphasis on maternal and child health care. The health subcentres are located at the level of the *kecamatan* or *desa* (village).

3. Pos Pelayanan Terpadu (Posyandu or Integrated Health Service Posts), offer five basic services, namely: immunization; nutrition, education, and baby weighing; diarrhoeal disease control; family planning; and maternal and prenatal care. These centres are located in villages and towns. They do not have permanent staff. Instead, health care workers will travel to the villages periodically and hold group meetings and individual consultations. The Posyandu have fewer facilities than the Puskesmas and focus above all on preventive medicine and maternal and child health care. The Posyandu were set up at a very rapid pace in the 1980s, until before long one could be found in most of the *villages* and *towns* throughout the country. The PKK has been very active in helping to build and maintain the Posyandu network.

The initial thrust for Indonesia's health care programme came under the auspices of the Inpres programme. In 1974, Indonesia began an intensive programme of rehabilitating and building the Puskesmas. Every district received a per capita grant for the purchase of medicine with a minimum of Rp 5 million per *kabupaten* (Booth and Glassburner,

1975: 18). Throughout the 1980s, the government expanded the system to reach more of the population. What distinguished Indonesia's effort and what was most important to its accomplishments is that it brought the simplest and most widely needed services to the broadest population.

The policy to concentrate on simple and inexpensive community health centres rather than sophisticated and expensive hospitals and clinics was based on Indonesia's experience and logic. First, because Indonesia built many health centres, people did not need to travel far to use them.[13] Second, the centres placed a great deal of emphasis on preventive medicine; their objective was to try to help people avoid getting sick, rather than curing illness. Preventive medicine is much cheaper than curative medicine since it relies above all on education and the supply of nutritional supplements rather than hospitalization and treatment with expensive drugs. Lastly, although hospitals offered more comprehensive health care facilities, villagers were more comfortable using local health centres and drew on these services more readily than those of the hospitals.

By the end of Repelita III, Indonesia had constructed about 55,000 Puskesmas and Puskesmas Pembantu, among which some 5,700 were renovated. (A summary of the development of community health centres appears in Table 7.2.) During Repelita III, the government decided to expand those Puskesmas experiencing high patient volume. The size of the facilities was increased from 80 square metres to 135 square metres. Also, the government decided to provide housing for the attending physicians at the Puskesmas.

In 1978, the government launched a village outreach programme intended to supplement the standard services provided by the health care facilities. The scheme, which relied mostly upon primary health care nurses,

TABLE 7.2
Number of Community Health Centres in Indonesia, Repelita I–V

Community Health Centres	As at End of				
	Repelita I	Repelita II	Repelita III	Repelita IV	Repelita V
Construction					
Puskesmas	2,343	4,353	5,353	5,642	6,889
Puskesmas Pembantu		6,636	13,636	17,338	24,102
Posyandu			25,000	213,000	244,843
Rehabilitation					
Puskesmas		5	2,500	4,351	11,817
Puskesmas Pembantu		208	3,000	5,723	18,932
Total	2,343	11,202	49,489	246,054	306,583

Source: Lampiran Pidato Presiden/Mandataris MPR, various issues.

was called the Pelayanan Kesehatan Masuk Desa (PKMD or Village Community Health Development programme). The focus of these efforts was to intensify efforts to incorporate preventive medicine into the community life of the village. The PKMD evolved into one of the government's leading primary health care programmes by training health care workers at the village level to provide education on nutrition and illness treatment. The PKMD even helped devise local health insurance schemes.[14]

The government recognized the limitations of the community health centres and between 1973/4 and 1983/4 the government constructed nineteen new hospitals. The hospitals were intended to handle the more serious disorders from throughout the region. With the new hospitals, Indonesia had an average of 1 hospital bed for every 1,850 persons in 1985.[15] By international standards this is very low. By comparison, in 1980 the ratio for the United States was 1 bed for every 171 people. For Japan, the ratio was 1:89. Indonesia was in need of much more progress, but it was moving in the right direction. On the other hand, hospitals were intended as health service providers of last resort, with primary care coming from the community health centres. By the end of Repelita IV, the services of the Puskesmas and the Posyandus were available to almost all members of society. Starting in the mid-1980s, the private sector recognized the need for advanced health care facilities and has been very active in building hospitals (Table 7.3). This is important because it shows that medical services can also be provided effectively through private sector institutions. It also meant that the government's health care services increasingly went to meet the needs of the poor and less affluent Indonesians, while the wealthier Indonesians relied on private health care providers. In most respects, this has been a positive development in that it allows the government-provided services to be drawn on most heavily by those who were least able to pay for them.

TABLE 7.3
Number of Hospitals and Hospital Beds, Repelita I–V

	Repelita I	Repelita II	Repelita III	Repelita IV	Repelita V
Hospitals					
Total	581	612	666	747	802
Private [a]	113	132	167	223	277
Beds					
Total	63,643	72,405	81,109	90,281	95,323
Private Hospitals[b]	11,874	15,515	19,704	24,489	28,497

Source: Lampiran Pidato Presiden/Mandataris MPR, March 1994.
[a]Number of private hospitals out of the total number.
[b]Number of beds in private hospitals out of the total number.

There is no value in having a nation-wide network of community health centres without trained personnel to staff them. Finding the means to train the large number of needed medical professionals was a difficult long-term task for the government. The difficulty was not only in training the large number of medical personnel needed; what was equally challenging was to ensure that health care professionals were practising in all regions of the country. The government observed that if doctors were left to decide on their own, after graduating from medical school, most would establish their practice in urban centres. To bring medical services to Indonesia's widely dispersed population, the government determined that it would have to engage in some unconventional market interventions. To induce doctors to take up practice in rural areas and especially outside of Java, the government heavily subsidized medical school fees. The 'catch' was that to practice medicine after graduation, doctors had to accept a temporary position as government employees, during which time they were obliged to accept an assignment in a rural area for a minimum of three to five years, depending on the location. After the period of 'field-work' was completed doctors were free to leave the civil service and set up private practice anywhere in the country. Most doctors would then return to the cities, where they were able to build lucrative practices. Many, however, after having developed close ties with the community, decided to stay in the villages.

The physicians were supported and complemented by an extensive corps of primary health nurses and midwives. In those areas where no doctor was available, nurses would serve as the main health care providers. The increase in health care services in rural Indonesia was substantial. None the less, the supply of qualified physicians has remained insufficient and the training received by health care practitioners has generally been inadequate. Furthermore, as civil servants, doctors have been seriously underpaid, especially given the sacrifices that they were required to make in relocating to remote areas of the country. Low income has forced many physicians to seek supplementary income by taking on second jobs. Thus, overworked and underpaid, the quality of their services has suffered. Regrettably, these conditions have discouraged many potential candidates from entering the field.

The PKK which had an important role in assisting in educating Indonesian families on proper nutrition also had an important role in working with the government to bring general health services to the country. The Posyandu were usually staffed by volunteers rather than paid professionals. During the 1980s, the PKK, in their volunteer capacity, worked with the government to set up some 200,000 Posyandu throughout Indonesia. In recognition of its contribution, in 1988, the United Nations

Children's Fund (UNICEF) awarded the PKK with its Maurice Pate
Award for dedication to child survival. (See Figure 7.1 on changes in the
child mortality rates during the period 1969–83, corresponding to
Repelita I to Repelita III.) The PKK also received the World Health
Organization's (WHO) Sasakawa Health Prize for the implementation of
immunization programmes and the improvement of public nutrition.

The system has significantly added to the nation's effort to bring health
care services to Indonesia's huge rural population. The economic gains
from improved health care are impossible to calculate with any precision,
but they have certainly been very substantial and the personal benefit
resulting from healthier lives has been priceless. As mentioned earlier, in

FIGURE 7.1
Infant Mortality, 1969–1983

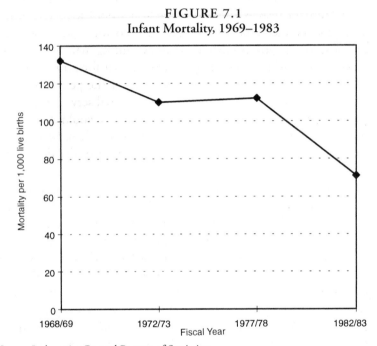

Source: Indonesia, Central Bureau of Statistics.

1969, the average life span for Indonesians was 47 years, and infant mortality was 132 per 1,000 live births. By focusing on preventive medicine,
volunteer services, and education, the government was able to bring low
cost but effective health care to the people of Indonesia. By 1983 infant
mortality had dropped by 53 per cent to 71 per 1,000 live births.
Additionally, the average life expectancy of Indonesians reached 55 years
in 1980 and 64 years in 1995.[15]

Besides the reduction in child mortality and increase in life expectancy, through institutions such as Puskesmas and Posyandu, and with the help of volunteer organizations like PKK, Indonesia spread new health care services across the country. Whole communities that had never before had any contact with modern health care practices now are regularly in contact with doctors and nurses. Births are mostly handled by midwives. And through seminars and informal meetings Indonesians have become more knowledgeable about nutrition and hygiene. Some of life's harder edges have been softened as more parents are able to watch their children grow to maturity, living their lives without the relentless assault on their health that so frequently accompanies childhood in the developing world.

FAMILY PLANNING: HARMONIZING INNOVATION WITH TRADITION

Scholars estimate that at the beginning of the twentieth century the population of Indonesia was probably about 40 to 45 million. Although the fertility rate among Indonesian women was high, so was the mortality rate, and this slowed the expansion of the population. By the 1950s, however, it became evident that the population was growing very rapidly. When Indonesia undertook its first comprehensive national census in 1961, the government determined that the country had a population of approximately 97 million people and that the annual population growth rate was about 2.3 per cent.[16] This meant that the country's population would double every thirty years. By the year 2000 Indonesia would have a population of approximately 236 million, and in 2020 the population would climb to 371 million. The trends were portentous. Indonesia's economy would have to grow at 2.3 per cent in real terms simply to prevent the country from slipping into deeper poverty. And even with economic growth, there was no guarantee that the environment could support so many people.

According to the population theories of Thomas Robert Malthus, war, famine, and disease were nature's way of controlling population. Indonesia in the late 1960s looked like a prime candidate to confirm Malthus' dreadful predictions about population growth overtaking economic resources. Population pressures in certain parts of the country, notably on Java and Bali, were already straining the environment. In 1971, with a population of 76 million, Java was already the world's most densely populated among areas of its size.[17] If the population growth continued unabated, it could easily cancel out the nation's economic gains. Even improved agrarian technology offered no guarantees. Furthermore, the consequences from overtaxing the nation's ecology—from excessive water consumption to pervasive environmental pollution—could be calamitous. The government determined that measures had to be taken to slow the nation's population growth. For this reason, it incorporated family planning into Repelita I and continued to build upon it in the years that followed.

Population Growth in Context: Traditions of Our Ancestors

In 1969, an Indonesian woman had on average 5.6 children over the course of her child-bearing years. By comparison, there is a growing number of industrialized countries in which women on average have less than two. Uniformly, one finds higher fertility rates among women in the poorest countries. The reasons may vary from country to country. However, for the government to succeed in bringing down the birth-rate, it had to first understand the reasons that led Indonesians to have large families. Only after answering this would the government be in a position to take appropriate countermeasures.

One of the most basic factors that led to large families in Indonesia was the traditional attitude toward the family. By centuries-old custom, the family is an exceptionally strong unit in Indonesian life, and this generally holds true for the many subcultures that collectively comprise the Indonesian nation. The individualism that is so admired in the West has almost no place in Indonesian culture. From birth to death, Indonesians are almost never alone. A small village ethos pervades the entire country, even in the sprawling metropolis of Jakarta. The group orientation of Indonesian life begins with family, and is evident in child-rearing practices from birth onward. Indonesian children may be among the most pampered in the world—if not in terms of material wealth, at least in love and attention. It is said, that for the first two years of life, the feet of children rarely touch the ground because they are always being carried, usually by their mothers. To Indonesians, being surrounded by family—both nuclear family and extended family—is the image of the world as it should be. In all this, there is the implied value that 'the good life' or the 'Indonesian Dream' is a home with many children. As a popular Indonesian saying goes, 'More children, more blessings'.

From the perspective of an Indonesian agrarian household, children bring financial benefits as they are expected to provide labour both in the fields and around the house. Children bring security since they are expected to take care of their parents in their old age. However, because the rate of child mortality was high, parents felt more confident having many children.[18] Indonesians' hedge against the rigours of life has always been the family.

Besides these factors that led couples to have more children, most Indonesians simply lacked the means to control their fertility. Few

Indonesians had access to contraceptives, and even when available, there were strong taboos against using them. Since the great majority of Indonesians lived in the countryside, life was regulated according to agrarian norms. Until recently, there was no room in the Indonesian village ethos for the idea that a couple would deliberately seek to interfere with the course of nature when it came to bearing children.

Reinforcing this attitude was the prevailing sense of decorum. Indonesia, like all agrarian cultures, has a tendency to be conservative. Public discussion of anything pertaining to sexuality was taboo for women. To compound the problem, especially in the early years of Indonesia's effort to promote family planning, many of the professionals associated with the programme were men. The idea of an Indonesian woman talking to any man, even her husband, about sexual matters was simply stepping beyond the limits of propriety.

There were religious taboos that discouraged family planning as well. For example, despite the grave ramification of Indonesia's rapid population growth, under President Sukarno, the country's family planning policy was to *not* have a policy. When asked by community groups to institute family planning programmes, Sukarno declined, asserting that the growing population would add to the nation's strength. President Soeharto later wrote (1984: 204) that Sukarno had admitted to him privately Indonesia's need for family planning, but had believed that opposition from the Muslim clergy would not permit it. Believing he had no options, Sukarno tried to make a virtue of necessity.[19]

Besides reasons of custom and religion, there were practical factors that inhibited the acceptance of family planning. For example, in the 1970s, most Indonesian women of child-bearing ages were illiterate. They had minimal contact with technology, and even the consumption of vitamins was foreign to them. Without the ability to read or count, it was more difficult to follow the proper procedures to regulate conception effectively.

Strategies for Change: Steps to Smaller Families

The forces opposing family planning were thus widespread and deeply rooted. The government needed to devise a strategy that would lead to a culture in which family planning was not only considered acceptable, but openly encouraged. Here we will review six of the government's strategies and associated measures taken to promote family planning in Indonesia.

Redefining the Ideal Family and Role of Family Planning

Indonesia's approach to family planning went well beyond birth control; instead, it aimed to assist in the general improvement of family welfare.

The government emphasized that small families were good for the family itself and the community. In this respect, family planning was seen as both an individual and community responsibility that was an integral part of nation building. To the traditional view that equated many children with the ideal family, the government offered a new norm: 'The small family is a healthy, happy and prosperous family.' This was an ideal the government hoped people would accept *en masse*, in much the same way as people had incorporated televisions, motor cycles, and electricity into their everyday life.

Indonesia's policymakers were mindful of the sacred position of the family in Indonesian culture. They respected this deeply. Under no circumstances did any of the nation's policymakers want to undermine the strength of the family in Indonesian culture. The heart of the Indonesian family planning strategy, therefore, was to challenge not the basic concept of the family, but simply the size. The main thesis of Indonesia's family planning policies was that smaller families were better suited to satisfy the Indonesian ideal on the good family life. This was a big jump, given that on average women bore almost six children during their lives. Success in family planning would require, therefore, a change in cultural norms that amounted to reweaving the basic fabric of society.

Not long after its founding in 1970, the Badan Koordinasi Keluarga Berencana Nasional (BKKBN or Family Planning Co-ordinating Board) began an enormous communications campaign that carried the family planning message to every member of society. If the traditional Indonesian attitude toward the family could be summarized as seeking familial 'strength in numbers', the BKKBN vision was epitomized in the simple motto, 'two children are enough' (*dua anak cukup*). This motto and the BKKBN logo—depicting a father, mother, and two children—became a ubiquitous feature of Indonesia's public communication, rivaling the Coca-Cola and Sony trademarks in terms of public recognition. The motto and logo together conveyed repeatedly the simple BKKBN message that the ideal family is one that is healthy, happy, and prosperous with no more than two children.

Providing a Strong Institutional Base for Family Planning

In 1969, Indonesia incorporated family planning as part of Repelita I. The plan proposed limiting its activities to the islands of Java and Bali because, as the plan said, '66 per cent of the whole Indonesian population is found on these two islands totaling only 7 per cent of the area of the country' (Department of Information, 1969: Vol. 2C, p. 70). The plan aimed at

enrolling 3 million participants ('acceptors') in the family planning programme before the end of 1973. With this, the programme projected that
some 600,000 births could be avoided. This was a step in the right direction, but the plan's major flaw was its conservatism. As envisioned, the
programme would have almost no impact whatsoever on the overall
expansion of the population.

To empower the nation's family planning efforts, in 1970 the government established BKKBN. This marked the debut of a tremendous effort
to reverse the population trends that threatened to undermine the nation's
future. Soon thereafter, Haryono Suyono, a sociologist trained in the
United States, assumed the leadership of BKKBN and, thereafter, the
agency distinguished itself as one of Indonesia's most efficient and effective
governmental departments. In less than two decades BKKBN did what
seemed impossible: it helped to substantially reduce Indonesia's birth rate.
BKKBN had the strong support of the government. The agency has a
remarkable record of organizing campaigns, creating coalitions, building
popular support, and providing services on a massive scale. Equally important, BKKBN accomplished its aim without force, coercion, or even
including abortion as one of its methods for limiting births. Instead,
BKKBN skillfully balanced education, access to appropriate forms of contraception, and community support to bring about a radical change in the
nation's view of the family and of the appropriateness of measures to regulate births.

Building A National Support Network

Perhaps the most important factor contributing to the success of
Indonesia's family planning movement was a network of support that
extended through every social group and region. Through this network virtually every adult member of society was made aware of the value of family
planning and the channels available for participating in family planning.

1. *The President.* At the centre of the network was the programme's
chief exponent, President Soeharto. Besides ensuring that the programme
received adequate funding, over the years the president provided moral
support through efforts that were highly visible and symbolic. To recognize successful family planning centres the president travelled to villages
from one end of Indonesia to another. Every year, he presented couples
with awards for their participation in the programme. And when
Indonesia opened its first condom factory, photos of the President touring
the factory appeared in every newspaper in the country. The President's
actions communicated an unmistakable message to all Indonesians that

family planning had the unqualified support of the nation's leader and the central government.

2. *The Armed Forces*. Beneath the President was the ABRI, the nation's military forces. As early as 1972, ABRI leaders began a concerted campaign to enlist participation of their ranks in family planning. The director of BKKBN at the time was a medical doctor in the military, Brig.-Gen. Suwardjono Surjaningrat, who also served as Indonesia's Minister of Health. Suwardjono vigorously promoted family planning. Even among this primarily male constituency, he emphasized that family planning was as much a responsibility of husbands as of wives.[20] As one of Indonesia's strongest organizations, the support of ABRI bolstered the official commitment to family planning.

3. *Women's Groups*. ABRI's involvement was complemented by several women's groups, including Dharma Pertiwi, the Organization of Military Wives, and Dharma Wanita, the Association of Civil Servants' Wives. Together, these associations constitute the largest women's organizations in the country. Whereas ABRI communicated mostly with men, Dharma Pertiwi and Dharma Wanita brought the family planning message to women across the nation. The backing of Dharma Pertiwi and Dharma Wanita not only assured a large number of acceptors, it conferred legitimacy on the programme and enhanced its prestige, especially among women.

4. *Religious Leaders*. Essential to the success of Indonesia's family planning programme was the support it received from the nation's religious leaders. About 85 per cent of Indonesia's population is Muslim. The nation's Islamic leaders initially were unprepared to support the programme. Muslim scholars, however, found scriptural justification for family planning so long as it did not promote abortion or sterilization. Abortion is illegal in Indonesia, and sterilization, while available, is not promoted as a contraception option. Given these policies, Indonesia's family planning programme received the acceptance and support of the nation's clergy of various faiths. This support was indispensable in helping persuade many villagers that family planning was acceptable, not only from a social perspective but also from a moral and spiritual perspective. Statistical evidence later demonstrated that there was a greater number of acceptors of family planning in villages where the religious leaders supported the goals and methods of the programme (Warwick, 1985: 17). Indonesia has been a family planning pioneer among countries with large Islamic populations, and in this capacity has worked with Islamic leaders from around the world to affirm the positive role of family planning in an Islamic context.[21]

5. *The Family Welfare Movement and Volunteer Groups*. If Indonesia

relied only on paid employees to deliver the message and services of family planning, the programme would have remained small and ineffective due to the government's financial limitations. Fortunately, the spirit of volunteerism was alive and well in Indonesia and many volunteer groups joined with BKKBN to help support the family planning movement, among which the most prominent was the PKK. Earlier it was mentioned that the PKK was instrumental in establishing and staffing thousands of integrated health posts or Posyandu throughout Indonesia. One of the main services in the country's Posyandu was to provide contraceptives and information on family planning. Because of the efforts of the PKK and other volunteer groups, millions of Indonesians—who otherwise would have been unreachable—became active participants in family planning.

6. *Community Group: The Balinese Banjar*. Bali offers a striking example of community support for family planning, in this case from a men's community group, the *banjar*. In Bali, membership in a *banjar* is compulsory for married men. There are more than 3,700 *banjar* on the island. In 1974 BKKBN worked with the heads of the *banjar* to include family planning as one of the topics on the agenda of the meetings held every thirty-five days. At the meetings, a chart was displayed indicating whether or not married couples were family planning acceptors. Within three years after beginning the co-operation between BKKBN and the *banjar*, some 60 per cent of the couples of child-bearing age were registered as family planning acceptors. By the early 1990s the population growth rate of Bali dropped to 1.7 per cent, the lowest in Indonesia at that time.

7. *Village Leadership and Acceptors Groups*. In its effort to achieve comprehensive participation among eligible couples in the family planning programme, BKKBN enlisted the support of the village head in villages across the country. This local leader would act as an unofficial sponsor of the family planning programme. In most cases, his wife would assume a leadership role as the organizer or facilitator in family planning meetings and in the distribution of contraceptives to acceptors. It would not be enough simply to admonish Indonesians to have fewer children. Acceptors needed to be given the 'tools' needed to participate in family planning, and BKKBN had to have the institutional strength to meet the challenge of the job it set for itself. By enlisting the village head, BKKBN insured that the message would reach every couple in a village. To consolidate the participation within a village, BKKBN encouraged individual acceptors to join together to form 'acceptor groups' comprising fifteen to thirty families. The family planning acceptors would act as a close-knit support group that served as an example for non-acceptors in the surrounding community. By the active participation of the village head and acceptor groups, the taboo against publicly discussing family planning was

gradually displaced with an attitude that regarded family planning as an everyday measure taken to fulfil the aspiration for a healthy, happy, and prosperous family.

Through this network the family planning message was spread both extensively and intensively. The network spread vertically from the President through every level in the government. And horizontally, the BKKBN network connected every village and city in the country. In this way, virtually every couple in Indonesia was well aware of the family planning message and the methods for controlling the size of their family. As Indonesians everywhere became more aware and supportive of family planning, the nation's culture gradually grew to embrace the view of the small family as the appropriate norm for contemporary Indonesian society.

Health, Education, and Income Enhancements: The Broader Context of Family Planning

As already stated, the objectives of Indonesia's family planning programme went beyond population control. Instead, BKKBN sought to encourage a new vision of the ideal family, which equated the small family as the healthy, happy, and prosperous family. For that reason, BKKBN's family planning activities reached past issues associated with birth control and embraced activities associated with health care, education, and income enhancement.

BKKBN's efforts were so tightly linked with health that the agency grew in tandem with the Ministry of Health. In many cases, they shared the same facilities. Throughout the 1970s and until this day, the Ministry of Health has been busily setting up a nation-wide network of health centres independent of BKKBN. Since family planning in Indonesia was viewed primarily as a health matter, the synergy between the two organizations was obvious. Where a village did not have a health centre, BKKBN would construct its own centre for family planning services and contraceptive distribution. In 1974 there were 2,343 Puskesmas concentrated primarily in Java and Bali, most of which offered family planning services. By 1983 the number had grown to over 184,000 centres located in provinces throughout the country. By the late 1980s there were hundreds of thousands of volunteers working in over 220,000 family planning centres. These were supported by 8,630 family planning clinics, 6,834 private doctors, 1,445 pharmacies, and 65,608 village family planning posts, and 136,760 weighing centres for children (BKKBN, 1989).

The linkage between health care and family planning was not to economize on overhead costs. As noted, one of the factors that led

Indonesians to seek large families was the high incidence of child mortality. However, large families contributed to poverty and increased the incidence of maternal mortality in childbirth. Because the objective of Indonesia's family planning programme was to encourage the healthy, prosperous family, BKKBN always linked its programme with activities to promote mother and child's health, and to an extent, income generating activities.

Midwives and nurses had a central role in the BKKBN programme. The presence of midwives in the birthing process helped prevent complications from difficult births or from unhygienic conditions. Furthermore, having midwives working for BKKBN was a strong testimony for the agency because the livelihood of these women depended on birth. Yet, as BKKBN employees, midwives served the dual function of supporting healthy births while counseling on the wisdom of small families and good child care. As a result of better birthing conditions and fewer births per woman, the incidence of maternal mortality in childbirth decreased from 800 per 100,000 live births in 1980 to 450 per 100,000 in 1985.

In villages across the country, BKKBN held seminars on infant care, nutrition, and hygiene with the aim of safeguarding the health of mothers and children. Mothers were encouraged to frequently bring their children to the local Posyandu or Puskesmas for weighing. If a baby's development appeared to deviate from healthy norms, the health care adviser would investigate further to try to determine the cause. If necessary, the mother would be advised to seek additional medical attention. Otherwise, she was given advice on how to help her child grow healthily through the critical early years of life and, if appropriate, supplies of vitamins and other nutritional supplements were given.

Additionally, BKKBN launched programmes to help increase the income of family planning acceptors. The most important programme was called Usaha Peningkatan Pendapatan Keluarga Akseptor (UPPKA or Efforts to Increase the Income of Acceptor Families). UPPKA directs working capital to acceptor groups, especially in rural areas. These programmes enabled the participants to pay for contraceptives, afford medical treatment and help in the activities of the Posyandu, and above all to increase their own income. Many of the UPPKA members are women who have had only two children because of their adherence to family planning practices. This enables them to invest more of their time in income generating activities. UPPKA sometimes received aid from both BKKBN and PKK, which would then be disbursed for use by acceptor groups in small business enterprises, such as weaving and handicraft. UPPKA was created to help such women make the most of having a small family.

A number of other income enhancing programmes have been introduced for family planning acceptors. For example, millions of coconut seedlings—which could eventually serve as a dietary supplement and source of income—have been given by the government to family planning acceptors. Another income enhancement comes as a discount card given by BKKBN to family planning acceptors after three years consistent contraceptive use. Grocery stores, cinemas, insurance companies, and many local merchants honour the card with a 10 per cent discount. By thus linking family planning with health, education, and even income enhancements, Indonesians witness tangible benefits to having small families.

Supplying the Tools for Change: Logistics for Family Planning

Central to the family planning programme is the distribution of contraceptives. Acceptors are offered a variety of options including birth control pills, IUDs, implants, injections, and condoms. BKKBN hold frequent meetings with the community to explain and promote the use of contraceptives.

To monitor the daily changes of the enormous family planning network, during the 1970s, statistics were compiled on a monthly basis and sent back to the BKKBN headquarters in Jakarta where they were processed and analyzed. With this compiled information BKKBN was able to estimate the number of family planning acceptors on a national and local basis, as well as contraceptive usage, participation in programmes, and other related data. Originally, this data was transmitted by post. Since the 1980s, however, BKKBN has computerized its operations and now receives a steady stream of information that travels electronically from regional centres directly to the central computers in Jakarta. This system helps BKKBN officials to identify quickly what areas are experiencing the greatest success and which are having the most serious difficulties. This information is then used to modify and improve the general programme as well as to respond to issues affecting specific districts and even individual centres. The computer information is also essential for maintaining a steady stock of contraceptives. Contraceptive distribution centres are kept well supplied based on the inventory information the managers of distribution centres send to BKKBN. In response to the data supplied, the distribution centres will be supplied automatically with a few months' stock without a manager having to specifically request more supplies. In this way, BKKBN has developed one of the most sophisticated logistics operations in Indonesia. The beneficiaries are the family planning acceptors who have been given the tools to regulate the size of their family due to the efficient system developed by BKKBN.

Self-reliant Family Planning

With so many new couples entering the childbearing age every year, BKKBN is encouraging a third 'community' to assist in promoting family planning: the private sector. Over time, family planning has become a natural and integral part of Indonesian family life. As more couples attempt to regulate their fertility without government encouragement or subsidy, private doctors are counselling couples on family planning and more private companies are marketing contraceptives, particularly condoms. The government's aim is to have more and more of the nation's acceptors seek family planning services through private channels rather than relying on BKKBN.

Indonesia's New Family

Indonesia's achievements in family planning have been remarkable. The proportion of eligible couples practicing family planning rose from 2.8 per cent in 1971/2 to 62.6 per cent in 1984/5. As indicated in Figure 7.2, between 1969 and 1993 total fertility dropped from 5.6 children per woman to 2.9.

Overall, Indonesia's population growth rate has fallen from 2.3 per cent in the 1970s to 1.98 per cent in the mid-1990s. As a result, instead of

FIGURE 7.2
Average Fertility Per Woman, 1969–1993

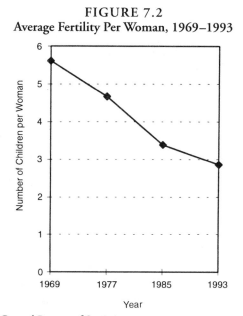

Source: Indonesia, Central Bureau of Statistics.

FIGURE 7.3
Population Growth at Constant versus Actual and Projected Rates, 1961–2020

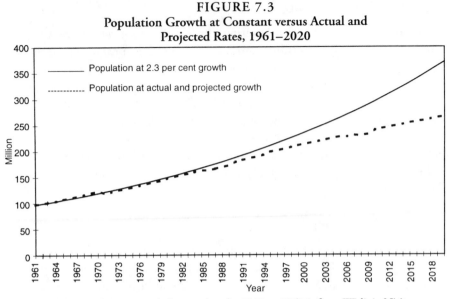

Sources: For declining growth figures, data for 1950 to 1962 is from Widjojo Nitisastro as quoted in *Statistical Pocketbook of Indonesia*; for 1964 to 1968 data is from *Bank Indonesia Report 1968*; for census years 1971, 1980, and 1990 data quoted from *Statistical Year Book of Indonesia 1994*.

Note: Growth rate is 2.8 per cent annually from 1965 to 1968 and 2.3 per cent for previous years; 1969 and 1970 are calculated using 2.8 per cent annual growth rate; in between years are calculated as follows: for 1972 to 1979 using 2.32 per cent annual growth rate; for 1981 to 1989 using 1.98 per cent annual growth rate; for 1990 to 2020 from population projections derived from 'Penduduk Indonesia Selama Pembangunan Jangka Panjang Tahap I' as quoted in World Bank (1990) on the assumption of moderate growth; for 1990 a growth rate of 1.88 per cent; for 1995 a growth rate of 1.73 per cent; projected growth rates for these years are: 2000 = 1.49 per cent, 2005 = 1.25 per cent, 2010 = 1.15 per cent, 2015 = 1.08 per cent, and 2020 = 0.99 per cent.

having the predicted population of 236 million by the year 2000, Indonesia's population will be approximately 213 million. Furthermore, if the current trends continue, by the year 2020 Indonesia will have about 100 million fewer people than it would have had if the population had continued growing at the rate of 2.3 per cent as was the case when Indonesia launched its family planning programme (Figure 7.3).

By focusing on health, education, and income enhancement, Indonesia's family planning programme was consistent in its espoused objective of helping couples to achieve healthy, happy, and prosperous families. In this way family planning was spared the ill associations of population control programmes. Instead, family planning was seen as a humane endeavour to assist communities via the family unit. This approach once again demonstrated the pragmatism of Indonesia's planners. The government's support of family planning, rather than undermining the family, created a context in which Indonesia's family ideal could be better realized. Indonesian married couples participated in the family planning programme because it was in their self-interest to do so. In this respect, the interest of individual families is harmonious with the interests of the nation. Because of the convergence of interests, Indonesia's population in the mid-1990s was 20 million less than it would have been without the family planning programme.

FACTORIES OR TEXTBOOKS?: REFLECTING ON THE RETURNS FROM SOCIAL INFRASTRUCTURE INVESTMENT

There are infinite means by which a government can affect the lives of its citizens but probably none that touch people quite so directly as social infrastructure programmes such as education, health care, and family planning. These types of programmes share two important features: they are highly interrelated and the return on investment is difficult to assess. Because they are interrelated, investment in one will enhance the value of the others. It is more difficult to educate a sickly child than one who is healthy. Conversely, education contributes to health. The education of parents can have a strong influence on the health of their children. For example, a study by J. N. Hobcraft (1993) showed a reduction of at least 20 per cent in child mortality (defined as death by age 2) when parents received schooling of four to six years. When parental schooling increased to seven or more years, there was a 50 per cent reduction in child mortality when compared to parents with no schooling. The link between health and education is clearly very strong.

Governments, however, must make difficult choices in allocating scarce funds for development. Investment in social infrastructure can be difficult to justify when the 'payback' may not be apparent for a decade or more. Especially when governments are facing pressures from local constituencies, a bridge or a road may offer more tangible return for the taxpayers. Furthermore, investing in social infrastructure is risky. The literature on economic development has many examples of investments in education that failed to produce the hoped-for economic gains.[22] For these reasons, a government may find it 'safer' to invest in factories and roads rather than education and family planning. Despite this caveat, Indonesia's experience confirmed to the country's economic team that the investment in the nation's social infrastructure resulted in considerable financial and social benefits. These 'returns on investment' will be felt for many generations to come. For that reason they are impossible to estimate. No doubt, however, the contribution has been enormous.

The following paragraphs review and recap a few of the key lessons learned during the long effort to build the nation's social infrastructure.

1. *The Importance of Culture*. Economic development is fundamentally about cultural transformation. As a country develops, inevitably it must part with some of the ways of its past. One of the difficulties of the economic policymaker is to recognize how to balance modernization with tradition. Indonesia's new commitment to education, health care, and family planning all brought great benefit to the people. There was, however, a price—many traditional ways had to be abandoned. Indonesians, for example, were asked to accept that it is more practical, indeed better, to have two children rather than six. Here, tradition had to give way to new norms that supported economic development. Changes of this sort could be particularly unsettling for conservative rural communities. If policymakers push too hard in ways the community is not ready to accept, they can provoke a backlash that defeats the policy. The policymaker, therefore, must balance the need for change with a community's ability to absorb change. When there is a gap between the two, either the policymaker has to accept a compromise or devise a way to make the change acceptable to the community. Education is usually one of the best means of helping a community adapt to the changes that come with economic development. It may take years, however, before the community can fully experience the benefits of investment in education.

2. *Intergenerational Economics and the Necessity of a Long-term Vision*. One of the great difficulties in developmental economics is to manage properly the expectations of the people. In a sense, we can say that developmental economics is 'intergenerational economics'. The challenge of policymakers is to have their constituencies accept that it is in everyone's interest to build for the future, rather than focus on immediate needs. This is particularly difficult when those who are most in need, the poor, are often asked to be the most patient. In this respect the New Order government generally conducted its planning according to three time frames: the annual budget, the five-year plan, and the twenty-five year plan. The most important contribution of the first twenty-five year plan was that it communicated to the Indonesian people that the development process requires time and perseverance. The plan is more of a vision statement than a blueprint for action. Yet, it was in this long-term time frame that the tremendous return on investment in social infrastructure became evident.

3. *Maximizing Returns on Social Infrastructure Investment*. Although

Indonesia spent a great deal on social infrastructure programmes, given the magnitude of these undertakings, the costs were very small. The key was to invest in programmes that had low unit costs and to draw heavily on the support of volunteers. This strategy not only saved money, it involved the community in the services they were receiving. This created a greater sense of personal and community commitment to the projects and services which in turn added to their impact.

4. *Governments Must Succeed where Markets Fail.* Indonesia's economic planners have generally been inclined to trust in the power and effectiveness of the market. However, governments must consider carefully those places where markets may fail and selectively decide where to take steps to compensate. Social infrastructure is a prime example. For a poor country like Indonesia, there was little economic incentive for the private sector to invest in educating the nation's children, to organize family planning acceptors' groups, or to construct village health centres. Yet, it was in areas such as these where investment was indispensable to long-term economic growth. In trying to determine if a government should fund a project or service, it should consider two basic questions: a) is the investment essential or optional to the development process?; b) without government investment, would the private sector take over the investment? If the investment is essential yet unlikely to be assumed by the private sector, then the government should consider intervening. In Indonesia's experience, education, health care, and family planning were sectors in which government intervention was fully justified and ultimately well rewarded.

Lessons from School

1. *Setting Standards.* Universal primary school was the right goal for Indonesia during the 1970s and 1980s. The government could certainly have chosen numerous other strategies. Yet, the economic returns were greatest for primary education, and the universal availability was equitable. No Indonesian citizen was left out for any reason. In aiming for universal primary education, Indonesia set for itself a national educational standard based on what was feasible and practical. Universal primary education was feasible in that it was within the economic reach of the government, although it required an enormous portion of the government's budget. It required a strong commitment, but especially when the country obtained the oil windfalls during the 1970s, the government was able to mobilize the resources to make substantial progress to reach that goal. Universal primary education was also a practical standard as it led to the literacy levels needed for industrialization.

Standards in school are not like standard measurements or even industrial standards. Educational standards must always change in a way that reflects the evolving needs of society. Current standards should set the foundation upon which a new foundation is built. As Indonesia prepares for the twenty-first century, intellectual training is increasingly important. In the face of global competition, Indonesia must continually raise the standards of its educational system higher both in terms of the number of required years in school and the quality of the educational experience.

2. *Building Bridges through Decentralization.* When Indonesia was in the energetic process of building thousands of new schools every month in the 1970s, the approach it took was to offer villages the money for construction materials. The villages had to provide the land, hire the labour, and manage the construction. This was an excellent policy. Because of the responsibility taken by the village, the school represented the community's desire for their children. Furthermore, by drawing on local support in the designation and construction of schools, the pace of school construction was able to proceed much more quickly than if the central government had to oversee every aspect of school development. The school construction programme also helped in the nation-building process as it created a direct and positive link between Indonesia's central government and the villages. This development was a powerful example of the potential of well-managed but decentralized decision-making.

3. *Paying Where Due.* One area where the government was mistaken in its policies to build the educational system was in the area of school fees. The justification for the early policy of charging fees for students to attend public schools was purely economic. The government had little money and wanted parents to help defray the costs of services for their children. However, if the government could have chosen between constructing a new state-owned enterprise or eliminating school fees, it would probably have chosen more wisely if the funds had gone to education. In 1984, school tuition fees were eliminated. However, costs for primary education were still beyond the financial means of some of Indonesia's poorest. Although parents no longer had to pay tuition fees, they still faced other official and unofficial costs. Official costs included (and still do) the purchase of school uniforms, parent–teacher association fees, student association fees, sports fees, and other related fees, the total of which can amount to more than the former tuition fees. To this can be added unofficial fees, such as 'seat fees', used by school authorities to make up the budget deficiency due to the insufficiency of central government funding. If a parent cannot afford to pay these fees, there are options to have them waived. It is probably unrealistic to expect schooling costs ever to be reduced to zero. On the other hand, the government should carefully monitor these matters to ensure that there are no parents unduly

burdened by supplemental school fees, and no children are being denied an education for financial reasons. The procedures for waiving school fees should be clear and uniform.

Lessons from Indonesia's Health Care Efforts

1. *More Thoughts on Centralization and Decentralization.* Although much of the planning and evaluation of Indonesia's health care took place in Jakarta, the system was otherwise quite decentralized. This decentralization led to the creation of programmes that were close to the people they were supposed to serve. As this system evolves it will need continual adjustments and improvements to meet local needs. With an ever increasing corps of experts and technicians, many of the planning functions that have been centrally organized may be most effectively delegated to planning organizations at the provincial, district, and even subdistrict or village level.

2. *Appropriate Technology.* By spreading health care services widely, Indonesia was able to extend the reach of the programme. Doing so, however, meant that the country had to try to maximize its investment by selecting health care services that were relatively inexpensive yet responsive to community needs. By necessity this led to a focus on preventive medicine, nutritional improvement, and increased hygiene. This was a case of applying the philosophy of appropriate technology to medicine. This was the right approach for the early stages of health care delivery, not only for reasons of costs, but because the policy was aimed at helping people to help themselves. Rather than having teams of doctors ready to help a community in which the people are frequently ill due to preventable causes, it is better to teach people how to avoid illness from the start. When serious illness or injury did strike, the weakness of the system was most evident. The best solution may be to continue to build on the medical training institutions and keep the nation's economic development going forward. As the nation's income increases, Indonesia will have the means to pay for the medicines and equipment to treat illness. In the meantime, the focus on preventive medicine and on the policy of subsidized medical education followed by assignments in the countryside were good ones that should continue.

Lessons from Family Planning

1. *Respect the Local Culture.* There is probably no better example of nation-wide community participation than Indonesia's family planning programme. The success of the effort was due in part to programme leaders who took great pains to work constructively within the confines of local

customs and culture. Essential in this respect was the decision to seek the support of Indonesia's religious and community leaders. The government could have pushed the programme forward without consultation or community involvement. The programme would have been technically feasible and no doubt it would have failed. By accommodating the culture and norms of the communities in which it sought to operate, the government was able to address very sensitive topics without alienating the constituencies it wanted to reach. Instead of trying to change the culture by force, the government worked with the people to build a new culture in which family planning received widespread support.

2. *Build Allies and Link Programmes.* The family planning programme reached virtually every person in the country because it allied itself with a diverse group of established organizations from ABRI to the PKK. The family planning effort also established links to many complementary programmes such as health care, baby weighing, nutrition education, and income enhancement schemes. This strategy of creating organizational and programmatic links greatly expanded the reach of the BKKBN and this contributed to the rapid incorporation of family planning as an integral part of Indonesian daily life.

3. *Small Families and Economic Development.* It has become an article of faith of development economists that the most effective form of family planning is economic development itself. Demographic statistics from around the world have confirmed this theory repeatedly. Economic development and family planning go hand in hand. Family planning helps to accelerate economic development; and as an economy develops, family size declines. In the case of Indonesia, the government believed that after cultural obstacles were removed, individual self-interest would be sufficient to sustain the family planning movement in the long run. Family planning services and the supply of contraceptives should then become a lucrative market for the private sector. When this happens, the government will be able to reduce its role in the family planning programme and direct its attention to other concerns.

*   *   *

Indonesia's accomplishments in the area of building its social infrastructure have been impressive, both for what has been accomplished and the ingenuity of the approach to meeting the needs of such a large and diverse country. Still, there is much work ahead. To put Indonesia's accomplishment in perspective, it is instructive to consider the development criteria established by the UNDP. The UNDP publishes a summary statistic encompassing many aspects of both physical and social infrastructure called the 'human development index' (HDI). The HDI attempts to provide a more comprehensive indicator of socio-economic progress than economic indicators such as per capita income. The HDI is a composite of three basic components of human development: longevity, knowledge, and standard of living. According to the UNDP's 1994 rating, Indonesia ranks forty-one out of all ninety-seven developing countries using the HDI. This means, according to the UNDP's broad way of evaluating the state of economic development, Indonesia ranked somewhat better than average when compared with other developing countries. What is noteworthy, however, is how the UNDP ranks Indonesia's progress over time. In that respect, the UNDP ranks Indonesia among its top ten performers in human development over the period 1980 to 1992 (United Nations Development Programme, 1994: 102–3).

The UNDP analysis confirms what many less scientific observations would suggest, which is that Indonesia has shown remarkable progress in a relatively short period of time. What this analysis does not tell us is how this progress was possible. The short answer is that the nation made major strides in improving its social infrastructure through the creation of schools, clinics, and contraceptive dispensaries. Those tools, however, would have accomplished little without a change in culture. By creating programmes that reached out and were accepted by the Indonesian population at large, Indonesia engineered a quiet and peaceful cultural revolution. This revolution in culture was needed for the country to make the transition from a society that was geared toward coping with the insecurities of economic subsistence to one that was firmly on the road to industrialization.

Indonesia's social infrastructure policies were among the most important decisions made by the New Order government. The societal changes from the advances in social infrastructure have been so great as to be all but irreversible. If the government eventually decided to abolish the family planning programme, it is virtually certain that the nation's birth rate would never again rise to the six children per woman average that prevailed for centuries past. Indonesia's investment in social infrastructure was an investment in social equity. By investing in social infrastructure, all Indonesians—urban and rural, rich and poor—were offered the same tools to help themselves live better lives. This created a new national community and with it a change in attitudes about what a person can reasonably expect from life. Indonesians are not only living longer, their lives are more secure and their options more varied. Unlike their grandparents, the parents of today firmly expect the lives of their children to be more secure, healthy, and prosperous than their own. This belief in a better future is shared by all Indonesians because the benefits from development of the nation's social infrastructure are being experienced by all.

1. Figures from the Ministry of Finance and Bank Indonesia *Annual Report 1984/85*.

2. *Sinar Harapan*, 1 March 1971, p. 3.

3. This data is from the State Employment Agency as quoted in Tilaar (1995: 327).

4. In the fiscal year ending in March 1984, statistics show that 108 per cent of eligible Indonesian children attended primary schools. In fact, probably around 93 per cent of all children of the appropriate age group attended schools. The statistics indicate that attendance exceeded 100 per cent because also attending school were individuals older than the designated ages for this level of schooling.

5. This fact was reported in the text of Repelita I, Vol. 2C, p. 11. The problems in medical education were symptomatic of the crisis afflicting the entire educational system.

6. Information in these two paragraphs comes from several sources, specifically, Soeharto (1973), the World Bank (1990), the World Bank (1995a), and Indonesia's Central Bureau of Statistics. It should also be noted that in 1974, the World Health Organization (WHO) declared Indonesia free from smallpox.

7. This 1996 data is drawn from Central Bureau of Statistics materials. Other data is drawn from *Secretariat Jenderal Dewan Pimpinan Pusat Golongan Karya. Orde Baru dalam Angka, Jakarta, May 1992*. It is worth noting that according to a study conducted in 1969/70 by the Food and Agriculture Organization (FAO), 57 per cent of the households in Java consumed only 1,400 calories per day and 34 grams of protein of which 3 grams were animal protein (Booth and Sundrum, 1981: 206). There is a significant discrepancy in the different data on caloric intake reported in these two studies. It is impossible to tell what may be behind the differences. In any case, both sets of data point to prevalent malnutrition.

8. Other PKK activities are discussed below under 'sanitation', 'health centres', and 'family planning'.

9. PKK's Taman Gizi programme followed a very similar programme started by the government in 1974. Called the Usaha Perbaikan Gizi Keluarga (UPGK or Family Nutrition Improvement programme), it also emphasized the nutritional needs of mothers and young children. As with the Taman Gizi programme, the UPGK supported sound nutritional practices and encouraged mothers to bring their children to health centres for regular weighing. If a child's weight showed deviation from expected norms, then after trying to determine the cause, the health workers would make recommendations on dietary changes to restore health and weight to normal. The programme was launched in 1,500 villages in eight provinces and eventually was extended to 50,000 villages in every province.

10. In many of Indonesia's cities one will find pockets which inner-city mini-communities have developed that greatly resemble the villages in the countryside. In sections of many 'urban villages', the paths among the houses are unpaved and homes are constructed closely together. In these areas, only people walking on foot or pushcarts can pass, but not motor cars. When villagers make the transition from the countryside to cities, they often first take up residence in 'urban villages'. It was primarily in this type of city community where the government constructed urban MCKs. As Indonesia develops, these

villages are being replaced by modern residential areas, complete with the facilities one would expect in any modern city.

11. This data was reported in the attachment to the President's January 1993 budget address.

12. This section refers to material contained in the World Bank document (1991: 48–53).

13. Distance is an important factor. Although the poor have the greatest health care needs, they also have less access to transportation than the rich. For those residing in urban centres, distance is not such an important issue. But for the rural poor, distance may determine whether they seek treatment or not. This is a challenging issue for the government because Indonesia's population is spread across such a large area.

14. For more on this see Hugo et al. (1990: 112–13).

15. The data for 1969 and 1980 is from the World Bank (1995). The life expectancy data for 1995 comes from Indonesia's Central Bureau of Statistics, *Welfare Indicators 1995*.

16. For an extensive discussion of the 1961 census and an analysis of various demographic trends, please see Widjojo (1970). This seminal work on Indonesian population trends was written by the chief architect of Indonesia's economic development. Therein, Widjojo constructs four scenarios offering four distinct projections of the country's population growth. Based on these projections, in 1991, the population was expected to range from a minimum of 197.8 million to 227.0 million (Widjojo, 1970: 206). The actual population in 1991 was 191.9 million. If Widjojo's estimates were high, it was not due to faulty methodology or improper analysis. Instead, the success of Indonesia's family planning programme exceeded all expectation. Part of the credit for this achievement must go to Widjojo himself, whose research helped galvanize the government's attention on this urgent issue.

17. By way of comparison, Java is similar in size to the state of New York. Yet, in 1991, New York—one of the most densely populated states in the United States—had a population of 18 million while Java had a population of 109 million.

18. Besides the high rate of infant mortality, McNicoll (1982: 813) notes that during the 1960s, one quarter of all children died before the age of 15.

19. As we shall discuss later, the reluctance of religious leaders to support family planning did not constitute doctrinal opposition.

20. See the newspaper, *Suara Karya*, 8 September 1972, p. 2.

21. In February 1990, President Soeharto hosted the International Congress on Islam and Population Policy in Jakarta and Aceh, Sumatra. Additionally, BKKBN has endeavoured to work closely with leaders in the Indonesian Muslim community as well as with Hindu, Christian, and Buddhist leaders. Without the firm backing of the Hindu leadership in Bali, for example, it is doubtful that the programme would have successfully taken hold in that community.

22. See, for example, Gannicott (1990: 41) who stated, 'In sub-Saharan Africa, the bright hopes for post-independence education have been replaced by stagnation in enrolments and deterioration in the quality of schooling.'

PART III

1983–1993
THE DEREGULATION DECADE:
MOVING TOWARD CONSENSUS

Introduction

IN March 1983, President Soeharto installed a new Cabinet. While the composition of the Cabinet remained quite stable, the process of global economic restructuring that had been unfolding during the previous two decades was now coming to a head. As important as these economic developments were, the political drama that was taking place was perhaps the most spectacular in modern history.

In the early 1980s, tensions mounted as the American–Soviet arms race showed no signs of abating. In a March 1983 speech, United States President Ronald Reagan provocatively castigated the Soviet Union, calling it an 'evil empire'. As if to corroborate the charge, in September a Soviet jet fighter pilot deliberately shot down a Korean Airlines civilian passenger plane that had strayed into Soviet airspace. Everyone on board was killed. Then, a shift in the river of history occurred a year and a half later when Mikhail Sergeyevich Gorbachev became Secretary-General of the Soviet Union's Communist Party. Over the next five years, Gorbachev introduced economic restructuring (*perestroika*) and openness (*glasnost*) in political and cultural affairs. His great accomplishment, unintended as it was, was to preside over the dissolution of the Soviet Union without permitting the forces of change to degenerate into a violent revolution or war.

The trend toward democratization had been building for years in many countries. In 1983, Argentina returned to democratic rule after eight years of military dictatorship. Two years later Brazil followed and the trend continued throughout most of Latin America. The East European countries reacted to the *glasnost*-crack in the Soviet wall with an overwhelming flood of will-power. In 1989, throngs of jubilant Berliners, with sledge-hammers in hand, personally tore down the Berlin Wall. With that symbolic act, Communism was defeated. In rapid succession Hungary, East Germany, Czechoslovakia, Bulgaria, Romania, and the Baltic states all asserted their independence and commitment to democracy and market economics. When the Soviet Union itself collapsed in 1991, under the leadership of its new leader, Boris Yeltsin, power was devolved to the now independent former Soviet republics. These newly independent countries also declared their commitment to democratic governance and the free market.

The economic turbulence that rocked the industrialized world during the 1970s continued well into the 1980s. There was, however, a difference. Countries were finding more adequate solutions to difficult economic problems. Moreover, there were signs of growing consensus on how to manage many international economic problems and a greater willingness among governments to work collaboratively to find solutions to these problems.

By 1984, the United States pulled itself out of recession. Its economy grew by 6.8 per cent, the highest rate since the 1950s. This surge was due in part to the steep drop in international oil prices. The fall in oil prices dealt a harsh blow to many oil-producing countries, among them Indonesia. Hardest hit, however, were the developing countries who borrowed beyond their means during the 1970s when the leading international commercial banks—flush with petrodollars—became too liberal in their lending. When the world oil shortage became an oil glut, the oil-producing developing countries found themselves indebted beyond their means. The debt was enormous, and the impact was global. As the decade advanced, there was a co-ordinated effort among the multilateral financial agencies, such as the IMF and the World Bank, as well as the governments and banks in the industrialized countries, to seek collaborative solutions. Consequently, most countries were able to resolve the problem. For some of the most severely indebted, however, the problem persisted. None the less, the 'Third World debt crisis', as it was called, was an example of crisis management on an international scale, and the effort was largely successful.

The exchange rate volatility that began to wreak havoc in the 1970s continued to destabilize the world economy well into the 1980s. Then on 22 September 1985, the finance ministers of the United States, Japan, Germany, the United Kingdom, and France, agreed to what became known as the Plaza Accord, named after the New York hotel where the meeting was held. The Accord called for the appreciation of other currencies against the dollar. A day later, the dollar dropped by over 4 per cent, and continued to slide for several years thereafter. For Indonesia, given the structure of the nation's debt and exports, this was a painful development. The Accord, however, was an important step in creating a free but relatively stable international monetary system, backed by co-ordinated intervention among the major economies. As such, it was an example of the extension of the emerging economic consensus to international monetary policy.

The international economic solidarity exemplified by the Plaza Accord was quickly put to the test. The return to growth among the industrialized countries following the oil crisis in the 1980s did not go unnoticed by the world's major stock markets. At first, market growth was in step with the economic recovery. However, before long, many of the major markets were growing at a pace that generated its own momentum. Then on 19 October 1987, Wall Street's Dow Jones Industrial Average fell by 22.6 per cent. This was the worst drop in a single day ever—almost 10 per cent more than the drop that precipitated the crash of 1929. Like dominoes, stock markets around the world fell. The losses were so severe that the event could have easily plunged the world into a deep recession. Unlike 1929, however, governments and central banks from all the industrialized countries acted quickly and in concert to moderate the effects of the fall. Their actions succeeded in averting an international economic catastrophe.

Considered together, it would be easy to interpret the 1980s as a string of economic disasters. In fact, this was springtime for a new, stronger, and more resilient economic order. The process is still young. Yet, while the world economy looked as if it were breaking to pieces in the 1970s, as the 1980s were drawing to a close it seemed as if a new equilibrium was starting to appear. The competition between the communist–capitalist camps had become irrelevant. Instead, the central policy issue became how to make markets work more effectively. In capitals from Jakarta to London, governments were recognizing that there was no value in using state-owned enterprises to do what the private sector could do better. The urgent questions governments faced were less concerned with ideology and more with practical applications. They were questions such as how to best manage exchange rates so that volatility is curtailed while currencies are permitted to float; how to determine when regulations are needed and when they are excessive; and how to open trade while minimizing negative repercussions on domestic industries. In short, the important question of this time—and it is one that remains with us over a decade later—is how to define the best role of government in an open economy.

During the 1970s until the late 1980s, Indonesia's economy ran counter to the mainstream of world economics. The oil shock that brought recession to the industrialized economies was a boom to Indonesia. The drop in oil prices in the 1980s, which was essential to the recovery of the industrialized economies, was a devastating blow to Indonesia. In 1983, however, Indonesia began a process of economic deregulation. In so doing, Indonesia was on the forefront of a consensus that was emerging among economists and policymakers around the world, namely, that markets work best when allowed to function with minimal government intervention. The openness that came with deregulating the economy permitted Indonesia to integrate its domestic economy more thoroughly into the international economy. Equally important, deregulation created the conditions for the private sector to become more deeply and extensively involved in the nation's economic development. The strengthened private sector contributed to economic growth and enhanced equity by involving more of the economy in the development process. The next three chapters will discuss the process and significance of Indonesia's economic deregulation and restructuring. We will conclude the book by reflecting on the implications of an increasingly global economy on the Indonesian economy and the evolution of our understanding of the economic development process. In the Epilogue, we will briefly consider the significance of Asia's economic turmoil that emerged in 1997.

8
The Economic Phoenix: The Financial Sector and the Origins of Indonesia's Deregulation Movement

As the 1980s progressed, many observers feared Indonesia's economic progress was transitory and insubstantial: like a straw house floating atop a crest of oil. They predicted Indonesia would be unable to sustain itself without the artificial life-support system of oil money. As it became increasingly evident that the oil boom was over, there was growing concern that Indonesia might be among the first casualties to be culled in a Darwinian triage of international economics. Fortunately, they were wrong. Around the same time, in April 1982, Gunung Galunggung, the volcano in West Java, suddenly erupted. Volcanic ash filled the skies over much of Java. The sun was hidden and days were dark. The rain fell like mud from the sky. Superstitious Indonesians—and there were many—saw in this as a portent of great difficulties that would afflict the nation. Unfortunately, events would prove them correct.

For almost a decade throughout the 1970s, Indonesia's economic progress had been sustained through the remarkable windfall of two oil booms. With the arrival of the new decade, however, this phenomenon was coming to an end. Indonesia's 'easy money' was almost finished. From 1970 to 1979, Indonesia's per capita income had grown more than five-fold.[1] Growth of this magnitude was remarkable. Still, it was too early to celebrate: Indonesia's per capita income in 1970 stood at only $80, hence even a 500 per cent increase brought it only to the level of $410 per capita.

Indonesia needed to begin the process of building a more diversified economy that could continue to develop without an excessive reliance on oil money. Rather than attempting to redirect the cumbersome machinery of state toward that end, Indonesia's economic team recognized that the state could no longer serve as the dominant generator of economic growth. Instead, the government tried to restructure the economy to tap into the power of the market. To do so, however, meant a significant change in the rules of the game. Hence the economic team began the

1980s with the task of dismantling the pre-existing regulatory framework so that the various sectors of the economy could, with unaccustomed freedom, create and respond to conditions best suited to their success. This process of redefinition and reorientation of the economy very soon became known as the 'deregulation movement'.

The process started in earnest in 1983 out of a conviction that the way to reinvigorate the overall financial system would be to give more freedom to the institutional lifeblood of the system, the banks. By 1986, when the price of oil plummeted and Indonesia faced the immediate and unrecoverable loss of more than two-thirds of its revenue, deregulation became an absolute necessity. The success that was to follow would not have been possible but for an earlier series of decisive and wide-ranging actions, through which the core principles of deregulation had already been put into place. As the deregulation movement proceeded, no aspect of the economy was untouched. In this chapter we will focus on the changes as they applied to the financial sector while in the next chapter we will focus on deregulation of trade and investment.

THE END OF INDONESIA'S OIL ECONOMY

The oil boom that began in 1979 with the revolution in Iran was short-lived. In January 1981 oil prices peaked above $35 per barrel and then declined. In 1982, the global economy slowed and slipped into a debilitating recession. Indonesia's economic growth was hit by constricting forces from two sides: the decline in global energy consumption and hence in the demand for Indonesia's oil, paralleled by shrinking markets for Indonesia's non-oil commodities as well.

In aggregate, this led to an abrupt contraction among Indonesia's exports of all types. Indonesia's appetite for imports, however, remained strong. Indonesia's balance of trade, which had long run a surplus, suddenly became negative. The heady 7 per cent annual growth in GDP that had been the norm for much of the 1970s was over. In 1982, Indonesia's economy grew by an anaemic 2.2 per cent.[2] The impact on the economy was devastating. The national psyche was shaken. The optimism of the 1970s suddenly disappeared and Indonesians began to doubt the promise of economic development. In a speech mirroring the temper of the times, President Soeharto said in January 1983 that the year ahead 'looks gloomy, but not without hope'. The state of the world economy, he said, 'poses an obstacle to the forward movement of our economy'.[3]

By mid-1983, it seemed as if the oil shock had been successfully absorbed and the crisis weathered. The government announced details of

Repelita IV that would begin in April 1984. The plan was predicated on an average growth of 5 per cent for the period. The targets appeared feasible, perhaps even excessively conservative. Indeed, given the annual population growth of 1.98 per cent and 1.8 million new entrants to the job market every year, 5 per cent growth was necessary for there to be any substantive progress in the economy. That year, Indonesia's GDP grew by 4.2 per cent and in 1984 the figure rose to 7.0 per cent. Across the nation, and in particular among Indonesia's economic team, the collective sigh of relief was almost audible. The renewed growth in Indonesia's economy, together with the signs of a recovery in the global economy, appeared to confirm that the recession of 1982 had been an anomaly.

Indonesia's respite was brief. In 1985, oil prices again began a further period of decline. The budget for 1986/7 was based on the assumption that oil might drop from $28 to $25 per barrel. Analyst reports in early 1986 predicted that while oil prices might dip as low as $20 per barrel, they would average around $22 to $24. A decline in oil prices of that magnitude threatened to decimate the government's budget. As a general rule of thumb, a decline of $1 per barrel of oil resulted roughly in a $400 million contraction in export earnings.[4] Indonesia ran the risk of a current account deficit that dwarfed all previous deficits. The only stable sector of the economy was agriculture, yet, it too faced serious problems since all of Indonesia's agricultural commodities, except coffee, faced depressed export markets.

Then in 1986, oil prices fell like a stone, dropping from over $25 per barrel in January to less than $10 per barrel in August. In one stroke, Indonesia faced the worst economic crisis since the New Order came to power in the mid-1960s. There were only two possible routes to restore the economy: oil prices would have to rise again and quickly or the economy would have to be rapidly and drastically restructured away from its heavy dependence on oil. There was no basis to expect oil prices to return to their previous levels any time soon. Fortunately, three years earlier, in 1983, Indonesia's economic team had begun a process of economic reform designed to make the economy more market-oriented, especially in the allocation and distribution of financial resources. These reforms gave a greater role to the private sector and—equally important—competition. At the same time, fiscal reforms had been introduced both to wean the budget from oil revenues and to make the taxation system more equitable. Systemic reforms would make economic signals more transparent, and thus assist the necessary restructuring into new and efficient non-oil production. In 1986, the urgent question was simply how quickly a country of 163 million people could reconfigure the basic structure of the economy.

COPING WITH CHEAP OIL: INITIAL STEPS

After his re-election in March 1983, President Soeharto installed a new Cabinet. Most of the economic team was retained. Although Widjojo Nitisastro's position as Co-ordinating Minister was given to Ali Wardhana, Widjojo remained an integral and leading member of the economic team as an economic adviser to the government.[5] J. B. Sumarlin became head of the planning agency, Bappenas, and Minister for Development Planning. Former Bank Governor Rachmat Saleh was made Minister of Trade. Arifin Siregar was selected as Governor of Bank Indonesia. Subroto became Minister of Mines and Energy. Emil Salim became Minister of Population and the Environment, and I was appointed Minister of Finance. Only Arifin Siregar was new to the team, but he was already well known to all the economic ministers. This continuity in the team was invaluable. It meant that the team members could focus immediately on the job at hand rather than spending time getting to know one another or manoeuvring for position within the Cabinet. Again, Indonesia would face severe hardships, and again teamwork and co-operation among the economic ministers—together with the support and confidence of President Soeharto—were crucial in meeting the challenges of reinvigorating the Indonesian economy.

The factors that led to the oil price collapse of 1986 first began to emerge with the oil decline in 1983. This was one instance when it was no exaggeration to say that a national hardship was 'a blessing in disguise'. The initial steps the government took to cope with the problem involved monetary, fiscal, and exchange rate policies. However, at the same time, the government had begun a long-term process of reorienting the country's basic model of development. The significance of these changes would not be apparent for several years. However, had the government not begun the reform process in 1983, the crises ahead could have thoroughly devastated the economy.

The 1983 Devaluation

In 1983, the new Cabinet faced a depressed economy, lower oil revenues, and the rapid depletion of the nation's foreign reserves. The situation was made worse by the nation's currency, which had grown steadily overvalued since the previous devaluation in November 1978. Once again, the rupiah's misalignment was hurting trade. In early August 1982, the *Asian Wall Street Journal* voiced the widely held belief that Indonesia would soon be forced to devalue the currency:

Nearly all economists, bankers and government officials seem to agree that a devaluation is coming—and probably sooner than later. That consensus has sent Indonesian importers and foreign businessmen scurrying for protection. It has also caused a run on US dollars from the Indonesian treasury, prompting Finance Minister Ali Wardhana to warn recently of a 'serious flow of foreign currency out of the country'. What's made a devaluation almost inevitable, bankers say, is the continuing deterioration of Indonesia's balance of payments position. Official foreign exchange reserves have dropped nearly 38 per cent in the past 10 months to slightly more than $5 billion (Manguno, 1982).

A little over a week later, on 16 August 1982, President Soeharto, in his annual speech commemorating Indonesia's independence, went on record affirming that the rupiah would not be devalued: 'The government believes and hereby states that a devaluation of the rupiah is not necessary. The rupiah's current managed float against foreign currencies will be maintained' (*Kompas*, 1982). The President's speech reflected the government's genuine desire to use all available means to avoid a devaluation. However, in the months to follow, the assault on the nation's current account persisted unabated. By March 1983, Indonesia's foreign exchange reserves had fallen to $3.3 billion. During the same month, OPEC cut oil prices by $5 a barrel. Under these circumstances, the government was faced with three possible courses of action: a) launch a programme of massive deficit spending, thereby reversing a long-standing core policy; b) greatly increase the level of offshore borrowing; or, c) devalue the currency. The government chose to devalue. For these reasons, on 30 March 1983 the rupiah was devalued by 27.5 per cent, from 702 to 970 rupiah to the dollar.[6] The benefits were indisputable: in a single move, it served to stimulate exports, draw back much of the flight capital that had moved overseas in anticipation of the devaluation, and helped to strengthen Indonesia's current account.

Although painful, since it brought an immediate decline in international purchasing power, the devaluation nevertheless achieved its purpose. Furthermore, the country had learned from the previous devaluation and was much more successful in controlling inflation than had earlier been the case. Without resorting to price controls or any other extraordinary measures, the 1983 inflation rate rose only to 11.5 per cent. By 1984, Indonesia's balance of trade returned to an export surplus, a position that has been maintained every year since. A crisis was averted.

Fiscal Restraint

The devaluation was an important policy for regaining control of the declining economy. Simultaneously, the government also chose to enact a range of supporting fiscal measures. In 1982, the government had already introduced an austerity budget. However, the economy had deteriorated so badly during the year that even those standards of austerity were insufficient for 1983. The government's routine operating budget had already been cut to the bone. The only place where expenses could be further reduced was in the development budget. Thus, in May the government announced that it would rephase billions of dollars worth of projects that were being planned or in the early stages of construction. Some of the specific projects selected for rephasing[7] were a $1.6 billion olefin plant, a $1.5 billion aromatic plant, a $1.35 billion oil refinery, and a $600 million alumina plant. The government decided to continue work on a downstream aromatics plant. However, it abandoned plans to build the upstream feeder facilities, opting instead to import the chemical inputs. This decision was taken to save foreign exchange in the short to medium-term. Given the conditions of the time, the government had to gear its decisions to accommodate short-term financial constraints while upholding its commitment to a balanced budget.

These particular projects were selected for suspension or cancellation largely because they were highly capital intensive. In particular, these projects were to be financed with loans from abroad that had to be matched by expenditures from the Indonesian government; hence rephasing them would release the government from large debt obligations in the future, while also lowering the amount that Indonesia would need to pay out immediately in local counterpart funds. From a market perspective, it should also be noted that, at the time, the regional market was glutted with some of the petrochemical materials that these plants would produce. Given these conditions, there were no compelling reasons to make these investments—either in the secondary plants or in the oil refinery itself.

In the months that followed, the government cancelled or rescheduled other projects as well, including a rail project, a large purchase of buses, and various shipping investments. In the end, during 1983 some $10 billion in projects were cancelled or rescheduled. These were difficult decisions to take because the New Order had staked its existence on its ability to advance the nation's economic development. The economic team was especially vulnerable. Following the cut-backs, a host of critics—especially those expecting to be directly involved in the cancelled projects—strongly criticized what they saw as the excessive conservatism of the country's economic policymakers. This, they claimed, slowed the country's economic development. Conservative or not, for the economic team the decision to rephase was based on careful and thorough economic analysis. If politics had been permitted to rule, the projects would have gone forward. This, however, did not occur.

THE NEW SPIRIT OF DEVELOPMENT

The devaluation of the rupiah and the cutting of projects were defensive measures. They were an attempt to reverse quickly and forcibly the growing current account deficit and arrest the depletion of the nation's foreign exchange reserves. They did little, however, to promote growth.

Without further reform, a devaluation is like performing surgery and leaving the incision unstitched. In such cases, even a successful operation would likely kill the patient. A devaluation is a temporary measure intended to facilitate an economic transition. But for the devaluation to be worth the pain, economic policymakers must address the underlying problems that led to the need for devaluation. For Indonesia in the early 1980s, it was becoming clear that the principal obstacle to growth—besides an overdependence on oil—was overregulation and excessive bureaucratic involvement in the economy. Both domestic commerce and external trade were too highly regulated. The result of this was that conducting business in Indonesia was notoriously inefficient and expensive. Through years of overregulation, Indonesia's products had become exorbitant for domestic consumers and were increasingly uncompetitive in international markets. If the 1983 devaluation was to have any salutary, long-term effect, it needed to be accompanied by reforms that addressed these underlying problems. With this as a starting point, the government in 1983 set in motion a long and arduous process of economic reform that ultimately would transform the basic structure of the Indonesian economy.

The spirit of the new approach was captured above all in one word, 'deregulation'. Starting around 1986, people in Indonesia began talking about 'deregulation' similar to the way people in Britain talk about football. A decade earlier, Indonesians everywhere—from field labourers to the President—saw themselves as 'agents of development'. Now, Indonesians had become ardent advocates of deregulation. The deregulation movement took on an aura that was both revolutionary and almost mystical. Many naively thought that deregulation was a 'magic bullet' that would quickly cure Indonesia of its economic ills. These views were somewhat extreme. Starting in the mid-1980s, however, the government began a long-term process of consciously and systematically peeling away layer upon layer of rules and regulations, procedures and protocols that had built up over time to the point where they had come to constrict economic freedom in the name of protection and stability. In so doing, a whole new movement was begun.

The 1983 Bank Reforms

The first shot in the battle to deregulate and reform the economy took place on 2 June 1983 with a series of measures intended to redefine the nation's banking environment.[8] At this time, banking in Indonesia was conducted through the central bank, a group of state-owned banks (consisting of five commercial banks, one development bank, and one savings bank), twenty-seven provincial development banks, seventy-two private domestic banks, and ten foreign banks.[9]

The original banking law, introduced in 1968, provided guidelines for the management of the central bank and the nation's state and private banks. Generally, this law has served the country well and continues today to be the basic legal foundation upon which Indonesian banking is established. But many of the regulations governing banking were created during the stabilization period and were intended to satisfy the needs of business and the economy during those difficult years. For example, the government had deliberately created a system that favoured the state banks because the government could direct these banks to support economic development policies. However, because the government exercised tight control over state banks, they were less responsive to the commercial interests of the private sector. The banks complied with government policies by supporting priority projects and sectors, and by implementing government programmes such as the selective credit programme, differential lending rates, and various savings schemes. The profit motive ran a distant second to satisfying government economic policy.[10]

State banks were in a curious situation. Although they were also given preferential treatment that ensured that they would grow large and dominate the nation's banking, their operations were truncated to support government policy objectives. State-owned corporations, for example, were obliged to do their banking with state banks. Additionally, state banks generally got preferential credit rates from the central bank. Furthermore, no matter how poor their performance, state banks would never be permitted to go bankrupt. Under these conditions, state banks were able to strongly dominate banking in Indonesia.

The Essence of the Reforms

The essential elements of the bank reforms, enacted on 2 June 1983, include the following:
- Credit ceilings were removed for all banks;
- All banks were given authority to determine their interest rates on deposits and loans;

- Taxes were eliminated on interest, dividends, and royalties on foreign currency deposits in all state banks;
- The differential interest rate system—according to which state banks determined interest rates according to the sector for which the loan was to be used—was abolished.

The abolition of the credit ceiling came as a great surprise and was heartily welcomed by the banking community. By raising or lowering the limits on the amounts that banks could lend, Bank Indonesia had a very direct way of managing the money supply. The government knew that by increasing bank autonomy in managing credit, the central bank would experience a corresponding decrease in its ability to regulate the money supply. The government accepted this risk as a necessary step in making Indonesia's banks more competitive. As a safety check, the Indonesian banking system was conservatively managed, with reserve requirements remaining at 15 per cent. Therefore, despite the removal of direct controls, banks were still required to conform to other indirect controls designed to maintain bank standards.

The differential interest rate system had been used to encourage investment in priority areas. The procedure was very helpful during the stabilization period, but during the 1960s and early 1970s, Indonesia's economy was much smaller and less complex. There were fewer banks and they were all more easily amenable to government directives. Furthermore, since financial resources were so scarce, it was appropriate for the government to intervene in the market to channel resources to those areas where they could most benefit long term development. In the 1980s, however, the economy had grown too big and complex to justify the differential interest rate system. Bankers often found it difficult to determine to which category a project should be classified. The system led to inefficient allocations of credit. There were instances of low interest loans going to inefficient projects, while efficient and potentially profitable projects had to pay high interest rates because they were not considered 'priority'. Finally, there was always the temptation of collusion: as a 'favour', a banker could classify a project as belonging to a low interest category when it should have been placed in a high interest category.

The government still provided subsidized loans to farmers and small businesses through Bimas, the KIK, and similar programmes. Apart from some special interventions such as this, the banks were free to charge what the market would bear and lend to whomever they determined was an acceptable credit risk.

A few months after the main banking reforms, in February 1984, Bank Indonesia introduced two new instruments for managing the money supply, the Sertifikat Bank Indonesia (SBI) and the discount window. Similar to the United States treasury bill, the SBIs were commitments to pay the holder, upon maturity, the purchase price plus accrued interest. Weekly, Bank Indonesia auctioned SBIs in varying denominations and maturities to banks and non-bank financial institutions, which could trade them on the market or hold them until maturity and then sell them back to Bank Indonesia. The government's main objective in selling SBIs was to establish an intermediate money market. Once this was established, the government could add or drain liquidity to the banking system by buying or selling SBIs. The excess liquidity resulting from the June 1983 reforms made this an opportune time to introduce this instrument. A year later, on 1 February 1985, the government added another instrument to its arsenal, the Surat Berharga Pasar Uang (SBPU). SBPUs were promissory notes that were widely used to pay off obligations and smooth out potential liquidity problems.

The discount window formalized Bank Indonesia's role as lender of last resort. One window was available to member banks with short-term liquidity problems; they could borrow from it for terms up to two weeks. A second window was used for somewhat longer term borrowing—periods of up to two months—which under certain circumstances could be extended to four months, though at relatively high interest rates. By controlling the rates charged on these discount windows, Bank Indonesia could also exert indirect control over the country's money supply.

Significance of the Reforms

The reforms were a giant step forward for banking in Indonesia as well as in the management of the economy. Despite the depressed economy, bank lending grew vigorously. Before the reforms, the state banks had a market share of almost 80 per cent, and this was virtually guaranteed through regulations. Under these conditions, they exhibited the typical characteristics of oligopolists in a high-demand market. There was little incentive to innovate, there was little competitive pressure, and there was little progress. The new laws forced the state banks to compete head-on with private banks. An ancillary effect of the reform was that the banks were forced to redefine their relationship with the government. Instead of state banks acting as instruments of the bureaucracy, they had to recast themselves as service providers in competition with private banks for the government's business.

With credit ceilings removed, there was a rush to increase lending. Predictably, the private banks responded more quickly. According to the

Bulletin of Indonesian Economic Studies, in the fifteen months following the June decree lending by the domestic private banks increased by over 90 per cent and that of state banks by 42 per cent (Booth, 1984: 13). The Indonesian economist, Anwar Nasution (1984: 28), using more colourful language, said that because the state banks had been 'fat cats for a decade' it would take them longer to remember how to catch mice. Although this was true at first, the state banks soon adopted a competitive spirit, picked up speed and held on to their dominant position into the 1990s. To sustain this surge in lending, banks needed to increase their deposits. They did so by raising interest rates on deposits. This served not only to mobilize domestic capital, but to draw back much of the flight capital that left the country before the 1983 devaluation.

Because the reforms had such a major impact on the banking system, some problems were inevitable. For example, in late 1984 there was a surge in demand in the interbank market, which triggered a huge increase in interest rates on overnight loans. Bank Indonesia had to open a special credit facility and limit the amount banks could borrow in the interbank market. With this, rates returned to their previous levels. There were several other difficulties as well. In 1985, Bank Perkembangan Asia failed and some of Bank Pacific's shares were taken over by Bank Indonesia. Moreover, early the next year, an investigation revealed that over 50 per cent of the loan portfolio of the Indonesian Development Bank, Bapindo, was considered bad or doubtful.

Despite these problems, the changes brought considerable progress to Indonesian banking and helped to accelerate growth while demonstrating convincingly the power of deregulation. Commenting on the reform, the *Asian Wall Street Journal* quotes an executive from the Indonesian Private Bankers Association as saying 'this whole package of policies... should lead to revitalization of the banking industry in Indonesia, which had grown lazy. And it should help our Indonesian businessmen get going again after the shocks of budget cutting, devaluation and price increases' (Manguno, 1983). That was the intention of the reform, and it succeeded. There was more. The reforms helped answer the question, 'If freed of unnecessary regulatory constraint, how will the banks react?' The market's response was unmistakable. According to Bank Indonesia data, between 1983 and 1988, credit for private sector business tripled—from Rp 15.7 trillion to Rp 46.9 trillion. This happened despite the depressed conditions of the time. Perhaps what was most significant is that deregulation of banking represented the beginning of what would be a long-term effort to deregulate the entire economy. This early experience confirmed the power of deregulation and encouraged the government to push the process forward.

A TIME TO BE TAXED

In the early 1980s, Indonesia could still count on oil as a source of export revenue for at least another two decades. With new discoveries, Indonesia might even remain an oil exporter for three or more decades. In the not too distant future, Indonesia was in fact likely to become a net oil importer. With oil and gas supplying some 70 per cent of government revenues, the depletion of oil reserves together with declining prices had serious implications for government revenues and, hence, the government's role in development. The most promising alternative source of revenues was the nation's people. Up to that time, compared to the citizens of most other countries, Indonesians were seriously undertaxed. Most Indonesians paid no taxes at all, and for those who did, collection consistently lagged behind expectations. If the Indonesian government expected to continue to develop the economy, non-oil taxes were the government's only avenue for raising the needed revenues.

Ever since the founding of the New Order, the government knew it had to overhaul the tax system. The job, however, was so enormous, and potentially so disruptive, that it was continually deferred. During the first decade and a half of the new government, instead of the massive reform needed, the government enacted numerous minor changes in hopes of extracting incremental improvements from the existing system. These efforts met with some success and during the 1970s government revenues from non-oil sources kept pace with the economic expansion. The problems with Indonesia's tax system, however, were far more serious than could be solved by tinkering. The entire system needed to be reconstructed from the ground up. This was finally accomplished with the enactment of the Income Tax Law of 1983, introduced on 31 December of that year and hence in effect from the start of 1984.

Origins and Development of Taxation in Indonesia

The 1983 Income Tax Law replaced three laws: the 1925 Corporate Tax Ordinance, the 1944 Income Tax Ordinance, and the 1970 Tax Law on Interest, Dividends, and Royalties. These complex laws were rendered all but incomprehensible by an assortment of over 20,000 supporting regulations promulgated since 1925. The pre-1983 tax system comprised a bewildering forty-eight rates for individuals and ten for corporations. The system consisted of a huge collection of decrees and amendments, many of which contradicted each other. To this was added a morass of exemptions and exclusions that could be applied for any number of reasons, such as promoting or supporting a particular group or activity. The system was entirely inaccessible to modern accounting practices.

Indonesia's tax system was so arcane that the only way for taxpayers to determine their tax obligations was by visiting the tax office and reviewing their financial data with a tax officer. The officer would then assign a tax rate to the individual or corporation. The taxpayer would then proceed to the Government Cash Office to pay, usually in cash. Although the tax assessment should have been determined based on objective criteria of income and legitimate exemptions, in reality taxes were highly 'negotiable'. It was well known that a job as a tax collector was one of the surest roads to riches in the government bureaucracy.[11] For this reason, there was a perversely 'rational' resistance to change within the tax department. For the tax collectors themselves, 'tax reform' was nothing more than a euphemism for income reduction.

To remedy this situation, in 1981 the government began a comprehensive study with the ultimate aim of creating an entirely new tax system. To this end, it drew on the services of a team of foreign consultants from the United States, Europe, and Japan to research world taxation systems and provide counsel to the Indonesian officials dealing with tax reform. Concurrently, the government sent a team of Indonesians to study modern taxation systems abroad. Critics both inside and outside the government chastised the government for employing foreign consultants. The economic team's argument, however, was that if we waited until Indonesians were sufficiently trained, this would delay the introduction of the new system by several years—something the government could not afford. For three years the government worked intensively on the new tax system. Except for a core group of advocates, including the President, the Cabinet, and the director-general of taxation, A. T. Salamun, the effort met with widespread resistance on every front—from the tax department, to the Parliament, to the public at large. Despite the resistance, the economic team knew that reform was imperative and pushed tax reform forward with the priority normally accorded to matters of national security. What was at stake was nothing less than the ability of the government to finance its future operations.

The Elements of the New Tax System

There were four basic objectives to the new law:

1. *Simplicity.* To ensure popular compliance, the new tax system had to be simple. As a general principle, it was agreed that the average taxpayer should be able to determine clearly and with certainty his tax obligations without retaining the services of a tax specialist or requiring contact with officials from the tax department. Simplicity was also needed to make the tax system *transparent*. The government reasoned that if the system were

simple, tax obligations would be less susceptible to interpretation. Simplicity should thwart the 'negotiability' of tax liabilities. This would benefit taxpayers, who would no longer need to worry that they could find themselves liable for a host of mysterious and seemingly arbitrary tax obligations. Simplicity was seen as essential to remove much of the aura of tyranny and corruption that hung over the tax system like a black cloud.

2. *Equity.* The tax system should be equitable for all citizens. To Indonesia's economic team, this meant that taxes should be progressive, that is, the burden of taxation should be borne most heavily by those with the highest income.

3. *Enforceable.* The tax system had to be designed so that taxes could be easily collectable. Despite the size of Indonesia—both in terms of geography and population—tax evaders do stand a good chance of being apprehended under the new system.

4. *Revenue Enhancing.* The new system should lead to an increase in the government's revenues. With this in mind, the government aimed at creating a system with relatively low tax rates but with a wide base. Furthermore, the system should be sufficiently efficient that the cost of administering the tax collection would be a small fraction of revenues collected.

Following extensive research, Indonesia devised an income tax system that satisfied these objectives. Some of the key provisions of this law are described below.

Taxing Income

The new law contained three basic rates for taxing income: 15 per cent, 25 per cent, and 35 per cent.[12] At the time of introduction, the lowest rate was applied to people in an income bracket of up to Rp 10 million (then about $10,000); the second rate was for individuals whose income was between Rp 10 million and Rp 50 million. The last rate was for individuals who earned over Rp 50 million. A few essential exemptions applied to all taxpayers. Notably, the taxpayer had an exemption for himself of Rp 960,000, plus additional exemptions of Rp 480,000 for a non-income-earning spouse and each dependent, up to three. Thus, for a family of five, with a non-income-earning spouse, the taxpayer began with a deduction of Rp 2,880,000, or about $2,880 at the time of introduction in 1984. With these few basic deductions, the majority of Indonesians were exempted from paying taxes. In this way, the system succeeded in its objective of being both simple and equitable.[13]

Another significant characteristic of the tax system was that collection was based on *self-assessment*. Tax officials were instructed to perform 'spot audits' and to investigate those cases for which there were grounds for suspicion. Otherwise, the tax system was expected to run with little or no contact between the taxpayer and the tax officials. In this way, the new system reduced the cost of tax collection (since fewer tax collectors were needed) and minimized the temptation for collusion.

Two other important measures put in place by the government to support this initiative were to computerize the entire taxation process and to institute a serious programme of job training. These measures were both intended to enhance the efficiency of the system and to aid in the accuracy of tax collection. There can be little doubt that for a country the size of Indonesia, the tax system had to be automated. Here again, however, many employees from the tax department adamantly opposed the change. They claimed that computerization would do little to enhance efficiency, while it would create a technical élite within the department on whom the rest would all depend. The 'tried and true' manual approach, they asserted, was more equitable in terms of work distribution. Furthermore, they argued that the manual methods might even be more accurate because, in some cases, human judgment was needed to properly process a tax return. The opponents to computerization were clearly wrong, but their arguments were similar to those of workers in other industries and countries around the world: they feared that machines would eliminate their jobs. While this may be a legitimate concern, nevertheless improved efficiency in tax processing was a matter of national interest that had to go forward. Another unspoken concern of some employees in the tax department was that computerization might well make the whole system of informal payments more difficult. Indeed, that was one of the intentions of the government and this was an intention that no one could publicly oppose. Ultimately, the computers were bought, and—to the dismay of some—they accomplished their intended purposes.

The Value Added Tax

For taxes to compensate for the loss in oil revenues, Indonesia needed to have a source of tax revenues beyond the income tax. Indonesia's economic planners selected the value added tax (VAT). Writing on the VAT, economist Arnold C. Harberger (1990: 27–8) said 'it is a robust and good tax, which can be designed to raise substantial revenues at small economic cost. ... No public finance development of the last half century can rival the emergence and spread of the value-added tax.'[14] In time, the VAT became a corner-stone of the Indonesian taxation system. Its success exceeded all projections and expectations.

In Indonesia, the VAT applies to all manufactured goods and imports, as well as to construction services. The tax does not apply to cigarettes, nor does it apply to agriculture because raising crops or livestock is not considered manufacturing. Otherwise, there are no exemptions. Most important, in Indonesia, unlike in most other countries, the VAT is applied at one rate only, 10 per cent, and is applied at all stages of goods being sold—but not at the retail level. It is 'invisible', therefore, to consumers. This made it a less contentious tax. Furthermore, unlike sales taxes, the VAT is not a cascading tax. In Indonesia, the new tax replaced a sales tax that was complex and essentially unenforceable.

With only one rate and with universal applicability, the greatest strength of Indonesia's VAT was its simplicity. It would be harder to find a simpler tax. Although Indonesia received its inspiration for this tax from Europe, the European approach was very complicated as it applied to both goods and services at many rates. The second strength of Indonesia's VAT was the method by which it was collected. A company that pays a VAT when it buys a good, will get a refund when it sells its product that contains the good for which the VAT was already paid. To take the classic example, if a baker sells bread to a supermarket chain, he will pay the VAT when he buys the ingredients and collects the VAT when he sells his own products. It is in a company's interest to collect the VAT because only then can it be compensated for the VAT it has already paid.[15] In order not to discourage exports, the VAT was made refundable on exports for which a VAT had been paid.

Taxing Luxuries and Property

Indonesia adopted two more taxes during this period: the property tax and the luxury tax. As a compromise to some members of Parliament, Indonesia adopted a tax on goods considered luxuries. This tax was applied at two rates, 10 per cent on such items as consumer appliances and carbonated beverages, and 20 per cent on various items including sedan cars and private aircraft.

Lastly, Indonesia completed its arsenal of taxes with a property tax. The introduction of this tax was particularly troublesome. Since the colonial period, Indonesia had land and property taxes on record. These taxes, and especially the land tax, were generally ignored because the government considered the old tax to be unenforceable. Even if it could have been enforced, it would have placed the tax burden on the nation's farmers, people who were usually not wealthy enough to tax. The objective of the new property tax law was to collect taxes primarily from the relatively wealthy owners of residential urban real estate or commercial property. As with the other elements of Indonesia's taxation system, the property tax

FIGURE 8.1
Non-oil Tax Revenues, 1984/85–1995/96

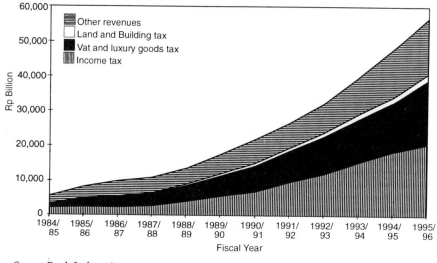

Source: Bank Indonesia.

Note: Figures are in current rupiah. Other revenues include: import duties, excise duties, export tax, other tax and non-tax receipts.

was designed to be simple. Buildings valued at less than Rp 2 million were exempted from tax. Otherwise, the tax rate of 0.5 per cent applied to 20 per cent of the land and building's assessed value. The logic behind this rather unusual formula was 'psychological'. Many members of Parliament were concerned that the property tax would prove too onerous to them personally. To get the law passed and taxes collected, the economic team's strategy was to keep taxes low. By keeping the tax at only 0.5 per cent and saying that only 20 per cent of the assessed value was taxable, the members of Parliament were willing to agree to the tax. Although this tax could not compare with the VAT or the income tax in terms of its revenue generation capacity, it was an important step forward in capturing a source of potential revenue among Indonesia's wealthy 'propertied class'.

Since their introduction, the VAT and the luxury taxes together have contributed between 29 and 34 per cent of total non-oil revenues. Overall, non-oil tax revenues have increased almost ninefold in just over a decade (Figure 8.1).

The Problem of Exemptions

The most important step in bringing equity to the tax system was the elimination of a plethora of exemptions and loopholes. This may have been the most difficult aspect in the reform of the nation's tax system.

Under the previous taxation regime, there were so many exemptions that a person could easily avoid paying taxes simply by claiming affiliation to a tax-exempt group. Hence the elimination of exemptions and loopholes was particularly alarming to the wealthiest segment of the population, which was also a politically powerful group. However, the designers of the new tax code reasoned that by exempting even one group, the government was opening the door for other groups to lobby for special tax status. Two huge and powerful constituencies that had previously been exempted from paying taxes were the nation's civil servants and the co-operatives. Obtaining consensus that these groups would be taxed for the first time was an enormous challenge. In the end, the principle of equality prevailed and these and other formerly exempted groups were for the first time required to pay taxes.

Foreign investors were another powerful vested interest that had grown accustomed to preferential tax treatment. For decades, many governments, in their efforts to woo international investors, were engaged in a battle to give their country a competitive edge over others. The chief lure to bring in the big investors has always been tax incentives. Governments around the world have demonstrated great ingenuity in adjusting the tax system in the quest for foreign investment. Indonesia was no exception. Before introducing its new tax law, Indonesia offered tax holidays to foreign investors as an incentive to invest in the country. When Indonesia was preparing to enact the new tax law, it faced a serious dilemma: could Indonesia remove exemptions from domestic taxpayers such as civil servants and co-operatives and still extend them to foreign investors? The most compelling argument in favour of tax holidays was that without such inducements, investors would choose another country for the site of their business. However, this raised other questions. If tax holidays were given to foreign investors, what about domestic investors? Further, if the exemption were given to them, then what other groups should be exempted? And so on. The government eventually took the difficult decision to eliminate the tax holiday for foreign investment. The government argued that its new tax regime was sufficiently fair, simple, and economical that it should serve as an incentive in its own right. As an added enhancement to businesses, the government introduced a liberal and progressive depreciation schedule that applied to all businesses.

The reaction was explosive. The government heard from many quarters that Indonesia would lose out in investment. Business executives and chambers of commerce asserted that without tax incentives Indonesia was simply not sufficiently attractive to bring in foreign investment, especially given the tough competition from other countries in the region. The result? The critics were right—but only to a point. Indeed, Indonesia's overall investment environment was not attractive. Removal of the tax exemptions was a black mark against an investment regime that was still suffering under the nationalist distortions that grew out of the 1970s. But the government was also right. The tax holiday had added to the distortions in the economy. The investors who argued that they needed a tax holiday during the start up period of their business were often the same who later insisted that they needed protectionist measures to stay in business. Such investors contributed to Indonesia's 'high cost economy'. Indonesia decided to gear its tax regime to attract companies that were strong enough that the tax holiday would not be a decisive factor in the decision to invest.

The decision to halt the tax holiday was a painful one, particularly for BKPM, the organization charged with promoting and co-ordinating investment. In the short term, the *status quo* was preferable to the new investment environment. However, by abandoning the tax holiday, Indonesia was trying to shift its focus from a short-term to a long-term strategy. The transition period was difficult. None the less, the government stood firm in its decision and for three years, 1984–6, foreign investment levels declined considerably. Eventually, however, the investors returned, for reasons we will discuss in the next chapter.

The question remains, however, whether the tax holiday is economically justifiable. The argument that the holiday is needed to match conditions in countries competing for the same foreign investment is not without merit. Before selecting a site for investment, foreign businesses will have an extensive list of factors they will use to determine where they believe they can obtain the best return on their investment. For example, in 1997, among Indonesia's neighbours, China, Vietnam, Myanmar, India, Sri Lanka, and others do offer various forms of tax holiday. By not matching that incentive, Indonesia may indeed be putting itself at a competitive disadvantage in this respect. Of course, Indonesia offers many other advantages which may offset that one disadvantage. In the final analysis, whether a country offers a tax holiday is probably of relatively little significance to the investor or the government. This is especially true because firms are usually not profitable in their initial years of operation. What is most important, however, is to create an environment that is attractive and supportive of all investment. The most attractive investment environment is the one that is efficient, free of corruptive distortions, and low in cost. The lack of these qualities represent a kind of tax to investors and one from which the government derives no benefit.

Building Support and Maintaining It

No one likes taxes.[16] Without taxes, however, there can be no public infrastructure, public schools, and national defence. In short, organized society would cease to function without taxes. This notwithstanding, when news surfaced that a new tax system was about to be introduced, many newspapers and individuals were very critical, especially regarding the new income tax law. To counter this, the government—working with private institutions—launched a nation-wide contest to build public awareness and support. The contest gave cash prizes to the writers of outstanding articles explaining the new tax system and its benefits. The contest organizers suddenly found themselves inundated with articles, the best of which were selected and reprinted in publications throughout the country. These were supplemented with books that were given to legislators for distribution to their constituencies. These efforts helped to reduce the public opposition to the new tax system and accelerated acceptance of the new law.

No matter how well crafted the law may have been, its success depended on having people qualified to implement it. As mentioned earlier, the government sent many officials from the Directorate General of Taxation to training programmes in the Netherlands, the United States, and Japan. Several of these officials engaged in specialized studies in accounting, auditing practices, and taxation procedures. Others were enrolled in MBA and Ph.D. programmes in subjects from public finance to computer science. From these highly trained individuals, the Directorate General of Taxation formed an élite auditing team. When the new tax law was introduced, corporate and individual taxpayers were given an initial amnesty period during which time they were asked to voluntarily report their current tax obligations. For those who complied with the terms of the amnesty, all previous tax violations would be forgiven. Few, however, availed themselves of this offer. After this period ended, the élite auditing team went to work. They were quickly able to uncover billions of rupiah in unreported revenues. Equally important, the team succeeded in sending a powerful message to the taxpaying community, that is, for the first time, the government was serious about collecting taxes. This team had an important role in building and maintaining the credibility of the tax system.

Assessing the New System

In 1984, the year the new tax law took effect, Indonesia obtained about 30 per cent of its tax receipts from non-oil and gas sources. Two years later, in 1986/7, when Indonesia was facing a crisis from falling oil prices, the new tax system was coming on stream. Then, 61 per cent of tax receipts came from non-oil and gas sources. Reversing a long-term trend, non-oil taxes leaped beyond oil revenues and in fiscal year 1994/5 contributed over 76 per cent of the government's revenues. The new tax system worked. The most important factor behind the success was that it was created in the spirit of deregulation: thousands of complicated rules and qualifications were collapsed into a simple and relatively easy to understand system. Furthermore, the collection process was much less labour intensive. Lastly, the VAT was particularly ingenious in the way in which it transferred the burden of collection to the merchants. During Repelita V the government collected Rp 45.2 trillion in VAT, representing one-fifth of government revenues.

This is not to suggest there were no problems. To this day, the system still needs improvement. Although collusion and evasion have been reduced, they have not been eliminated. In this regard, Anwar Nasution (1991: 15) wrote:

In spite of encouraging progress, however, the 13 per cent ratio of non-oil revenues to non-oil GDP in 1990/91 remains low by international standards. In 1989 the ratios of tax to GNP for Thailand and the Philippines, for example, were 18.9 per cent and 17.2 per cent respectively. The low collections of non-oil tax revenue [in Indonesia] are a sign of low tax compliance, which indicates a need for further improvements in tax administration as well as in the legal and accounting systems.

Nasution raises a very important point. The new system succeeded in increasing the number of corporate and individual taxpayers. The government's non-oil revenues increased substantially at a time when alternative revenue sources were desperately needed. However, despite the increase in number of income tax payers, compliance is Indonesia remains low, even in comparison to our neighbours. There is still a large segment of the population who pay no taxes or who pay far less than their legal obligations. Because taxation is so vital to Indonesia's development efforts the country must be vigilant in its efforts to improve the tax system. Indonesia needs to refine the system so that taxpayers understand their tax obligations more clearly and so that the opportunities for evasion or collusion are eliminated. Otherwise the momentum of progress may be lost and the tax revolution that began in 1983 will end up being no more than another example of the country's inability to overcome the inefficiency and malfeasance that have tainted so many of the nation's tax collection efforts for decades.

THE NEXT PHASE IN FINANCIAL REFORMS

Following the oil market crash of 1986, Indonesia's programme of financial sector reforms moved into high gear. Although economic difficulties prompted the movement, it was maintained because deregulation and debureaucratization revitalized the economy. In the mid to late 1980s, the Indonesian economy underwent a rapid metamorphosis. The country that had been frequently looked upon as the 'sick man' of South-East Asia was suddenly being touted as one of the next generation of Asian 'dragons' or 'tigers'.[17] However, the transition from oil collapse to a revitalized economy was tense and distressing.

1986: Indonesia's Last Devaluation?

The 1986 crash of the oil market created a situation with many parallels to 1983, except the situation in 1986 was far more extreme. One unfortunate parallel was that despite the devaluation that took place in April 1983, in 1986 Indonesia's current account deficit once again slid into the danger zone.[18] With oil trading below $10 a barrel, Indonesia's revenues from oil dried up. Demand for imports, however, remained strong. This put pressure on Indonesia's balance of payments. The situation was exacerbated by the frequent, extreme gyrations in the world currency markets. For several years, the relative exchange rates of the dollar, yen, mark, and franc had been so volatile that it was difficult for the smaller currencies to find an appropriate equilibrium rate on which to peg their currencies. The September 1985 Plaza Accord was intended to bring greater stability and co-ordination to the major world currencies. In the long run, greater stability in the currency markets would aid Indonesia. In the short run, however, the principal effect was to cause an appreciation of the yen, which added another serious difficulty to Indonesia's already embattled economy as so much of Indonesia's debt repayment obligations were denominated in the Japanese currency.[19]

Since 1983 the rupiah had been placed on a so-called 'crawling peg'. In other words, the currency was expected to float against the US dollar, with the range of fluctuation moderated to maintain exchange rate stability. That range would be adjusted over time. In reality, the rupiah crawled too slowly, moving from Rp 994 to the dollar in 1983 to Rp 1,134 in September 1986. Given the level of inflation Indonesia had experienced over these three years and the seriousness of the country's balance of payments deficit, the rupiah had again become overvalued. The government needed to take immediate action. Again, as in 1983, Indonesia had the same mixture of options: drawing down its foreign exchange reserves, increased overseas borrowing, deficit financing, or devaluation. Again, as in 1983, the government chose to devalue. On 12 September 1986, the government cut the value of the nation's currency to the new rate of Rp 1,644 to US $1.00, a 31 per cent reduction in value. That, however, is where the similarities with 1983 stop.

Most notably, the government was successful in holding down inflation after the 1986 devaluation. That year, the inflation rate was only 5.9 per cent, the next year it rose to 9.1 per cent, in 1988 it dropped to 5.8 per cent and in 1989 it stood at 6.0 per cent. To have kept the average rate of inflation less than 7 per cent after such a large devaluation is unusual. This accomplishment signified that Indonesia had made considerable progress in learning how to manage inflation following a devaluation. The principal factors that contributed to such low inflation were tight control over the money supply, fiscal restraint, and good co-ordination between Bank Indonesia and the nation's other banks. Helping further, world inflation during that period was relatively low, averaging less than 4 per cent among the OECD countries.

On paper, a devaluation is a simple numerical adjustment, a change in ratios. In reality, devaluations are disruptive and traumatic. No reasonable government would undertake a devaluation lightly.[20] A devaluation shakes the confidence of the people in their currency and in the government they have charged to act as steward of the economy. In 1986, the government realized it needed to approach exchange rate management differently so that, if at all possible, the nation could avoid having to experience the trauma of devaluation again. What was especially important with the 1986 devaluation, therefore, were the measures that followed. This devaluation was designed to be Indonesia's last.

Since the 1986 devaluation, the rupiah has been governed according to a liberal 'floating' system against a basket of currencies. Under this system, the exchange rate was adjusted daily with the rupiah rising or falling against the dollar and other currencies in a way that more accurately reflects the market value of the currency. A float can be a double-edged sword. On occasion, changes in the relative values of currencies had prompted the government to raise the exchange rate of the rupiah against the dollar and other currencies. When this happened, there were often vociferous complaints from those who had made investments or engaged in currency speculation on the assumption of a steadily declining rupiah. This, however, was one of the 'costs' of adopting a floating exchange rate system.

The process of determining exchange rates is an imprecise science at best. Since 1986, and throughout my tenure in office, the government's exchange rate policy was conservative and tended to err on the side of having the rupiah somewhat undervalued. Consequently, after the 1986 devaluation there were no instances when the economic team further considered devaluation. A devaluation is a blunt instrument that should be avoided if at all possible. By moving the rupiah to a float that permitted the currency to accurately reflect the market conditions, the economic team tried to create the conditions that would render devaluations a thing of the past.[21]

The 1988 Bank Reform

In October 1988, Minister of Finance Sumarlin announced a new package of measures aimed primarily at deregulating the banking system. Building on the 1983 reforms, the 'October 1988 Package', or 'Pakto' as it was called (for 'Paket Oktober'), was designed to stimulate growth and innovation among state, private, and foreign banks operating in Indonesia. Some of the highlights of this measure are as follows:

1. *Foreign Banks.* For the first time, foreign banks were permitted to set up branches outside Jakarta in any of the nation's six major cities, provided that 50 per cent of their loan portfolio went to export-oriented businesses. The new cities now open to foreign banks were: Surabaya, Semarang, Medan, Bandung, Ujung Pandang, and Denpasar. Furthermore, foreign banks were permitted to open joint ventures with Indonesian banks.

2. *Domestic Banking.* Measures were taken to facilitate lending, enhance competition, and strengthen export financing.

   i) The requirements for establishing a bank or opening branches were relaxed. The reserve requirement was reduced from 15 per cent to 2 per cent, which enabled banks to expand lending as a proportion to deposits.

   ii) State-owned enterprises were freed of the obligation to deposit all their funds with state banks. Instead, state companies needed to keep only 50 per cent of the funds in state banks. As for the rest, no more than 20 per cent of a state-owned enterprise's funds could be deposited in a single commercial bank. This regulation, obviously, was intended to force state banks to compete even more directly with private banks as well as to foster competition among private banks.

   iii) Bank Indonesia extended the time covered by foreign currency swaps from six months to three years. This gave traders security against devaluations and exchange rate variations. This provision benefited investors by reducing the risk of holding rupiah. It also benefited the government by reducing the inducement for capital flight.

3. *Taxes on Interest Income.* A 15 per cent withholding tax was applied to interest on savings and time deposits. This was an essential step to help add some vitality to the country's stock exchange. Before Pakto, interest on bank accounts was tax exempt, whereas dividend income and capital

gains from stocks were taxed. Because interest rates on bank deposits were so attractive, there was no incentive to invest in stocks. By taxing interest from bank deposits, the tax bias in favour of bank deposits was removed, and this led the way to a significant increase in investment in stocks.

Development of the Capital Markets

Indonesia has had a stock exchange since 1912. The original equities market was established under Dutch rule in Jakarta when the city was still known as Batavia. Later, a second exchange was established in Surabaya. Trading stopped on the exchange in 1956 after the Indonesian government began nationalizing foreign firms. From the early days of the New Order the government recognized the value of a stock exchange as a vehicle for mobilizing capital and fostering growth of the private sector. There were, however, several inhibiting factors, the most important of which was the government's uncertainty about its ability to regulate a large and active market. The government had limited ability to collect taxes on dividends and capital gains. Furthermore, Indonesia had a shortage of qualified accountants who could perform credible audits of listed companies. On the corporate side, there were few companies in Indonesia prepared for the rigours of financial reporting required of companies that are publicly listed. Owing to these and other factors, the Jakarta Stock Exchange (JSX) was modestly launched on 10 August 1977, with a single listing, that of the cement company PT Semen Cibinong. Despite the constraints, by 1984 the number of listed companies had risen to twenty-four and remained frozen at that level for the next five years.

Throughout this period, there was little activity in the Indonesian equity market, a phenomenon that resulted directly from stringent regulations put in place to ensure market stability. In 1976, the government established a 'middleman' agency—PT Danareksa—to buy and sell shares of publicly listed companies with the express mandate that price fluctuations must be kept within a 4 per cent band. Danareksa intervened in the market by buying and selling shares to maintain stability. Stocks served essentially the same purpose as a certificate of deposit. There was little risk of loss, but equally little hope of gain.

After the Pakto measures, a new set of deregulation policies was introduced on 22 December, known as Paket Desember (Pakdes or 'the December Reform Package').[22] This package was intended to help invigorate Indonesia's capital markets by permitting the creation of new, privately operated stock exchanges in several provincial cities and by removing the 4 per cent fluctuation limit on listed shares. The package also included measures intended to guard against capital market abuses. This it did by prohibiting insider trading and limiting the board of any exchange from holding more than 10 per cent of the exchange's total shares. The package also provided guidelines for advanced financial services such as factoring, leasing, securities trading, and credit cards.

Consequences of the Reforms

The market's reaction to the 1988 deregulation packages was swift and intense. Both the banking sector and the capital market expanded at a remarkable pace. The measures also illustrated the extent to which the public was influenced by banking regulations. The immediate reaction to the new measures was a rush on bank deposits. Customers sought to withdraw funds before 14 November when the 15 per cent tax on deposit income was due to take effect. The sudden drop in liquidity caused interbank interest rates to jump suddenly by 10 percentage points pushing rates up to around 32 per cent.[23]

Despite these initial problems, banks of every size and form started to reassess their operations in Indonesia and most tried to expand. According to the Biro Pusat Statistik (BPS or Central Bureau of Statistics) data, the number of banks grew from 83 in 1987 to 213 in 1995, and during the same period the number of branches grew from 1,283 to 4,601. Binhadi (1995: xxi) notes that the total volume of funds mobilized quadrupled from $21 billion in December 1988 to $85 billion in December 1994, while during the same period bank loans leapt from $28 billion to $99 billion.

More important than sheer volume have been the qualitative changes in bank operations, namely:

- Improved efficiency of financial intermediation due to the market mechanism in determining interest rates;
- Greater competition among banks;
- A much broader and improved range of financial products available to bank customers.

More far-reaching still, the 1988 reforms changed some fundamental characteristics of the economy. The effort begun in the 1970s to monetize the countryside came to full fruition in the late 1980s. It was then that the private sector recognized the enormous potential of this huge, yet underbanked market. Indonesia's banking infrastructure began to expand as never before. The proliferation of bank branches and financial services created a tremendous force that reached out to those who previously had been overlooked and excluded from the formal banking system. Bank branches could be found in small, remote villages that just a few years earlier would never have been given a moment's thought by commercial banks. Villages across Indonesia were fully integrated into the formal economy as virtually everyone was encouraged to open an account, no matter how small. Farmers, who previously would have bartered their goods in local markets, now dealt in cash, held their income in bank deposits, and collected interest on their savings. More than ever, farmers chose to hold their savings in banks rather than as bags of rice.

In all this what was perhaps most astounding was not the expansion of the banking network but the extent to which banks fought to build their customer base, from the largest cities to the small towns and villages. Some banks held lotteries to attract new depositors. Others offered gifts. Others promoted themselves through slick advertising, while others tried to offer rates and fees that were more attractive than those of their competitors. For the first time, the forces of a highly competitive financial market spread across the Indonesian archipelago. This laid the foundation for an economic chain reaction that led to the influx of other goods and services. In the process, a kind of economic transformation spread throughout the country, pushed with such determination that the 'invisible hand of the market' almost seemed to assume physical characteristics.

The sudden surge in banks and branches led to some problems:

1. There was a serious shortage of qualified staff, which led to a frenzy of employee hunting and executive 'hijacking'. The turnover in staff was enormous and disruptive to stable management. People with little experience were being rapidly promoted to positions of responsibility for which they were unqualified. The demand for employees led to a rapid and extreme escalation of salaries especially for executive staff.

2. The growth in banks and branches proceeded more quickly than Bank Indonesia's capacity for supervision. Bank Indonesia was pushed to the limits and this increased the risk of bank mismanagement.

3. Because the reserve ratio was lowered from 15 per cent to just 2 per cent, banks suddenly found themselves with a surplus in loanable funds. The combination of lower reserve requirements and intensified competition put pressure on banks to increase lending. Consequently, there was an increase in bad loans, bank failures, and fraud.

4. Lending increased rapidly, and the money supply increased accordingly, which created inflationary pressure. The economy become overheated. Therefore the government had to exert great efforts to control inflation.

The first major problem occurred in 1990 when the private bank, Bank Duta, lost some $420 million in misguided foreign exchange transactions. The bank would have collapsed were it not for a group of foundations that stepped in to provide the bank with the cash needed to weather the emergency. The next major banking crisis occurred in 1992 when Bank

Summa, one of Indonesia's top ten banks, was suffering under bad debts associated with Indonesia's volatile property market at that time. The bank was owned by the Astra group, one of the nation's leading conglomerates and its largest manufacturer of motor cars. Astra's principal shareholder pumped millions of dollars into Summa, hoping to rescue the bank. In the end, the effort was unsuccessful. Summa was forced to suspend operations in 1993, representing the most serious blow to the nation's banking system since the new banking regulations were passed ten years earlier.

As with the banks, the stock market demonstrated rapid but erratic growth. As with banking services, Indonesia's stock market also took off. Trading grew at a rate previously unimaginable. The hitherto 'sleepy' exchange was suddenly infused with a surplus of energy. In 1988 trading values rose by 490 per cent. The following year trading value rose by 3,052 per cent! The JSX, which for so long had been virtually invisible, suddenly became the 'rock star' of the Indonesian economy. For a brief period from 1989 to 1990, virtually the entire nation was fixated on the stock exchange. The exchange seemed to be a machine for generating overnight millionaires. Indonesia was suddenly hit with *demam bursa*, or 'stock exchange fever'. Taxi drivers, housewives, and villagers stood overnight in long lines, frequently carrying with them their life's savings, to be among the first to buy shares in initial public offerings.

Inevitably, the bubble burst. In 1990, the JSX was among the fastest growing exchanges in the world. A year later, its composite index declined by 41 per cent in rupiah terms and 44 per cent in dollar terms, the sharpest decline of any major stock market in the world. The crash was unfortunate, but not surprising. What was most regrettable was that the sharp decline in the market certainly harmed many of the small investors who believed the stock exchange was a fast route to quick and easy wealth. The extreme swings were a sign of immaturity for the exchange as an institution as well as for the people who naively gambled with their scant savings, only to see them disappear.

To extract itself from the business of running the exchange, the government privatized the JSX in April 1992 through the creation of PT Bursa Efek Jakarta (BEJ), with its own directors, managers, and shareholders. Through this means, the government hoped to encourage greater efficiency through private sector management. In May 1995, the JSX moved to a new high-rise building and in October of that year the exchange adopted a fully computerized trading system. It was a rough ride, but in a matter of a few years, the JSX did make the transition from a small and ineffective exchange to a serious capital market. In the years ahead, it will certainly play an increasingly important role in mobilizing funds to support the nation's business development (Figure 8.2).

FIGURE 8.2
Jakarta Stock Exchange Index, 1977–September 1997

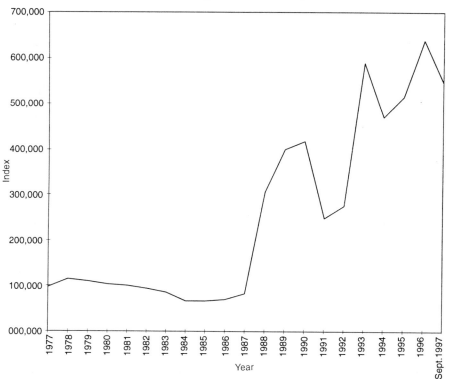

DEREGULATING THE FINANCIAL SECTOR:
SOME LESSONS

With the bank reform of 1983, Indonesia began a process of financial reform and deregulation that was to last for more than a decade. It was an opportune time for change. In 1982, Indonesia had passed through serious economic difficulties. These problems were minor compared to the disaster of 1986. Yet, in 1982 Indonesia's GDP growth rate was 2.2 per cent, whereas in 1986 it was 5.9 per cent. Indonesia was able not only to survive the utter collapse of the oil economy in 1986, it even managed a high level of growth. The growth of 1986 seems to defy logic. Without doubt, the reason Indonesia was able to maintain its economic growth during the collapse of the oil market in 1986 was because three years earlier the country had already begun the process of deregulation and tax reform.[24] Though we would not have said it at the time, the deregulation process begun in 1983 was Indonesia's 'declaration of independence from oil'. When the oil market collapsed in 1986, the Indonesian economy was already significantly more diversified than it had been just a few years earlier.

These reforms were important because through them the government changed the nature of financial intermediation in Indonesia. Banking, the stock market, and exchange rate management, all became simpler and more market-oriented. The economy became more flexible and stronger as a result. The changes in financial intermediation were complemented by changes to the taxation system that equally reflected a spirit of simplicity and market-orientation. The VAT, in particular, was designed with business in mind. Together, these financial and fiscal reforms laid the foundation for the restructuring of the economy. Indonesia's economic team learned many important things from this restructuring process. A few key lessons are summarized below:

1. *Flexible Exchange Rates.* Ever since Indonesia abandoned the multiple exchange rate system in the early 1970s, Indonesians have been permitted to convert and move currencies into and out of the country with complete freedom. The philosophy that was behind the free convertibility of foreign currencies, however, was not extended to the management of exchange rates: one was market-oriented, the other was not. For many years Indonesia vainly tried to maintain a stable exchange rate by keeping the rupiah tightly pegged to the dollar. The fixed exchange rate or 'crawling peg' gave the illusion of stability, nothing more. In reality, Indonesia's trade was hindered by a currency that was repeatedly subject to devaluation and persistently overvalued. Experience has shown that exchange rates should be permitted to float with as few distortions in setting rates as possible. The government's first job is to ensure that the economy overall remains healthy—free of oppressive regulations and unencumbered by excessive public or private sector debt. Government intervention in exchange rates should be confined to efforts to moderate temporary extreme rises and falls in the currency. When such intervention is needed, it should be forcible in order to send a clear message to currency traders. Otherwise, government authorities should not try to fix exchange rates; efforts to do so will always fail and end up damaging the economy.

2. *Balancing a Liberal Banking System and Capital Market with Appropriate Regulations.* It was not until the 1980s, after Indonesia began deregulating the banking system, that the country experienced the enormous potential of banks to mobilize funds and energize commerce. The deregulation of the capital markets had a similar function. Indonesia's stock market had been virtually comatose for over a decade, in large part because the state company Danareksa was charged to intervene in the market to suppress volatility of any sort. Soon after Danareksa was relieved of this function, Indonesia's stock market experienced huge gains and losses. Some might interpret these gyrations as vindicating the stabilizing role of Danareksa. A more appropriate interpretation would be to accept that

when a market is freed from extreme and oppressive controls, there is a risk of volatility. By freeing the market, investors should expect to see fluctuations similar to those in every stock exchange. Overall, however, the market should be far more effective in satisfying its primary functions as a vehicle for raising funds and sharing profits. On the other hand, it is equally important to recognize that there is a limit to deregulation, as good regulations are also essential to the proper functioning of markets. With a stock market, for example, it is important to recognize the necessary and salutary role of both fair regulations and strict regulators. Market regulators must be watchful to guard against insider trading and other abuses that could destroy the exchange. As already stated, Indonesia's deregulation effort was not aimed at removing all regulations. Furthermore, in extreme cases, intervention in the stock market may be needed to prevent panic selling. This will become increasingly a threat as the market grows larger and more computerized. Here, as throughout the deregulation process, the government's intention was not deregulation for its own sake. Instead, the government sought to streamline regulations so that they would not act as impediments to efficient economic growth.

3. *The Value of Fiscal Conservatism.* During this period there was a great deal of pressure on the government to abandon its commitment to a balanced budget and to engage in deficit spending as a way to stimulate the economy. The government resisted this approach and was still able to reactivate the economy without relinquishing its commitment to prudent monetary and fiscal policies. Moreover, for some time Indonesia has had to cope with a very heavy debt repayment burden. It is to the government's credit that when it faced serious economic difficulties, it never tried to respond through deficit spending, excessive borrowing, or through the deliberate draw-down of foreign exchange reserves. Such 'solutions' would have postponed problems only to create new troubles in the future.

4. *The Dangers of Excessive Deregulation.* In retrospect, certain aspects of the 1988 deregulation package went too far, most notably the 2 per cent reserve requirements for banks. Some might argue that the previous 15 per cent requirement was too high. That conservatism, however, at least ensured stability and security to banking. Because of the reduction in reserve requirements, Indonesia created conditions that inevitably led to new problems. Fortunately, the problems, such as those met at Bank Duta and Bank Summa, were resolved without inflicting long term damage to the economy or to the banking system. Although the government's commitment to deregulation remained steadfast, these difficulties confirmed the value of deregulating cautiously and in stages.

5. *The Strength of Simplicity.* Throughout the deregulation process, the government emphasized simplicity. The deregulated economy was a

simpler, more 'transparent' economy. Therefore, it worked better. Businesses and individuals are always in a better position to make accurate judgments if the regulatory environment is simple and clear. On the other hand, complicated and incomprehensible regulations—even if originally well intended—can readily be used as a veil behind which inefficiency and corrupt practices grow. Simplicity was a guiding principle in Indonesia's attack on its overregulated and bureaucratic economy. Greater simplicity has made Indonesia's economy freer and stronger.

With the collapse of Indonesia's oil economy in the mid-1980s it would have been reasonable to expect Indonesia to move into a catastrophic recession. Instead, by taking measures to deregulate the nation's financial system, Indonesia showed it was capable of continuing its economic development without overreliance on oil. Just as the phoenix is reborn among the ashes of its own destruction, so too Indonesia's economy emerged from the crisis of the mid-1980s stronger and more resilient than ever before.

1. These estimates are based on World Bank (1995a) data using the Atlas method of calculation.

2. Here, as throughout this book, the economic data is drawn from official Indonesian sources. Generally, these figures are the same or similar to those used by the World Bank. For the period under consideration, however, the World Bank calculates GDP growth using a different base year than that used by the Central Bureau of Statistics. According to their estimates, in 1982 the Indonesian economy shrank by −0.3 per cent.

3. Quoted in *Kompas* (1983).

4. The figure derived is based on the volume of Indonesian oil output plus the impact on Indonesia from a drop of $1.00 on the spot market. In fact, the change in value of Indonesia's exports was not identical to the change on the spot market since there was not a one-to-one correspondence between the two. According to various analyses, during the mid-1980s the estimated loss to Indonesia from a $1 decline in a barrel of crude oil ranged from $300 million to $400 million.

5. It should be noted that Widjojo's position as 'adviser' was in no way ceremonial. Although he no longer held a ministerial portfolio, Widjojo maintained the confidence of the President and retained his considerable stature among the economic ministers. For this reason, he continued to attend most meetings that involved significant decisions on economic policy. Indeed, Widjojo's influence was evident in all of Indonesia's important economic policies from the beginning of the New Order to the present time. In the ensuing Cabinet five years later, installed in March 1988, I succeeded Ali Wardhana as Co-ordinating Minister. As with Widjojo, Wardhana continued to serve as a close adviser to the President without ministerial portfolio and as an active and highly valued member of the economic team.

6. This was my first major decision as Minister of Finance. Barely two weeks after my appointment, I had a long one-on-one meeting with President Soeharto in which I explained to him why I believed the devaluation was Indonesia's best option—indeed, its only option. The President listened intently and said he would carefully study my analysis and recommendations. About a week later, the rupiah was devalued. Ironically, the day

after the devaluation, on 31 March 1983, the *Far Eastern Economic Review* published an article profiling the new Cabinet. Commenting on my appointment, the article expressed concern that 'the new Finance Minister Radius Prawiro may not be strong enough to take painful decisions' (Awanohara, 1983). I will leave to others to assess my strength. However, I will say that I am certainly one of the few ministers of finance that devalued the currency during his first month on the job, bringing to a precipitous end one of the shortest honeymoons a new minister could ever have.

7. 'Rephasing' (*penjadwalan kembali*) is the term that was used to indicate that the future of a project was in doubt and temporarily suspended. In some cases, 'rephasing' was a way of indicating that a project had been put 'on hold'. In other cases, 'rephased' projects were simply terminated. And in other instances, the term was used to describe projects that would be continued up to an appropriate stopping point and then sold. The government deliberately chose an imprecise term because it wanted to avoid committing itself either to cancellation or continuation of these projects. Instead, the government adopted a position of 'studied ambiguity'.

8. I can trace the origins of my personal involvement in the deregulation movement to a day spent with Widjojo. A few weeks after being appointed Minister of Finance in 1983, I spent the day travelling with him and other government officials to several industrial sites around Java. Deregulation as a general concept had been circulating among economists and academics, but the government had not embraced it, nor had the government decided to try to deregulate any particular industry or sector. At one point Widjojo and I were seated in a Hercules military airplane between inspections and engaged in an intense conversation. Given my new responsibilities, I wanted to find some way to reinvigorate the banking system. As the conversation progressed, we concluded that the only way to help the banking sector was to give it more freedom. The exact nature of that freedom needed to be studied, but in that conversation we both confirmed our conviction that progress in the financial sector would require deregulation. Upon returning to Jakarta, we immediately set ourselves to the task of developing a deregulation strategy for banking. That day with Widjojo again confirmed his central role in identifying what would become the core principles of Indonesia's economic policies for the 1980s.

9. For a discussion of banking in Indonesia from the colonial period through the early days of the New Order please refer to the Prologue and Chapter 1 of this book, as well as Panglaykim (1974). As will be discussed later in this chapter, this situation was significantly altered under the new banking law of 1988.

10. Despite the constraints under which state banks operated, they have performed a remarkable service in assisting in the national development process. The modernization of the rural sector, for example, would never have occurred so quickly were it not for the extensive network of branches and lending facilities created by the state bank, BRI (see Chapter 5 on Agriculture).

11. The other position in which government employees had abundant opportunity for 'supplemental income' was by working as a customs agent. This is addressed in the next chapter.

12. Under the old system, the uppermost tax rate was 50 per cent. According to the 1983 law this was reduced to 35 per cent. Then in 1995 the uppermost tax rate was reduced to 30 per cent.

13. In his lucid review of the Indonesian tax system, Malcolm Gillis (1989: 90) notes that before the introduction of the new tax law, the poorest third of the population paid 5 per cent of their income in taxes, whereas the richest decile paid only 9 per cent of theirs. It was the explicit objective of the new taxation system to redress such inequity.

14. In advocating the tax to Indonesia's Parliament, my description was more blunt: 'It is a money machine', I said. This was no exaggeration. The returns from the VAT were remarkable.

15. The way Indonesia's VAT operates is illustrated through Table 8.1 and the comment that follows.

TABLE 8.1
Comparison of the Value Added Tax to a Cascading Sales Tax (Rp)

VAT		Markup (percentage)	Pre-tax Sale Price	VAT at 10 per cent	Price with Tax	VAT Rebate	Total Tax to Government
Step 1	Trader imports good		1,000	100	1,100	–	100
Step 2	Trader sells to miller	100	2,000	200	2,200	100	100
Step 3	Miller sells to baker	100	4,000	400	4,400	200	200
Step 4	Baker sells to public	100	8,800	–	–	–	–
	Retail sales price with tax				8,800		
	Total tax collected						400

Sales Tax (Cascading)		Markup (percentage)	Pre-tax Sale Price	Sales Tax at 10 per cent	Price with Tax	Sales Tax Rebate	Total Tax to Government
Step 1	Trader imports good		1,000	100	1,100	–	100
Step 2	Trader sells to miller	100	2,200	220	2,420	–	220
Step 3	Miller sells to baker	100	4,840	484	5,324	–	484
Step 4	Baker sells to public	100	10,648	1,065	11,713	–	1,065
	Retail sales price with tax				11,713		
	Total tax collected						1,869

Let us suppose a trader imports a kilogram of special Australian wheat at a cost of Rp 1,000. At the time of importing, he will have to pay the government a VAT of 10 per cent, that is, Rp 100, for a total cost of Rp 1,100. The trader then sells the raw wheat to a miller for Rp 2,000 to which is added the VAT of Rp 200 (a 100 per cent mark-up, which excludes the cost of the tax, since the trader will be reimbursed for his tax payment). The miller pays a total cost of Rp 2,200. The trader would collect the VAT of Rp 200 and from this he would retain the Rp 100 that he previously paid in VAT and remit to the government only the additional Rp 100. After the miller had ground the raw wheat into wheat flour, he sells it to the baker of the very popular 'Indo-Australian Bread' for Rp 4,000, (assumes another 100 per cent mark-up) to which is added a VAT of Rp 400. The miller collects Rp 400 in VAT, retains the Rp 200 he paid previously for VAT and remits Rp 200 to the government. The baker—famous throughout Jakarta—again marks up his costs by 100 per cent and sells his specialty bread directly to the public for Rp 8,800 a loaf. No VAT is collected on the retail sale or paid to the government. The total VAT collected on the loaf of 'Indo-Australian Bread' is Rp 400. The beauty (in the eyes of a former Minister of Finance) of this tax is that it is in the interest of everyone who pays the VAT to collect it. Once the VAT is paid at the initial stage, collection is virtually guaranteed at every successive stage. Furthermore, the retailer is free to charge whatever price he wants, while the cost of the tax is invisible to the consumer.

The table compares the scenario described above under a VAT and a 'cascading' sales tax regime. For simplicity's sake, let us assume that the sales tax is uniformly 10 per cent, although in reality sales taxes tend to be more variable. The cascading sales tax results in taxing the price including previous taxes. It therefore adds tax upon tax. The VAT avoids this problem. Only vertically integrated companies can avoid the escalating costs from sales taxes since they do not sell the goods to themselves. As Harberger (1990: 27) notes, 'It is quite obvious that this cascade type of taxation gives an artificial incentive to vertical integration—that is, for a retail chain to raise its own wheat and make its own flour and bread, so that the only taxable event takes place when the bread is sold to the final consumer.'

16. Not even all politicians like taxes. Indeed, the technical elegance and economic cogency of Indonesia's new tax law were not enough to ensure it warm reception on the political front. In November 1983, I introduced the new tax laws to Parliament. Many of Indonesia's parliamentarians were adamantly opposed to the new law, for many reasons, most of which were based on wrong assumptions about the impact of the law on the average Indonesian taxpayer. In a Parliament of 460 representatives, there were almost as many views on how the law should be modified. One faction wanted to add more rates than three, another refused to believe that self-assessment would work, while others wanted to have more deductions included. Some groups opposed the VAT and others preferred the *status quo*. The situation seemed certain to lead to an acrimonious deadlock. At this point, I requested leaders from various factions to visit me individually in my office. Away from the frenzy and group pressure that had built up in the Parliament, I reminded each of these representatives that the tax laws we were trying to replace were inherited from the Dutch and were designed to support a colonial regime. That system, I asserted, was utterly ill-suited for the needs of a modern country that aspired to become an industrialized nation. I reminded them that we had all fought in the war for independence and that as patriots we had pledged then, as we must continue to pledge today, to rid the country of all detrimental vestiges that prevented us from progressing. With this in mind, I entreated them to join with the Cabinet to create a new basis for fiscal independence. The proposed tax system, I said, was designed not only to replace an antiquated tax system, but also was essential to the government's effort to rid itself of its oil addiction that had dominated the Indonesian economy for so long. After many hours of such talks, most of the opponents were convinced, and the proposed tax system was passed with very few alterations. Further, the new law took effect at least about a year earlier than anyone had projected.

17. In a conversation with me, one journalist used a more colourful phrase. Indonesia, he said, had become the 'flavour of the month' in investment circles.

18. Bank Indonesia reports that the current account deficit was $1.97 billion in 1984/5 and $1.83 billion in 1985/6 and jumped to $4.05 billion in 1986/7.

19. It is noteworthy that despite the dire implications for the Indonesian economy of

the fall in oil prices and currency realignments, the economic team never lost its confidence in the economy's ability to rebound. This was one of those moments when one had to balance one's impression of the quality of Indonesia's leadership and the resilience of the Indonesian people on the one hand against economic projections on the other hand. The projections did indeed point toward an economic disaster. None the less, the team had an inexplicable—one could say, irrational—confidence that Indonesia would emerge from this crisis stronger than before. That confidence was shared by many Indonesians and was in itself an important contributor to the nation's quick recovery from its economic difficulties.

20. Among all the decisions I had to take during my twenty-seven years as a Cabinet official and Governor of Bank Indonesia, there were none more personally stressful than the decision to devalue the currency. My colleague, Ali Wardhana, who as Co-ordinating Minister would normally make the announcement, shared that stress. Several hours before the announcement was to be made, I received a call from Minister Wardhana. He had just been admitted to the hospital and asked me to speak on his behalf, which I did. Unlike other devaluations, this one came as a surprise to the nation, and a very unhappy surprise, indeed. Still, some commentators also recognized the appropriateness of the move. Whatever the objective merits, when I returned home, I learned that a day earlier my brother-in-law called my wife and informed her that he was considering making an investment but would hold off if the rupiah was about to be devalued. She told him that she knew of no plans for a devaluation. He then went ahead with the investment. With this devaluation not only did I have the wrath of the country to face, but also that of my wife and brother-in-law. My wife and I have a policy of being very honest and open with each other. Where I draw the line is with devaluations. Until it was announced, only the President and a small circle of Cabinet ministers were aware of the decision. To the best of my knowledge there have been no studies on the effects of devaluations on the marriages of Ministers of Finance. In my case, I am happy to report that despite the stress, our marriage has withstood the rigours of several devaluations.

Besides their impact on marriages, devaluations can be hazardous to one's career. Woo, Glassburner, and Nasution (1994: 87) refer to a study by Cooper that concludes that 'a devaluation appeared to double the probability that a ruling party would be removed from power, and to triple the odds that a minister of finance would be ousted'. I have the dubious distinction of having devalued the rupiah twice during my tenure as Minister of Finance, something few Ministers of Finance can claim. By Cooper's calculations, that would suggest that my chances of being removed from office had been increased by three to the second power (3^2), that is, nine times. Indeed, that was my one and only term as finance minister, but in the next Cabinet, President Soeharto rewarded my stamina by appointing me to the position of Co-ordinating Minister for Economy, Finance, Industry, and Development Supervision.

21. By allowing the rupiah to float, the government virtually eliminated the possibility of a government orchestrated devaluation. However, as the decline of over 50 per cent in the value of the rupiah against the dollar during the period of July to December 1997 graphically demonstrated, a floating exchange rate provides no guarantee of monetary stability. The plunge in the value of the rupiah followed in the wake of the devaluation of the Thai baht in July 1997. Currency traders, speculators, businesses, and individual savers in Indonesia and throughout South-East Asia became extremely nervous. The Indonesian rupiah came under a punishing assault in September and again in January 1998. As a result, the value of the currency fell of its own accord more than would have been the case if the government deliberately imposed a devaluation. There are many reasons we could

give to explain why the value of the rupiah dropped so suddenly and extremely. Rather than offering an explanation or theory, I will simply note that floating exchange rates bring their own risks. The strength of a floating rate is that the currency is permitted to find the market level of value. The risk of floating rates is that a currency is unshielded against the volatility of the market. Furthermore, floating exchange rates require greater subtlety and sophistication on the parts of both a nation's central bank and its private commercial banks. It would be naïve to think that a monetary instrument as sensitive and powerful as floating exchange rates could be risk free. None the less, despite the pain that can be inflicted by a floating rate, there is little doubt that it is the most accurate indicator of the market value of a currency. A floating exchange rate can render a currency more vulnerable to speculators and on occasion this may require extraordinary actions, including international intervention. However, if the economy is managed according to sound monetary policies, a floating exchange rate represent a necessary step in the creation of a developed market economy.

22. In the interval following Pakto, yet another reform package was enacted, on 21 November 1988. Because this package dealt primarily with trade related matters it is discussed in the next chapter .

23. For more on this see Brown (1988).

24. Perhaps Indonesia's good luck in this instance was fortune's way of compensating for particularly bad luck in 1978. As Chapter 7 suggests, I continue to defend the decision to devalue the currency in 1978 as a good one. With the 1978 devaluation, export commodities that were difficult to sell because of the unrealistic rupiah–dollar exchange rate were finally competitive in international markets. The timing, however, was horrible, falling as it did just over a month before the start of the second oil shock. On balance, however, fortune has dealt fairly with Indonesia.

9
Indonesia's Paradigm Shift in Trade and Investment

INDONESIA has a saying, 'The cornered cat becomes a tiger.' The global oil market collapse of 1986 had all the makings of turning into Indonesia's equivalent to the great stock market crash of 1929. Indonesia's economic team indeed felt cornered as the dreadful shadow of the crisis loomed before us. A sense of intense and purposeful focus took hold of the team as we set ourselves to the task of devising strategies to deal with the dire circumstances we faced. No economy ever starts with a clean slate. Each day builds upon the day before it. For Indonesia, the oil collapse, however, provided a pivotal moment in which the basic course of economic development changed directions. By the mid-1980s, the task the economic team faced could no longer be measured according to the traditional parameters of economic development—the challenge was to redefine the basic model of development.

The deregulation process that began with the financial sector in 1983 was a crucial step in the right direction. This alone, however, was insufficient. Although financial deregulation removed many of the obstacles and bottlenecks in the process of economic intermediation, Indonesia's commerce remained bound up by excessive regulation. While the deregulated monetary sector could lubricate the gears of the economy, the machine itself was in need of serious repair.

For over a decade Indonesia's economic development had been based on an inward looking economic paradigm sustained through heavy doses of oil money. With the collapse of the oil market, the fatal flaws of that approach were starkly evident. If the Indonesian economy did not collapse along with the price of oil, it was because the government somehow managed to, as it were, switch the nation's 'engine of growth' while the train was in full motion. The change represented a 'paradigm shift' that can occur only rarely in a nation's development process. In this case, the government orchestrated the shift progressively, through a series of reform 'packages', each of which reconfirmed the fundamental correctness of deregulation and the inherent wisdom of the market economy.[1] In essence, Indonesia's economic team took steps to allow the market to reconstruct itself. The following pages highlight the steps taken pertaining to two crucial aspects of the economy: trade and investment.

TRANSITION TO A NEW PARADIGM

The essence of the economic vision that had guided Indonesia through two oil booms was a cluster of policies that emphasized import substitution, Indonesianization, and leaned toward autarky. During those years, Indonesia's economy grew less hospitable to foreign investment and international trade. By contrast, the new economic paradigm that Indonesia adopted in the 1980s was far more 'outward looking'. The essential characteristics of the new approach were as follows:

- Deregulation and debureaucratization;
- Export-led growth;
- The creation of a regulatory climate conducive to foreign investment;
- Transfer of economic power from the government to the private sector.

Among these four, probably the most important was deregulation: without deregulation, none of the other three would have been possible. One could give a variety of names to describe Indonesia's new economic model. However, we will here refer to this new approach as the 'outward looking paradigm' or simply the 'deregulation movement'.

The basic ideas of this approach were not new or revolutionary. Many countries had embraced deregulation in their domestic reform policies to some degree, including Indonesia. None the less, the change did indeed represent a 'paradigm shift' in the sense that it had a sweeping impact on virtually every economic policy and every aspect of the economy. This shift provided startling proof of the impact that government policy has on economic development.

Before the deregulation movement, the government had imposed controls on the economy primarily for three reasons: a) to direct industrial development specifically to assist indigenous Indonesians; b) to protect domestic industries from more effective offshore competition; and c) to conserve foreign exchange. To an extent, these controls all achieved their intended purposes. In so doing, however, they exacted a heavy toll on the economy. The controls led to market distortions that, in turn, resulted in countless costs spread widely across the economy. Ultimately, Indonesia paid for the old paradigm by sacrificing part of its economic growth and by failing to prepare fully for the day when oil could no longer finance the nation's economic development.

To attack Indonesia's 'high cost economy', the government had to deregulate. Apart from deregulation of the nation's financial sector, the bulk of Indonesia's deregulation efforts was concentrated in the areas of trade and investment.[2] There is a close link between the two. Trade and investment have a direct impact on the nation's current account. Both exports and foreign investments bring foreign exchange into a country. Both inject capital into the economy that can accelerate growth beyond levels obtainable exclusively through domestic resources. Specifically, Indonesia needed investment to develop export-oriented industries and it needed export-oriented industries to provide a steady supply of foreign exchange. Without foreign exchange, industrial development was impossible. The linkages between trade and investment were strong, and because of these linkages, the restrictions placed on one directly affected the other. Similarly, deregulation in one affected the other as well.

It may seem ironic that the people who were pushing for deregulation were largely the same group of policymakers who had guided the nation's economic development since 1968. The changes they began to espouse in the 1980s were not so much a repudiation of past policies as they were recognition that the country needed new policies to maintain development under radically different circumstances. Not only were the economic conditions in the 1980s very different from the 1970s, but the politics had changed almost as drastically. Almost a decade separated Indonesia from the upheavals of the mid-1970s. Much of the residual fear and suspicion of foreign participation in the economy had faded. By the mid-1980s, the country's mood had shifted. The previous heavy involvement of the government in every aspect of the economy began to seem inappropriate and ineffective. The people were ready and desirous of change, and the economic conditions of the time required it.

External Influences on Indonesia's Economic Development

Many external factors led Indonesia to place its economic policies under careful review. The world economy that Indonesia faced in the 1970s and early 1980s had become more protectionist. The major markets for Indonesia's exports were Japan the United States, Western Europe, and Australia. Indonesia was able to maintain a steady and positive trading relationship with Japan largely through the latter's continued reliance on Indonesia for energy and natural resources. For Indonesia's manufactured goods, however, the situation was not so easy. Indonesia's exporters faced a growing number of tariffs and quotas as well as trade restrictions linked to concerns on intellectual property, the environment, and labour conditions, among others. Such conditions made it increasingly difficult for trading nations to penetrate export markets.

The difficulties were exacerbated by the inadequacies of the main forum for guiding world trade, the General Agreement on Tariffs and Trade (GATT). GATT was established in 1948 on the principle of non-discriminatory trade practices among its members. Only twenty-three countries were then GATT members, and they were the leading trading nations. By the late 1970s, however, there was a growing consensus, among GATT members and non-members alike, that the organization was no longer capable of addressing the needs and interests of contemporary world trade. Developing nations felt particularly underrepresented and unprotected. Many countries urged that a new round of international trade talks be held quickly. Many traders and politicians hoped that a renewed trade agreement could add greater uniformity to the trade regulations among nations. This, they hoped, would help create more equitable trade conditions for both the established trading countries and the developing countries who were trying to build their trading capacity. Despite years of complaints, the new round of GATT negotiations did not begin until 1986 and was not concluded until 1994. In the meantime, Indonesia's exports, like those of other countries, were hampered by the many inconsistencies in trade regimes from one country to another. As with many developing countries, one area of particularly strong growth potential was in the area of textile and apparel production. One important international accord, however, the Multi-Fiber Agreement (MFA), greatly restricted Indonesia's trade development in this sector.

Indonesia's challenge in the early to mid-1980s was to find the means to replace foreign exchange earnings lost through declining oil prices. Moreover, for the economy to grow, Indonesia had to do more than simply replace the loss from declining oil revenues with non-oil revenues. It had to greatly expand non-oil foreign exchange earnings and the only viable route was an aggressive policy of export promotion. However, by the mid-1980s Indonesia's export capacity was limited by three basic factors: first, Indonesia's trade sector was seriously overregulated; second, the manner in which the country had developed in the 1970s was imbalanced and unconducive to a broad export orientation; and third, protectionism had become more entrenched world-wide.

Other than adding its voice to the chorus of developing countries calling for easier access to international markets, there was little Indonesia could do to influence the patterns of international protectionism. Where the government could make a difference was through domestic reforms that addressed the structural weaknesses in the economy. Without oil to rely on, Indonesia needed to achieve greater diversity in the products it offered on world markets.

FREEING TRADE

Indonesia has always had the makings of a great trading nation. After independence, Indonesia began the process of building its trading capacities by exporting its principal commodities, that is, plantation crops, specifically rubber, coffee, tea, copra, and palm oil. However, before the 1970s, Indonesia was a minor player among the international trading countries. The oil boom, however, had a surprising side effect: oil served as a lure to induce Indonesia to engage wholeheartedly in trade. In just over a decade, Indonesia moved from being an insignificant trading country to become Asia's largest exporter of oil. Almost by accident, Indonesia became a significant trading country.

When the oil sector began its decline in the early-1980s, Indonesia needed to rethink its model of development. The choices were few. The country could try to return to its pre-colonial agrarian economic model. In the early 1980s, this kind of pre-industrial autarchy was clearly unworkable for a country of Indonesia's size. Alternatively, Indonesia could simply accept the decline in revenues from lost oil prices as a fact of life. In other words, Indonesia could accept poverty as its destiny. Such extreme fatalism was never seriously considered.

Indonesia's only real choice was to try to compensate for the loss in oil revenues through trade in non-oil commodities. Among Indonesia's neighbours, there were already several celebrated export-led growth models. Although countries such as Japan, South Korea, and Taiwan were inspirational examples of the potential for rapid development, the model they embodied was of limited use to Indonesia in the 1960s and 1970s. Indonesia was much poorer than any of these nations were when they began their process of rapid development. Furthermore, Indonesia's population was much larger, and managing development among a widely dispersed archipelago added many logistical problems unique to the country. Therefore, although Indonesia could not simply adopt outright the export-led growth model from these countries, the country's economic leaders tried to formulate policies that would move the economy in a similar direction. Because the economy had become so overburdened with regulations and non-tariff barriers, the transition was difficult.

An Assault on Imports

Since the 1970s, part of Indonesia's strategy for maintaining a positive balance of trade had been to restrict imports. The country hoped to conserve foreign exchange and stimulate development of domestic industries by promoting import-substituting industries. Because of this policy, businesses had little incentive to invest in export-oriented industries.

Protectionism gave many firms a virtual guarantee that they would be profitable, no matter how inefficient they may have been. This, however, contributed to the creation of Indonesia's 'high cost economy', which in turn drove up the costs of locally manufactured goods.

Import substitution was sustained by shielding the economy behind a wall of tariff and non-tariff barriers (NTBs) including quotas, monopolies, bans, or regulations designed to restrict market access by specific product or country of origin. Although tariffs and NTBs are both market distortions, economists generally agree that tariffs are a less inefficient and more equitable form of market distortion than non-tariff barriers. Over the years, however, Indonesia relied heavily on NTBs—especially licences, quotas, and product bans—to regulate its trade. The most frequently used restrictions were sole-importer licences.

Sole-importer status awarded a single agency—whether a private company or a government board—a monopoly on the importation of a particular type of product. Initially, the government drew on this policy to stem the flow of foreign exchange that went to satisfy Indonesia's ever-increasing appetite for imports. The government awarded sole-importer licences to help stabilize markets since the government reasoned it could exercise more influence on the importation of goods if they were channelled through a limited number of importers rather than through the free market. NTBs such as sole-importer licences were originally used on a small scale that they had almost no impact on the Indonesian economy. The government created regulatory boards to reduce market volatility, and sole-importer licences were awarded to control imports and conserve foreign exchange. Over time, however, the cost of non-tariff barriers was unmistakable.[3] The sole importer could raise the price of goods, delay shipment, or direct goods to preferred customers. Buyers were entirely at the mercy of the sole importer. Such practices could disrupt manufacturers business plans and force them to adjust output and prices largely according to the wishes of the importer. By raising the costs of inputs, sole importers had a significant impact on the prices of domestically produced goods. This contributed to the high cost of goods in Indonesia and it reduced the competitiveness of its exports.

Restrictions on trade grew throughout the 1970s and early 1980s as the government took further steps to protect the domestic industries that were proliferating under the auspices of the country's oil windfalls. The downward trend in Indonesia's trade in the early 1980s reinforced the use of NTBs. After slipping to near recession in 1982, the country experienced a trade deficit for the first quarter of 1983—the first since the founding of the New Order. As it turned out, by the next quarter Indonesia achieved a positive balance and has maintained it ever since. However, there were serious implications from this deficit. At Indonesia's level of development and given its heavy debt burden, it could not afford to maintain a deficit for long. If the trend had continued, it would have had devastating effects on the economy (Figure 9.1).

The government first responded to the drop in its balance of trade by introducing measures to curb imports. This was the only option available to the government that could be implemented quickly and bear significant results. The alternative strategy—export promotion—required time to build industrial and business capabilities and international markets. The government's first priority was to return the economy to a positive trade balance, and this could be done fairly quickly simply by controlling imports.

Although the government introduced sole-importer licences to stabilize the market for selected goods and services, sole importers were invested with too much power. The sole importers were an expedient means of trying to restrict the flow of foreign exchange. Unfortunately, this approach was inefficient, costly, and difficult to remove after having been introduced.[4]

Building the Nation's Non-oil Exports

The government's other option for achieving a positive balance of trade

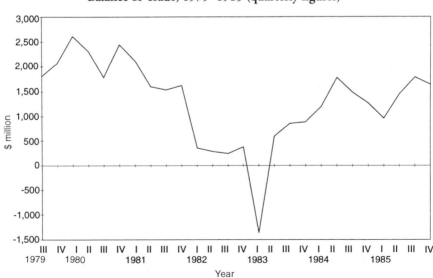

FIGURE 9.1
Balance of Trade, 1979–1985 (quarterly figures)

Source: Indonesia, Central Bureau of Statistics.

was to promote exports. This it tried to do through a variety of methods. Generally, however, given the government's import-substitution bias in the 1970s and early 1980s, most policies to build exports during this period met with limited success.

One positive measure Indonesia took in the late 1970s to promote non-oil exports was to create the National Agency for Export Development (NAFED). NAFED established representative offices in Europe, the United States, Japan, and in the Middle East all with the purpose of promoting Indonesian exports. Through its overseas office, trade missions, and its information services, NAFED has done a laudable job in promoting Indonesian exports. However, in the 1970s to mid-1980s Indonesia had a chronically overvalued rupiah, a high cost economy, and an import-substitution bias. These conditions ensured that NAFED's efforts to promote non-oil exports were destined to meet with limited success.

The weakness in Indonesia's trading regime was exacerbated by the fact that so much of its traded goods went to one country, Japan, and these exports were concentrated in a narrow band of products—primarily oil, LNG, timber, and a few other commodities. During the late 1970s, agricultural commodities constituted some 80 per cent of Indonesia's non-oil exports, with timber and rubber the two leading exports. In the early 1980s, manufactured goods were hardly represented among Indonesia's total exports. Except for a few commodities, such as coffee and oil, Indonesian products were uncompetitive in world markets.

Although Indonesia had managed to avoid many of the most debilitating aspects of the 'Dutch disease', (see Chapter 4 for a discussion of this topic) the non-oil trade sector had not kept pace with the overall growth in the economy. So when oil prices began to decline in the early 1980s, there was no alternative sector ready to take its place. The economic decline of 1982–3 sent a strong message that alerted the government about the vulnerability of the economy. Indonesia had to address the structural weaknesses in the economy by building a non-oil trade sector. This would require a shift in economic strategy and a substantial long-term effort. The main obstacle the government faced in engineering this change in economic orientation was a shortage of funds. With the sudden disappearance of the government's oil revenues, the government could no longer finance development through its own direct intervention. To achieve a similar end, the government had to create a favourable regulatory environment that would induce the private sector to take greater economic initiative.

There was, however, an important structural impediment to trade development—Indonesia's customs service. For years, the country's customs service had demonstrated its capacity to slow trade rather than facilitate the process. To build the nation's foreign exchange reserves without significant oil wealth, Indonesia needed to develop a dynamic trading capacity. An essential prerequisite was to have an efficiently functioning customs service.

Reforming Customs

In every country, customs services act as the gatekeepers of trade. Indonesia was no exception. In 1985, Indonesia's customs service employed 13,000 people in fourteen regional offices responsible for monitoring fifty-two ports. Besides inspecting goods crossing the nation's borders, Indonesia's customs service also inspected goods intended for transhipment between the major Indonesian islands. The customs service exercised tremendous influence over the country's trade. Its power over the Indonesian economy was enormous.

Indonesia's geographic conditions render customs control an inherently challenging task. As an archipelagic nation of over 17,000 islands, Indonesia's borders were inherently porous. The country was a smuggler's paradise. Ultimately, however, the problem of smuggling was more than just one of geography, but rather of collusion.[5]

Indonesia's customs service had become a law unto itself according to which the entire trade process was readily manipulated to serve the interests of a retinue of customs officials. Because of the importance of trade, the entire economy suffered as a result. What evolved was a kind of symbiosis in which traders learned to accommodate the inefficiencies and demands of the customs service, the government obtained some approximation of the duties expected, and many customs officials greatly expanded their incomes. An unfortunate effect of this situation was that it increased costs and slowed the flow of goods. Goods could remain on the docks for weeks or months while traders 'negotiated' with customs officials for their release. To protect against this, businesses were forced to hold inordinately large inventories. Besides being costly, businesses often found themselves saddled with obsolete products for which they had been flagrantly overcharged. These expenses were then factored into the price of goods, thereby adding further to the cost of doing business in Indonesia.

On many occasions, the government had tried to improve the customs services through regulatory reforms, personnel changes, and periodic disciplinary actions. In February 1976, the government resorted to threats when President Soeharto declared smuggling a 'crime of subversion'. In 1982, the government adopted a set of policy measures intended to revive trade. Therein the government appealed to a sense of civic duty of the customs officers. The policy called on the customs department to spare no efforts to expedite the flow of goods. The department was unmoved. Nothing worked. In the eyes of Indonesia's business community, the country's customs agency was hindering the nation's economic development by deliberately creating a bottle-neck that choked trade. The pervasiveness and extremism of corruption damaged the reputation of the entire country. On 14 October 1983 the *Jakarta Post* reported, 'An executive of a warehousing and forwarding firm (EMKL) complained that customs officers at the port "are becoming impudent and greedier. Normally they would accept any amount (of graft) we offered but now they fix the amount we have to provide."'

The only solution was to take drastic action. Customs services were under the Ministry of Finance. In February 1985, as Minister of Finance, I relieved the Director-General of Customs and Excise of his position and assumed his responsibilities myself, a position I held for almost two years.[6] Over the next few months, the government conducted investigations to gain a more thorough understanding of the extent of the problems. Then in April 1985 the government issued Presidential Instruction (Inpres) No. 4, which laid out a set of reforms intended to reduce excessive bureaucratic intervention and add transparency and efficiency to Indonesia's customs service.

The corner-stone of Inpres No. 4 was a drastic new initiative according to which most customs inspection duties were transferred to the Swiss firm, Société Générale de Surveillance S. A., known by the abbreviation SGS. The government gave SGS—a totally outside body, brought in under contract—responsibility to inspect in the country of origin all goods bound for Indonesia with a value over $5,000. After SGS inspected the goods, they were placed in sealed containers and needed no further clearance in Indonesian ports unless the seal was broken or customs officials had good reason to believe that the container contained illicit goods. Simultaneously, about half the customs employees were given 'indefinite leaves of absence'. They continued to receive their government salary even though they were no longer authorized to continue with their government duties. Thus, no one could argue that the government treated them unfairly. Some of those employees were ultimately fired, some were given early retirement, and others returned to work at the directorate-general of customs, but usually in different capacities from their previous positions.

Inpres No. 4 also aimed to improve Indonesia's trade by deregulating or streamlining inter-island shipping and port operations. The decree eliminated the need for customs inspections on goods shipped between islands within Indonesia. According to the measure, the management of ports was reformed by greatly increasing the number of ports open for foreign vessels, reducing port costs, and strengthening the role of harbour-masters with the purpose of enhancing trade efficiency.

Despite a few minor 'teething problems', the value of the new system was readily apparent. According to the *Bulletin of Indonesian Economic Studies*, 'before the implementation of Inpres 4/1985 a Japanese manufacturing affiliate found that customs clearance of its goods averaged 43 days.... Recent reports now say that goods rarely stay in Jakarta's Tanjung Priok port for more than one week. Also importers and exporters have reported up to 40 per cent declines in charges of freight forwarders' (Muir, 1986: 21n. 6). Further more, the number of signatures needed to import goods was reduced from twenty to one.

Perhaps most significant, Inpres No. 4 was a landmark that affirmed in unmistakable terms that the government was prepared to take extreme actions to put its trading house in order. Through these measures, Indonesia took a major step forward in removing one of the most important structural impediments to trade.

Subsidizing Exports

Any government that faces pressures on its foreign reserves has a duty to take corrective measures. Although Indonesia's initial response was to limit imports, the government knew that for Indonesia to regain economic growth in a post-oil economy, it had to develop its non-oil exports. Instead of trying to limit demand by imposing tariff and non-tariff barriers, the government chose to foster exports. The measures first adopted were unorthodox but indicative of the government's determination to restructure the nation's trade regime.

In January 1979, the government launched an export certificate programme that offered subsidized credit to exporters of Indonesian products. Initially only Indonesian exporters could avail themselves of the subsidy, but eventually it was extended to all exporters, regardless of their citizenship. Traders reacted enthusiastically and rushed to take advantage of the opportunity.

Although the government's intentions were good, the programme was short-lived. International critics insisted that the programme was an unfair trade practice. Moreover, domestic traders soon discovered that the programme had loopholes that rendered it readily susceptible to abuse. To take advantage of the subsidized credit, for example, some unscrupulous traders set up fictitious 'paper companies' or even sent empty containers.[7] In March 1985, Indonesia became a signatory to GATT. Indonesia's export certificate programme was determined to be in contravention of the GATT prohibition on export subsidies and, accordingly, Indonesia agreed to phase it out. In June 1986, the government ended the programme.

The elimination of Indonesia's export certificate programme was for the best. The programme tried to compensate for deficiencies in the economy, but did nothing to correct them. The export certificate programme was inherently flawed: first, the underlying reason Indonesian exports needed subsidies was because the economy was too expensive or 'high cost'. Second, the subsidy created economic dependencies that were unsustainable. Finally, the subsidy was costly. Exporters should have been contributing to government revenues rather than consuming them. The export certificate programme created an incentive for businesses to export, but this incentive did not reflect market forces. Despite the good intentions of the programme, the subsidies added new distortions to the economy, when Indonesia needed to remove them. The eventual termination of the export certificate programme was another step that led the government inexorably toward deregulation as the most effective method for developing the country's export capacities.

Freeing Exports

The free market is an economic ideal that serves as a standard against which economic policies can be judged. It is also an ideal that has no counterpart in reality. Every market around the world is distorted to a greater or lesser degree. The tools of trade policy all tend to distort the economy in some way by protecting certain sectors, by promoting others, or by reacting to the trade policies of one's trading partners. Trade policy is largely a process of deciding what distortions to apply, when to apply them, and when to remove them. Obviously, most distortions end up being harmful, but some can actually be helpful in achieving certain economic objectives in the short-term. In Indonesia's case, even though the economic team was predisposed to favour free trade, trade policy was driven by pragmatism rather than by a philosophical commitment to free trade. The policies that were appropriate in the 1970s had to be succeeded by new policies to meet the new conditions of the 1980s. The most important distinction between the two periods was that the policies of the 1970s were more appropriate in a booming oil economy. In the 1980s, Indonesia tried to make the transition to an economy that did not depend on oil wealth. What transpired over a period of about two decades was an evolution in trade policy that ultimately led to a freeing of trade from most non-tariff barriers and a reduction of tariffs. Relatively free trade became the pragmatic choice for Indonesia. The next few paragraphs review some important highlights of the route taken by Indonesia that led the country in this direction.

When the second oil boom ended in 1981, the economic team recognized that trade reform was needed. The process, however, was daunting if for no other reason than that the matrix of industrial protection was so extensive, complex, and mutually reinforcing. The government had regulated so many products and services that it took considerable research to compile a comprehensive inventory of tariff and non-tariff barriers. Furthermore, there was little consistency in trade restrictions from sector to sector or even within one sector. Indonesia's economic policymakers had to keep in mind that deregulation in one sector would have an impact on other aspects of the economy. To create conditions that would move Indonesia to become an export-oriented economy, the government had to add greater consistency to the trade environment and remove the distortions that resulted in Indonesia's 'high cost economy'.

The growing call from the private sector for deregulation strengthened the government's resolve. One of the first efforts to deregulate trade and investment occurred in April 1985 when the government eliminated seventeen categories of licences previously required to carry out designated economic activities. Most of the licences in this deregulation package were industry-specific and did not have a significant impact on the economy as a whole. One, however, had a more significant impact on economic activity overall. That was a decree revoking the need for licences for domestic inter-island trading. This was very important in stimulating growth of the domestic trade sector.

Overall, progress was slow until the oil market collapsed in 1986 and placed the entire economy at risk. The measures that had been implemented to inhibit imports and stimulate exports were underpowered. The government's long-term economic plans and annual budget were rendered virtually irrelevant. The economic team responded with a strategy that more than ever signified that the government was embracing a new outward looking and more market-oriented paradigm for economic development. The essence of this new strategy was encapsulated in a group of deregulation measures known as the May 6th Package of 1986.

Beginning in 1986 and continuing to this day, Indonesia generally issues its economic reforms in policy bundles called 'packages', each of which is generally identified by the date of issue. Among all the reform packages, probably the most celebrated was that of 6 May 1986. Whether the policy reforms contained therein were the most comprehensive or radical is unimportant. What distinguished the May 6th Package was that it represented the government's most firm and explicit confirmation of what would be a long struggle to restructure the Indonesian economy without the prop of oil. Although measures to deregulate the economy had already taken root in the financial sector, the May 6th Package focused on trade and investment, the aspects of the economy most directly responsible for contributing to Indonesia's high cost economy.[8]

The following highlights some of the salient characteristics of the May 6th Package pertaining to trade. The package also included measures pertaining to investment. Those will be discussed in the next section.

1. *Elimination of NTBs and Export Competitiveness.* The May 6th Package represented the government's first systematic assault on the array of non-tariff barriers constraining Indonesia's trade. Logic would suggest that the government should be able to remove NTBs with as much ease as it implemented them. That, however, was not the case. Behind every non-tariff barrier was at least one major beneficiary who risked considerable loss with the removal of protection. The sole-importer licence was one of Indonesia's most pervasive NTB. As a first step to break this cycle, the May 6th Package stipulated that companies that exported 85 per cent or more of their products were permitted to bypass sole importers and directly import intermediate goods. This regulation also allowed manufacturers of exported goods to import the necessary components free of quota restrictions. This measure greatly reduced the influence of NTBs in the Indonesian economy.[9]

2. *Import Duty Drawback System.* The Pusat Pengolahan Pembebasan dan Pengembalian Bea Masuk (known as P4BM or Centre for the Management of Import Duty Exemption and Restitution) was an innovative service within the Department of Finance. Its purpose was to reimburse companies for the payment of import duties on intermediate goods meant for re-export from Indonesia. P4BM was given strict guidelines for processing duty drawbacks. According to the original stipulations, complete reimbursement should take no more than sixty days. If the forms were properly completed, P4BM was generally able to complete the process in less than a week. Furthermore, to reduce the temptation for collusion, applications had to be made by mail and inquiries could only be made by mail or telephone. The office did not even have a waiting room to receive guests. On this agency, Thee Kian Wie (1992: 234) stated, 'From the outset, this agency impressed businessmen and observers alike with its efficient administration of the duty free and drawback measures. In fact, the very effective operation of this agency and its efficient administration has to a large extent been responsible for the success of Indonesian government in effecting a relatively smooth transition from an import-substituting to an export-promoting strategy of development.'

3. *Bonded Zones.* The May 6th Package permitted the creation of

bonded zones—the first being in Jakarta's port facilities at Tanjung Priok. This permitted goods to enter the country without paying any import duties or VAT. Customs officials did not have to inspect goods entering the bonded zone until they were leaving the country as exports. The bonded zones could also be used as transhipment points where goods could be stored and reshipped as is or after repackaging. The bonded zones, however, went beyond simple transhipment points. They served as export processing zones where businesses could set up manufacturing facilities for goods that would later be re-exported, all done without paying any duties whatsoever.

4. *Tariff Reduction*. Indonesia's average weighted tariffs were reduced from 22 per cent to 13 per cent by import value.

The May 6th Package contained policies both to remove obstacles to trade and to facilitate trade development. The Package addressed only a portion of Indonesia's impediments to trade. However, more than the deregulation of 1983, or any future deregulation package, the May 6th Package signalled the beginning of Indonesia's 'deregulation movement'. As such, perhaps more than any other event or policy, the May 6th Package was emblematic of the paradigm shift in the New Order's economic policy.

In the months and years following 6 May 1986, the government sustained the drive to reform Indonesia's trade regime. Policy packages were launched October 1986, January 1987, July 1987, November 1988, May 1990, June 1991, July 1992, May 1995, and June 1996. In the process, the reduction in Indonesia's tariff structure has been comprehensive and many non-tariff barriers were eliminated. Some of the reforms were sector specific, for example, to facilitate shipping, or deregulate particular industries, such as textiles, pharmaceuticals, animal husbandry, and the automotive sector. Although Indonesia's economy is still beset with too many NTBs, the series of policy packages greatly improved Indonesia's position as a trading country.

Exchange Rates and Trade

Trade policy is, of course, tightly linked to exchange rate policy. Since the founding of the New Order government, the government has devalued the rupiah on several occasions. Devaluations at once made Indonesia's exports relatively cheaper while making imports more expensive. For that reason, the impact of a devaluation on trade is particularly strong. Following each of the devaluations in 1978, 1983, and 1986, there was a surge in exports, but the benefits were temporary. Devaluations are, then, powerful tools in redressing trade imbalances, but they offer no long-term solution. It is therefore wrong to consider devaluations as simply one among several tools in trade policy. Indonesia never undertook devaluations as a means to promote trade, but rather to correct an exchange rate that had become misaligned. Because of these misalignments, Indonesian exports were at a disadvantage. To rectify the problem, the government chose devaluation. In every case, it would have been preferable to have maintained a strong currency based on a consistently realistic exchange rate so that no devaluations were needed. The trade regime would have been stronger and confidence in the rupiah higher. Unfortunately, it took the New Order almost two decades to learn that lesson fully.[10]

A NEW CLIMATE FOR INVESTMENT

Without investment, economic development is impossible. This simple idea is one of the essential truths of economic development. Since developing countries always face a shortage of capital, foreign investment is particularly important in promoting economic development. This notwithstanding, measures such as forced Indonesianization, strict limitations on the sectors open to investment, and even restrictions on the right to expand existing investments, all served to reduce the attractiveness of Indonesia as a site for investment.

Little of value came from these highly restrictive policies. Rather, these restrictions had a similar effect on foreign investment as non-tariff barriers had on trade: the regulations served to keep foreign investment out to protect existing investments. The lack of foreign investment resulted in fewer jobs, a smaller capital base, and reduced technology transfer. Furthermore, because Indonesia's investment policy was geared to protect 'infant industries', the competitive potential of the market was never realized. This was another factor contributing to the 'high cost' of Indonesia's economy. One scholar on the Indonesian economy, Richard Barichello (1991: 277), described the situation thus:

Given the inefficiency and relatively low labour intensities of highly protected sectors compared to the less protected ones, it was possible to give some indication of the perverse employment and foreign exchange earning effects of these policies.... The usual argument of advocates of protection was that it generated employment and saved foreign exchange. Using numbers from this and other studies, it was possible to show that investments induced by high protection of import substitutes generated only one-quarter of the jobs as would the same investments in export production. Similarly, a switch of investment from import sectors to exports would result in four US dollars worth of new foreign exchange earnings in the growing sector for every dollar lost in the shrinking sector.

Barichello's point is an important one. All evidence suggests that protectionism achieves exactly the opposite of its stated objectives. Rather than build the economy by fostering the growth of young companies, protectionism leads to the creation of fewer companies, fewer jobs, and generates less foreign exchange than would have been the case in an open export-oriented investment policy.

Despite the government's desire for greater foreign investment, the confusing and restrictive policy environment during those years ensured that investment levels remained relatively small and unstable. Foreign investment approvals rose in 1982 and 1983 only to fall in 1984. Some analysts have surmised that the rise may have been induced by a rush by investors to secure the tax holiday before its elimination after the new tax law took effect in 1984. In that year, foreign investment approvals decreased by more than 100 per cent and the downward slide continued during the next two years. Besides tax provisions, foreign investors were concerned about the stability of the economy in the midst of the collapsing petroleum market. Whatever the cause, foreign investment remained low, especially when considering the size of the Indonesian market, the country's need for capital and employment, and the volume of investment flowing into other countries in South-East Asia.

In March 1985, with foreign investment levels still well below 1975 levels, the government began an intensive effort to reform the nation's investment climate. The government reduced the number of licences required from twenty-six to thirteen and removed the levies associated with the investment application process. This measure responded to the desires of investors to simplify the investment process. It was a modest beginning as the government left untouched many of the most problematic issues, such as rules on equity and divestiture. But the momentum was building. A year later the government launched the May 6th Package. Some of the highlights of this package affecting the investment regime include the following measures:

1. *Increased Foreign Equity.* The package permitted up to 95 per cent foreign ownership for export-oriented firms—defined as those firms that export at least 85 per cent of their products. Similarly, firms that were valued at $10 million or more, or were located in selected provinces, generally in eastern Indonesia, were permitted 95 per cent foreign ownership. Within five years, the portion of domestic ownership should increase to a minimum of 20 per cent. For other investments, a minimum of 20 per cent of capital should be Indonesian and after ten years, this should be raised to 51 per cent.

2. *Expanded Access to Finance for Foreign Joint Ventures.* Joint ventures would be treated the same as domestic firms and would be permitted to borrow from state banks and participate in government credit schemes provided the foreign partner had divested of at least 75 per cent of the

company or had listed at least 51 per cent of the shares through the stock exchange.

3. *Duration of Permits*. Permits for investment were awarded for thirty years from the time the firm was established or expanded.

4. *VAT Exemption*. All direct investments were exempted from the VAT on imported capital goods.

Over the next few years, the government implemented a series of measures designed to improve the nation's investment conditions. The number of sectors closed to foreign investment was systematically reduced. Investors were permitted to diversify their product line without seeking new licences. The government lowered the minimum capital investment from $1 million to $250,000. In May 1989, the government gave investors much more freedom in terms of the areas in which they could invest. Until this point, BKPM had issued a list known as the DSP which specified the sectors in which the government permitted companies to invest. What the DSP implied was that a sector was closed unless specifically declared open. The new regulations took the opposite approach: the DSP was abandoned and in its place was the Daftar Negatif Investasi (DNI or Investment Negative List). The DNI listed those sectors specifically closed for investment. If not indicated, then the sector was considered open.

After moving to a negative list, the government maintained its effort to expand investment opportunities by progressively reducing the number of sectors declared 'off limits'. In 1991, 1992, and 1993, previously closed sectors were opened. With the 1993 regulations, only six business sectors were closed to foreign investment for national security, environmental, and other narrowly defined reasons. In April 1992, the government announced that it would soon be dropping the long held prohibition on 100 per cent foreign ownership for investments in Indonesia. This promise became official policy in 23 October 1993. Parallel to this, the divestiture policies became less stringent. Enterprises with 100 per cent foreign ownership were permitted twenty years to divest their holding to 51 per cent. In 1996, the government agreed to restore the tax holiday to industries in selected sectors.

Deregulation of Indonesia's foreign investment sector also promoted innovation. One important example was the role of private foreign investment in areas that are typically the exclusive domain of the government, such as telecommunications, roads, the provision of potable water, and power generation. In these and other areas, the government recognized that development would be slow unless the co-operation and support of the private sector were sought in selected infrastructure development and maintenance projects.

THE MARKET RESPONDS TO
DEREGULATION

The process of economic restructuring was a difficult transition that required several years to accomplish. Despite the devaluation in 1983, non-oil exports were not restored to 1980 levels until 1986. In 1981, with a value of $4.5 billion, non-oil exports comprised less than 18 per cent of total exports. By 1987, the value of non-oil exports had risen to $8.6 billion, slightly surpassing oil revenues for the first time since 1971. The trend did not stop there. Between 1985 and 1996 non-oil exports rose by 649 per cent (Figure 9.2).

Indonesia's total exports declined from a high of $25.2 billion in 1981 to a low of $14.8 billion in 1986. Exports then began to climb again and by 1990, Indonesia's exports surpassed the previous record. In the process, the composition of Indonesia's trade had fundamentally changed. Growth was no longer being generated from oil, but from non-oil exports, above all manufactured goods. Oil, as a percentage of total export revenues, fell from 82.4 per cent in 1982 to only 43.1 per cent in 1990.

In these laudable achievements, Indonesia's manufacturers and traders showed initiative and their capacity to compete when freed from a

FIGURE 9.2
Oil and Non-Oil Exports, 1971–1996

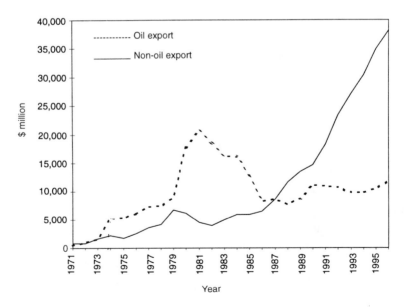

Source: Indonesia, Central Bureau of Statistics.

needlessly oppressive regulatory environment. On the other hand, if exports had levelled off there, the accomplishment would have been little more than compensation for a loss. Fortunately, the growth trend continued. One of the most striking indicators of the restructuring of Indonesia's trade sector occurred in 1993. In that year Indonesia's non-oil exports exceeded the value of Indonesia's non-oil imports for the first time since 1955. The phenomenon was repeated with an even greater margin in 1995. The trend has been lasting. For the five-year period 1980–4, Indonesia's non-oil exports averaged $427 million per month; between 1985 and 1989, the monthly average was $767 million; and in the five years between 1990 and 1994, $1.89 billion. In 1995 and 1996 trade continued to grow, although the growth has been somewhat below government targets.

There are some other noteworthy characteristics of Indonesia's trade development. First, Indonesia's trade became more diversified. Besides the obvious shift from oil to non-oil exports, Indonesia's trade shifted from primary commodities to manufactured goods. Second, during this period, Indonesia expanded its trade with a wider group of countries. More and more trade was conducted within Asia and in particular with the member countries of the Association of South-East Asian Nations (ASEAN). The increased diversification in terms of products and markets and the higher proportion of manufactured goods in Indonesia's trade mix meant that Indonesia's trade was less exposed to the volatile swings of commodity markets.

The success in trade could never have occurred were it not for a concomitant increase in investment. Foreign investment approvals for the 1976 to 1985 ten year period averaged $950 million per annum; during the next decade the average increased more than elevenfold to $11.1 billion of approved investment per annum (Figure 9.3). The link with deregulation was unmistakable. The growth in investment that began in 1987 after deregulation was launched accelerated over time. Investment was spread across a broad range of industries, but as hoped, it tended to be concentrated in the export-oriented manufacturing sector. Furthermore, because the minimum amount of investment was lowered to $250,000 this reduced the barriers to smaller investments, which tend to be more labour intensive than investments requiring large capital outlays. This was a positive trend given Indonesia's need to expand employment opportunities for the 2.4 million entrants to the labour force annually in the late 1980s. This investment not only served to stimulate the economy through the direct injection of capital into the market, but was also essential to the efforts to create an export-oriented economy freed from overdependence on oil.

FIGURE 9.3
Foreign Investment Approvals, 1967–1996

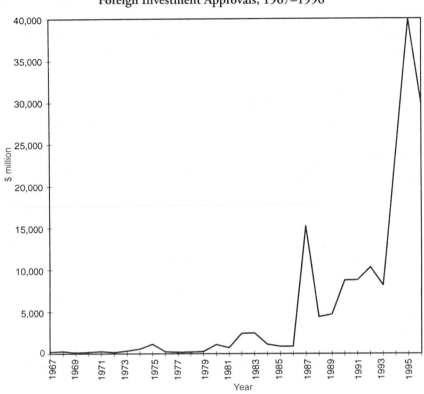

Source: Indonesia, Central Bureau of Statistics.

ON THE SIGNIFICANCE OF THE DEREGULATION OF INDONESIA'S TRADE AND INVESTMENT

The restructuring of the Indonesian economy through expanded trade and investment in the non-oil sectors was remarkable; to have realized this transformation so rapidly was almost miraculous. Part of the credit must go to exogenous factors. By 1981, the second oil shock was over and the world economy was growing again. This increased the opportunity for Indonesia's exports on the one hand, and created an international economic climate more conducive to foreign investment. None the less, while the importance of exogenous factors should be recognized, the critical factor behind the growth in Indonesia's trade and foreign direct investment was what amounted to a paradigm shift in the nation's economic policies. During the 1980s, Indonesia largely abandoned its inward-looking economic policies in favour of outward-looking policies that relied on deregulation to empower the private sector.

The reforms in customs and investment procedures begun in 1985 set the stage for the more intense efforts to deregulate the economy with the May 6th Package. The movement continued and was responsible for creating an economic environment conducive to the flourishing of the private sector. Growth was a natural outflow. Indonesia's experience is consistent with many studies on the effect of economic orientation on economic growth. Referring to economic analysis by the well-known economists, Jeffrey Sachs, Bela Balassa, and others who saw the management of the exchange rate and trade regime as two of the most critical factors in determining economic growth, the economist David Dollar (1992: 524) states: 'Outward orientation generally means a combination of two factors: first the level of protection, especially for inputs into the production process, is relatively low (resulting in a sustainable level of the real exchange rate that is favourable to exporters); and, second, there is relatively little variability in the real exchange rate, so that incentives are consistent over time.'

Ranking 117 countries, including 95 less developed ones over the period 1976–85, Dollar found that 'outward-oriented' countries grew at a faster rate than did those whose orientation was inward. In Dollar's ranking, Indonesia was in the middle of the second quartile, behind such first-quartile countries as the Asian 'tigers', as well as Spain, Malaysia, and Mauritius. However, in the years since the 1985 cut-off date of Dollar's comparative study, Indonesia greatly opened its economy through deregulation. Since then, the level of trade protection has been greatly reduced and the exchange rate moved to a realistic level, thereby rendering further devaluations unnecessary. Indeed, progressive policies toward foreign investment, trade, and monetary controls, have turned Indonesia into one of the more open and outward-looking economies in the world. Based on the fundamental shift in the development paradigm that was to follow, one can safely surmise that if Dollar had conducted his study based on the Indonesian economy during the 1986–93 period, Indonesia would undoubtedly rank among those outward-looking economies in the first quartile.

By deregulating trade and investment, Indonesia integrated itself into the international economy more tightly and extensively than ever before. Indonesia made the world its market-place and reciprocated by inviting the world to take a stake in the nation's development. Investors from around the world have responded most obligingly. The link between trade and investment has been strengthened by deregulation measures that have opened both sectors.

The restructuring of the Indonesian economy has not been without difficulties. Trade and foreign investment have both served as Indonesia's commercial window on the world. Through trade and investment,

Indonesia has exposed itself to the rigours and risks of international competition. Many businesses have suffered, and many have chastised the government for abandoning protectionist policies. However, Indonesia as a nation has profited. Most of Indonesia's businesses have risen to the challenge of international competition. The competition has made them stronger and all Indonesians have benefited from lower costs, as well as better quality and a broader range of goods and services.

The philosophy behind Indonesia's import-substitution policies was that greater self-sufficiency meant greater security. Proponents of autarky could point to the havoc caused by the collapse of the oil market as demonstrating the ill effects of exposure to the international economy. However, Indonesia's cure to the problems caused by the collapse of oil was to avail itself of many opportunities for increased international trade and investment. By rejecting import substitution in favour of export orientation, Indonesia began a process of redefining the basic philosophy upon which the country's economic development was based. This process began slowly. By the time the deregulation of trade and investment was openly embraced, there was already ample evidence from the initiatives in the financial sector and customs service that deregulation worked. Economic theory, however, was insufficient. What was needed, above all, was the political will to begin a process that would fundamentally alter the basic paradigm upon which economic development had been based.

Although the May 6th Package was a turning point in Indonesia's economic policy process, in some respects the May 6th Package could be better understood as a conclusion rather than a beginning. The devaluation in 1978 was Indonesia's first step to wean the country from its oil dependence by creating the monetary conditions favourable for exports. That process was temporarily sidetracked when the second oil boom occurred in 1979. However, the government returned to its commitment to 'oil independence' in 1983. Had the government not taken steps to reform banking in 1983, taxes in 1984, and customs in 1985, the May 6th Package would have done little to compensate for the 1986 oil collapse. That package represented not only the launch of deregulation as a movement, but also the conclusion of Indonesia's oil-driven economy.

While Indonesia was still shell-shocked from devaluation and the collapse of oil prices, the *Far Eastern Economic Review* early in 1987 quoted a World Bank report that stated, 'Even if manufactured exports increased dramatically, they are starting from such a small base that it will be a number of years before revenues come close to those from primary products' (England, 1987). Even the World Bank, it seems, had greatly underestimated Indonesia's capability for trade development. They were not alone. What no one could have predicted in 1986 was the extraordinary resilience and initiative of the Indonesian people. When the government changed its policies to create a more conducive environment for private sector development, the people of Indonesia demonstrated their remarkable productive capabilities.

It was fortunate that Indonesia's government accurately assessed that its role in the post oil boom years had changed. Instead of clinging to the *status quo* in which the economy was dominated by the government through state-owned enterprises, Indonesia's economic policymakers consciously engineered a paradigm shift in the nation's economic order, which ceded power to the private sector. In the process, Indonesia moved from one economic paradigm that was inward looking, emphasized import substitution, and was inhospitable to foreign investment, to one that was more outward looking, emphasized export promotion, and unabashedly welcomed foreign investment. From this new paradigm emerged an economic environment that was more resourceful, flexible, and responsive to market forces. Indonesia had succeeded in shifting the economy from oil-led growth to trade-led growth. This change in the basic order of the economy allowed Indonesia to cast off its gloom and insecurity associated with reduced oil earnings. Instead, the country faced the future with expanded economic opportunities, better equipped to meet the new challenges of an international economy that was rapidly changing due to the forces of globalization.

1. For more on this, see my paper, 'Back to the Wisdom of the Market Economy', presented at the Institut Pengembangan Manajemen Indonesia, Jakarta, 15 December 1989.

2. The term 'investment' refers to foreign and domestic investment. In this chapter, however, the focus is on foreign investment because the restrictions on foreign investment in Indonesia were particularly severe. This, therefore, was where the policy changes were most significant.

3. In this regard the Australian economist, Heinz Arndt, proved himself to be a perspicacious observer of the Indonesian economy. Some of Indonesia's earliest NTBs were commodity boards that were created to stabilize product markets and help promote Indonesian goods. Commenting in 1971 on Indonesia's sugar board and rubber organizations, Arndt (1971: 20) states, 'All these may be mere teething troubles in the early stage of new policies. But they illustrate the two key points at which policies of intervention in the market are most vulnerable: the risk of black markets and other illegal evasion of direct controls and the risk of political pressure on the controlling authority by vested interests, whether for privileges which yield monopoly profits or for protection of high cost producers.'

4. An interesting study on Indonesian trade protection was conducted by Pangestu and Boediono (1986). They found many direct and indirect forms of protection to be in effect in Indonesia, besides the standard tariffs and customs duties. The authors examined

twenty-two different policy instruments used to protect domestic manufacturing. Seen in this light, the study shows the considerable creativity of Indonesia's policymakers in protecting the market.

5. When I assumed my position as Minister of Finance, I agreed to the President to undertake two major tasks: reform the nation's taxation system and its customs systems. The effort to reform taxes was already underway when I began my new duties in 1983. Soon after launching the new tax law, my colleagues in the economic team and I set ourselves to the job of reforming customs. We all knew that trade needed to be deregulated, but there was no point in deregulating trade until customs had been reformed.

Instead of acting purely as an enforcement agency, Indonesia's customs officials held strong views on what should be the government's policy on tariffs, quotas, and other trade-related matters. If, for example, the economic team argued that Indonesia needed to lower tariffs, customs officials would object based on the assertion that the country relied on duties for its income. This had been true in the past, but the government's new strategy was to rely less and less on duties (on imports) and more and more on taxes (on income and sales) for its revenues. Tax reform provided the fiscal passageway that permitted customs reform. The customs department resisted this change as they wanted to hold on to their position as one of the primary financiers of the government. This attitude rendered the reform process more difficult.

6. This was an extreme and highly unorthodox action on my part, but I saw no other alternative. It was clear to the economic team that the revival of the Indonesian economy would in large part depend on trade. Trade however could never truly flourish so long as the customs service was unreformed. Customs officials had been given numerous reproaches and warnings, but to no avail. Under these circumstances, we planned in secrecy a strategy for the rapid and thorough reform of this government agency. To this end, I personally assumed the position of the Director-General of Customs. With these measures, the government took an essential step in the process that would lead to a complete restructuring of the nation's customs service.

7. See, for example, the work by Mari Pangestu (1996) which provides a good overview of deregulation policies and the export certificate scheme.

8. The Minister of Trade who replaced me in 1983 was Rachmat Saleh. I told Pak Rachmat that he now had a mandate to review all the regulations that had accumulated during my tenure as Minister of Trade and to cut them mercilessly. For my part, I had to perform the same exercise for those regulations that pertained to finance. In essence, I had to undo the work done by my predecessor, Ali Wardhana, who had become the nation's senior economic minister—the Co-ordinating Minister for the Economy, Finance, Industry, and Development Supervision.

9. This was just the beginning of the process. Several other deregulation measures continued the same process. For example, the 25 October 1986 Package specified that 165 products controlled by sole importers were open to competition.

10. As mentioned in Chapter 8, by allowing the nation's currency to float, there is a risk that the market fluctuations can have a similar impact on the currency as a devaluation. Under a floating exchange rate regime, the government's job is not one of arbitrarily setting an exchange rate and maintaining it through rigid government regulations. Instead, with floating rates, the government needs to adopt measures (both through domestic interventions and in co-operation with other countries) that will be conducive to maintaining exchange rate stability. This is a complex task, but its virtue is that it ensures that the currency will accurately reflect market values.

10
An Economy Restructured:
Reflections on Indonesia's Deregulation Movement

LIKE many nations, Indonesia has alternated between periods of being primarily an inward-looking country and other times when it was more outward looking. The qualifications 'primarily' and 'more' are important because, of course, no nation ever fully adopts all one stance or the other. There are extreme examples, Myanmar or Albania in previous decades on the inward looking side of the spectrum; or perhaps the Netherlands, as a nation that has been persistently—and successfully—outward looking. But the policies and predispositions of most nations are generally a balance of the two.

As the preceding chapters have shown, during the 1970s, fueled by oil money, Indonesia was mostly inward looking. Although much of the windfall revenues were used to underwrite the physical development of the country, the focus on diversifying and expanding trade and investment was minimal. The abrupt decline of Indonesia's oil income changed all that.

In 1989, the Indonesian scholar Hadi Soesastro wrote,

The 1980s will be recorded in Indonesia's history as the decade of deregulation, a time when measures to deregulate the economy were undertaken as part of the broader effort toward economic structural reform. But the significance of the deregulation policy perhaps lies in its systemic effects and longer-term implication for the country's economic management and the equally significant influence these effects could have upon the direction of the nation's sociopolitical development. Deregulation implies both a reduced role for government intervention and a wider and more creative participation by the public (p. 853).

Soesastro was correct. Just as the 1970s were Indonesia's oil decade, the 1980s were Indonesia's deregulation decade. Now, as we are about to enter a new millenium, the process of economic evolution continues. Deregulation has represented a sweep far wider than a reduction in red tape.

Ultimately, deregulation has embodied Indonesia's effort to redefine the government's role in the economy and its relationship with the private sector.

Although deregulation was at first embraced only reluctantly, it led to the creation of a fresh intellectual climate in which it became safe, even necessary, to question, test, and re-evaluate the rules and assumptions that had guided economic policymaking since the early days of the New Order government. With the full-blown collapse of the oil market in 1986, deregulation fever swept the country and was quickly embraced as New Order orthodoxy. Deregulation gave a fresh start to Indonesia's ongoing process of economic development.

Few countries have restructured their economy so thoroughly and with such success as Indonesia. In the 1980s, however, when deregulation was proceeding at an aggressive pace, some decisions that had to be made in a near-crisis atmosphere led to excesses in policy reform. In other cases, mistakes were made as a result of sheer over-optimism. Hence the question: What was special, effective, or important about deregulation in the Indonesian context? Over the next few pages, we will briefly reflect on the significance of deregulation as the defining characteristic in Indonesia's economic development for over a decade and the factors that contributed to its success. We will begin this discussion by considering an important theoretical justification for deregulation: making the most of comparative and competitive advantages.

COMPARATIVE AND COMPETITIVE ADVANTAGE

In his article in the *Indonesia Quarterly*, Ali Wardhana (1989) noted that economic reform is rarely if ever undertaken for its own sake. Pressures for reform generally emerge from some crises: external price shocks, abrupt changes in domestic economic conditions, or shifting political circumstances and pressures. This was true for Indonesia. It was also true that the necessity for change was not solely due to the decline in oil prices but to a larger reconfiguration of the world economy. Along with the decline in oil prices, there was renewed economic vigour among many of the world's industrialized countries. Transnational investment grew rapidly and East and South-East Asia were emerging as the high growth areas in the global economy.

In the late 1980s, to adapt to the changing world economy, one of the primary theoretical considerations behind the economic team's support for embracing deregulation was our conception of Indonesia's comparative and competitive advantages. It was obvious to the economic team that

Indonesia was endowed with a set of abundant factors of production that could provide the country with many benefits. In themselves, however, these would be insufficient to achieve the nation's economic development goals.

Since the nineteenth century, one of the primary theoretical justifications for international trade has been the concept of comparative advantage. The term 'comparative advantage' is generally attributed to the renowned classical economist David Ricardo (1772–1823) in his 1817 *Principles of Economics*. The theory of comparative advantage states that it is worthwhile to import goods that the country can produce more cheaply than another country, provided it can pay for the imports with exports that are still more cheaply produced at home.

This idea was further developed by two Swedish economists, Eli Filip Heckscher and Bertil Ohlin, into what has come to be known as the 'factor-proportions theory'. This theory states that a country should export those commodities that intensively use the productive factors which it possesses in relative abundance, as compared with the relative abundance of these factors in the rest of the world (for more on this, see for example, Baldwin and Richardson, 1974: 1). This theory demonstrates the mutual advantages of international specialization, or 'territorial division of labour'. If all countries produce according to their comparative advantage and trade for other goods, the net result is a larger world output than would occur if all countries pursued policies of national self-sufficiency.

The theory of comparative advantage continues to be considered a pillar of sound economic reasoning about international trade, even in modern times, despite some attempts to revise and/or discredit it.[1] One interesting attempt to create a theoretical framework to correct some of the perceived deficiencies in the theory of comparative advantage is the theory of *'competitive advantage'* developed by the American economist Michael E. Porter.

According to the competitive advantage concept, success for firms operating in a competitive environment derives as much from exploiting product differentiation—developing and marketing a superior quality product —as it does from exploiting cost differences. Porter's 1990 book, *The Competitive Advantage of Nations*, extends the concept to the national level and in so doing deals explicitly with international trade issues. In this book, Porter explicitly criticizes the theory of comparative advantage, calling for a new model to replace it. Porter argues that while the theory of comparative advantage has intuitive appeal and does help explain trade patterns in many industries, it leaves many patterns unexplained. He notes, for example, that in some instances, real-world evidence is hard to reconcile with the theory of comparative advantage. For example, South

Korea's relative success in exporting capital-intensive products such as steel, cars, and ships since the Korean War, is at odds with the theory because capital was relatively scarce in that country. Porter and others concluded that the theory of comparative advantage is based on unrealistic assumptions. The standard theory assumes no economies of scale, identical technologies everywhere, undifferentiated products, and fixed factors with no factor mobility across national boundaries. By doing so, the theory assumes away many facets of real-world competition, including the importance of firm strategy, such as product differentiation. Finally, the theory of comparative advantage helps explain broad tendencies in patterns of trade, but is less useful in explaining whether a nation will export or import in individual industries.

Many scholars have criticized Porter's view for various reasons. For example, one scholar of Indonesian economics, Peter Warr, argues that the concepts of competitive and comparative advantage are complementary and should not compete for the attention of policymakers. He suggests that the supporters of competitive advantage attack the concept of comparative advantage based partly on a false analogy—that between the determinants of success of a single firm and the success of a nation. The theory of comparative advantage, Warr (1994: 7) contends, was never intended to explain the superior performance of one country over another; rather, the theory provides principles to help guide an efficient allocation of resources in an open economy. Therefore, 'the theory of comparative advantage is most relevant for the exploitation of cost-based advantages, while the literature of competitive advantage is most salient for the development of successful differentiated products. The literature on competitive advantage thus reveals important lessons for individual firms.' Furthermore, according to Warr, the Porter critique misses a crucial implication of the theory of comparative advantage; that trade is mutually beneficial 'even when one country is absolutely more—or less—productive in terms of every commodity' (Samuelson, 1969: 9).

The purpose in raising this issue is neither to provide a detailed review of the arguments associated with comparative or competitive advantage nor to extend the debate. Instead, however, these ideas provide a useful theoretical and strategic backdrop against which Indonesia's deregulation policies can be measured and assessed.

Indonesia's comparative advantages are by now well known; they include a large and inexpensive labour pool, an abundance of natural resources, and a strategic location straddling many of the world's most important sea lanes. Even if Indonesia relied solely on the strength of its comparative advantages, it could expect to engage beneficially in international trade. Merchant vessels would always pass through Indonesian waters. The country's oil, gold, tin, rubber, coffee, and palm oil would practically sell themselves. Moreover, as long as the nation remained poor, it could always serve as a supplier of inexpensive labour. However, the risk Indonesia would face by excessively relying on its comparative advantages is that it would remain at the mercy of cyclical commodity markets, as well as the market for cheap labour. The markets for oil, tin, and palm oil are set internationally, and Indonesia would always be in a weak position to increase the wages of labour so long as there were other countries who offered cheaper labour. In other words, by relying on comparative advantage alone, Indonesia could expect the national economy to reap economic gain, but the extent of the gain would rely heavily on exogenous market forces, such as international commodity prices and the lowest prices for unskilled labour. To rely *solely* on comparative advantage might well amount to the easy road to nowhere. Despite the limited benefits from trade, Indonesia could count on remaining a poor developing country for many years to come.[2]

Long before anyone in Indonesia's government had heard about Porter or his theories, Indonesia's economic team was devising economic policies that were of a similar spirit to his idea of competitive advantage. In the 1970s, the team knew that if Indonesia traded the nation's oil wealth for consumer goods or unproductive projects, we would be like the prodigal sons living off our father's inheritance. When the oil was finished, the party would be over. For Indonesia, the key to competitive advantage was to take strategic measures to maximize the benefits from the nation's resources and investments. The theory was simple. It was the implementation that proved more challenging.

Textbooks on economic development are overflowing with examples of developing countries that have been unable to break the cycle of poverty, in part because their governments wasted the nation's money on grandiose projects that were monuments to the egos of a few bureaucrats, but brought little benefit to the people. Because developing countries by definition are poor, it is imperative that government investments be directed to projects that bring high and relatively quick returns to the country. In Indonesia's case—as discussed in an earlier chapter—in the 1970s, the economic team devised strategies to optimize the benefit from the nation's wealth first by trading oil for schools and health care, even state-owned enterprises, and infrastructure to support agrarian development. It is to the credit of the government that most of the nation's resources were used meticulously in ways that laid the groundwork for achieving competitive advantage. In several cases, when the government was about to engage in mega-projects that were beyond the nation's means and of dubious value, it had the wisdom and courage to assess the projects objectively and cut them.

With much of the essential infrastructure put in place, the Indonesian government recognized that the most direct path to competitive advantage no longer lay with the government, but with the private sector. For this reason, in the 1980s, the government embraced deregulation. Considering the above analysis, we can say that the economies with the greatest chance of advancing in the competitive international market will be those which *build on their comparative advantage while simultaneously seeking competitive advantages as well.* Strong development-oriented economies should encourage competition and the innovation and efficiency it fosters. Competitive advantage is a continuous process of self-reinvention both for firms and for countries. Those that are unwilling or unable to cultivate competitive advantages will not fare well. Protectionism may sustain a poor performer, but such a 'success' helps no one, nor does it constitute a valid argument for opposing deregulation.

REGULATION AND DEREGULATION IN THE INDONESIAN CONTEXT

During the more than fifty years since Indonesia achieved independence, the government's economic philosophy has oscillated between episodes of stricter and looser government control of the economy. As already discussed in an earlier chapter, after the New Order assumed control of the government in 1966, it initially scaled back the extent of government control of the economy. Conditions in the 1970s, however, led the government to create a more highly regulated economy—a trend that persisted until the 1980s. In some instances, the government instituted imaginative regulations that accelerated growth. The selective credit policy in the late 1960s and early 1970s is one such example.[3] This policy enabled the country to channel its very limited resources to areas that were considered vital for the nation's economic development. As the country's wealth grew and the economy increased in complexity, it was no longer practical for the government to try to control credit with such precision. The central government then abandoned this type of intervention.

The deregulation movement did not affect the full extent of Indonesia's regulations. Indeed, many of the regulations introduced over the course of the New Order were, and still are, sound and constructive. Some of the principal objectives for introducing regulations were as follows:

• To maintain security, usually in terms of personal safety, financial or institutional integrity, or environmental health;

- To set standards in products and services so as to ensure transparency and minimum levels of quality;
- To ensure fairness in the execution in matters of business and other civil affairs, free of collusion, fraud, or other illegal or immoral practices.

These three justifications for regulation are usually not controversial. However, where problems *did* tend to occur is when the government introduced regulations to influence prices, limit competition, or otherwise manage markets to protect selected industries. These types of regulations tended to be more troublesome and controversial. Indonesia's deregulation movement focused on changing or eliminating these market-distorting regulations.

The principal tools Indonesia used to protect industries were NTBs. As earlier discussed, these embraced a wide range of mechanisms, including import bans, quotas, sole-importer licences, preferential access to credit, closure of sectors to new investment, and a complex array of special licences and levies. In many instances, these regulatory barriers succeeded in providing a protective shield behind which local companies could grow. The unintended side effect was that Indonesia's cost structure became distorted with domestic prices usually exceeding international prices. Furthermore, entrepreneurship was stifled, as sectors became the exclusive domains of designated companies.

When Indonesia began to deregulate the economy in a systematic manner, the government's intention was not to attack regulations per se. Rather, deregulation was an attack on the distortions and inefficiencies caused by useless or misguided regulations. Anwar Nasution (1991: 5) provides the following astute and concise summary of the objectives of deregulation: 'From a microeconomic point of view, deregulation in Indonesia has had three connotations: one, lower barriers to market entry; two, relaxation of constraints on the activities of the business sector; and three, limited privatization in the sense of transfer of enterprises from public ownership to the private sector.' This summary is correct. However, to it should be added that the impact of deregulation on state-owned enterprises was not only in terms of transfer of ownership to the private sector, but also removing the regulatory barriers that protected state-owned enterprises from free market pressures. Deregulation was intended to force many state-owned enterprises to emulate the private sector in terms of competitiveness.

We can summarize the objective of Indonesia's deregulation movement even more concisely: Indonesia's deregulation movement aimed at removing any unnecessary regulatory constraints on economic activity, to enhance efficiency, and facilitate the structural adjustments that would lead to a freer and more responsive economy. Deregulation can come in many forms. Any simplification or elimination of regulations—from the procedures in applying for a driver's licence to the requirements in producing feasibility studies—involves deregulation. From a broader, more theoretical perspective, Indonesia's deregulation movement represented a more deliberate and determined adherence to the principles of neo-classical economics over more interventionist and inward-looking economic policies. Neo-classical economics emphasizes the importance of prices and free markets. In every economy, prices are important economic signals to which people respond. In a market economy, the prices of goods and services are determined according to the laws of supply and demand. Deregulation represents an effort to remove those regulations that distort prices and markets.

Deregulation is somewhat of an economic enigma. How is it that economists can speak so positively, even reverentially, about something that is inherently negative? Deregulation only makes sense in terms of regulation. If deregulation merits celebration, does this mean every regulation represents failure? Should yesterday's regulators (who are often today's deregulators) be seen as ill-informed, misguided, or perhaps even economic saboteurs? And if deregulation is a sign of progress, then should a country aspire for some sort of primal chaos, a pre-civilized state without rules or laws? To these questions, the answer, of course, is 'no'. Regulation and its corollary, deregulation, are among the most basic responsibilities of a government. Regulations embody the rules according to which a society defines itself. All soundly functioning economies operate according to well-crafted and appropriate regulations. Oddly, while we tend to regard the policymaker as a statesman, we see the regulator as a bureaucrat. In reality, we need both.

The art of policymaking is built upon a foundation of regulations, laws, and accepted norms. Good governance may rest in large part in understanding when, how, and what to regulate, deregulate, and even re-regulate. As with much in economics and politics, the lines between good and bad policies are often unclear and shifting. The ambiguity of policymaking is frustrating to the scientist and mathematician in every economist. However, it is in this 'gray zone', between the absolutes of black and white, yes and no, on and off, where the policymaker can find the opportunity for creativity, innovation, and compromise that is essential for progress. If there is anything special about the branch of economics we call 'development economics' it may be this: a healthy developing country must change rapidly to progress. Without change, there is no development. The challenge of the policymaker in a developing country, therefore, is to recognize that the development process requires that policies be reviewed and adjusted frequently so that the policy environment remains support-ive of the rapidly changing economy. Similarly, if economic policies are promulgated and ignored or removed frivolously, then the business cli-mate will lack stability and the credibility of the government and its pol-icies will suffer. A government must seek, therefore, to enact regulations that will strengthen a society and support its economic development. When conditions change and the regulations no longer serve a useful pur-pose, the government must deregulate or re-regulate.

The process of regulation, deregulation, and re-regulation is a funda-mental cycle of economic policymaking. Because a regulation 'in the books' will stay there indefinitely until effort is made to remove or modify it, regulations tend to accumulate. Hence, bureaucracies grow more bureaucratic. As the corpus of dysfunctional regulations grows, the entire economy must pay the price in wasted time, lost opportunities, and sacrificed growth. One of the major obstacles to development is an eco-nomy overburdened with the weight of accumulated, outmoded regula-tions. This said, the objective of deregulation should not be simply to cut regulations. The objective of deregulation is to create an efficient eco-nomy, free of unnecessary distortions.

In practical terms, when the government of Indonesia began its effort to deregulate the economy starting in 1983, the intent was to remove a specific set of constraints on the banking system. These measures were the first step in a long effort to effect a major structural change in the eco-nomy. Indonesia's economic team was convinced that by clearing away many of the regulatory constraints on the economy, prices and markets would work more efficiently, and this would provide an opportunity for the inherent strength in the economy to thrive. Indonesia's approach to deregulation was both effective and unconventional.

METHODS OF DEREGULATION: STRATEGIES AND SEQUENCES

Scholars have written extensively on the proper sequencing of deregula-tion. Economists hold that the sequencing of policies is important because good policies implemented in the wrong sequence can yield negative results. Even free market zealots recognize that deregulation should be done in stages. Were it possible to remove in one stroke all forms of pro-tectionism, redundant bureaucratic procedures, and inefficient regula-tions, the trauma would be so devastating that it would undoubtedly do more harm than good. Such simplistic liberalism could easily plunge an economy into recession as the networks of economic interdependencies are suddenly disrupted.[4] To avoid this, economists generally recommend that deregulation be introduced sequentially with each phase building on the previous. According to the theory, the first sector to be deregulated should be the 'real' sector, including trade, industry, and services, such as transportation. Liberalization of imports and lifting of price controls, for example, can help restore producers' incentives. This should be followed by deregulation of the financial sector, meaning banks and other domestic financial institutions. Finally, the theory holds that the institutions and regulations that govern the flow of foreign capital into and out of the country should then be deregulated. The reasons behind this approach to sequencing are as follows. Economists generally recommend that the deregulation process begin with the real sector to give businesses the chance to grow and seek out new market niches, but within the constraints of the tightly regulated banking system. The deregulated real sector will have the opportunity to grow, but because the financial sector is still highly regulated, it is less likely that banks will hastily accumulate an excess of risky loans. After the real sector adjusts to its new freedom, the government should then free banks from onerous rules on lending and bank management. Besides permitting growth in the financial sector itself, this will further stimulate business development. Finally, the restrictions on the movement of capital into and out of a country can be removed. According to the theory, it is risky to open the capital account if the economy is not sound, because with a lack of controls there is a strong risk of capital flight, which could cripple development.

This is a reasonable theory. Indonesia, however, followed exactly the opposite sequence. From 1966 to 1970, Indonesia moved in stages to permit the free convertibility of the rupiah. In April 1970, the multiple exchange rates were eliminated and everyone was permitted to freely purchase and use foreign exchange. In that year, just after emerging from a prolonged and arduous stabilization effort, Indonesia's total national foreign reserves stood at only $56.6 million! In this precarious state, the government took the bold move of removing all restrictions on the flow of capital into and out of the country. Indonesia's laws governing the flow of capital thus became some of the most liberal in the world, more so even than those of many of the most developed countries.

Indonesia's decision conformed to a persistent theme in Indonesia's economic policy management, that is, recognition of the powers of money, and the futility in trying to regulate it through non-market-oriented controls. In 1971, Indonesia was just recovering from its devastating experience of hyperinflation—itself due primarily to fiscal and monetary mismanagement. Despite the restrictions on capital imposed by the Old Order, Indonesians with the means to do so transferred much of their monetary holdings abroad seeking shelter in foreign currency deposits.

The New Order's economic team recognized that money is also called 'liquidity' because if there is even the slightest crack in the monetary controls—and there are always plenty—money will find a way to flow out of the system if that is what people want. The team saw only two workable approaches to controlling the capital account: either the flow of capital had to be airtight or capital should be allowed to flow freely. Any attempt to create a compromise would simply lead to ingenious methods to escape controls. This would create conditions for the development of a black market in foreign exchange. An open capital account, on the other hand, was workable so long as a country maintained sound monetary policies. This would result in the creation of an environment where people would not feel compelled to hold their money outside the country. Indonesia adopted the open approach, and the theory held true. Naturally, there were periods of unusually high inflow and outflow of capital, but the government accepted these as unavoidable. Eventually, Indonesians and foreign businesses saw that the government was seriously committed to the open capital account no matter what the circumstances. Their confidence then increased, and they were much more willing to hold money in the country. For this reason, Indonesia began by first deregulating the capital account in the 1970s. It is a decision the country's economic team never regretted.[5]

If this logic were applied to the financial sector, the government would have also deregulated it by the mid-1970s. Here, however, economic theory met face to face with political realities and theory was forced to yield. By 1973, Indonesia's oil money was beginning to grow rapidly and the national mood had become more nationalistic and protectionist. It was not until a decade later, in 1983, when Indonesia had experienced two years of declining oil prices that the time for a change in economic strategy had arrived and Indonesia decided to deregulate the financial sector. The decision to deregulate banks—especially state banks—reflected above all the government desire to give a greater role to the market in promoting growth. With deregulation, the government stopped using banks as direct tools of development policy. Despite the economic downturn in 1983, the government calculated that the risks from deregulation were minimal and the potential gains from an energized banking system were very large. Deregulation of the banking system was essential in the post oil boom period. The government no longer had the means to act as the primary financier of economic development. By freeing up the banks, competition would lead to a more responsive and dynamic banking sector, and this in turn would help to revitalize the economy as a whole.

The deregulation of the real sector, that is, trade and industry, was also strongly influenced by conditions in the oil sector. With oil prices high,

Indonesia adopted protectionist policies, believing that this was an acceptable price to pay to cultivate the domestic industrial sector. Deregulation of the real sector did not begin until 1985 when the customs system was overhauled.

The deregulation of the real sector as a deliberate and intense government strategy coincided with the government's adoption of an aggressive export strategy for non-oil products. With the benefit of hindsight, here again it would probably have been better to have begun this process much earlier. In this case, however, Indonesia's policies were guided by more cautious political considerations. Sometimes, it takes an $18 drop in oil prices to create the right political climate. That is what happened in 1986. Deregulation of trade and investment offered Indonesia the best chance to bring down the pervasive 'high costs' in the economy and to create an environment conducive to private sector growth. During the tough years in the mid-1980s, when Indonesia most needed to change, it did so with exceptional speed and accuracy.

Indonesia's experience seemed to prove that the sequencing of deregulation was less important than the act of deregulating itself. Perhaps more important than the sequence was that when the government did deregulate, the measures were conceived and executed in a way that recognized the complex interdependencies in the economy. When the government determined to deregulate a particular sector, it tried to introduce policy changes in related sectors that were needed to support the deregulation. For example, the measures to open the capital account in 1972 were preceded by a devaluation in 1971 and followed by the continuation of high interest rates that served as an incentive to keep money in Indonesian banks. Similarly, deregulation of banking in 1983, and trade and investment in 1986 were both preceded by devaluations and followed by a series of supporting measures. Devaluations are not the only measures that should accompany deregulation. However, it is unlikely that deregulation of industry and trade would have succeeded if the exchange rate had not been adjusted. In Indonesia's case, even more important than the devaluations was tax reform, without which the government could never have been able to compensate for the loss in revenues from the decline in oil prices.

Related to the sequence of deregulation is the matter of *pace*. Decisions on the appropriate pace of deregulation must be determined by the context in the individual country. In Indonesia's case, the government implemented its stabilization programme at a rapid pace, while in its movement toward deregulation the chosen pace was more gradual. Had the stabilization effort not been executed rapidly, it probably would have failed. Having said that, deregulation of the capital account in the early 1970s did not serve as the launch of Indonesia's deregulation movement. Important as this move was, it would be more accurate to view it as an extension of the economic reform movement inspired by the stabilization efforts. Another decade would pass before Indonesia was prepared to take a leap into serious deregulation.

Deregulation Strategies

In Indonesia's case, the pace and sequence of deregulation were determined in a way that balanced economic exigencies with political realities. The basic instincts of Indonesia's economic team led it to favour free markets with minimal government intervention. However, in the early years of development, the country's policymakers accepted that the economy needed a relatively strong degree of government intervention to stimulate broad-based growth. This interventionist approach was adopted because the government believed that in the transition to a more industrialized economy, it needed to protect the nation's younger industries. Furthermore, Indonesia wanted to assist local companies to enable them to cope with the difficulties associated with international quota systems in such areas as textiles, coffee, cocoa, sugar, tin and other metals, and so on. The other important factor was the political climate. Indonesia's oil wealth in the 1970s virtually guaranteed that the level of intervention would remain high during the decade. With the surge in petrodollars, Indonesia could afford popular protectionist policies. During the 1980s, Indonesia's economy advanced while oil prices declined and the world economy grew more open. These conditions were more conducive to deregulation.

Neither the deregulation of the capital account in 1972 nor banking in 1983 and 1988 met with much resistance. In both cases, the private sector benefited, and the public sector was in no position to oppose the measures. Deregulating trade and investment, however, was more complicated. When the deregulation process began in 1985, the price of oil was falling and the financial assumptions for the 1986 budget were in doubt. Naturally, Indonesia's economic team was apprehensive. This, however, was a group whose nerves had been tempered in the heat of several crises. It is here that we can say that Indonesia's approach to deregulation switched from being initially almost *ad hoc* to one that was strategically conceived, systematically implemented, and executed with a long-term perspective. As oil prices dropped, the team determined that the trade and investment sectors needed to be deregulated quickly. The economic team was able to identify broadly the areas it believed were most in need of deregulation. To add greater precision in policy formulation, however, the team would often confer with the director-generals (DGs) responsible for the sectors for which deregulation was being considered. The DGs in turn would hold discussions with leaders from various trade associations and business groups to gather from them the areas in which their business sectors were most in need of help. For example, a director-general or one of his associates might hold discussions with the leaders of the textile association, a palm oil producers' association, a chamber of commerce, and others. After such discussions, the DGs would report to the economic team on the conditions in the sector they had studied, together with their recommendations for improving the business environment. The economic team then had an abundance of data and recommendations for reform. With this in hand, the team tried to identify the top priorities for deregulation and the associated sectors or industries that would be affected, positively or negatively, by the deregulation. After weeks of research and numerous discussions and debates, the team agreed to a list of targets for deregulation. As mentioned earlier, deregulation measures were always issued in 'packages' because the collections of measures were intended to be mutually reinforcing.

A small group, usually consisting of the Co-ordinating Minister for the Economy, Finance, and Industry, the Minister of Finance, and a few other senior officials such as the Governor of Bank Indonesia, the Minister of Trade, Minister of Industry, or the Chairman of BKPM, would present a brief to the President that identified the purpose and targets for deregulation. The group would explain the rationale behind each of the regulations and how the package was expected to work as a whole. The President would then study the recommendations for a few days. If something was unclear to him, he would ask for clarification from the co-ordinating minister and the minister whose sector was directly related to the issue, such as trade, finance, or industry. When the President's questions were answered and he was satisfied that the package was a good one, he would give his final approval, sometimes with modifications or qualifications. The team would then make any final adjustments needed to the package after which it was presented to the public as a government decree.

The economic team's deregulation strategy was based broadly on three criteria. First, the team considered the general state of the economy. We tried to identify those broad-based measures, which if implemented would have a significant impact on the economy as a whole. An example of a very broad deregulation measure was the reform of customs. Second, on a more micro-economic level, the team would identify the specific industries for which protection had become particularly extensive and hence damaging to the economy. Third, the team had to consider the political feasibility of deregulating a particular industry.

Opposition to deregulation came from elements within both the private sector and the government. For many companies, deregulation meant a loss of monopoly rights or a decrease in tariff protection. While this translated eventually into lower prices for consumers, it also brought with it the risk of lower profit margins for the producers.[6] Not surprisingly, to the industries targeted, deregulation was as welcome as an increase in income taxes. If a business or industry suspected it was about to lose its protected status, it would often lobby the government vigorously against deregulation. Some groups wielded such influence that it was very difficult or impossible to remove the protection they enjoyed. Initially, these groups were spared the withdrawal of protection. The delay in removal of protection was usually temporary, rather than an indefinite exemption.[7] Later, when the time was right, the team would return to those protected industries. Again the team would propose deregulation measures and frequently, with the passage of time, the industry was then ready to accept operating in a non-protected environment.

Throughout Indonesia's deregulation movement, the term 'deregulation' was often coupled with the term 'debureaucratization'. The government's commitment to debureaucratization was a way of applying the philosophy of deregulation to itself. Most deregulation measures had a direct impact not only on the targeted business sector, but on an associated government agency as well. Every licence, every permit, every government application, every inspection, and every licence renewal resulted in work for a government bureaucrat. Deregulation and debureaucratization were an assault on much of the day-to-day work, and the resulting authority of many civil servants. It was hardly surprising, therefore, that there were pockets of government insiders who were highly resistant to deregulation. Although deregulation almost never resulted in outright lay-offs, the streamlining of government procedures did create job redundancy. In some cases, deregulation also meant that government employees would have fewer opportunities for the 'gratuities' that were frequently conferred for expediting the processing of a licence or the performance of some other government service. Deregulation, therefore, bred insecurity and led to frequent tensions and insecurity.

One of the primary concerns of the economic team was how the economy as a whole would react to deregulation. Especially from 1986 to 1988, the introduction of each deregulation package was followed by a period of suspenseful watchfulness: how would the economy respond? How would the public react? And ultimately, how should the government respond if the deregulation measures did not achieve their objectives? If deregulation failed to revitalize the economy, the government's contingency options were very limited. Fortunately, in virtually all important respects, deregulation proved successful and the success increased the leverage of the advocates of deregulation.

It is apt to speak about a deregulation 'movement' because one deregulation measure led to another, in a long-term effort to reform the entire economy. After one package was introduced, the economic team was able to draw on the success to justify the extension of the deregulation process to other sectors. In this, the public played a leading role in the deregulation movement. If the public reaction had been negative or even indifferent, the deregulation of trade and investment might have begun and ended with the May 6th Package of 1986. Instead, the public gave such enthusiastic and uniform support that this energized the deregulation movement. In addition, numerous other groups gave their support as well. This included businesses whose opportunities had been previously restricted because of protectionism as well as chambers of commerce, intellectuals, the media, foreign businesses and governments, international organizations, and many other groups.

Ultimately, the most important determinant of the success of deregulation was the correctness of the measures. Deregulation spoke for itself, and it was a most convincing orator. The improvements in the economy that followed deregulation were irrefutable. The very success of deregulation generated its own momentum.

Various critics of this approach have described Indonesia's deregulation process somewhat disdainfully as 'piecemeal'. It is true that Indonesia's deregulation process was done in a series of 'packages' over more than a decade, and this is a process that continued well into the 1990s. Rather than interpret this as a plodding nature or a lack of commitment or an inconsistent vision, this method reflected a pragmatic strategy that permitted a steady and systematic transformation of the entire Indonesian economy. Every deregulation package was no more than one step in a long journey to redefine and reconfigure the economy.

Deregulation embodied a change in the basic economic principles underlying the Indonesian economy. In a well-reasoned critique of the deregulation process, the economist Djisman S. Simandjuntak (1991: 265) stated:

Unlike Singapore where the 'New Directions' were intensively discussed prior to their announcement, Indonesia went through a process of deregulation and privatization in which the government exercised a very high level of discretionary power. The criteria for reform have never been clearly spelled out.... This ad-hoc approach to deregulation and privatization has, admittedly, an advantage in that it made it possible for the government to initiate a policy change any time it wants. The reverse may also be true, however.

Simandjuntak is correct that deregulation measures were introduced without extensive public debate or consultation. There would have been merit to an open discussion in the spirit of dialogue and consensus (*musyawarah* and *mufakat*). However, especially in the mid-1980s, the government had to act quickly and often under duress to engineer a thorough transformation of the basic structure of the Indonesian economy. It is correct that deregulation was never incorporated into Indonesia's five-year plans, or even the annual budgets. It was, however, addressed in numerous speeches, debated in public fora, and covered extensively in the media. The public was acutely aware of the general movement and supported it strongly.

Although Simandjuntak makes a good point, rather than see the deregulation process as *ad hoc*, a better description might be 'strategic expediency'. The economic team was largely entering 'uncharted territory'. No one knew in advance what were the limits to deregulation, or how effective the government's methodology would ultimately prove to be. For Indonesia at this time, the deregulation movement was akin to an economic revolution. As with all revolutions, once the forces of change were unleashed, no one knew with certainty where they would lead. For this reason, to an extent an *ad hoc* or opportunistic attitude was needed. In the seeming randomness of the deregulation process, however, there was a definite strategy, that is, to deregulate in steps, observe the results, build support, and move to the next step—wherever that might be. In this way, over a period of years, the government engineered a sweeping reform of the entire economy. One experience laid the foundation for the next. The deregulation movement was created by a series of incremental steps that conformed to a long-range vision. The economic team had an idea where it wanted to take the economy, and it knew the general strategy it would use—deregulation. What the team did not know, however, was how the economy would react or what obstacles it would meet along the way. For this reason, especially during the 1986 to 1988 period, the government was very clear on the general strategy for restructuring the economy, but the specific elements were not well-defined. It was here that advanced research and follow-up analysis were essential. In the end, perhaps no one was more surprised at the effectiveness of deregulation than the economic team itself. Whatever this approach lacked in theoretical elegance was compensated for in tangible results.[8]

In 1992, economist Erik Thorbecke published a study that constitutes one of the most sophisticated evaluations of Indonesia's deregulation experience. He compared Indonesia's structural adjustment programme in the 1980s with that of various other developing countries. In his analysis, Thorbecke employed statistical analysis to assess the effectiveness of Indonesia's deregulation policies during the 1980s. In this analysis, he entered various actual and hypothetical levels of production, consumption, prices, savings, and the like into an econometric model. He then ran five alternative policy scenarios, varying levels of government investment, money supply, exchange rate management, and others. Thorbecke (1992: 77) found Indonesia's deregulation experience was a marked and positive contrast to the difficult and often unsuccessful experience of most developing countries. His assessment was that Indonesia's reform 'package, including the timing and sequencing of adjustment measures adapted voluntarily by the government was arguably close to optimal under the prevailing conditions and constraints'. He (1992: 106) then concludes as follows: 'A comparison of alternative counterfactual policy scenarios within a computable general equilibrium model indicated that the adopted reform package ... was superior to practically all other alternatives in its impact on growth, income distribution and the restoration of internal and external equilibrium, in both the short run and the medium to long run.'

Thorbecke's assessment that the execution of Indonesia's deregulation programme was 'close to optimal' is quite remarkable given the degree of inventiveness that was necessary in designing and implementing Indonesia's deregulation movement. Indeed, it was this flexible style to policymaking that led so many to criticize the government. Ironically, that was the government's strength. For a few years, during the mid-1980s, the attention of Indonesia's economic policymakers was intensely fixated on the one issue of restructuring the economy through deregulation. In rapid fire, the team launched reform after reform in an effort to reconfigure the basic structure of the economy. The data describe a remarkable transformation that restored vitality to an economy that had come perilously close to ruin along with the collapse in the oil markets.

DEREGULATION AND STRUCTURAL CHANGE

Over a dozen years have passed since Indonesia's deregulation movement began. The goal of deregulation was to hasten a structural change in the economy along four lines: a) the elimination of oil dependency; b) expanded export capacity; c) industrial growth; and d) private sector development. Indonesia achieved all of these objectives.

1. *Growth without Oil Dependency.* The dominance of oil in the Indonesian economy during the 1970s was inherently unstable. Yet, despite the sharp decline in oil revenues, Indonesia's GDP continued to grow vigorously. During Repelita IV (1984/5–1988/9), the economy grew at an average rate of 5.2 per cent per year. During Repelita V (1989/90–1993/4) the rate of growth increased to 6.9 per cent. This positive trend was maintained in 1995 when the economy grew at a rate of

7.6 per cent. According to Central Bureau of Statistics estimates, the economy grew in 1996 by approximately 8.5 per cent. The declining importance of oil has been more than compensated by growth in other sectors of the economy.

2. *Expanded Export Capacity.* In 1983, Indonesia's non-oil exports amounted to $5.01 billion. By 1995, non-oil exports had increased almost sevenfold to $34.95 billion. Besides increasing the volume and value of its exports, Indonesia also increased the diversity of its export products and markets. Thus, Indonesia has increased its trading capacity, while reducing its exposure to the volatility inherent in international trade. For the foreseeable future, therefore, it is unlikely that Indonesia will again become excessively dependent on any one export product or market.

3. *Industrial Development.* After deregulation of trade and industry was begun, there was a remarkable surge in industrial development. According to the Central Bureau of Statistics, production in ninety-two standard trade categories more than doubled in the period between 1988 and 1990. In 1991, the value of Indonesia's industrial exports surpassed those from the agricultural sector as well as oil and gas. The next year, in August 1992, another landmark was reached when Indonesia's manufactured exports surpassed $2 billion for the month. Indonesia's industry has now grown to become the leading sector in the economy, a distinction that had been firmly held by agriculture since time immemorial. In this, Indonesia demonstrated that by emphasizing agrarian development during the 1970s, it created a stable economic environment that permitted industry to flourish without creating severe dislocations in either sector.

4. *Private Sector Economic Leadership.* In 1983, Indonesia's government budget comprised 19.5 per cent of GDP for the year. In 1995 the government budget decreased to 17.6 per cent of GDP. What is more important, rather than seeing an ever increasing array of state-owned enterprises, industrial and business growth has been overwhelmingly concentrated among private sector firms. This trend is certain to continue as more state firms are privatized and the government relies almost exclusively on taxes to finance routine government expenditures. (This topic is discussed in greater detail in the next section).

Table 10.1 illustrates the change in the sectoral composition of Indonesia's economy between 1983 and 1996.

The extent to which the composition of Indonesia's economy changed in a little over a decade is remarkable indeed. The most dramatic change was that out of the nine basic sectors, manufacturing moved from the fifth ranking sector to become the economy's leading sector. The second most important change is that the mining and energy sector—which includes oil—dropped from its second place rank to fifth. As would be expected,

TABLE 10.1
Changes in the Sectoral Composition of GDP in Current 1983
and 1996 Prices (Rp billion)

Sector	1983			1996		
	Current Prices	Rank	Percentage GDP	Current Prices	Rank	Percentage GDP
Agriculture, forestry, and fishery	17,696.20	1	24.01	88,040.80	3	16.53
Mining and quarrying	13,967.90	2	18.95	45,915.70	5	8.62
Trade, hotels, and restaurants	12,009.40	3	16.30	88,877.80	2	16.69
Services	8,712.30	4	11.82	46,299.40	4	8.69
Manufacturing industries	8,211.30	5	11.14	135,580.90	1	25.45
Construction	4,597.20	6	6.24	42,024.80	7	7.89
Finance, ownership, and business	4,001.00	7	5.43	44,371.40	6	8.33
Transportation and communication	3,978.00	8	5.40	34,926.30	8	6.56
Electricity, gas, and water supply	524.30	9	0.71	6,593.70	9	1.24
Total	73,697.60		100.00	532,630.80		100.00

Source: Indonesia, Central Bureau of Statistics.

the sector that lost ground most after mining and energy was agriculture. Its ranking declined from first to third place while the sector was growing substantially in absolute terms. One other remarkable development is in the area of tourism, under the category of trade, hotels, and restaurants. By 1996, tourism's contribution to the economy had surpassed that of agriculture. Indonesia expects vigorous growth to continue in this area in the years ahead. Lastly, although the relative importance of services has declined, their absolute contribution has increased substantially. The relative decline in services is an outcome of the huge growth in manufacturing. In this early stage of development, Indonesian workers have moved from low paying and unstable positions in the service sector to more secure and higher paying jobs in manufacturing. If Indonesia follows a typical pattern of development, the relative share of agriculture in the economy will continue to decline. Many workers leaving the rural sector will enter the service sector.[9]

It is not only the composition of Indonesia's economy which changed significantly, but also the structure within individual sectors. Let us take industry as an example. In 1983, the food, beverage, and tobacco industrial group was responsible for almost half of the total industrial output. In

1995, 80 per cent of industrial output was shared by five industrial groups, with no single category having a heavily dominant position.

Behind this comprehensive structural change in Indonesia's economy, another trend was transforming the economy: the private sector was assuming the leadership role in the nation's industrial development, while the state sector decreased in importance.

THE PRIVATIZATION OF STATE-OWNED ENTERPRISES

Article 33 of the 1945 Constitution declares that 'branches of production important for the State and of dominating interest to the livelihood of the masses of the people have to be controlled by the State'. This Article served as the legal justification for the development of an extensive network of state-owned enterprises. Still, in the late 1950s, Indonesia's state-owned enterprises had a negligible role in the economy. However, the state sector grew rapidly in the 1960s following the nationalization of many industries. In 1986, the number of state-owned enterprises had grown to 215, in projects ranging from paper production to tin mines and tea plantations. Some, like Pertamina and Krakatau Steel, developed into very large multibillion dollar corporations.

After the founding of the New Order, state-owned enterprises first grew rapidly and then declined in their relative importance to the Indonesian economy. This trend reflected the government's changing view on what constitutes the most appropriate role of the state and the private sector in the economy. In 1967, after the build up of the state sector under the Old Order, the government announced it would endeavour to create an economic climate that removed favouritism toward the state sector. In 1969, the government changed most state-owned enterprises into limited liability corporations (known by the Indonesian abbreviation 'PT' for Perseroan Terbatas). The culture and business practices of state-owned enterprises, however, were slow to change. Then, with the surge in oil wealth, the government became more interventionist, which led to a proliferation of state-owned enterprises.

In 1987, Thee and Yoshihara published a study on the relative importance of foreign companies, state enterprises, and private Indonesian companies in seventeen industries, from soft drinks to motor cars. They found that state enterprises dominated the capital-intensive material industries (the 'upstream sector') and private enterprises (foreign and Indonesian) dominated the less capital-intensive finished products industry (the 'downstream sector'). Thus, they characterized Indonesian industry as 'upstream socialism, downstream capitalism'. There was some truth to this observation. This dualism in the Indonesian economy resulted from the belief within government circles that there were few private Indonesian entrepreneurs with the financial resources to undertake capital-intensive 'upstream' investments. This changed with the deregulation movement. After determining to reduce its industrial holdings, the government issued decrees in 1988 and 1989 with specifications to determine the soundness of state-owned enterprises.[10] Firms were grouped into four classifications: very sound, sound, less sound, and unsound. After firms were classified, the government was able to choose the steps that were needed for privatization.

Despite the government's avowed intention to privatize the nation's state-owned enterprises, progress has been slow. Some of the principal obstacles Indonesia faced were as follows:

1. *Cut-rate Sales.* Many state-owned enterprises were poor performers that depended on subsidies for their continued operation. After years of dependence, these companies were of little interest to private sector investors. They could be only be sold, therefore, at an enormous loss. The government reasoned it would be better to hold a state-owned enterprise and attempt to improve it rather than 'unload' the company at cut-rate sale prices or close it down altogether.

2. *Unemployment.* Because Indonesia suffered from high levels of unemployment and underemployment, the government did not want to exacerbate this problem by closing state-owned enterprises. The government has always resisted dismissing state employees for reasons other than wrongful acts or gross incompetence. As above, the government preferred to try to improve the company's performance with a view toward eventual privatization, rather than see government employees suddenly made jobless.

3. *The Problem of Indonesianization.* One of the objectives for developing state-owned enterprises was to help promote a class of managers and entrepreneurs among indigenous Indonesians. There was a risk that through privatization, ownership would pass into the hands of non-indigenous Indonesians, including foreign corporations or local conglomerates. There were few private Indonesian businesses with the capital or the entrepreneurial and administrative expertise to successfully acquire and manage these enterprises. If privatization constituted a transfer of assets out of Indonesian hands, it would be a set-back to the government's Indonesianization efforts.

4. *Transfer of Monopoly Rights.* Many state-owned enterprises had some limited monopoly rights, such as the exclusive rights to import certain types of goods. If the government sold state-owned enterprises together with their monopoly rights, the sale could result in a *de facto* transfer of a

market monopoly to the buyer. This was unacceptable to the government as well as to most Indonesians. Without such monopoly rights, however, many state-owned enterprises were unsaleable.

5. *Obstacles to Public Listing.* Other than outright sale, state-owned enterprises could be partially or totally privatized by listing the company on the stock exchange. This was the government's aim. The principal shortcoming to this approach was that the public listing was likely to fail unless the firm was profitable. The government was unwilling to list a company unless it was confident the listing would be a success.

The process of privatizing state enterprises has progressed slowly although the results have been positive. In 1988, Presidential Instruction (Inpres) No. 5 ordered an investigation of state-owned enterprises with the aim of determining which were suitable for eventual privatization. In 1989, the government indicated its intention to privatize fifty-two state-owned enterprises. By the beginning of 1997, however, only five have been listed on the JSX: PT Semen Gresik, the cement manufacturer; PT Indosat, the satellite communications company; PT Tambang Timah, the tin mining and processing venture; PT Telcom, what used to be Indonesia's telecommunications monopoly; and, the first Indonesian state bank, Bank Negara Indonesia 1946 (BNI). Soon, one of the crown jewels of Indonesia's state-owned enterprises, Krakatau Steel, is expected to be publicly listed.

It should be noted that besides the 187[11] state-owned enterprises, there are also a very large number of companies under the provincial governments. There is no consolidated record of all provincial enterprises. If, however, such enterprises were taken into account, the number of public enterprises would be considerably larger. If the task of privatization were extended to the provincial level, then the scale of work ahead would be far greater and the potential influence on the economy greater still.[12]

The difficulty in privatizing state-owned enterprises results in part from the conservative nature of the government. The goal of privatization remains. Implied in this goal is the question whether the government should retain any state-owned enterprises whatsoever. It is important first to recognize that there are many examples of successful state-owned enterprises. One such example is the state bank, BRI, the bank that has predominately served Indonesia's farmers and rural businesses. BRI achieved stunning results in support of the government's efforts to monetize the rural sector. Its continued growth and development show that state enterprises can be competitive with the private sector, even while remaining responsive to their guiding mission of supporting the government's economic development objectives. Although more study is needed, it seems likely that the determining factors for success of a state-owned enterprise are management skill and work incentives, rather than ownership. There-fore, although on average the performance of state-owned enterprises has been weak, this does not mean that state-owned enterprises are inherently hopeless as commercial ventures.

This acknowledged, with more than thirty years of experience by which to judge, the position of Indonesia's economic team was as follows: to pri-vatize where so doing could be done without incurring undue loss; other-wise, to assist state-owned enterprises to progress to the point to where they could be privatized. In extreme cases, when a state-owned enterprise shows little hope of rescue, it should be liquidated. Despite the excep-tional performance by companies such as BRI, it would seem that the best policy is for the government to avoid the creation of new state-owned enterprises. As an alternative to state-owned enterprises, the government should pursue the following two options. First, to fund research institutes such as the Bogor Agricultural Institute, the benefit of whose research should be made readily available to domestic companies and individual practitioners. Second, to work in partnership with private sector firms through grants or public tenders. In this way the government can encour-age competition and efficiency among local firms, influence their policies and activities and yet avoid entering the business of business—an endeav-our for which governments are ill-suited. This would permit the govern-ment to focus its efforts on raising the living standards of all Indonesians through public service activities such as infrastructure development, edu-cation, environmental protection, and public health programmes. The government's active encouragement of private sector development may have been the most significant implication of Indonesia's deregulation movement.

BALANCING DEREGULATION WITH APPROPRIATE REGULATION: THE FOREIGN COMMERCIAL DEBT TEAM

Earlier we said that the process of regulation, deregulation, and re-regulation is a fundamental cycle of economic policymaking. Because deregulation was so fundamental to Indonesia's economic restructuring, we have called it a paradigm shift in the country's economic orientation that was tightly linked to what was popularly known as 'the deregulation movement'. None the less, we should not lose sight of the fact that deregulation was a means and not the end. The end that Indonesia's government sought through deregulation was a stronger, more prosperous, and dynamic eco-nomy.

Deregulation was not the sole route to the restructured economy. In many cases, new regulations were needed, and in other instances, modification and redefinition of former regulations were most appropriate. An important example of this principle occurred in 1991. Indonesia then faced a rapidly increasing current account deficit that threatened the nation's financial stability. Steps needed to be taken to regain control of the situation. Indonesia's deregulators had to change hats and become regulators in a very public and controversial way. It was for the good of the country, but the return to the role of regulator instead of deregulator was not a position to which we aspired.

In the early days of the New Order, Indonesia had already experienced two crises pertaining to debt, the first concerning the inheritance of the Old Order debt in the late 1960s, and the second when Pertamina incurred enormous debts in the mid-1970s. Having learned from these difficult experiences, Indonesia was able to avoid another debt crisis similar to those that plagued most oil-producing developing countries during the 1980s. Problems, however, often have a way of appearing when they are least expected.

In the late 1980s and early 1990s, the government faced new problems with debt, but in this case the source of the troubles was the private sector. On the government's side, through careful planning and discipline, the nation's public debt was shrinking as a proportion to the nation's export earnings. Indonesia's official debt-service ratio had decreased from over 30 per cent in the late 1980s to just over 20 per cent in the early 1990s. However, whatever gains were being made in terms of government debt were being negated by the rapidly growing levels of debt incurred by the business community. The nation's growing current account deficit—which in FY 1989/90 stood at $1.8 billion—was of great concern to the country's economic leaders. The next year that amount more than doubled, reaching $3.8 billion. A principal factor contributing to the growing current account deficit was the rapidly escalating private sector debt originating from offshore loans. The ability to assess this situation was difficult then, as it continues to be, because the information on private sector offshore loans is not readily available.

The primary source of this problem can be traced to a heightened level of investment and other business activities that stimulated a corresponding increase in imports. The other major element was a group of planned mega-projects valued in billions of dollars. Most of these were led by the private sector, but often had with some affiliation with one or more government agencies. While the government has often spoken glowingly of the value of the 'public and private sector partnership', this is one time when the partnership worked to the disadvantage of the country. The main drawback was that links to the government—however tenuous—

made a local investor seem to have strong credentials when seeking off-shore loans. Furthermore, if a loan were linked in any way to the government, it was considered a sovereign debt. The government would then have to assume responsibility for the loan if the associated business went bankrupt.

The mega-projects that were behind Indonesia's sudden debt build up in 1990 and 1991 were mostly related to infrastructure development, such as roads, electricity generation, and telecommunications. Several other mega-projects were in the oil and petrochemical sectors. What made the situation particularly disturbing, however, was that even after the brief economic windfall that accompanied the 1990 Gulf War, the nation's current account continued to deteriorate. If Indonesia went ahead with all the proposed mega-projects they would certainly lead to serious monetary problems, such as higher inflation and debt repayment difficulties.

The government's response came as Presidential Instruction No. 39 (Keppres 39/1991). This instruction led to the formulation of a team comprising eleven ministers known as the Foreign Commercial Debt Team (FCDT).[13] The purpose of the FCDT was to serve as a gatekeeper for commercial borrowing that was in any way associated with the government. Concessional loans such as those obtained through the IGGI—and later the CGI, which was the consortium that succeeded the IGGI—were not covered by the FCDT, nor were loans that were entirely private sector. Soon after its formation, the FCDT announced an annual cap on offshore borrowing and declared that four mega-projects would not be permitted to go forward. All four consisted of petroleum-related facilities: a $1.26 billion aromatics plant, a $3.7 billion oil refinery, a $2.5 billion oil refinery upgrade, and a $2.4 billion olefins project. Cancellation of these projects was not done lightly. The projects had merit. They would have helped to create a more vertically integrated petrochemical industry, which would have taken advantage of Indonesia's abundant natural gas and oil reserves. It would also have served many downstream industries, from textile manufacturing to plastics production. Furthermore, these investments were projects backed by some of Indonesia's most influential business leaders. When the team first announced that these projects would not be authorized, some executives said they would push ahead with the projects anyway. At this point, President Soeharto confirmed that the decisions by the FCDT would be observed.

There was some bitter irony in this experience. The main thrust of the deregulation movement was to relegate more power to the private sector. The private sector had reacted to deregulation in a way that almost seemed drawn directly from an economics textbook. Investment, consumption, and per capita income all grew. Along with these, the nation's current account deficit grew as well, as the increase in imports and borrowing outstripped the country's export earnings. Keppres No. 39, which resulted in the creation of the FCDT, was an appropriate and necessary re-regulation to address this problem.

The lesson in this is that deregulation created a new set of problems that required a new set of regulations. This is a predictable cycle. As important as deregulation was to Indonesia, economic restructuring could not be achieved through deregulation alone. The increase in private sector debt was a warning to the government of the need to be vigilant in adapting the nation's regulatory environment to address newly emerging problems. In the case of the FCDT, the new regulations achieved their purpose. The country's economy continued to grow strongly, but the nation's current account deficit was kept to acceptable levels. In the process, the government showed that it was still prepared to make difficult decisions to sustain economic development, even if that meant taking positions that were strongly opposed by elements of the private sector.

DEREGULATION AND INDONESIA'S LONG-TERM DEVELOPMENT EFFORT

Under the best of circumstances, economic development takes time. Especially for a country with a population now surpassing 200 million, the process requires Herculean effort sustained over many years. Policymakers must alternate their focus between the most recent economic data and developmental goals for the distant future. In business, managing for short-term gain is risky; in national development, it is disastrous. To combat the myopia of judging economic development in terms of short-term gain, Indonesia's economic and political leaders have continually emphasized the nation's long-term development goals.

Since 1969, Indonesia's economic planning has been guided by annual budgets, Five-Year Development Plans (Repelita), and even twenty-five year plans, which are perhaps better described as broad statements of guiding economic principles and objectives. At every level of planning, the government has sought to base its policies on the Development Trilogy consisting of stability, growth, and equity.

The government used the popular idea of 'take-off' as a way of focusing public attention on the long-term objective of moving the nation from subsistence to a market-driven middle-income economy. Rather than representing a firm set of economic criteria, take-off was a symbolic idea that gave shape to the national aspiration for economic progress. Without going into detail, it seems safe to say that Indonesia has in fact achieved the take-off that was once a distant dream. The newfound strength of industry, trade, and banking as well as the progress in the nation's educational system have created the conditions for sustainable growth.

Besides the nation's budgets and five-year plans, the country's economic progress was also assessed in broad concepts that were indicative of levels of national development. For many years, for example, Indonesia's policy-makers looked forward to the day when the country would move from the stage of a 'less developed country' (LDC) to a 'newly industrializing country' (NIC). Authors using specific economic criteria have defined these terms in various ways. For example, in a recent study, *The Newly Industrializing Countries of East Asia*, authors Anis Chowdhury and Iyanatul Islam (1993) enunciate four criteria to determine if a country has reached the stage of newly industrializing economy. The criteria in their definition are as follows:

- The domestic savings ratio is at least 15 per cent.
- Real GDP per capita is at least $1,000.
- The share of manufacturing in GDP and employment reaches 20 per cent.
- The United Nations human development index, or HDI, reaches 0.75.

The most decisive evidence to support the idea that Indonesia's economy has achieved take-off is that in 1995, for the first time, Indonesia's per capita income crossed the $1,000 threshold. In addition, that year, Indonesia's gross domestic savings as a percentage of GDP was 29.5 pe cent. Manufacturing comprised 24.3 per cent of GDP. In 1992, Indonesia's HDI ranking was 0.586—below the threshold specified by Chowdhury and Islam. In 1997 the UNDP issued its HDI based on 1994 data. Indonesia's HDI increased to 0.668.[14] Indonesia's standing in this regard has since improved. In any case, the HDI measure is very imprecise and not as widely accepted as other indicators of development. For this reason, it is fair to state that by the above standards, with qualifications on the HDI, Indonesia has achieved the status of a newly industrializing economy.

Despite the turbulence and difficulties Indonesia experienced in the 1980s, Indonesia was able to quickly restructure its economy and restore economic growth. Deregulation provided the economic freedom that permitted the rapid remobilization of money and manpower into those sectors where they could best contribute to economic development. Deregulation was indispensable to the restructuring of Indonesia's economy, and restructuring was necessary to maintain economic growth without overreliance on oil. Without deregulation, therefore, it is virtually impossible that Indonesia would have entered so early the ranks of the world's NICs. Deregulation empowered the private sector, and the private sector propelled Indonesia's growth.

DEREGULATION AND THE FUTURE OF INDONESIA'S ECONOMY

For the first forty years of Indonesia's existence, the dominance of the government in the country's economic affairs was an established fact. Indonesia's economic development remained government-driven. In the 1980s, however, the model of development of the 1970s was no longer capable of meeting the new demands on the economy. With the drop in oil prices, the government had to operate under severe fiscal constraints. Resources were particularly tight in light of the growing dimensions of the economy. On the other hand, the level of development that the Indonesian people had come to expect had changed. Indonesia needed a new approach to development that could sustain economic and social growth. The government responded to the new challenge with deregulation. Deregulation, however, was more than the simple elimination of regulations. By putting economic power directly into the hands of the people, deregulation was the government's most important tool for restructuring the economy.

Earlier we said that deregulation was instrumental in switching the engine of growth from the government to the private sector. In fact, it would be more accurate to say that through deregulation, the powerful growth engine of the government continued working as hard as ever. Deregulation, however, allowed for the creation of not one new engine of growth, but millions. Every new entrepreneur, every new shop, bank, and farmer—all were invited to join more directly in the nation's economic development. Deregulation, and the freedom it implies, gave the people of Indonesia the opportunity to build a new economic future for the country. It is this economic freedom and the opportunity that it permitted that is the ultimate legacy of Indonesia's deregulation movement.

1. See, for example, the extensions and revisions discussed by many prominent economists in Baldwin and Richardson (1974).

2. For the sake of brevity, we are limiting our discussion of comparative advantage. Our point, however, is not that comparative advantage is static and progress is impossible. However, without complementing the benefits of comparative advantage with the aggressive pursuit of competitive advantage, Indonesia's progress would have been slower.

3. The selective credit policy is discussed in some detail in Chapter 1.

4. Theoreticians may try to justify simultaneous lifting of all regulations and distor-

tions (see Krueger, 1986: 29–30, for some theoretical arguments). Still, from the pragmatic point of view of our economic team, the task seemed not only daunting but also excessively risky.

5. Experience and monetary theory informed Indonesia's economic team that an open capital account should also be accompanied by a floating exchange rate. Otherwise, if a currency becomes overvalued, people will transfer their wealth into a 'safer' currency to avoid the risk of devaluation. Until 1986, Indonesia did not do this, and it created a kind of monetary dualism in which exchange rate management was incompatible with open capital account. This 'dualism' was inherently unstable and potentially injurious to the economy.

6. Businesses are consumers as well. Even businesses that lost the benefits of protectionism gained from the general lowering of input costs.

7. The plastics and the steel industries provide telling examples. These were strategic industries, both with influential backing within the government and outside. These industries were among the early candidates for deregulation. They were temporarily 'spared' to give them more time to prepare for the time when they would have to operate without the benefit of government protection. When we first raised the idea of deregulating the state steel company, Krakatau Steel, Minister of Industry Hartarto rightly pointed out that the company was unable to compete with foreign competitors. Deregulation might well mean the end for the company. Rather than abandoning plans to deregulate the steel sector, the government took steps to restructure the capital and management of the company. Then, in November 1988, the government deregulated both the steel and the plastics industries. Deregulation helped to bring down prices for both products and this helped the industries grow faster and stronger. Today, Krakatau Steel is not only large, but it is efficient and profitable. In the very near future, the company will be privatized.

8. Although in the mid-1980s it would have been impractical and even dangerous to put the deregulation process at risk by engaging in time-consuming and potentially acrimonious public debates, things have since changed. Indonesia is a participant in the ASEAN Free Trade Area (AFTA) and the Asia–Pacific Economic Co-operation (APEC). These two organizations have given detailed schedules for achieving specific targets for trade liberalization. By agreeing to these principles, the government has committed itself publicly to achieving certain deregulation objectives.

9. Many studies have examined the relationship between the stages of development and the pattern of structural change in manufacturing and industry. These studies have found a systematic relationship between the size and structure of the manufacturing sector, the level of per capita income, and the size of the country. (A classic study is H. B. Chenery and M. Syrquin's (1975) *Patterns of Development, 1960–70*). Such studies indicate that after a certain stage of development is reached, the share of manufacturing in GDP tends to fall, while the basic underlying forces of industrialization, including technological change, specialization, and trade, continue to propel output per capita upward. In other words, in a country's early stages of industrialization, the share of manufacturing in GDP and per capita GDP both grow. In a more advanced stage, however, although per capita GDP continues to rise, the share of manufacturing in GDP begins to fall. The decline in manufacturing is usually taken up by services. This would represent the shift in an economy from early industrialization to advanced industrialization. Indonesia still has a long way to go before it reaches this point. None the less, there has been a very important change in the nature of service employment in Indonesia as more people enter service-sector jobs, such as in banking, medicine, legal services, and others. It is likely that in the early

years of the next century, Indonesia will see its service sector develop at least as quickly as the industrial sector in the 1980s.

10. For additional discussion on the privatization process see Pangestu (1991).

11. This is the number of state-owned enterprises in early 1997. Besides those state-owned enterprises that were listed on the stock exchange, a number of firms were sold directly to private investors and others were liquidated.

12. If there has been any mistake in the government's privatization policy, it is that the process has proceeded too slowly. For the reasons already described, the government of Indonesia had wisely chosen to be cautious and methodical before privatizing any state-owned companies. None the less, privatization has helped the economy and the effort should continue with redoubled vigour. In the end, the companies will benefit from more autonomy, consumers will benefit from the enhanced competition, and the government will benefit from the expanded tax base.

13. The FCDT was also informally referred to as the Commercial Offshore Loan Team (COLT). The chairman of the FCDT was the Co-ordinating Minister for Economy, Finance, Industry, and Development (myself). The members consisted of the Minister of State; the Minister of Finance; the State Minister of Development Planning/Chairman of Bappenas; the Minister of Industry; the State Minister for Research and Technology/Chairman of BPPT; the Minister for Communications; the Minister for Tourism, Post, and Telecommunications; the Minister of Mining and Energy; the Minister of Public Utilities; and the Governor of Bank Indonesia.

14. This data was drawn directly from the UNDP's home page on the World Wide Web.

11
Beyond the Outward Looking Economy:
Embracing a Global Future

ECONOMIC development is never finished. Unlike a book that ends with its last sentence, or a painting on which the artist adds the final brush-stroke, an economy is always 'work in progress'. This is true not only because the 'wheels' of the economic machine are perpetually in motion, but because our understanding of the economic process is continually growing deeper, broader, and moving into whole new dimensions. In economics, as in many areas of scientific endeavour, we are living in a period in history in which the cycles of discovery, development, and succession are compressed. In some instances, one model displaces its predecessor. In others, one builds upon the other. When Copernicus, for example, developed a system of astronomy that recognized that the earth revolved around the sun, it replaced the Ptolemaic system that saw the earth as the centre of the universe. The two were fundamentally incompatible. In the twentieth century, Albert Einstein's relativistic physics was revolutionary, but it subsumed Newtonian physics as a special case. Einstein's ideas did not refute Isaac Newton's but expanded them in ways Newton never imagined.

The development of Indonesia's economic ideas and policies followed a similar course. Indonesia's outward-looking paradigm displaced the inward-looking paradigm. The latter was flawed and Indonesia needed to reject it. It would be wrong, however, to consider the outward-looking policies that Indonesia introduced in the 1980s as the final word on the country's economic development. Less than a decade later, in the early 1990s, it became apparent to the economic team that the world economy was changing in very important ways. Through a variety of causes and circumstances, economies everywhere, including Indonesia, were becoming increasingly international. This has important implications for economic development. Indonesia's economic team believed that to maintain the nation's development, Indonesia needed to prepare for an economic future where Indonesia's local economy would be well integrated into the global economy.

Globalization is neither a specific policy, nor a precisely defined phenomenon. We will use the term globalization to signify an approach to economics whereby the world is treated as a single market. The globalist vision seeks an integrated world economy. Nations—individually and collectively—support globalization by removing barriers to international commerce, thus permitting the free flow of trade, investment, currencies, and information across national boundaries.[1] Globalization applies to consumers and businesses alike. For the consumer, globalization implies having ready access to the products of the world at international prices. For business, globalization implies the ability to establish operations or market goods or services anywhere without restrictions based on national origin.

As Indonesia entered the last decade of the century, the economic team believed that the country had to begin preparing for the time when globalization could serve as an appropriate paradigm to guide the nation's economic policy. In the years that followed, the government took many important steps to move in this direction. The globalist outlook did not replace the outward-looking paradigm, but expanded it. In this chapter, we will consider several of the prominent arguments for and against globalization, in both general terms and as they apply to Indonesia.

ANTECEDENTS TO A GLOBAL ECONOMY

Although the word 'globalization' appears only in the most recently published dictionaries, the trend to move from a local economy to a global one has been building for several centuries. One could trace the origins of the globalization movement back at least four centuries—to September 1522—when members of the Magellan expedition returned to Seville, Spain, after the first known circumnavigation of the earth. Although Ferdinand Magellan was killed in the process, one of the five ships in his armada returned full of the spices that paid for the three-year expedition. In the process, Magellan's breakthrough gave conclusive proof that the earth was spherical with ocean routes that permitted circumnavigation. Then, as now, commercial interests were behind the push for globalization. In the years since, the trend toward global economic integration has continued. However, despite growing international trade, investment, and the steady build up of international institutions, most of the world economy has remained small, local, and isolated. Even by the first half of the twentieth century, in Indonesia as in most of Asia, Africa, and Latin America, most households had no electricity or running water. There were no telephones with which to chat with friends and relatives in the cities, no television sets, and very few radios.[2] This has changed quickly, above all due to technological and political changes.

During the last few decades, one of the most important catalysts for the internationalization of commerce was technology, or more specifically, information technologies, such as computers, software, and telecommunications. Indonesia recognized the importance of information technologies and in the 1970s was one of the early countries to build a national telecommunications system around satellite technology. During the 1980s, the advances in information technologies reached a breakthrough in terms of power, ease of use, and availability. The rapid advances in computers and software, and their consolidation with telecommunications led to the creation of a host of supporting technologies, from fax machines to satellite television broadcasts, corporate computer networks, and the global Internet. Together, these technologies have made possible the transmission of information on a scale and with a speed that was utterly inconceivable even three decades ago. Naturally, these advances have had an important impact on the development of Indonesia's economy. In the early 1980s, only the most sophisticated Indonesian businesses had had access to telex machines or other modern technologies. However, as technology increased in power, it decreased in cost. In a developing country like Indonesia, by the early 1990s even small-scale businesses were suddenly able to adopt technologies, such as fax machines and numerous computer applications which enabled them to partake more readily in the global economy.

The second major catalyst of globalization was political. The world witnessed a turning point in history in November 1989 when the Berlin Wall fell. With that symbolic event, the scourge of communism was exorcised in a matter of months. In all but a few strongholds, communist dictatorships gave way to the forces of capitalism and democracy. Even the last of the communist giants, China, has accommodated market economics while officially espousing communism. The fall of communism helped unify what had been a bipolar world. With this change, for the first time it has been possible to talk about a global economy.

During this period, Indonesia's economy was already in a state of remarkable change as the government pushed ahead with deregulation. None the less, Indonesia's economic policymakers recognized the momentousness of the changes taking place in the world economy. As one of their final policy objectives, the economic team began to prepare the country for a new order in international economics.

AGENTS OF GLOBALIZATION

The emergence of information technologies and the fall of communism helped create conditions conducive to globalization. The movement, however, depends additionally on the support of two principal agents: governments and business.

Government-led Globalization

All governments, including Indonesia's, tend to regard globalization with some ambivalence. The duty of a government is to the nation; it is through the nation that the government obtains power and legitimacy. Globalization, however, requires that nations conform to global conventions, which may conflict with domestic interests. These issues are particularly sensitive for a developing country like Indonesia since many Indonesians have worried that opening the economy too widely could lead to foreign domination of the economy.

Over the years, Indonesia had taken many steps to open the economy gradually and systematically to foreign trade and investment. One important step has been the pursuit of greater regional integration within ASEAN. Soon after its founding in 1967, the ASEAN nations had discussed the idea of eliminating all trade barriers within the region. Until the early 1990s, Indonesia had opposed the move. However, after the nation's successful experience with deregulation, Indonesia proposed that the organization move forward quickly to create the ASEAN Free Trade Area (AFTA). The ASEAN members agreed and designated the year 2003 to achieve its goal of regional economic integration.[3]

AFTA, along with the European Union (EU) and the North American Free Trade Agreement (NAFTA), are among the most important examples of regionalism, rather than globalization. None the less, they are representative of the trend to move incrementally toward global economic integration. The government of Indonesia, like many others, was more comfortable moving first toward free trade within a smaller, well-defined group of neighbouring nations. AFTA is beneficial in its own right, but it also serves as a bridge toward growing global integration. This reflects the cautious and empirical attitudes of most governments. They would rather take a chance to work with their neighbours to test the results of trade liberalization than to open the doors of trade 100 per cent to the entire world. When governments are satisfied that regional free trade initiatives are beneficial, they may then be more willing to include more countries or merge with other trade blocs. In the meantime, however, regional trade blocs constitute a cautious step toward global free trade and, as such, add strength and momentum to the globalization movement.

The Indonesian government did not stop with the proposal to create a free trade arrangement within the ASEAN region. The government held that the new trade group known as the Asia–Pacific Economic Co-operation (APEC) forum offered an enormous opportunity to redefine international economic co-operation. At the initiative of Indonesia, in November 1994, APEC declared its intention to create a free trade area among its members.[4] What makes APEC a true example of government-led globalization is that—unlike regional trading blocs such as the EU, AFTA, or NAFTA—APEC is committed to 'open regionalism'. This means that APEC tariff reductions will apply globally, to APEC members and non-members alike. APEC, therefore, has the potential to be a platform for government-led globalization on a scale never before imagined. We should underscore the word 'potential' since we are many years away from realizing the APEC objectives. The goal remains, however, and it is without any parallel in history. This said, we should note that many observers seriously doubt APEC's ability to achieve its stated objectives. The *Far Eastern Economic Review* (1996) for example, reported:

The truth is that APEC has never been more than a travelling photo op, with this year's backdrop the Philippines. If the Asia of 2020 proves as open and integrated as we hope, it will not be because its governments agree on a vision. It will be because its businesses will have already made it a fact.... Seven years after APEC's birth and two years after everyone shook hands on free trade, we don't know of a single business deal that has gone through because of APEC.

The *Review* critique represents a skepticism shared by a number of observers. Yet within a few weeks after this article was printed, APEC held its annual summit in Manila and each member country outlined their individual plans for achieving the APEC goal of free trade. These plans were collectively known as the Manila Action Plan for APEC (MAPA). The MAPA trade liberalization programmes went into effect in January 1997. According to MAPA, each of the eighteen members created their own strategy for achieving free trade by 2010 for the industrialized countries, or 2020 for the developing countries. APEC members do appear to be moving toward the realization of their objectives on or ahead of schedule. Moreover, APEC members pledged to 'eliminate substantially tariffs by the year 2000', on all information technologies, the technologies essential to the globalization process. Less than a month after APEC's Manila summit, the World Trade Organization (WTO) held its first ministerial meeting at which all members of the WTO agreed to the same principle of free trade in information technologies. Without APEC's initiative it is unlikely that the information technologies agreement would have been adopted by the WTO.

These experiences affirm the significance of APEC. Still, it is too early to tell if APEC can realize its ambitious objectives. The organization is still in its formative stage. It should be borne in mind that the Treaty of Rome, which established the European Common Market, was signed in 1957. It took thirty-five years before the Europeans were ready to create a workable economic union among the EU members. If APEC members fulfil their commitments to achieve free trade by 2010 for the advanced countries and 2020 for the developing countries, this will be an extraordinary accomplishment for such a diverse and important group of countries.

Business-led Globalization

Parallel to government-led globalization, the other driving force has been business. The primary vehicles for business-led globalization are trade and investment. Through growing world trade and investment, we are experiencing a melding of international markets. World trade has grown at an impressive rate. According to the IMF, from 1987 to 1994, total world trade in goods and services increased from $3.1 trillion to $5.3 trillion. In 1994, world trade increased by 8.75 per cent over the previous year and was expected to continue to grow by 8 per cent in 1995.[5]

The trend in overseas private investment has been even more impressive. According to the United Nations Conference on Trade and Development (UNCTAD), on a global basis, total overseas foreign direct investment rose to an estimated $325 billion in 1995, an increase of 46 per cent over the previous year. The benefits of this trend have not been lost on Indonesia. Among all developing countries, Indonesia was among the top four recipients of foreign direct investment.[6] In their desire to expand markets, businesses are aggressively spreading their goods and services to countries around the world.

Globalization is redefining the economy in virtually every country. With so much at stake, however, power struggles are inevitable. The opposition to globalization is strong and broad-based. Some oppose globalization through shrill public attacks and open calls for protectionism.[7] Others prefer more stealthy manoeuvres. Today, the world is in the midst of a fairly quiet, but very intense battle between competing visions for the future—one open and global, the other closed and local. Countless government leaders and bureaucrats, businessmen, farmers, and other economic actors in every country are leading the opposition to globalization. Although it currently seems as if the momentum of change is behind the advocates of globalization, the movement could be easily derailed. The primary obstacle to globalization is fear of global competition.

COMPETING IN GLOBAL MARKETS

When markets are free for international competition, old rules, former practices, and familiar customs frequently are no longer applicable. Globalization changes the nature of the competitive engagement and this is frightful to those who are unable to adapt to the change. Globalization is a nightmare for companies whose profitability relies on tariffs and quotas. Should Indonesian firms worry? They need not if they are competitive.[8]

Despite the internationalization of commerce, all markets depend on the decisions of individual buyers. For global firms to succeed in local markets, they must adapt to local customs, local tastes, and needs. Businesses, therefore, must balance globalization with localization and mass production with individual tailoring or mass customization. We find, therefore, that globalization creates a situation in which markets become bigger without losing their local quality.[9] Often it is the small, local firms that are best attuned to the needs of the surrounding market. Without the bureaucratic overhead, they can move more quickly in response to new opportunities. Local firms will be better able to exploit market niches. Often today's niche is tomorrow's norm. It was not so long ago that Coca-Cola marketed its product as a 'nerve tonic' to a few loyal customers in Georgia. Today it is the most widely marketed product in the world. Where Coke has led the way, others will follow. And in between the giants, new opportunities arise for those in touch with the needs of the market. Indonesia's economy has become stronger from the contribution of foreign firms. Local firms can benefit from exposure to successful international firms. Local firms, however, are in a better position to respond to local needs. By learning from international companies and developing a strong presence in their home markets, Indonesian firms will be better positioned to expand into the international arena. Local firms that are inefficient or produce goods that are overpriced or of poor quality will find it difficult to compete. This is the nature of the free market, and it is a mistake for a government to try to protect uncompetitive businesses behind a shield of tariffs, quotas, or other regulations.

GLOBAL IMPLICATIONS

The implications of globalization are enormous and certainly beyond the scope of this discussion. Over the next few pages we will reflect on a few prominent implications of globalization and consider the relevance for Indonesia. In most cases, the implications for Indonesia would hold true for other developing countries.

Increasing Wealth

One of the by-products of globalization has been both a redistribution and increase in wealth world-wide. When, for example, the American clothing manufacturer, Levi Strauss, contracts for apparel or sets up its own factory in Indonesia or in another developing country, the wages paid to local labour are low by American standards but high domestically. Consequently, local people are wealthier. When consumers in the United States buy imports that are of comparable quality but cheaper than domestically made goods, they have increased the purchasing power of their income. Consequently, they are wealthier. There are, however, two prominent counter-arguments: first, an American worker may have lost a job; and second, based on American standards, the Indonesian garment worker is underpaid.

Despite these arguments, there are more compelling arguments to commend overseas investment. The loss of a job by an American garment worker—regrettable as it is—means that America is subject to the same cycle of job migration as the rest of the world. The garment worker's job that is in Indonesia in the 1990s was in Japan in the 1950s, Taiwan in the 1970s, and in the year 2010 may well find itself in Vietnam or Tanzania. For its part, the United States has shown itself to be among the most resilient nations in terms of job generation. Moreover, Japan and Taiwan, both of which have partaken in the apparel manufacturing cycle, have ably moved on to become prosperous industrialized nations. If Indonesia can sustain its economic development, Indonesian industry should move beyond heavy reliance on low-skilled labour-intensive products to higher margin products in the years ahead.

For those who criticize Indonesia for being a source of 'cheap labour' it should be borne in mind that in just fifteen years Indonesia's real per capita income has increased from about $400 to over $1,000. This has resulted in a growing middle class as well as a growing population of skilled industrial workers. Although Indonesian workers are paid less than those in the industrialized countries, if the country can maintain its economic growth, per capita incomes will continue to rise. Undoubtedly, Indonesia's wage rates will eventually reach levels comparable to those in the West.

The evidence clearly points to the benefits of trade to all countries, developing and industrialized. According to one study on the impact of exports on the United States economy, export-related jobs pay 15 per cent more than the average wage. Worker productivity at exporting firms is 20 to 40 per cent higher. Export firms expand employment faster and are less likely to fail.[10] According to the World Bank (1995b: 3), among a group of export-oriented East Asian countries, manufacturing wages rose 170 per cent in real terms between 1970 and 1990. These and much other data provide compelling evidence that globalization is contributing to the increase in wealth in the global economy.

The Dark Side of Globalization

One of the prominent risks that accompanies globalization is that the problems in one economy will be shared by others. The linkage is evident in the daily movement of stock markets around the world. This was painfully evident during the stock market crash on 19 October 1987, the worst one-day decline in the New York Stock Exchange. In a chain reaction, all the world's major markets suffered serious losses. Were it not for the rapid and coherent intervention by governments from several major economies, the crash of 1987 could have led to another deep and prolonged world recession. This points to the danger created by international economic interdependence. Ironically, during the crash of 1987, Indonesia's stock market—which was almost uniformly referred to as 'moribund'—lived up to its reputation and was unaffected. Since then, Indonesia's economy has grown substantially, and the JSX has not only expanded in size, it has become a market for international investors.

The risks to global economic integration extend beyond the linkages among financial markets. For example, on 1 January 1994, NAFTA went into effect, uniting the markets of the United States, Canada, and Mexico. Within a year, Mexico faced a financial crisis that required the devaluation of the peso, and an emergency $52 billion international loan. Mexico's economy has since recovered, but the incident was another harsh reminder of the risks that accompany interdependence. On the other hand, because of the rescue, Mexico's economy—which could have been utterly devastated—quickly recovered. Therefore, although the problem was spread wider because of the tighter integration created through NAFTA, for the same reason, the recovery also came more quickly.

Many other potentially troublesome associations may accompany globalization. Drugs, pornography, and even criminals themselves can spread more easily among countries with open trade regimes. Indeed, closer international economic integration increases the need for nations to co-operate with each other in many other ways, from matters of law enforcement to technical co-operation. These matters are becoming ever more pressing for Indonesia as AFTA and APEC move from theory to reality. However, for Indonesia and other countries, global problems will require global solutions. Ultimately, international co-operation will bring much greater progress and security than would efforts to fight problems in isolation.

Globalization, Protectionism, and National Sovereignty

One cannot travel long on the globalization road without soon running into the problems of protectionism and national sovereignty. It is here that the fissures between the 'cultures' of economics and politics can grow so wide as to seem almost unbridgeable. Economists are virtually unanimous on the benefits of free trade. Politicians are almost as unified in fearing the wrath of interest groups that oppose free trade.

Critics warn that globalization is a commercially driven process that tramples over national sovereignty and cultural norms.[11] They assert that if Indonesia opens the economy to free trade and investment, the whole country will be watching American videos on Japanese televisions, while wearing Italian shoes, as they eat food imported from Australia. Little will be left for Indonesia, and in the process, the nation will sacrifice its cultural identity. Furthermore, they claim that by adopting trade, investment, financial, and other conventions such as those specified by the IMF, WTO, APEC, or AFTA, Indonesia will be relinquishing control over its economic destiny. Globalization, they assert, is an assault on national sovereignty.

These are old and tired arguments, recycled from the advocates of protectionism in the 1970s and the opponents to deregulation in the 1980s. With more than three decades from which to judge, the weakness of inward-looking economic policies is well established. Furthermore, three compelling arguments speak in favour of Indonesia's support of the globalization process.

1. First, with respect to GATT, APEC, AFTA, and other such conventions, Indonesia has taken a prudent, active, and assertive role in the negotiations of the economic agreements to which it is a party. Therefore, as an example, we can state unequivocally that the latest GATT agreement that resulted in the creation of the WTO is much more consonant with Indonesia's interests than was the GATT in its previous form.

2. Second, unlike the treaties created during the colonial era, the modern economic conventions to which Indonesia is a party were designed to benefit all participants. The rules in most cases apply equally to both Indonesia and the other parties to the agreement. The biases that favoured colonial powers in earlier treaties were unfair and unequal. Such inequities were scrupulously avoided in the new agreements. If anything, in recognition of the special needs of developing countries, the international conventions sometimes provide extra leeway to developing countries such as Indonesia. For example, according to the APEC agreement leading to regional free trade, the industrialized nations pledged to eliminate tariffs

and quotas by the year 2010 while the developing nations had an additional ten years to achieve the same end.

3. Third, Indonesia's experience has plainly demonstrated that the outward-looking paradigm generates higher growth than the inward-looking paradigm. If properly managed, globalization will build on the strengths of the outward-looking paradigm and benefit Indonesia's economy as a result.

If governments could achieve globalization simply by reducing tariffs and quotas to zero, the process, though difficult, would be—at least conceptually—a simple matter. The matter, however, is more complex. International economic integration brings with it problems associated with international standards. Some standards, such as intellectual property rights, are already well established. Others, such as standards pertaining to the environment, labour, wage rates, human rights, and working conditions, among others, are handled very differently from one country to another.

Here again, globalization can ignite debates pertaining to national sovereignty. Some opponents will argue—particularly critics in developing countries—that if globalization is linked to internal politics, it exceeds the accepted norms of economic engagement and, therefore, should be rejected. Others—particularly those from the industrialized countries—take an equally negative position, but from an opposing point of view. These critics assert that they cannot support globalization because they claim developing countries are too lax in matters as diverse as environmental management and workers' rights. The policies of developing countries, they claim, are unacceptable to the industrialized countries and unless they are changed, they will oppose globalization.

These conflicts can be regarded as problems of norms and standards. Issues of norms and standards also include matters such as product specifications, legal liabilities, and accepted practices in the service sector. These are all difficult matters, with no easy solution. However, if they are deliberated in fora in which all nations are treated with equal dignity and rights, then there is no reason why international standardization cannot be achieved while respecting national sovereignty.

Growing Innovation

We stated earlier that technology was a catalyst for globalization. Indeed, globalization and technological innovation are symbiotic; not only is technology driving the globalization movement, but globalization itself is also contributing to technological innovation. International economic integration means that not only is the market-place of goods and services expanding, so is the market-place of ideas. The most powerful example of this is the Internet. For example, in the late 1990s, a student in a village in North Sulawesi, equipped with a relatively inexpensive computer, can access the Internet from one of about a half dozen Internet access providers now available in that region alone. Via the Internet, she can gain access to vast amounts of information from every continent. She can see up-to-the-minute news photos from around the world, read scholarly publications, and exchange electronic mail with people in every country. Because of this technology, the importance of distance and national boundary has greatly diminished. Although our student is located in a remote region, she has access to essentially the same corpus of information that is being accessed by students at Oxford University, Columbia University, or the University of Tokyo. She now has at her disposal information that was unimaginable even to her older brother.

Besides permitting the rapid dissemination of information around the globe, the Internet allows collaboration among 'virtual colleagues' working collectively on projects from different countries.[12] This global collaboration is being carried out by academics, scientists, business people, and artists around the world. Such collaboration permits the rapid dispersal of information and insights, which facilitates creativity and innovation. This is an exceptionally enabling technology for developing countries. Although the costs of personal computers, telephone services, and Internet access are beyond the financial reach of most people in developing countries, the costs are falling rapidly. Moreover, one computer in a library, school, or university can provide a connection to the Internet for thousands of people. Poverty will always constrain the availability of technology for developing countries. None the less, the Internet represents a breakthrough because after the basic Internet costs are paid, the wealthiest and poorest users have access to essentially the same information. This is an economic model with few parallels.

GLOBALIZATION AND INDONESIA'S FUTURE

Two decades ago Indonesia's industrial development was based on oil-fed protectionism. At that time, the government's main concern was national integration. Global integration, as we understand it today, was not considered. However, as we stated, economic development is perpetually 'work in progress', and for Indonesia, what the experience of two decades has wrought is remarkable. In the late 1990s, Indonesia is as committed to globalization as it was to protectionism two decades earlier. The nation has changed dramatically and will continue to do so in the years ahead. Hence the questions: *Should* Indonesia stay on the course to greater global integration? Yes. The net benefits of globalization are huge. *Will* Indonesia continue on the globalization course? Maybe. Between now and 2020—when Indonesia is committed to achieve free trade under the APEC agreement—Indonesia will have ample time to reverse itself. Undoubtedly, over the next two decades, many academics, politicians, and business executives will claim to have discovered a 'new and workable' twenty-first century form of protectionism. We must learn from the lessons of our past: protectionism, by whatever name, creates economic inefficiencies that hinder economic development. Protectionism should never be embraced as a national policy.

The following paragraphs list some policies and actions Indonesia should consider for maintaining the momentum for global economic integration.

1. *Adopt Globalization as a Foundation Policy.* The government of Indonesia should embrace globalization as a basic paradigm guiding economic policies in the years ahead. Indonesia should set for itself the goal of becoming a truly open economy—as open as the most open economies in the world. The ASEAN members are aiming to achieve free intra-ASEAN trade by 2003, and APEC is aiming for 2010/20. Indonesia, however, should commit itself to becoming an open global economy regardless of AFTA, APEC, or any other agreement or body. The reason for so doing is simply because globalization will strengthen the Indonesian economy.

This policy also implies that Indonesia should be firmly resolute in renouncing protectionism. This does not mean the government should forever renounce the occasional corporate rescues or emergency tariff measures. Such actions, however, should be rare and limited to those instances when not doing so would significantly hurt the economy. Furthermore, the terms of protection or assistance should be explicit, limited, communicated widely to the public, and non-extendible. In other words, they should be temporary interventions responding to emergency conditions that are of significant national interest.

Under ordinary circumstances, rather than resorting to protectionism, the government should seek to assist small and undercapitalized firms through training programmes, research grants, and access to low-interest loans. The goal of such programmes would be to improve the efficiency of weaker businesses rather than encouraging them to continue inefficient practices behind a wall of tariffs and quotas.

2. *Support Indonesian Overseas Investment and Trade.* In modern rapidly changing markets, one of the most important things the government can do is to assist Indonesian businesses through state-of-the-art information services. To this end appropriate government agencies, such as BKPM, the

Ministry of Foreign Affairs, the Ministry of Industry and Trade, and the National Agency for Export Development should work with the commercial attachés in Indonesian embassies and consulates world-wide in order to provide timely market intelligence and ongoing advice to establish, maintain, and expand operations of Indonesian firms in overseas markets. This information should be made freely available to Indonesian traders and investors. Furthermore, wherever possible, Indonesia should seek assistance from foreign governments and chambers of commerce in overseas markets. This co-operation can accelerate the flow of investment and trade between Indonesia and its foreign partners, as well as reduce the risk of business failure.

3. *ASEAN and APEC Leadership*. Indonesia should take the initiative within the ASEAN and the APEC forums, not by trying to dominate the agenda, but by setting an example as an advocate for globalization. If APEC fails to achieve its stated goals of 'open regionalism' by 2010/20, this will represent an enormous set-back for the globalization movement world-wide. To demonstrate its leadership, Indonesia should recommend that the commitment to intra-ASEAN free trade by 2003 within the AFTA arrangement be extended to all APEC members willing to reciprocate. Furthermore, Indonesia should challenge the world community to take APEC's plans for free trade under 'open regionalism' a step further. The community of nations should seek for 'open globalism', that is, global free trade.

4. *Look Westward to Europe*. APEC should by no means monopolize Indonesia's globalization efforts. The world's largest trading bloc is the EU. Despite its many public declarations that it is committed to open economic relations with the world at large, the EU's focus has been more inward since the 1992 signing of the Maastricht treaty that led to its formation. In March 1996, leaders from Asia and Europe met in Bangkok for the first Asia–Europe Meeting (ASEM). At this time, the leaders affirmed their shared interest in promoting closer economic ties between the two regions. These pronouncements, however, have not yet been substantiated with significant initiatives such as those under APEC. If ASEM is not backed with serious actions, then it may come to be regarded as nothing more than a 'talk shop'. That would be a set-back to Asian–European relations by illustrating the inability of the two regions to co-operate with each other in a meaningful manner. Indonesia should urge its European colleagues to demonstrate their commitment by agreeing to extend trade conditions equivalent to those APEC extends to others. In trade, the nations of APEC and the EU should set for themselves the goal of seamless integration.

5. *The South–South Initiative in Free Trade (SSIFT)*. There were two

unusual and noteworthy features of the APEC free trade initiative: first, the call for regional free trade originated not from an industrialized country, but from Indonesia, a developing country; and second, unlike most trade groups, the composition of APEC's membership is drawn fairly evenly from both industrialized and developing countries. Normally, most developing countries would not be inclined to participate in such an association for fear that they would become overrun with products from the industrialized countries. The principle behind APEC is that free and fair trade benefits developing and industrialized nations alike; and the benefits of trade are not a function of per capita income but reciprocity guided by sound trade regulations.

With its experience in APEC and AFTA, Indonesia is in agood position to carry the message of free trade and globalization to the developing nations of the South. Most developing countries are reluctant to open their markets to free trade with the industrialized nations. That reluctance, however, should not extend to other developing countries. For this reason, Indonesia should propose the South–South Initiative in Free Trade (SSIFT), with the objective of establishing a free trade association among developing countries around the world. This could be done under the aegis of NAM; alternatively, SSIFT could exist as a free-standing organization. SSIFT could serve as a stimulus to trade for many nations who thus far have missed the export boom that transformed much of East Asia. Besides a focus on the reduction of trade barriers, SSIFT should seek to enhance trade by emphasizing technical exchange and co-operative ventures. Here again, Indonesia could assume a leadership role by sharing its experience in trade development with less developed countries. By building trade relations gradually but steadily among developing countries, some of the world's poorest countries could participate more directly in the international economy.

* * *

It would be naïve and potentially injurious if one assumed that the movement toward free trade and globalization is inevitable or will be easily accomplished. The twentieth century was twice ravaged by world wars and since 1945, the world has continued to witness the horrors of war, revolution, terrorism, and a hundred shades of violent conflict. We should not expect the hostilities that divide peoples along the lines of nations, politics, race, culture, and ideology to disappear suddenly in commerce. Furthermore, the beneficiaries of protectionism will continue to work intensively to preserve their privileged position. Simply by stalling, protectionism wins by default by perpetuating the *status quo*.

Yet, as the twentieth century draws to a close, as never before in history, we talk about globalization as a meaningful concept. This is a dramatic and audacious movement, in which humanity is moving towards a unified world, aided by the vehicle of commerce. Obviously, we should not expect this movement to proceed with lightning speed or to progress without generating a whole new set of problems. As the world becomes smaller, tensions are bound to arise over differences of culture, religion, and lingering historical animosities. When countries are more isolated from each other, such conflicts may be less pronounced. As with family life, to live in a global community we must learn to respect the unique characteristics of every culture and be willing to work for the maintenance of international peace and co-operation.

Progress in globalization will take time, concerted effort by governments and businesses, goodwill, and flexibility. Ultimately, the world will move toward globalization because it is in its political and economic interest to do so. The question remains: will it be in two decades or two centuries? Indonesia can have a role in answering this question. Indonesia surprised the world in 1994 by advocating that APEC move toward becoming a free trade region. This was an auspicious beginning. The hard work ahead is to maintain that momentum, both within APEC and with other countries and regions around the world.

Many have said that the nineteenth century was the European century, the twentieth century was the American Century, and the twenty-first century will be the Pacific Century, or Asian Century. If the trend toward globalization is maintained, then it may be more accurate to call the twenty-first century, the 'Global Century'. Indonesia has set the stage to be a full participant in a global future. By building on the pragmatic, outward-looking economic foundation the country has built over the previous three decades, Indonesia may earn a rightful position on the forefront of the movement leading to that Global Century.

1. The term 'free flow' is not meant to imply no restrictions whatsoever. Even a nation committed to free trade will have restrictions according to security or legal norms. The restrictions, however, are not applied to limit competition.

2. The dominance of local markets was an enduring fact well into the twentieth century. For example, as a boy growing up in a town outside Yogjakarta, in Central Java, virtually everything I ate or wore, and all the goods within my house, and the materials from which my house was made, were all produced locally. Things foreign were just that: they were thoroughly foreign or alien to my life. In books and magazines we saw pictures and read stories about foreign ways and products. We also saw that the Dutch had many

things different from those used by Indonesians. Just sixty years ago, the economy in which I was raised was not even a national economy as much as it was a local economy.

3. For more on this see the *AFTA Reader, Vol. 1*, published by the ASEAN Secretariat (1993), wherein it states:

The ultimate objective of AFTA is to increase ASEAN's competitive edge as a production base geared for the world market. A critical step in this direction is the liberalization of trade in the region through the elimination of intra-regional tariffs and the elimination of non-tariff barriers....

As the cost competitiveness of manufacturing industries in ASEAN is enhanced and with the larger size of the market, investors can enjoy economies of scale in production. In this manner, ASEAN hopes to attract more foreign direct investment into the region.

4. APEC was founded in November 1989, when ministers from twelve countries in the Asia–Pacific region met in Canberra, Australia. In 1993, the United States launched what was to be the first of the annual APEC summit meetings. APEC membership has since grown to eighteen, namely, Australia, Brunei Darussalam, Canada, Chile, People's Republic of China, Hong Kong, Indonesia, Japan, Republic of Korea, Malaysia, Mexico, New Zealand, Papua New Guinea, the Philippines, Singapore, Taiwan, Thailand, and the United States. According to APEC statistics, the eighteen members comprise about 40 per cent of the world's population, 56 per cent of the world's GDP, and 46 per cent of the world's merchandise exports.

5. During this 1987–94 period, total world output rose from $17.0 trillion to $25.8 trillion at market exchange rates (International Monetary Fund, 1995: 28, 91, 120).

6. This information was reported in the *Jakarta Post*, 7 June 1996.

7. For example, free trade and globalization were intensely debated in the build up to the 1996 campaign for the United States presidency. Indicative of American ambivalence toward globalization, a few of the politicians who aspired for the office were vitriolic in their attacks on free trade and zealous in their calls for protectionism.

8. In her book, *Indonesia in ASEAN: Foreign Policy and Regionalism*, Dewi Fortuna Anwar (1994) argues that the major opponents to globalization in Indonesia have been the major private industrial companies which have enjoyed near-monopolies and a large captive market. With protected markets, these companies are uncompetitive in the international market and have had little incentive to improve their efficiency in domestic markets. Small and medium enterprises, she suggests, have a more open attitude toward opening the domestic market. Indeed, they may well benefit from the greater access to inputs from companies around the world.

9. Thus, to accommodate the sensibilities of both Hindus and Muslims in India, McDonald's, that archetype of homogenized fast food, sells 'mutton burgers', and vegetarian dishes.

10. This data from J. David Richardson and Karin Rindal, *Why Exports Matter: More!*, Washington: Institute for International Economics, 1996, quoted in Bergsten (1996: 118)

11. Between the opponents and supporters of globalization are some who reluctantly accept its inevitability. One such position is well represented by the prominent Indonesian scholar of international relations, Juwono Sudarsono, the vice-governor of the government's prestigious National Defence Institute. Sudarsono (1995) believes globalization will be dominated by the three major economies: the United States, Japan, and Germany, since they exercise such control over the factors that will be crucial to the future economy, including science, technology, skilled labour, capital, and many essential resources.

Furthermore, he argues that globalization, in Indonesia as elsewhere, tends to concentrate capital and expertise in a few hands and this could hinder the political and economic democratization of the country. Sudarsono argues that globalization is inescapable and for Indonesia to succeed in the globalization era it should adopt the following policies:

- Emphasize the development of science, technology, and the job skills that will help Indonesia to compete. He recommends that efforts be concentrated in eastern Indonesia which is less developed than the western part of the country;
- Mobilize capital through domestic savings and capital markets;
- Accelerate the development of economic and social infrastructure.

12. Even in the production of this book, I have benefited from information shared via the Internet from friends and information sites in Asia, Europe, and North America.

12
Conclusion: Evolving Models of Development

WHEN historians look back at the twentieth century, they will probably identify the great wars, towering skyscrapers, devastating economic depression, and astonishing scientific breakthroughs as representative of the landmarks of this remarkable era. However, among the marvels of modernity, there is probably none more important than the emergence of the discipline of economic development. Some of the treasures of civilization, like the Borobudur temple in Central Java or the cathedrals of Europe, involved the collective efforts of thousands of people. Others, such as the paintings of Leonardo da Vinci, required the inspired effort of a solitary individual. Economic development is unusual in that it draws on the efforts of entire societies stretched out across generations. The field of economic development informs us that if people are given the tools to help themselves, and provided with an economic climate conducive to growth, societies can advance at an extraordinary pace and achieve in decades what might have previously taken centuries. The masterpiece of economic development is populations freed from the oppression of extreme poverty, with longer life spans, and healthier and more fulfilling lives. Despite the progress, the study of development economics is still in its early stages. Indonesia's experiences can provide much data to advance the understanding of the economic development process. As we enter a new century, this relatively new discipline may become better recognized for its contribution to the betterment of humanity.

For Indonesia, a systematic approach to economic development has been at the heart of a dramatic process of national transformation stretching over more than three decades. The question that lingers as we conclude this book, is whether Indonesia can keep its development on track. We will not try to speculate on a specific answer; however, we can assert that for Indonesia to sustain its development, it must build on its successes and learn well the lessons of its past so that it can avoid repeating old mistakes. To build for the future, however, Indonesia must continually implement new models of development appropriate for the changing conditions of society.

THREE DECADES OF POLICYMAKING ON THE ROAD TO ECONOMIC DEVELOPMENT

By 1993, I, along with most of the 'technocrats' who formed the economic team, retired from office. However, during the period since 1966, when had held various positions, Indonesia dramatically transformed itself. Every budget, every Five-Year Development Plan, and every policy constituted an effort to address developmental needs within the context of the particular conditions of the time. The stabilization policies of 1966 were very different from the growth policies of 1976 or the deregulation policies of 1986. Yet throughout this profusion of policies and shifting economic conditions, there were themes that were 'woven into the fabric' of the period. In retrospect, we can discern a number of principles of economic development that were essential to the New Order's approach. We will briefly review six such themes: a) monetary management; b) establishing priorities; c) cultivating markets; d) managing debt; e) sustaining credibility; and f) the role of pragmatism.

Managing Money

Scholars who have studied the final years of the Old Order have tended to focus on the political turmoil that shook the nation during that period. Monetary mismanagement greatly magnified these problems. To a considerable extent, the history of Indonesia's economic development since 1966 has been a testimony to the importance of monetary management. The sweeping changes that took place during Indonesia's stabilization period were an extraordinary example of the power of money. Over the next twenty years, Indonesia vanquished hyperinflation, opened the capital account, learned to sterilize large inflows of foreign exchange, moved to a floating exchange rate, and generally became more knowledgeable about how to control inflation. In these and other ways, Indonesia's economic team had countless experiences that confirmed the idea that sound monetary management is essential to economic development. Indeed, so important is it, that we can infer that governments would be well advised to give priority, at least in the short run, to monetary management over social welfare programmes, infrastructure development, or other fiscal interventions. A sound monetary environment is an essential prerequisite for sustainable economic development.

Establishing Priorities

Through the process of economic development, the driving objective is to move a society from a state of pervasive economic scarcity to general sufficiency. Poor countries, like Indonesia, generally lack many of the

essential requirements to achieve prosperity. Yet even in the midst of pervasive scarcity, some things will be relatively more abundant than others.
Indonesia's government had to set priorities that responded to the most
urgent needs with interventions that promised the greatest returns. Setting
priorities is one of the most stressful aspects of economic planning as it
involves choices about who will be the most direct and immediate
beneficiaries of development. Every budget represents a vision on what are
the nation's most urgent priorities, and what programmes promise to
bring the greatest benefits to society. Indonesia took momentous decisions
when it decided to give priority to agriculture over industry, community
health centres over hospitals, and primary education over university
education. These choices were all strategic decisions in which priorities
were established to bring the greatest benefit to the largest number of
people over the long term. Inevitably, groups disagreed with the priorities
set by the government. Since it is impossible to please everyone,
Indonesia's policymakers tried to set priorities based on sound economic
principles that supported the nation's development priorities. Political
influences are always a factor in establishing economic policy, but as
much as possible and practical, Indonesia's economic team sought to
determine economic policy based on economic reasoning rather than
political considerations.

Working with Markets

Over two centuries ago, Adam Smith described the market as an 'invisible
hand' that efficiently allocates goods and services according to the law of
supply and demand. The role of the market continues to be one of the
central issues of development. As economic theory would predict, evidence
has shown that efficiency increases as distortions decrease. Efficiency considerations, however, do not imply a need for 'free-fight capitalism'. Free
markets should be guided by appropriate regulations designed to correct
market failures and ensure that markets operate smoothly and fairly. The
role of the economic policymaker, therefore, is to support market development, while intervening through the regulatory process to correct market
failures in the interest of fairness and efficiency.

One of the dilemmas the New Order faced for some three decades was
how to manage this tension between freedom and regulation. The economic team found no definitive and final answer to this problem, nor is it
likely that one will ever be discovered. As with so much in economics, our
theories and working principles will always have to be adapted to the current conditions in a real economy. This fact, however, does not detract
from the substantial progress that has been made in understanding how

markets operate. Perhaps the fundamental lessons we can derive from the New Order experience is that the principle of free markets is a valid one, but that the regulations needed to encourage economic growth may change according to the stage of development. The distortions that are likely to arise in a subsistence, non-monetized economy are entirely different from the distortions that frequently arise in an industrialized economy with sophisticated capital markets. In the former, moving from barter to money required new rules and conventions of exchange. By monetizing the countryside, Indonesia's farmers were brought into the modern market economy. About two decades later, Indonesia took the development of markets even further through the creation of a full-blown capital market. The development of Indonesia's capital markets, however, created conditions suitable for new and unexpected forms of economic distortions to appear, and hence new regulations were required to ensure that the markets operated properly. Experiences such as these confirmed that as an economy develops, the regulatory environment must be responsive to the threats of new market distortions, while also seeking to ensure that markets retain the freedom they need to grow vigorously.

If the economic team erred in the way we balanced market freedom and regulations it was not that we 'regulated', but that we 'overregulated' in ways that added new distortions to markets. Some believed that the deregulation movement would lead to free-fight capitalism. That is incorrect! Deregulation was needed to bring greater efficiency and transparency to markets that had become opaque and inefficient through overregulation. One of the most challenging and difficult problems of development is to ensure equity within a free market. Many countries have tried to legislate equity by adopting communism, socialism, or various income distribution schemes. Based on Indonesia's experience, among the most effective means for fostering economic equity is to provide the poorer segments of society with the tools for self-empowerment—especially education, delivery of health care services, and special provision of credit. Equity also requires greater transparency, which will result in the elimination of many of the economic practices that benefit some while working to the disadvantage of the poor. Although 'perfect markets' may be no more than an economic abstraction, Indonesia's experience confirms that a government can have a vital role in creating efficient yet well-regulated markets.[1]

Managing Public and Private Sector Debt

There is no development without investment. Wise investment is the most basic step to building wealth. Like individuals, when nations want to stimulate development, but lack capital for investment, they must borrow.

Governments have two borrowing options. They can borrow from outside sources—multilateral institutions, other countries, or commercial banks—or 'from themselves', through deficit spending. Although nations borrow to accelerate growth, it is also the easiest route to financial ruin. Indonesia's experience with external borrowing and deficit spending under the Old Order was so catastrophic that it led the New Order to adopt a balanced budget policy to avoid the risk of excessive debt. In so doing, the government accepted self-imposed limits to its own growth.

Developing countries face a double burden of having the greatest need for economic growth, but inadequate supplies of capital to finance development. Consequently, in order to finance their development, the poorer nations need access to credit on concessional terms. The loss of access to such credit can have disastrous effects on a poor country. For this reason, nations that find themselves indebted beyond their means should work to find collaborative solutions that balance their own needs for credit with their lenders' need for repayment. The resolution of Indonesia's debt problems in 1970 was one of the landmarks in the nation's development. Because of this experience, Indonesia has been a strong and consistent supporter of debt forgiveness of the most severely indebted countries. No matter how much Indonesia advances economically, we should never forget the benefits the nation accrued through multilateral and bilateral assistance. As was given to Indonesia, so Indonesia must give to others. As Indonesia becomes stronger economically, the country should join with other nations and multilateral agencies to find ways to increase assistance for the world's least developed countries.[2]

In addition to heavy external borrowing, a country can also slip easily into excessive debt through deficit spending. Indonesia's commitment to a balanced budget permitted it to incur a considerable debt load, without exceeding the government's financial means. This policy has been the corner-stone of Indonesia's economic policies since the mid-1960s and should remain as such in the years ahead.

Besides the balanced budget principle, Indonesia also took steps to avoid excessive debt through the creation of the FCDT, which has had oversight authority for commercial credit involving the government. Every government needs institutions to sustain its fiscal integrity. In the late 1990s, with a large and dynamic private sector, the risk from excessive and unsound commercial debt may be a serious threat to the nation's financial stability. For this reason, the FCDT has a more important role than ever. Efforts must be made to invigorate and strengthen this agency to safeguard the economy against the risks of excessive commercial indebtedness. Moreover, Bank Indonesia must be vigilant in monitoring commercial banks to prevent imprudent lending.

Credibility and Stability

What may be most important in sustaining the strength of a government is its credibility. If a government says one thing and does another, it will quickly loose the confidence of the people. Even a government backed by the most powerful army will eventually fall if it cannot fulfil its commitments to the people. The difference between words and actions is not simply a matter of sincerity or honesty; more often than not, it is an issue of competence. During the Old Order, the government was unable to create and execute national budgets. Planning was impossible and this damaged the credibility of the government.

Beginning with the stabilization programme, Indonesia's New Order government consistently delivered on its commitments and frequently exceeded projections. In this way, the government was able to maintain its credibility and this helped to ensure the success of many efforts. This is a very simple idea, but one that is essential to good and strong governance. A government cannot expect the support of the people as if it were a right. Popular support must be earned every day by living up to the vision of development to which the government and people are committed.

Pragmatism

Economic development is an evolving discipline. Our current understanding of development is more sophisticated than that of thirty years ago. Because Indonesia's economic team held pragmatism as an abiding principle throughout its tenure, the government was flexible and responsive in the way it formulated economic policy. The government, for example, rapidly altered its policies when the country faced a surge in oil wealth and readjusted policies even more quickly when oil prices dropped. The pragmatism of the economic team led it to maintain a spirit of flexibility and creativity that kept the policy process open and evolving. Pragmatism led the team to seek constantly to innovate and improve policies to sustain economic development. In this way, our knowledge and understanding of the development process has grown over time.

Indonesia's commitment to pragmatism was balanced by a firm commitment to sound principles of macro- and micro-economics. The success of Indonesia's economic policies confirmed the idea that, as much as possible, economic policies should be insulated from undue political influence. Moreover, experience has demonstrated that alternative schools of economic policymaking, including communism, socialism, and even 'supply side economics', in the long run, have all failed. In the meantime, the field of neo-classical economics is progressing steadily. It is here that policymakers should seek guidance in creating economic policies.

Outward-looking Orientation

According to some theorists, in the early stages of development, it may be appropriate for countries to embrace inward-looking policies, while an outward-looking orientation is suitable when a country becomes economically more advanced. Indonesia's experience does not support this view. In the early years of national independence, Indonesians were often wary of opening the economy to the outside world. They feared that this could lead to renewed foreign encroachment in the domestic economy. Through inward-looking policies, Indonesia gained a false sense of security. In the process, economic growth was sacrificed. With many years with which to judge, we can now say with confidence that economies in every stage of development—even the early stages—can benefit from economic openness.

CHALLENGES TO INDONESIA'S FUTURE DEVELOPMENT

This book has reflected on many lessons from three decades of development. These lessons have been paid—to borrow the words of Winston Churchill—with 'blood, sweat, toil and tears'. They merit reflection by Indonesians and non-Indonesians alike. As long as countries struggle for economic development, Indonesia's lessons will be valuable. It would be a pity and a waste, if these lessons were looked upon as museum pieces—nostalgic stories shared among an ageing group of technocrats. What we must remember is that in economic development the field of concern is not the past, but the future. If the lessons of this book have any value it should not be simply to help us better understand the past, but to build a better future.

Despite Indonesia's rapid development during the previous three decades, there is no guarantee that the progress can be maintained. In many respects, to sustain growth in the next three decades may be even more difficult than the growth since the mid-1960s. Indonesia's economic base was so low that growth was a matter of survival for many of the nation's most needy. To maintain growth in the years ahead, Indonesia will need to refine and improve on the economic practices and institutions of today. It will need to adopt new strategies for growth, develop new industries, and prepare Indonesia's work-force for a new global market-place. As Indonesia prepares for the next century, the challengers faces it are enormous. The following paragraphs reflect briefly on some of the implications of the recent past for Indonesia's future.

The Changing Roles of Government, Business, and Legal Institutions

In recent decades, it has been popular to speak about 'structural change' in the Indonesian economy. This term was generally used to refer to changes in basic elements of the economy, such as the shift to non-oil exports, or the sweeping reforms of the banking system. However, the most important 'structural change' was the new economic roles of the government and the private sector. It was not long ago when the government thoroughly dominated the economy, including the production of every important product. Indonesia's private sector was so weak that it was almost insignificant. Times have changed, and despite the large number of state-owned enterprises that still exist, the government's primary role in the economy is now more as regulator and provider of public services such as education, rather than a producer of goods.

In an economy such as Indonesia's, where the public sector traditionally dominated commerce, it may be natural to think of government as the primary 'market distorter'. What should also be borne in mind, however, is that with the growth in Indonesia's private sector, important distortions and imperfections can also be the product of the private sector; notable examples include price-fixing, cartel formation, the growth of monopolies and oligopolies, and insider trading, not to mention various forms of collusion, fraud, and misrepresentation of products and services. In the past, when the private sector was weak and undeveloped, the risks were less stark. The government's new challenge is to keep the economy as open and free as possible, while protecting against new market distortions. For this reason, Indonesia will need to strengthen its legal institutions so that they are capable of meeting the inevitable increase in litigation that accompanies a large, growing, and complex economy. Indonesia's legal system, however, like the former taxation system, was inherited from the Dutch colonial regime. Since the founding of the Republic, the government has amended and adjusted the legal system in countless ways. As with Indonesia's tax regime in the 1980s, however, the many *ad hoc* modifications have not led to the creation of a healthier legal system. The system is in need of substantive reform, from matters of procedure to the legal code itself. Without a major overhaul, judges will continue to be overloaded, rulings will be continually subjected to disputes and second-guessing, lawyers will find it difficult to advise clients, and the strength of contracts will be doubted. Together, these will undermine popular confidence in the legal system's ability to uphold justice. Lacking a well-organized, independent judicial system based on a clear legal code, Indonesia's economy will be unable to develop to its potential. Legal reform is needed both to protect the economy from improper business practices and to establish a regulatory environment supportive of economic development.

Ecology and Development

To promote development, governments generally concentrate on employment, infrastructure, and the production of goods and services. One of the unfortunate by-products of economic development, however, is pollution and environmental degradation. In rural societies with small populations, pollution is negligible. As human population and consumption expand, so does the potential for pollution. In contemporary Indonesia, the most prominent forms of pollution are air pollution, water pollution from industry and human waste, and solid waste, such as product packaging. Such forms of pollution has become a problem even in remote rural villages. The situation has become ever more grave with Indonesia's rapid urbanization and industrialization.

Early in the development of the New Order, the government recognized the need to care for the nation's environment through the establishment of a special Ministry for Population and the Environment. Although the Ministry has had an important role in managing the environmental impact of industrialization, the pace of development has been so rapid that adverse effects have been unavoidable.

The situation, however, is far from hopeless. Just as economic planners have been able to accelerate the development process by following appropriate policies, the same principle should apply to environmental management. Developing countries should take heart in the fact that for many years the most advanced industrialized countries were by far the world's worst polluters. It was not until the 1970s that environmentalism became a serious global concern, supported with tough governmental regulations. In the last quarter of a century, the progress in many industrialized countries has been substantial.

The problem Indonesia faces is to maintain high environmental standards without sacrificing economic development. Environmental protection can place a considerable burden on businesses. On the other hand, a society may pay a heavy price in the form of health problems and productivity loss because of lax environmental standards. As Indonesia's economic development advances, the government must find new and more efficient means to safeguard the environment without sacrificing development. The support of business and the general population will be needed to succeed in this effort.

Information, Education, and Development

In every stage of development, generally at least one industry, commodity, or activity serves as a kind of 'centre of gravity' for the economy. During Indonesia's colonial period, the economic 'core' was the nation's agricultural commodities, especially rubber, sugar, tobacco, tea, and coffee. In the 1970s, Indonesia's economic centre was oil, and in the 1980s and 1990s, the centre shifted to non-oil manufactured exports, led by plywood and textiles. In each of these periods, these dominant economic elements were also at the heart of the development model of the time.

Indonesia can expect to continue to reap considerable employment and revenues from commodities such as oil and gas, rubber and palm-oil. These commodities are unlikely, however, to help Indonesia advance to the next stage of development. Furthermore, Indonesia's economy has already progressed to the point where it can no longer rely on inexpensive labour to sustain its competitive position in global markets.

According to current projections, by 2005, Indonesia's number one foreign exchange earner will be tourism. This would lead one to suppose that tourism would assume the position as the 'core' of Indonesia's economic development model early in the twenty-first century. Although tourism is well poised to occupy the number one spot in industrial ranking, however, it also seems likely that Indonesia's economic development will not be driven by any one particular industry or commodity. Instead, Indonesia is entering the period of 'information-led development'. To sustain the pace of development and raise the nation's living standards, Indonesia's economic 'centre' will shift to *information*, and Indonesia's development model will be an economy that is information-driven. Information has always been essential to development, but many of the changes in the contemporary economy result from the breakthroughs in information technologies. The economies of the industrialized countries are undergoing a significant restructuring because of the 'information revolution'.

Many factors are contributing to this change, including satellite communications systems, the television, and inexpensive print technologies, but, as suggested earlier, the key technology is the Internet. The Internet is not only revolutionizing specialized academic fields, but it is also having an increasing impact even on everyday matters. The Internet is now being used by homemakers to share recipes for their favourite dishes, real estate agents to show pictures of property listings, and bookstores to reach global audiences. The information revolution is now for everyone.

For Indonesia to sustain its development in the next century, every sector of society will need to join the information age. Every business must recognize that information is essential to improved competitiveness.

Indonesian workers must make the transition from unskilled labour to skilled labour, and eventually become 'knowledge workers'. To succeed in the information age the Indonesian work-force—from factory workers to chief executive officers—must accept that to stay competitive in the contemporary economy, all workers must continually upgrade their skills and knowledge. More than ever, learning should be an integral and ongoing part of work.

To succeed in the information age, Indonesia must continue to give high priority to education in the broad sense of the term. The nation's commitment to education should be manifested not only in the number of years of schooling available for each student, but also in the quality and content of the curriculum. The government and corporations need to join forces to ensure that appropriate and advanced educational services are available to both children and adults. Moreover, leaders must recognize that the requirements for educational competence in contemporary society are different from those of yesterday. In Indonesia's future schools, blackboards and chalk must be supplemented with computers and Internet connections. In the years ahead, no Indonesian child should graduate from school without basic computer literacy. This means that the country will need to make a substantial investment in computer equipment, software, and telecommunications infrastructure.

Disciplines from economics to mechanical engineering are advancing at remarkable speeds because information is able to travel so quickly and inexpensively. If developing countries do not join this 'revolution', the gap between the advanced and the developing countries will grow wider than it is today. Alternatively, Indonesians can and should try to fully avail themselves of the explosion of information that is currently circulating the globe. In so doing, economic development is likely to advance more rapidly than ever.

Politics, Pluralism, and Development

When the New Order first set out on its effort to build the nation's economy, the political turmoil of that time had shattered the economy and resulted in widespread misery. During Indonesia's previous regime, politics was given priority over economics, and the economy suffered as a result. The factionalism and divisiveness that had paralyzed Indonesia for so long were eventually succeeded by a steady commitment to economic development. There can be no doubt of the wisdom of that policy. With most Indonesians then living in dire poverty, illiterate, and unable to be reached by the media or most other public information sources, there was limited opportunity for orderly and informed popular participation in the political process. In the three decades since the founding of the New Order, the government has never wavered in its commitment to economic development. This was reflected in the political system Indonesia adopted in the late 1960s; that system was designed to emphasize consensus and stability over the factionalism that paralyzed the former regime. The system worked, and therefore Indonesia has generally remained quite stable, which has permitted the economy to grow in a way benefiting all Indonesians.

Indonesia in the late 1990s faces a very different set of problems from those in the mid-1960s. Younger Indonesians are better educated than their parents were. Virtually every Indonesian has access to a television or radio. Indonesia now has a growing middle class, many of whom are travelling overseas and some who have studied abroad. Moreover, the majority of Indonesians now have been born after 1965. The younger generation of Indonesians, therefore, only has a second-hand knowledge of the pre-1966 struggles. The traumas of national disunity, the 1965 abortive *coup*, the ravages of pervasive poverty and economic paralysis are no more than the stories read in textbooks or heard from one's parents.

For the younger generation of Indonesians, the post-1965 generation, their point of comparison cannot be the hardships of the 1950s and early 1960s. Instead, they will judge Indonesia in light of recent developments. Because of Indonesia's successes, the expectations of the people have grown steadily higher. This is as it should be. For a country to progress, the hopes and expectations of the younger generation should exceed those of their parents. It is in this way that impetus of development can be maintained. The rising expectation of Indonesians is a sign of successful development and something for which the government should feel proud. These circumstances, however, result in new and growing pressures on the government. What was satisfactory for today's parents may no longer be adequate for their children. Therefore, just as the developing economy is continually 'work in progress', so too, Indonesia's political system must develop to meet the changing needs of contemporary society. To maintain progress in the political sphere, Indonesia must continually reaffirm its commitment to openness to new ideas and information and to strengthen the nation's democratic processes. The people of Indonesia are eager and qualified to participate more actively in their own governance. In response, the government must try to continually improve the nation's political institutions to make them more efficient and responsive to the will of the people.[3]

Indonesia is a highly diverse society, comprising people from many ethnic groups, local cultures, and religions. This diversity is one of the nation's greatest strengths. It is not surprising, however, that on occasion,

Indonesia has experienced periods of heightened tension based on ethnic and religious matters. In a few instances, these tensions led to outbursts that have resulted in damage to property and even loss of life. These incidents are incompatible with the civility and forbearance needed to develop a peaceful and prosperous society. As Indonesia strives to advance the society as a whole and its political institutions in particular, the people must never forsake the tolerance and respect for diversity that has been one of the enduring traits of the Indonesian culture.

CONCLUDING THOUGHTS ON INDONESIA AND THE EVOLUTION OF ECONOMIC DEVELOPMENT

The field of development economics is advancing every day. Although the progress is impressive, so long as there is a child born in poverty, a mother who dies in childbirth, or a young adult inadequately trained to earn a decent living, the work of development economists and policymakers is unfinished. The tools of economic development are continually changing and evolving. They remain, however, inadequate. More progress is needed. Development economics must create better models and more powerful methodologies to understand the problems of the communities they are trying to help, and the options available.

Over the past three or so decades, progress in the field of economic development may have been less than what we would hope, but it has been very considerable none the less. The more we learn about development, the better are we able to recognize the unfathomable complexity of economies and individual economic behaviour. Rather than a series of fixed and precise rules that limit choices and options, the most important lessons of development are general principles that can guide policymakers. In this conclusion, we have reviewed a few of the salient principles that were essential to Indonesia's development in the past, and some that we may need to consider in the future.

In the chapter on agriculture, we discussed the value of the great goal of seeking rice self-sufficiency. The achievement of that goal should serve as the stepping stone for even greater goals. Among these: in 1995, Indonesia achieved a GNP per capita of about $1,000. This was a developmental milestone for Indonesia. In 1996, the World Bank defined a high-income economy as one for which the GNP per capita was $8,956 in 1994. The GNP per capita of Switzerland in that year was $37,930. If we compare Indonesia to Switzerland, the world's wealthiest nation, the achievement of a per capita income of $8,956 is not far-fetched. It may take many years for Indonesia to become a 'high-income country'. It is, however, an attainable long-term goal and one that we should adopt just as we set our eyes on 'take off' some thirty years ago.

Earlier in the book, we said that social infrastructure must be managed in the context of 'intergenerational economics'. In fact, it would be accurate to say that the entire field of economic development must be conceived in terms of 'intergenerational economics'. This is not to negate the appropriateness of short-term goals since the long-term is composed of many shorter increments. However, those economists and policymakers who confine their focus to the daily rise and fall of the stock market and by measuring progress in fiscal quarters would do better not to enter the field of economic development. As we stated at the beginning of this book, economic development requires the protracted patience of evolution and evolution is tough business. Evolution in economic development requires a firm and clear vision and sustained effort across generations. Is it reasonable, for example, for Indonesia to aspire to become one of the world's high-income nations? Certainly it is. It is only by setting great goals that Indonesia will achieve great accomplishments. We should never expect, however, that we can achieve our goals without a good faith effort sustained over many years. One of the strengths of President Soeharto and the economic team was their ability to maintain their vision of economic development over some twenty-five years. This steady, pragmatic commitment was invaluable in keeping the country's economic development on track despite the difficulties the nation faced.

Yesterday's goals must always be displaced by new and more ambitious goals. With the advances of development, the marvelous accomplishments of yesterday quickly appear commonplace and hackneyed. To maintain the momentum of development, Indonesia must set new goals for a new generation—a generation that never experienced colonial oppression, a generation for whom independence is an accepted reality, and a generation which does not live in fear of pending food shortages. While the older generation focused on such essential concerns as rice self-sufficiency, the younger generation is more concerned with employment and quality-of-life issues. Indonesia's lessons of development should serve as the foundation on which a new society can construct an economy that responds to the expectations of a new generation. The next generation must accept new challenges of development and set new goals for a new century. When they do so, they would do well to build for the future having learned well the lessons of the past.

President Sukarno was fond of saying that Indonesia was the richest country on the earth. Put a stick into Indonesia's soil, he would say, and soon you will have a blossoming tree. Sukarno made this boast while fully aware that in economic terms, Indonesia was among the poorest countries in the world. Sukarno was a master of evocative imagery, but his assertion of Indonesia's wealth was more than poetry. Despite Indonesia's poverty, hunger, and sickness, what Sukarno saw was a nation that had newly achieved independence and with it, a sense of place on earth. After years of colonial oppression, Indonesia had discovered a new hope for the future. In this hope, Indonesia had suddenly become very rich indeed.

Once again we could say that Indonesia is among the richest countries on the earth. This wealth is shared by many nations. The countries that are richest are those which provide their people with the tools to help themselves so that the people and the government can have the confidence and capacity to work together for economic development. For such countries, the future is open to the creative potential of humanity. The poorest countries, by contrast, are those that are poor in spirit—those who lack hope. The poorest countries are those beset with the grief of war, ethnic conflicts, religious intolerance, harsh political oppression, or those for which state ideologies have created a tyranny that crushes personal freedom.

Indonesians are a resilient people. We have been tested as a nation in many ways and we have shown ourselves to be resourceful in coping with adversity. Despite three decades of growth, however, many Indonesians are still living today below the poverty line. The job of economic development is far from complete. The government must continue to strive to increase the income of most Indonesians. Even more important, economic development must respond to the aspiration of the people for full and meaningful lives. The challenge of economic development in the new century will be to build the new Indonesian community that is well educated, economically strong, and empowered to accept responsibility as caretaker of this large and diverse nation. If Indonesia can learn well the lessons of development and maintain its commitment to pragmatic economic management, guided by the spirit of consensus, dialogue, and mutual help, the nation will be well equipped to meet the challenges of the future.

1. For a related discussion, see Radius Prawiro (1989).

2. Lenders need to be creative and flexible in offering assistance. For example, Indonesia under the Abs settlement relied on reduced interest rates and an extended repayment period. In another instance, when Vietnam found itself ineligible for IMF assistance due to outstanding debts, Japan assumed the debt as a way of opening the door for Vietnam to receive loans of much greater magnitude.

3. In looking toward the 1998 elections, President Soeharto affirmed, 'The government is encouraging openness and democracy' (*Jakarta Post*, 1997: 1).

Epilogue:
The Struggle Continues

DURING the second half of 1997, with virtually no forewarning, waves of volatility struck the world economy with an intensity that recalled the market meltdown just a decade earlier. However, this time the epicentre of the economic turmoil was neither the United States nor Europe, but East and South-East Asia. The region that for the previous two decades had been the world leader in economic growth suddenly stumbled and fell. Many countries were affected by this instability, but the impact on Indonesia was particularly severe. As I write these words in mid-January 1998, the prominent economic issues facing Indonesia are complex, intertwined with those of many other countries, and in the process of unfolding. More time and data will be needed, therefore, before we can objectively assess the causes and significance of the economic instability that afflicted the Indonesian economy in late 1997 and continuing into 1998. I will refer to this recent disturbance as the volatility or instability of 1997 even though these difficulties have persisted into the new year. At this point, we cannot predict the depth or durability of Indonesia's economic difficulties. The purpose of this epilogue is to look back once again at some of the themes in this book in the light of the unfolding economic difficulties.

BACKGROUND: THE INDONESIAN FALL-OUT FROM AN ASIAN CHAIN REACTION

On 2 July 1997, after months of mounting pressure, Thailand devalued its currency, the baht. Although this was hardly a unique experience, this devaluation caught the attention of investors around the world. In recent years, Thailand had been among the fastest growing economies in the world and a favourite site for investors in the so-called emerging markets. Therefore, when the government devalued the baht, many investors interpreted this as a sign of serious weaknesses in the economy, particularly the banking sector. Initially, most analysts confined their worries to Thailand. Within a little more than a month, however, the fear of devaluation spread across the region and currencies across South-East Asia came under attack from foreign exchange traders, speculators, local businessmen, and even individual bank-account holders. On a massive scale, people traded their local monies for major international currencies, such as the dollar, yen, and mark. In response, the government of Indonesia tried to defend the rupiah by raising interest rates and maintaining a steady exchange rate. Although this made borrowing very expensive, the measure was intended to induce people to continue holding their wealth in rupiah. Before long, however, the pressures on the rupiah grew to a point that on 14 August, Bank Indonesia abandoned its efforts to steady the currency and the rupiah fell rapidly. This instability fed rumours that some of the nation's troubled banks would be closed. This exacerbated capital flight and put even greater pressure on the rupiah which on one day, Friday, 3 October, dropped by 8.5 per cent, capping a fall of over 30 per cent during the month.

During this period, one of the few economies in East Asia to remain unaffected was that of Hong Kong. When however, the Hong Kong stocks plunged 10.4 per cent on Thursday, 23 October, this proved to be the proverbial straw that broke the camel's back. Almost instantaneously, the 'Asian flu' travelled the globe and not a major market was spared. On Thursday and Friday, share prices on Wall Street tumbled and on Monday, 27 October, Wall Street's leading index dropped 554 points, a 7.2 per cent decline. The next day, Wall Street rebounded, gaining 4.7 per cent, the sixth largest single day's gain since the end of the Second World War. In sympathy, most markets also registered a quick appreciation.

Most observers expected Indonesia to bounce back with similar resilience. At the end of October, the IMF and Indonesia announced a multibillion dollar assistance package that was intended to restore confidence and stability to Indonesia's beleaguered economy. Commenting on the state of the international economy, on 3 November the President of the World Bank, James Wolfensohn, reassured the world that 'the worst is over'. Although his words were credible, the troubles afflicting Indonesia and its Asian neighbours were deeper and more intractable than had been presumed. Later in November, South Korea's economy showed signs of serious deterioration and was also in need of a massive rescue package.

In early January 1998, after Indonesia publicly announced the details of the state budget, the financial crisis worsened, with the rupiah's exchange rate exceeding Rp 10,000 to the dollar, a depreciation of over 70 per cent from a year earlier. This prompted a new round of negotiations with the IMF, which resulted in an adjustment package valued at $43 billion. Although the economy has shown signs of stabilizing, it will take months before one can assess the impact of these measures.

REFLECTIONS WITHOUT THE BENEFIT
OF HINDSIGHT

While the jolt to the Indonesian economy in the August to October 1997 period can be traced to the regional instability that was triggered by the devaluation of the Thai baht in July, the persistence of Indonesia's economic instability in the following months has probably been due to home-grown factors. Had Indonesia's situation stabilized in October, its condition would have been a remarkable example of economic contagiousness. What seems to have happened, however, is that when Indonesia caught the 'Asian flu' it became more vulnerable to some of its own internal economic weaknesses that had been kept in check so long as the economy was growing at a good pace. As Indonesia entered 1998, the nation was preparing to elect a new President. To some extent, the emotional concerns people had regarding their political future may have been manifested in their economic behaviour. These conditions render an analysis of the country's economy even more difficult. The following paragraphs are a few key themes that have emerged in the second half of 1997 regarding Indonesia's economic volatility and the nation's ongoing economic development efforts. Since these reflections are written without the benefit of hindsight, they are tentative thoughts intended to extend some of the ideas in the book.

Monetary Policy and Banks—The Backbone of
Economic Development

One of the abiding themes of this book has been the critical role of fiscal and especially monetary policies in managing economic development. Monetary instability was one of the factors that led to the decline of the Sukarno regime and my first priority as the Governor of Bank Indonesia in 1966 was to rein in the inflation that was crippling the economy. Indonesia's conditions in the late 1990s are very different from the mid-1960s, but once again we can see that monetary stability is one of the key determinants of economic strength. An editorial in the 12 January 1998 issue of the *Wall Street Journal* states, 'The first clue to solving the crisis in Asia is to recognize that it's a monetary crisis.' The article gives some recommendations for stabilizing currencies and concludes, 'Once exchange rates are stabilized, recoveries can begin. They will not begin so long as these currencies go on "floating", while what they're really doing is sinking, and dragging down with them otherwise viable economies.' This is an accurate and important point—one with serious implications. Indonesia has long maintained a firm commitment to a policy of the free convertibility of our national currency, the rupiah. A logical and valid extension of that policy was to embrace a floating exchange rate system. Both of these policies were intended to permit money to do what it is supposed to do—reflect the value of the goods and services produced and exchanged within the economy. The volatility of the rupiah in the last five months of 1997 was so extreme that it suggests that extraordinary factors were involved. One obvious factor was the 'Asian flu' phenomenon, whereby devaluation in one economy puts pressure on the currency of its neighbour. From that perspective, the rupiah was caught in the tide of local currency sell-offs that swept the region. Then on 31 October 1997, in compliance with a deal worked out with the IMF, Indonesia announced it would close sixteen insolvent banks. This was an appropriate measure in every respect except for one: it failed to account for the fact that for most Indonesians banking was a fairly new experience. Many Indonesians were wary of banks to begin with and when a small group of banks was closed, it aggravated the public's sense of insecurity. Many reacted by rushing to withdraw their money and converting their holdings into dollars. This caused the value of the rupiah to fall, which provoked more people to want to trade their rupiahs for dollars. Thus, the way in which monetary and financial issues were managed may have contributed to the downward cycle of the currency.

These events clearly illustrate the central role of monetary policy in influencing economic development. Indonesia's lessons of stabilization from the 1960s and early 1970s may be helpful in understanding the monetary volatility the country has been experiencing in the late 1990s.

Bank Indonesia and the FCDT: Responding to the Dangers of Growth and Debt

It is natural and suitable for a developing country to be impatient in seeking growth. Over the last three decades, Indonesia consistently has been among the world's fastest growing countries and no one wants to see this trend reversed. But even if Indonesia were to sustain a high rate of growth, it would take decades for the nation to achieve a standard of living comparable with the OECD countries. None the less, there are hidden dangers in high growth. Rapid growth can mask many troubles in an economy— bad bank loans are a significant case in point. There is evidence that some banks have depended on sustained high levels of growth as a means of offsetting the losses incurred by relatively large numbers of bad loans. Rather than instituting policies to minimize the percentage of non-performing loans, these banks accelerated their pace of lending and in the process expanded their portfolio of non-performing loans.

According to the *Economist*, 'On one estimate, the bad loans of East Asian banks now account for between 10% and 20% of their total loans, compared with a mere 1% in America, and that estimate may rise' (1997b: 19). A bad loan will hurt any bank, but banks with low reserves will find themselves especially vulnerable. Recognizing this, in April 1997 Indonesia raised the reserve requirements of banks to 5 per cent, its second increase since February 1996, when the reserve requirement was only 2 per cent. This was an appropriate measure but one that was introduced rather late in light of the fact that quite a few banks with very low reserves had already run up an excessively high percentage of non-performing loans.

The goal of the government, however, should not be simply to have banks increase their reserves but to minimize their exposure to bad debts. This situation recalls the early 1990s when Indonesia was faced with a serious current account deficit. In response, the government rescheduled a number of mega-projects and established the FCDT. As described in Chapter 10, the FCDT was created to serve as gatekeeper for any commercial borrowing in which the government had a stake. Because of FCDT intervention in the early 1990s, the government was better equipped to hold down the level of public and private sector debt through the banking system.

The FCDT continues to exist, but its oversight role has not kept pace with the massive expansion of commercial and public borrowing. One of the most significant challenges Indonesia faces is to ensure that the level of private sector debt does not rise to the point that it may pose a risk to the overall health of the financial system. The purpose of the FCDT is to supplement Bank Indonesia's normal supervisory and regulatory duties. Together these two can help ensure that exposure to potentially bad debts is kept to a minimum. Because successful development necessitates an ever-growing volume of capital, the regulatory and supervisory services of Bank Indonesia and the FCDT are needed more than ever. The need for prudent control of public and private sector debt that led to the creation of the FCDT in 1990 was a critical lesson of development for Indonesia. This lesson is as pertinent today in the late 1990s as it was almost a decade earlier when the FCDT was first established.

Planning a Trip for 200 million—Balancing the Social, Political, and Economic Sides of Development

The economic policymaker is a kind of weatherman. His job is to monitor constantly every instrument available to assess the strengths and weaknesses in the economy. However, unlike the weatherman, the policymaker's responsibility includes recommending interventions that will influence tomorrow's economic climate. Every economy is affected by a vast number of forces, ranging from real weather patterns to the vagaries of international politics. This is a job of incalculable complexity. In Indonesia's case, policymakers must contend with the daunting task of moving 200 million people from a traditional agrarian culture to an information-intensive industrial economy. This situation is further complicated by an unusual degree of ethnic and cultural diversity. Each manifestation of development brings new strains to the country as long-standing traditions are being forced to adapt to new conditions very quickly. The farmer who finds that his son no longer wants to till the soil, the weaver who finds that her hand-loomed sarongs are no longer in demand, and the government official who faces pressures from an increasingly independent electorate, all encounter strains born of economic development. The new economy brings new problems. The solution is not to reject economic change but to advocate change that will bring the greatest good for the country as a whole while trying to minimize the social dislocations that accompany development. All Indonesians are united in their desire to see an improvement in the nation's quality of life. Indonesians want more food on the table; everyone wants their children to receive better education; and urbanites and villagers alike want access to products of the world markets. Unfortunately, however, there is no way to support economic progress without some level of disruption to the prevailing norms. The difficult question, especially for a developing country, is how to manage economic development in such a way that the changes it brings are not too destabilizing to the society.

The nation of Indonesia was born in the chaos of revolution as the country struggled to extricate itself from its colonial past. During the two decades leading up to the establishment of the New Order government in 1966, Indonesia was beset with such political instability that economic development was all but impossible. The following three decades saw a dramatic change for the better. Peace and political stability returned, and though the nation was still poor, the economy grew rapidly. In the late 1990s, however, the steady growth of Indonesia's economy has been disrupted and throughout the country there is a heightened focus on political affairs. Our history has shown us that economic development cannot coexist with the turmoil of extreme political instability. For this reason, Indonesia once again must seek a meaningful and satisfactory way of addressing the political aspirations of its people while maintaining the stability needed to support economic development. This is a challenge, but one that should be well within the reach of the Indonesian society.

The Difficult Transition to a Global Economy

There are global implications to the economic instability that afflicted Indonesia in 1997. The volatility revealed weaknesses in Indonesia's economy and those of other economies in the region. However, rather than interpreting these events as isolated Asian problems, to an extent it might be more appropriate to see these events as a striking example of the dramatic reconfiguration of the world economy that has occurred in recent years. Just a decade ago, the economies of South-East Asia were too puny to exert any noticeable effect on Wall Street, the City of London, or Tokyo. Not so today. One of the remarkable aspects of the 1997 market volatility is that it demonstrated the new economic impact of South-East Asia on an increasingly integrated global economy. The time may have arrived to rethink the dualism implied in the traditional conceptions of 'North' and 'South', as well as 'industrialized' and 'developing' nations. The channels of economic influence no longer run one way from the industrialized countries to the developing countries. The economies of South-East Asia have developed to the point that the growth or contraction in these markets are felt around the world. This situation requires Indonesia and its Asian neighbours to recognize not only our new influence in world affairs, but also our new obligations to participate as full and responsible players in an emerging global economy.

Adapting to this new economic environment will be no easy task. There was more behind the economic volatility of 1997 than weak banks and unsuitable government policies. In Indonesia and much of Asia, many businesses, especially banks, and many government policies were designed to support outmoded economic paradigms—the paradigms of inward-looking autarchy or export-led growth that resisted true economic openness. In many respects, neither banks, nor businesses, nor governments were prepared for the changes brought by globalization. As a result, business and policy leaders have often been using yesterday's tools to shape tomorrow's economy. Although this is not an uncommon occurrence, the instability of 1997 showed that a significant dissonance had grown between the economic policies and practices of the time and the demands of the rapidly evolving economy. When this dissonance became too extreme, change was forced in a way that was sudden, traumatic, and potentially dangerous because it was so uncontrolled.

The actions that Indonesia and other countries have taken so far to respond to the economic crisis have been moving in the right direction, but they tend to address the problem only in domestic terms. This, I believe, is insufficient. In the introduction to Part II, I mentioned that the

Plaza Accord of 1985 was 'an important step in creating a free but relatively stable international monetary system, backed by co-ordinated intervention among the major economies', namely the United States, Japan, Germany, the United Kingdom, and France. Since 1985, the international community took another major step to foster economic co-operation and growth by establishing the WTO. The Plaza Accord and the creation of the WTO are positive examples of the maturation of the international economy. Of the two, however, only the WTO represents a truly global outlook. The WTO gives all the participating nations a new set of tools to deal with the globalization of trade. There is no comparable institution or process to help nations deal with the effects of the globalization of currency markets. Currencies, like most traded goods, should be permitted to move freely across national boundaries; this has long been a corner-stone of Indonesia's economic policy and one that should be retained. However, as Indonesia and other nations in the region investigate what changes to make to prepare for a global economy, we need to think creatively about the policies that pertain to currency flows and exchange rate volatility. Individual governments must continue to accept primary responsibility for the strength and stability of their nation's currencies. However, that job could be rendered more efficient if the task of co-ordinating monetary policies is undertaken by the advanced industrialized countries together with the newly industrializing and developing economies. The Plaza Accord offers a clue regarding the kind of tools to which I am referring, but this Accord was a loose agreement among a small group of large economies. With the WTO as a model, the community of nations should investigate how to extend the ideas behind the Plaza Accord to a broader constituency. If the volatility of 1997 only results in domestic policy changes without any corresponding changes at the international level to moderate currency volatility, then we will have missed an opportunity to create the tools needed to facilitate the development of a more smoothly functioning global economy.

* * *

It is regrettable, though not unexpected, that the most significant reforms are frequently born of crisis. No people, however, want to traverse history in a perpetual lurch from one crisis to another. Not only would that be neeedlessly painful, it would also be heedless of one of humanity's greatest gifts, our ability to learn from our past. The job ahead for Indonesia is to avoid those avoidable mistakes by learning well the lessons of development now available to us. While it is too early to discern what will be the lessons from Indonesia's economic turmoil of 1997, some of the themes that extend the major ideas of this book are as follows:

- Sound monetary policy is the foundation of economic development. The maintenance of a strong currency and sound banks is one of the most important responsibilities of a government.
- Debt, though necessary for development, is dangerous if not carefully monitored and regulated.
- In periods of rapid growth, a government may find that its regulatory machinery is both overtaxed and inadequate to deal with newly emerging business trends. In such times, extra vigilance is needed to safeguard against unacceptable business practices such as lax lending policies.
- Global problems require global solutions. Exchange rate volatility can become so extreme that the normal regulatory mechanisms are not adequate. For this reason, the international community should consider establishing an organization that can help co-ordinate efforts to moderate currency markets during instances of extreme volatility.
- Economic development by definition is a process that brings managed and generally positive change to a society. Change, however, brings with it stresses, often in ways that cannot be anticipated. By honing their sensitivity to changing social conditions and listening carefully to the people they serve, economic policymakers will be better able to respond to the social stresses that economic development can bring about. To this end, good governance requires close co-ordination between all branches of the government—executive, judiciary, and legislative. Only by working together can a government create coherent policies that effectively promote development while reflecting the will of the people.

In the wake of the recent market disturbances, there have been those who suggested that Asia's economic tigers were paper tigers, and that the East Asian miracle was no more than a mirage. There is no ground for such pessimism. For many years the savings rates in much of Asia—Indonesia included—have ranked substantially higher than in most other countries. Not only does the region have considerable supplies of 'home-grown' capital to finance development along with that supplied by outside investors but it also has the propensity to save. Among many Asian nations this will facilitate recovery when financial markets regain their equilibrium. Moreover, for over three decades Indonesia has been relentlessly developing its infrastructure, improving the health and welfare of its citizens, and expanding the educational opportunities available to the young. It has been Indonesia's long-term commitment to building its physical infrastructure and cultivating its human resources that have been the bedrock of its economic development. That foundation remains intact despite the problems in Indonesia's financial sector and the associated volatility in the currency and equity markets. However, perhaps the most important factor that will ensure that economic growth returns to Asia, and Indonesia in particular, is that our people are committed to development. So long as the people of Indonesia believe that they are capable of improving their economic conditions and they are prepared to work hard to achieve that end, then the country will continue to progress.

In many respects the development process is becoming more complex as Indonesia's economy progresses. Unlike the neat, logical equations that fill most economic textbooks, the challenges of development are often painful, stubborn, irrational, human, and messy. The volatility of 1997 reminds us of the limitations of our own forecasting abilities. Such conditions compel us to recognize the fragility of economic development and the serious need to address squarely economic, political, and social issues that could undermine progress if neglected. In the end, although we must acknowledge our inability to predict certain economic events, this in no way diminishes the important lessons that we have gained from our years of experience. To the contrary, such problems reaffirm the abiding strength of principles such as the Development Trilogy (stability, growth, and equity), pragmatism, and the need for economic policies to be firmly grounded on economic theory. The potential of the Indonesian people and economy is vast. Despite the nation's remarkable progress, however, the regional and domestic volatility of 1997 is a vivid reminder of the great distance Indonesia still must travel to create a sound, advanced, and prosperous economy. Indonesia's struggle for economic development must continue.

Appendices

SUPPLEMENTAL ECONOMIC DATA

APPENDIX TABLE A.1
Gross Domestic Product, 1969–1996 (Rp billion)

Year	Current Prices	Constant Prices (1973)
1969	2,718.0	4,820.5
1973	6,753.4	6,753.4
1978	22,746.0	9,566.5
1983	71,214.7	77,622.8
1988	142,104.8	99,981.4
1991	226,508.6	123,089.5
1996	490,316.6	Unavailable

Source: Indonesia, Central Bureau of Statistics.

APPENDIX TABLE A.2
GDP Growth, 1969–1996 (percentage)

Year	Annual Growth	Year	Annual Growth
1969	7.1	1983	4.2
1970	7.5	1984	7.0
1971	7.0	1985	2.5
1972	9.4	1986	5.9
1973	11.3	1987	4.9
1974	7.6	1988	5.8
1975	5.0	1989	7.5
1976	6.9	1990	7.4
1977	8.8	1991	6.8
1978	7.8	1992	6.2
1979	6.3	1993	6.5
1980	9.9	1994	7.5
1981	7.9	1995	8.2
1982	2.2	1996	7.9

Source: Indonesia, Central Bureau of Statistics.

APPENDIX TABLE A.3
Oil and Non-oil Exports and Imports, 1965–1996 ($ million)

Year	Total Exports	Total Imports	Oil Exports	Oil Imports	Non-oil Exports	Non-oil Imports
1965	707.7	694.7	272.0	12.6	435.7	682.1
1966	678.7	526.7	203.4	7.5	475.3	519.2
1967	665.4	649.2	239.6	12.6	425.8	636.6
1968	730.7	715.8	297.5	6.1	433.2	709.7
1969	853.7	780.7	382.9	10.9	470.8	769.8
1970	1108.1	1001.5	446.3	14.7	661.8	986.8
1971	1233.6	1102.8	477.9	20.4	755.7	1082.4
1972	1777.7	1561.7	913.1	30.3	864.6	1531.4
1973	3210.8	2729.1	1608.7	43.8	1602.1	2685.3
1974	7426.3	3841.9	5211.4	183.0	2214.9	3658.9
1975	7102.5	4769.8	5310.8	253.5	1791.7	4516.3
1976	8546.5	5673.1	6004.1	437.7	2542.4	5235.4
1977	10852.6	6230.3	7297.8	732.0	3554.8	5498.3
1978	11643.2	6690.4	7438.5	579.7	4204.7	6110.7
1979	15590.1	7202.3	8870.9	793.3	6719.2	6409.0
1980	23950.4	10834.4	17781.6	1744.0	6168.8	9090.4
1981	25164.5	13272.1	20663.2	1721.3	4501.3	11550.8
1982	22328.3	16858.9	18399.3	3544.8	3929.0	13314.1
1983	21145.9	16351.8	16140.7	4144.8	5005.2	12207.0
1984	21887.8	13882.1	16018.1	2696.8	5869.7	11185.3
1985	18586.7	10259.1	12717.8	1275.6	5868.9	8983.5
1986	14805.0	10718.4	8276.6	1086.4	6528.4	9632.0
1987	17135.6	12370.3	8556.0	1067.9	8579.6	11302.4
1988	19218.5	13248.5	7681.6	909.0	11536.9	12339.5
1989	22158.9	16359.6	8678.8	1195.2	13480.1	15164.4
1990	25675.3	21837.0	11071.1	1920.4	14604.2	19916.6
1991	29142.4	25868.8	10894.9	2310.3	18247.5	23558.5
1992	33967.0	27279.6	10670.9	2115.0	23296.1	25164.6
1993	36823.0	28327.8	9745.8	2170.6	27077.2	26157.2
1994	40053.4	31983.5	9693.6	2367.4	30359.8	29616.1
1995	45418.0	40628.7	10464.4	2910.8	34953.6	37717.9
1996	49814.8	42928.5	11721.8	3595.5	38093.0	39333.0

Source: Indonesia, Central Bureau of Statistics.

APPENDIX TABLE A.4
Per Capita Income, 1969–1996 (Rp thousand)[a]

Year	Income
1969	20
1973	46
1978	138
1983	436
1988	694
1991	1,038
1996	2,355

Source: Indonesia, Central Bureau of Statistics.
[a]At current values.

APPENDIX TABLE A.5
Population Below the Poverty Line, 1976–1996

Year	Poor (million)	Percentage of Total Population
1976	54.2	40.5
1978	47.2	33.7
1980	42.3	28.7
1981	40.6	27.0
1984	35.0	22.0
1987	30.0	18.1
1990	27.2	15.2
1993	25.9	13.7
1996	22.5	11.3

Source: Indonesia, Central Bureau of Statistics.

APPENDIX TABLE A.6
Daily Per Capita Consumption, 1969–1996

Year	Calories	Proteins (grams)
1969	2132	42.20
1973	2247	45.60
1978	2417	47.63
1983	2565	52.00
1988	2712	60.02
1991	2848	65.41
1996	3151	69.75

Source: Indonesia, Central Bureau of Statistics.

Bibliography

Abs, Herman J. (1969), 'The Problem of Indonesia's External Debt and Reflections on its Solution', Unpublished Report for the Indonesian Government and Creditor Countries, 30 July.

Ali, Mohamed (1964), 'Interview with Chairul Saleh', *Far Eastern Economic Review*, 28 May.

Anon. (1973), 'Ekonomi Tahun 1973: Cerah dan Suram Sela Menyela', *Kompas*, 29 December.

Anon. (1977), 'The Dutch Disease', *Economist*, 26 November, pp. 82–3.

Anon. (1982), 'Pidato Kenegaraan Presiden Soeharto, Pancasila Seharusnya Satu-satunya azas Setiap Parpol', *Kompas*, 16 August.

Anon. (1983a), 'Illegal Levies Rife at Tanjung Priok says Businessman', *Jakarta Post*, 14 October.

Anon. (1983b), 'Rancangan APBN 1983–84 Rp 16.5 Trilyun Lebih; Hany dengan Efisiensi dan Sikap Prihatin, Pembangunan dapat Ditingkatkan', *Kompas*.

Anon. (1996a), 'Just Do It: Why APEC Doesn't Matter', *Far Eastern Economic Review*, 31 October, p. 5.

Anon. (1996b), 'Overseas Investments Hit a Record $325 b. Last Year: UN', *Jakarta Post*, 7 June.

Anon. (1997a), 'And South-East Asia Thinks its all over', *Economist*, 8 November, pp. 41–2.

Anon. (1997b), 'How Far is Down', *Economist*, 15 November, pp. 19–21.

Anon. (1997c), 'Soeharto Promises Openness', *Jakarta Post*, 2 January.

Anwar, Dewi Fortuna (1994), *Indonesia in ASEAN: Foreign Policy and Regionalism*, Jakarta: P.T. Pustaka Sinar Harapan & Institute of Southeast Asian Studies.

Arief, Sritua, and Sasono, Adi (1987), *Foreign Capital, Foreign Debt Burden and the Indonesian Economy*, Jakarta: Institute for Development Studies.

Arndt, H.W. (1966), 'Banking in Hyperinflation', *Bulletin of Indonesian Economic Studies*, (5): 45–70.

_____ (1971), 'Survey of Recent Developments', *Bulletin of Indonesian Economic Studies*, VII(1): 1–18.

_____ (1975), 'Survey of Recent Developments', *Bulletin of Indonesian Economic Studies*, XI(2): 1–19.

ASEAN Secretariat (1993), *AFTA Reader*, Jakarta. Vol. 1.

Awanohara, Susumu (1983), 'Rejuvenation Revisited', *Far Eastern Economic Review*, 31 March.

Baldwin, Robert E., and Richardson, J. David (1974), *International Trade and Finance*, Boston: Little, Brown.

Bank Indonesia (1968), 'Laporan Tahun Pembukuan 1960–1965', Djakarta, pp. 25–6.

_____ (1970), 'Report for the Financial Year 1969/70', Jakarta, p. 38.

_____ (1978), 'Report for the Financial Year 1977/1978', Jakarta, p. 34–5.

Barichello, Richard R. and Flatters, Frank R. (1991), 'Trade Policy Reform in Indonesia', in D. H. Perkins and Michael Roemer (eds.), *Reforming Economic Systems in Developing Countries*, Cambridge: Harvard University Press.

Bartlett, Anderson G. (1972), *Pertamina: Indonesian National Oil*, Tulsa, Oklahoma: Amerasian.

Bergsten, C. Fred (1996), 'Globalizing Free Trade', *Foreign Affairs*, 75 (3): 105–20.

Bernard, Charles (1978), 'Pertamina Debt Reduced to $6 Billion', *Business Times*, 25 April.

Binhadi (1995), *Financial Sector Deregulation: Banking Development and Monetary Policy, the Indonesian Experience 1983–1993*, Jakarta: Institut Bankir Indonesia.

Bitterman, Henry J. (1973), *The Refunding of International Debt*, Durham, N. C.: Duke University Press.

BKKBN (1989), *Family Planning in Indonesia: New Paths for Development*, Jakarta.

Boeke, Jan (1946), *The Evolution of the Netherlands Indies Economy*, New York: Institute of Pacific Relations.

Booth, Anne (1984), 'Survey of Recent Developments', *Bulletin of Indonesian Economic Studies*, XX (3):1–35.

Booth, Anne and Glassburner, Bruce (1975), 'Survey of Recent Developments', *Bulletin of Indonesian Economic Studies*, XI (1): 1–40.

Booth, Anne and Sundrum, R. M. (1981), 'Income Distribution', in Anne Booth and Peter McCawley (eds.), *The Indonesian Economy During the Soeharto Era*, Kuala Lumpur: Oxford University Press.

Brown, John Murray (1988), 'Jakarta Money Market Squeezed', *Financial Times*, 9 November.

Bruton, Henry J. (1970), 'The Import-Substitution Strategy of Economic Development: A Survey', *Pakistan Development Review*, X (2): 123–46.

Chenery, H. B. and Syrquin, M. (1975), *Patterns of Development, 1960–70*, London: Oxford University Press.

Chowdhury, Anis and Islam, Iyanatul (1993), *The Newly Industrializing Economies of East Asia*, New York: Routledge.

Coggin, Dan (1975), 'Chilly, with Some Bright Spots', *Far Eastern Economic Review*, 7 November, p. 13.

Corbridge, Stuart (1993), *Debt and Development*, Cambridge: Blackwell Publishers.

Corden, Warner M. (1984), 'Booming Sector and Dutch Disease Economics: Survey and Consolidation', *Oxford Economic Papers*, Vol. 36, pp. 359–80.

Dahm, Bernhard (1969), *Sukarno and the Struggle for Indonesian Independence*, translated by Mary F. Somers Heidhues, Ithaca: Cornell University Press.

Daroesman (1971), 'Financing Education, Part I', *Bulletin of Indonesian Economic Studies*, VII: 61–96.

‗‗‗‗ (1972), 'Financing Education, Part II', *Bulletin of Indonesian Economic Studies*, VIII: 32–68.

Daroesman, Ruth (1981), 'Survey of Recent Developments', *Bulletin of Indonesian Economic Studies*, XVII (2): 1–41.

de Vries, Barend (1986), 'Future Capital Flows: Critical Improvements and the Role of Coordination', in Michael Claudon (ed.), *World Debt Crisis: International Lending on Trial*, Cambridge: Ballinger.

Dollar, David (1992), 'Outward-oriented Developing Economies Really Do Grow More Rapidly: Evidence from 95 LDCs, 1976–1985', *Economic Development and Cultural Change*, 40 (3): 523–45.

England, Vaudine (1987), 'Virtue From Necessity', *Far Eastern Economic Review*, 5 February.

Friedman, Milton (1968), 'The Role of Monetary Policy', *American Economic Review*, LVIII (1): 1–17.

Gannicott, K. (1990), 'The Economics of Education in Asian–Pacific Developing Countries', *Asian–Pacific Economic Literature*, 4 (1): 41–64.

Geertz, Clifford (1963), *Agricultural Involution: The Process of Ecological Change in Indonesia*, Berkeley: University of California Press.

Gelb, Alan and Associates (1988), *Oil Windfalls: Blessing or Curse?*, New York: Oxford University Press.

Gillis, Malcolm (1984), 'Episodes in Indonesian Economic Growth', in Arnold C. Harberger (ed.), *World Economic Growth*, San Francisco: Institute for Contemporary Studies, pp. 231–64.

‗‗‗‗ (1989), 'Comprehensive Tax Reform: The Indonesian Experience, 1981–1988', in Malcolm Gillis (ed.), *Tax Reform in Developing Countries*, Durham: Duke University Press, pp. 79–114.

Glassburner, Bruce (1971), 'Introduction', in Bruce Glassburner (ed.), *The Economy of Indonesia: Selected Readings*, Ithaca: Cornell University Press, pp. vii–viii.

‗‗‗‗ (1978), 'Political Economy and the Soeharto Regime', *Bulletin of Indonesian Economic Studies*, XIV (3): 24–51.

Grenville, Stephen (1973), 'Survey of Recent Developments', *Bulletin of Indonesian Economic Studies*, IX (1): 1–29.

Hagen, Evereet E. (1958), 'An Economic Justification of Protectionism', *Quarterly Journal of Economics*, LXXII (4): 496–514.

Hamengkubuwono IX, Sri Sultan (1966), 'Statement Politik Economi Dalam Negeri', *Business News*, 12 April.

Harberger, Arnold C. (1984), 'Economic Policy and Economic Growth', in Arnold C. Harberger (ed.), *World Economic Growth*, San Francisco: Institute for Contemporary Studies, pp. 427–88.

‗‗‗‗ (1990), 'Principles of Taxation Applied to Developing Countries: What

Have We Learned', in Michael J. Boskin and Charles E. McLure (eds.), *World Tax Reform*, San Francisco: ICS Press, pp. 25–48.

Hill, Hal (ed.) (1994), *Indonesia's New Order: The Dynamics of Socio-economic Transformation*, St. Leonards: Allen and Unwin.

Hobcraft, J. N. (1993), 'Women's Education, Child Welfare and Child Survival: A Review of the Evidence', *Health Transition Review*, 3(2).

Hugo, Graeme J. et al. (1990), *The Demographic Dimension in Indonesian Development*, New York: Oxford University Press.

Indonesia (1993), 'Lampiran Pidato Pertanggungjawaban Presiden/Mandataris Majelis Permusyawaratan Rakyat Republik Indonesia di Depan Sidang Umum Majelis Permusyawaratan Rakyat RI', Maret.

Indonesia, Central Bureau of Statistics (1995), *Statistik Indonesia 1994*, Jakarta.

_____ (1997), *Statistik Indonesia 1996*, Jakarta.

Indonesia, Departement Keuangan (1967), *Summary Budget for 1967 [Ringkasan Anggaran Pendapatan dan Belandja Negara Tahun 1967]*, Jakarta.

Indonesia, Department of Information (1969), *The Five-Year Development Plan (1969/70–1973/74)*, Jakarta.

Indonesia, Sekretariat Jendral Dewan Pimpinan Pisat Golongan Karya (1992), 'Orde baru dalam Angka: Hasil-hasil Pembangunan Jangka Panjang Tahap Pertama', Jakarta, Mei.

Indonesia, State Ministry (1994), *Gerankan 30 September Pemberontakan Partai Komunis Indonesia: Latar Belak, Aski, dan Penumpasannya*, Jakarta.

International Monetary Fund (1995), *World Economic Outlook*, Washington, DC.

Javasche Bank (1953), *Laporan Tahun Pembukuan 1951–1952*, Jakarta.

Kong, Cho Oon (1986), *The Politics of Oil in Indonesia: Foreign Company–Host Government Relations*, Cambridge: Cambridge University Press.

Lachica, Eduardo (1981), 'Indonesia Urged to Ease Rigid Rules on Business', *Asian Wall Street Journal Weekly*, 27 April, pp. 1, 20.

Lindert, Peter H., and Morton, Peter J. (1989), 'How Sovereign Debt Has Worked', in Jeffrey D. Sachs (ed.), *Developing Country Debt and the World Economy*, Chicago: University of Chicago Press, pp. 225–36.

Lipsky, Seth (1978), *The Billion Dollar Bubble & Other Stories*, Hong Kong: Dow Jones.

Manguno, Josephe P. (1982), 'Move by Indonesia to Devalue Rupiah Believed Imminent', *Asian Wall Street Journal Weekly*, 9 August.

_____ (1983), 'Jakarta Eliminates Ceilings on Lending, Interest Rates in Bid to Spur Investment', *Asian Wall Street Journal Weekly*, 13 June.

McCawley, Peter (1978), 'Some Consequences of the Pertamina Crisis in Indonesia', *Journal of Southeast Asian Studies*, IX(1): 1–27.

_____ (1981), 'The Growth of the Industrial Sector', in Anne Booth and Peter McCawley (eds.), *The Indonesian Economy During the Soeharto Era*, Kuala Lumpur: Oxford University Press, pp. 62–101.

McNicoll, Geoffrey (1982), 'Recent Demographic Trends in Indonesia', *Population and Development*, 8(4): 811–19.

Mears, Leon A. and Moeljono, Sidik (1981), 'Food Policy', in Ann Booth and

Peter McCawley (eds.), *The Indonesian Economy During the Soeharto Era*, Kuala Lumpur: Oxford University Press, pp. 23–61.

Muir, Ross (1986), 'Survey of Recent Developments', *Bulletin of Indonesian Economic Studies*, XXII (2): 1–30.

Musgrave, Richard A. and Musgrave Peggy B. (1983), *Public Finance in Theory and Practice*, Singapore: McGraw-Hill.

Myint, Hla (1971), 'The Inward and Outward-looking Countries of Southeast Asia', in Hla Myint (ed.), *Economic Theory and the Underdeveloped Countries*, New York: Oxford University Press, pp. 271–90.

Nasution, Anwar (1984), 'The Indonesian Economy: Problems of Adjustment to Global Recession and Lower Oil Prices', *Indonesian Quarterly*, XII (1): 16–31.

—— (1991), 'Survey of Recent Developments,' *Bulletin of Indonesian Economic Studies*, 27(2): 3–44.

Neary, J. Peter and Wijnbergen, Sweder van (1986), *Natural Resources and the Macroeconomy*, Oxford: Basil Blackwell.

Paauw, Douglas A. and Fei, John C. H. (1973), *The Transition in Dualistic Economies*, New Haven: Yale University Press.

Pangestu, Mari (1991), 'The Role of the Private Sector in Indonesia: Deregulation and Privatization', *Indonesia Quarterly*, XIX (1): 27–51.

—— (1996), *Economic Reform, Deregulation and Privatization: The Indonesian Experience*, Jakarta: Center for Strategic and International Studies.

Pangestu, Mari and Boediono (1986), 'The Structure and Cause of Manufacturing Sector Protection in Indonesia', in Christopher Findlay and Ross Garnaut (eds.), *The Political Economy of Manufacturing Protection: Experiences of ASEAN and Australia*, Sydney: Allen & Unwin, pp. 1–47.

Panglaykim, J. and Penny, D. H. (1968), 'Survey of Recent Developments', *Bulletin of Indonesian Economic Studies*, (9): 22–44.

Panglaykim, Y. (1974), 'Financial Institutions in Indonesia', *Indonesia Quarterly* 3(1).

Pearson, Scott; Naylor, Rosamund; and Falcon, Walter (1991), 'Recent Policy Influences on Rice Production', in Scott Pearson et al. (eds.), *Rice Policy in Indonesia*, Ithaca: Cornell University Press.

Penders, C. L. M. (1974), *The Life and Times of Sukarno*, London: Sidgwick & Jackson.

Penny, D. H. (1966a), 'The Economics of Peasant Agriculture: The Indonesian Case', *Bulletin of Indonesian Economic Studies*, (5): 22–44.

—— (1966b), 'Survey of Recent Developments', *Bulletin of Indonesian Economic Studies*, (3): 1–26.

Pohl, Manfred (1983), *Hermann J. Abs, A Biography*, Mainz: Hase & Koehler.

Porter, Michael E. (1990), *The Competitive Advantage of Nations*, New York: The Free Press.

Posthumus, G. A. (1971), *The Inter Governmental Group on Indonesia*, Rotterdam: Rotterdam University Press.

Prijono, Achmad (1983), 'Indonesia's Mining Production', *Indonesian Quarterly*, XI (4): 73–85.

Radius Prawiro (1966), 'Monetary Problems in the Framework of Economic Stabilization', Paper presented at the Second Army Seminar, Jakarta.

_____ (1989), 'Back to the Wisdom of the Market Economy', Paper presented at the Institut Pengembangan Manajemen Inconesia, Jakarta, 15 December.

_____ (1990), *Inter Governmental Group on Indonesia*, Jakarta: Menteri Koordinator Bidang Ekuin dan Pengawasan Pembangunan.

Reidinger, Jeffrey (1994), 'Innovation in Rural Finance: Indonesia's Badan Kredit Kecamatan Program', *World Development*, 22 (3): 301–13.

Roeder, O. G. (1966), 'The Impossible Dream', *Far Eastern Economic Review*, 2 October.

_____ (1968), 'Cabinet of Experts', *Far Eastern Economic Review*, 20 June.

Sadli, Mohamad (1974), 'Impressions on the First Japanese–Indonesian Conference', *Indonesian Quarterly*, II (2): 14–18.

Samuelson, Paul A. (1969), 'The Way of an Economist', in Paul Samuelson (ed.), *International Economic Relations*, London: Macmillan,.

Sapuan (1989), 'The Development of Rice Marketing in Indonesia', *Indonesian Food Journal*, 1 (1).

Simandjuntak, Djisman S. (1991), 'Process of Deregulation and Privatisation: 'The Indonesian Experience', *Indonesia Quarterly*, XIX (4): 263–370.

Simorangkir, J. C. T. and Say, B. Mang Reng (1980), *Around and About the Indonesian Constitution of 1945*, Jakarta: Djambatan.

Siregar, Machtarudin (1990), *Pinjaman Luar Negeri dan Pembiayaan Pembangunan di Indonesia*, Jakarta: Lembaga Penerbit Fakultas Ekonomi Universitas Indonesia.

Snodgrass, Donald R. and Patten, Richard H. (1991), 'Reform of Rural Credit in Indonesia: Inducing Bureaucracies to Behave Competitively', in Dwight H. Perkins and Michael Roemer (eds.), *Reforming Economic Systems in Developing Countries*, Cambridge: Harvard University Press, pp. 341–63.

Soeharto (1966), 'Statement Made on Behalf of the Indonesian Government at the Multilateral Conference in Tokyo', Jakarta.

_____ (1973), 'Address to the General Session of the People's Consultative Assembly', Jakarta: Department of Information, Republic of Indonesia.

_____ (1976), Keterangan Pemerintah tentang Rancangan Anggaran Pendapatan dan Belanja Negara Tahun 1976/77', Paper presented at the 1976/77 Budget Address to the DPR, Jakarta, Indonesia, 7 January.

_____ (1984), *Saksi Sejarah: Mengikuti Perjuangan Dwitunggal*, Jakarta: Gunung Agung.

Soesastro, M. Hadi (1989), 'The Political Economy of Deregulation in Indonesia', *Asian Survey*, XXIX (9).

Sudarsono, Juwono (1995), 'Globalisasi Ekonomi dan Demokrasi Indonesia', *Politik, Ekonomi, dan Strategi*, Jakarta: Gramedia Pustaka Utama, pp. 191–5.

Tabor, Steven R. (1992), 'Agriculture in Transition', in Anne Booth (ed.), *The Oil*

Boom and After: Indonesian Economic Policy and Performance in the Soeharto Era, Kuala Lumpur: Oxford University Press, pp. 161–203.

Thee, Kian Wie (1992), 'The Investment Surge from the Asian Newly-Industrializing Countries into Indonesia', *Asian Economic Journal*, VI (3): 231–65.

Thee, Kian Wie and Yoshihara, Kunio (1978), 'Foreign and Domestic Capital in Indonesian Industrialization', *Southeast Asian Studies*, 24 (4): 327–49.

Thorbecke, Erik (1992), 'The Indonesian Adjustment Experience in an International Perspective', *Jurnal Ekonomi Indonesia*, 1(1): 76–116.

Tilaar, H. A. R. (1995), *Pembangunan Pendidikan Nasional 1945–1995: Suatu Analisis Kebijakan*, Jakarta: Grasindo.

Timmer, C. Peter (1975), 'The Political Economy of Rice in Asia: Indonesia', *Food Research Institute Studies*, XIV (3): 197–231.

United Nations Development Program (1994), *Human Development Report 1994*, New York: Oxford University Press.

Wardhana, Ali (1989), 'Structural Adjustment in Indonesia: Export and the "High-Cost" Economy', *Indonesia Quarterly*, XVII (3): 207–17.

Warr, Peter G. (1992), 'Exchange Rate Policy, Petroleum, Prices, and the Balance of Payments', in Anne Booth (ed.), *The Oil Boom and After: Indonesian Economic Policy and Performance in the Soeharto Era*, Singapore: Oxford University Press, pp. 132–58.

_____ (1994), 'Comparative and Competitive Advantage', *Asian-Pacific Economic Literature*, 8(2): 1–14.

Warwick, Donald P. (1985), *Culture and the Management of Family Planning Programs*, Occasional Paper, Jakarta: Harvard Institute for International Development.

Widjojo, N. (1970), *Population Trends in Indonesia*, Ithaca: Cornell University Press.

_____ (1994), 'A Once-for-All Settlement of Foreign Debt', Paper presented at the NAM Ministers of Finance Meeting, Jakarta, 13 August.

Wilson, Dick (1964), 'Accounting for Konfrontasi', *Far Eastern Economic Review*, 8 October.

_____ (1972), 'Can "Non-Ideological Maoism" Work?', *Far Eastern Economic Review*, 22 January, pp. 38–9.

Woo, Wing Thye; Glassburner, Bruce; and Nasution, Anwar (1994), *Macroeconomic Policies, Crises, and Long-term Growth in Indonesia, 1965–90*, Washington, DC: World Bank.

World Bank (1979), *Indonesia: Cottage and Small Industry in the National Economy*, (2490-IND), Washington, DC 11/9.

_____ (1990), *Indonesia: Strategy for a Sustained Reduction in Poverty*, Washington, DC.

_____ (1991a), *Indonesia: Health Planning and Budgeting*, Washington, DC.

_____ (1991b), *World Development Report 1991: The Challenge of Development*, Washington, DC: Oxford University Press.

_____ (1993a), *The East Asian Miracle*, New York: Oxford University Press.

_____ (1993b), *World Development Report, 1993: Investing in Health*, Washington, DC: Oxford University Press.

_____ (1995a), *World Data 1995: World Bank Indicators on CD-ROM*, Washington, DC.

_____ (1995b), *World Development Report: Workers in an Integrating World*, Washington, DC: Oxford University Press.

_____ (1996), *From Plan to Market: World Development Report 1996*, Washington, DC: Oxford University Press.

Index

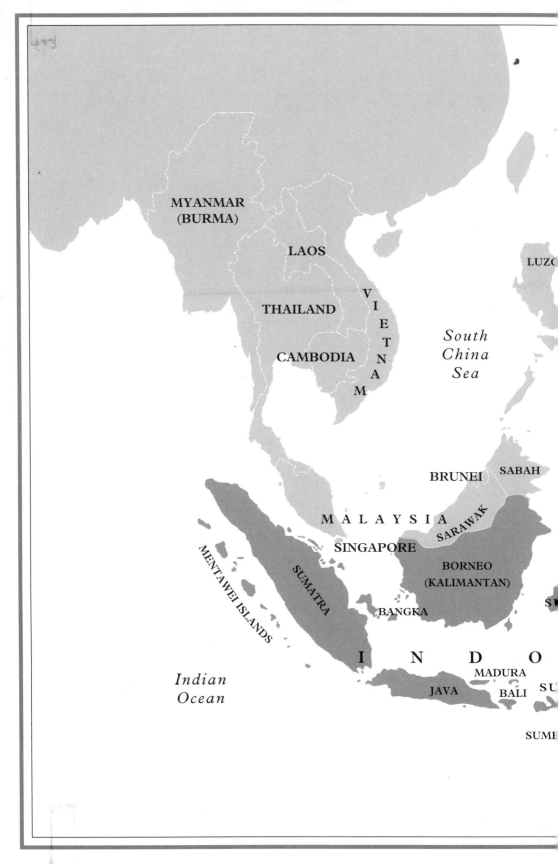